# THE JEWELLERY MATERIALS SOURCEBOOK

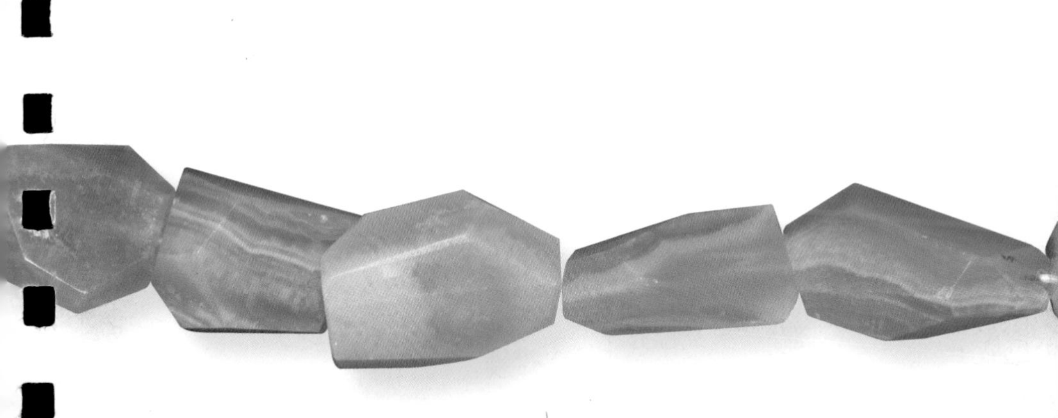

# THE JEWELLERY MATERIALS SOURCEBOOK

## THE ESSENTIAL GUIDE TO MATERIALS, GEMSTONES AND SETTINGS

Anastasia Young

A QUARTO BOOK

Published in 2008 by
A&C Black Publishers
38 Soho Square
London W1D 3HB
www.acblack.com

ISBN: 978 1408 105 801



Conceived, designed, and produced by
Quarto Publishing plc
The Old Brewery
6 Blundell Street
London
N7 9BH

QUAR.TJB

Senior editor: Katie Hallam
Copy editor: Mary Connell
Art director: Caroline Guest
Art editor: Natasha Montgomery
Designer: Jon Wainwright
Photographer: Martin Norris
Illustrator: Leon Williams
Picture researcher: Sarah Bell

Creative director: Moira Clinch
Publisher: Paul Carslake

Color separation by Modern Age Repro House Ltd, Hong Kong
Printed in China by Midas Printing International Ltd

9 8 7 6 5 4 3 2 1

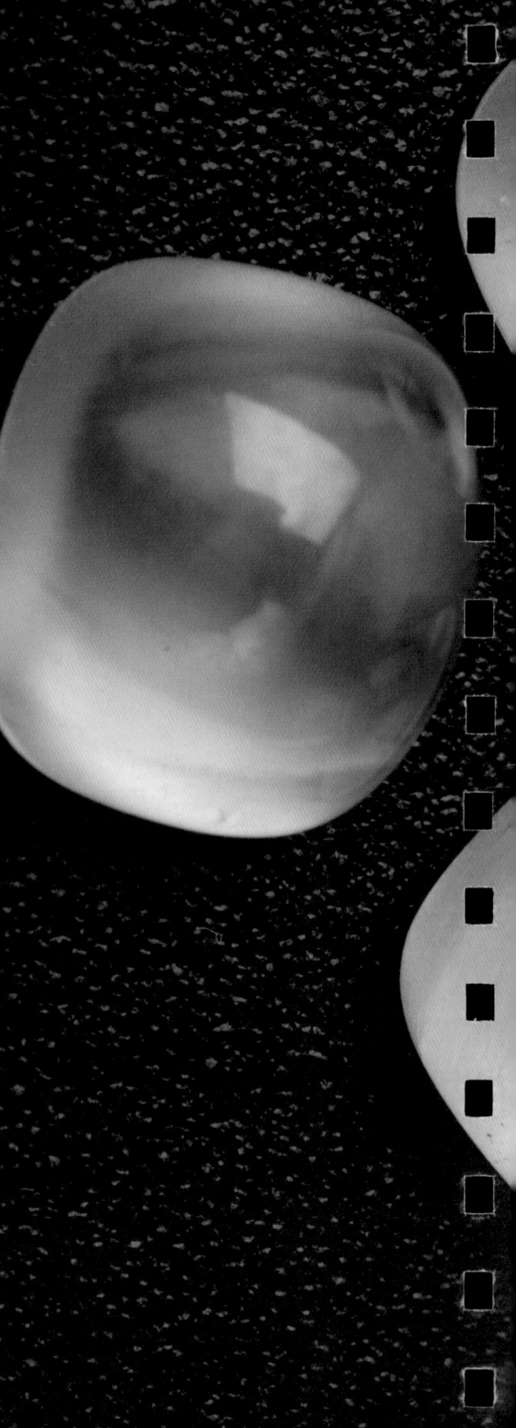

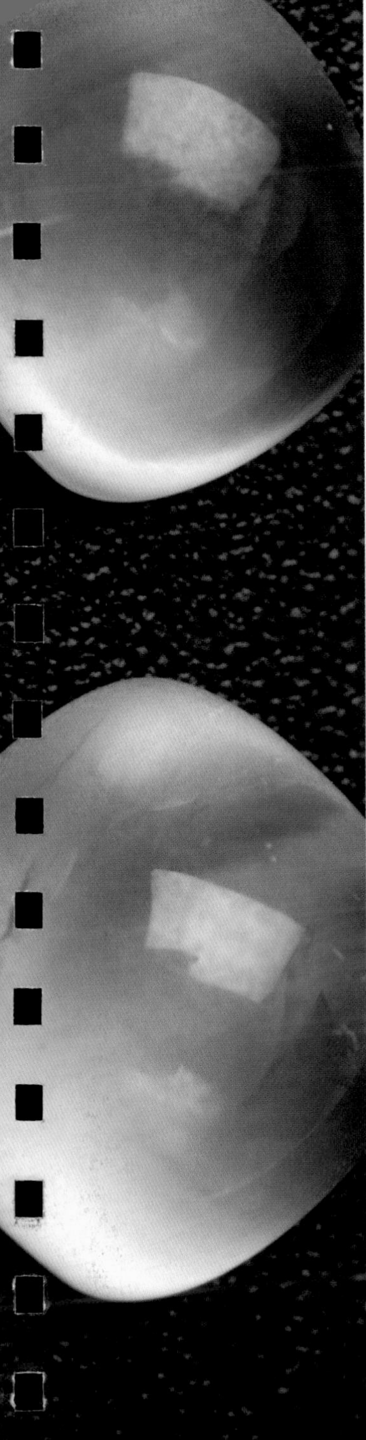

# Contents


| | |
|---|---|
| Foreword | 6 |
| About this book | 6 |
| Health and safety | 8 |
| **Part 1**: Base Metals | 10–55 |
| Copper, brass and gilding metal | 12 |
| Aluminium and refractory metals | 36 |
| Steel | 44 |
| **Part 2**: Precious Metals | 56–125 |
| Silver and gold | 58 |
| **Part 3**: Natural Materials | 126–163 |
| Wood | 128 |
| Bone, ivory, horn, shell and jet | 140 |
| Leather | 150 |
| Feathers, hair and quills | 158 |
| **Part 4**: Plastics and Rubber | 164–187 |
| **Part 5**: Other Media | 188–203 |
| **Part 6**: Stones and Settings | 204–241 |
| Stones | 206 |
| Settings | 230 |
| Recipes | 242 |
| Suppliers | 244 |
| Resources | 247 |
| Glossary | 250 |
| Index | 253 |
| Credits | 256 |

## FOREWORD

I have always enjoyed making things, but it wasn't until I discovered jewellery-making that I really found my creative voice. I was drawn to the permanency that working in metal affords, and also to small-scale objects. Jewellery provides a perfect medium in which to explore my ideas. Problem-solving is a driving force for me, and the technical challenges that making jewellery presents are made all the more interesting by the range of materials and processes available to the contemporary jeweller.

In writing this book, my aim is to inspire readers to explore avenues of jewellery-making that they hadn't previously considered, in terms of materials, techniques and aesthetic considerations. This guide serves as a starting point. Jewelry is a vast subject area that spans thousands of years and hundreds of techniques, and I hope I have communicated my enthusiasm for materials and the ways in which they can be made into beautiful objects.

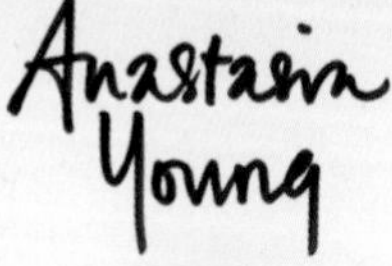

# About this Book

This book guides you through the essential materials used in contemporary jewellery-making – from base and precious metals through natural materials to plastics – and features a wide variety of techniques that can be applied to them to make stunning jewellery pieces. The final part of the book contains a gemstone directory, information on popular jewellery settings and a resources section with suppliers' details.

**INTRODUCTION**
*Each material is introduced with a summary of its available forms and their uses.*

Inspirational finished pieces show the possibilities achievable by applying certain techniques and combining materials.

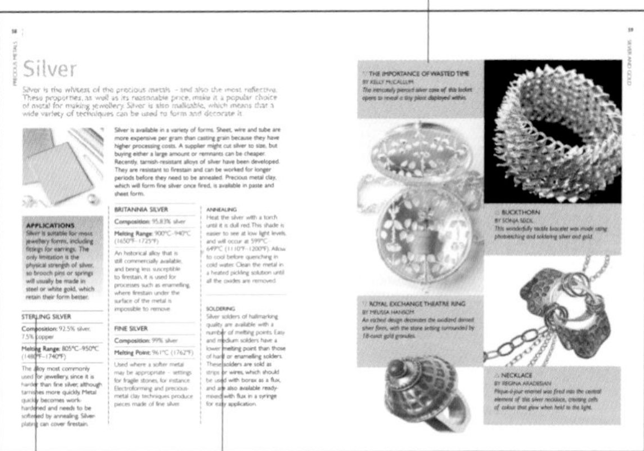

58
PRECIOUS METALS

Silver

Silver is the whitest of the precious metals – and also the most reflective. These properties, as well as its reasonable price, make it a popular choice of metal for making jewellery. Silver is also malleable, which means that a wide variety of techniques can be used to form and decorate it.

Silver is available in a variety of forms. Sheet, wire and tube are more expensive per gram than casting grain because they have higher processing costs. A supplier might cut silver to size, but buying either a large amount or remnants can be cheaper. Recently, tarnish-resistant alloys of silver have been developed. They are resistant to firestain and can be worked for longer periods before they need to be annealed. Precious metal clay, which will form fine silver once fired, is available in paste and sheet form.

**APPLICATIONS**
Silver is suitable for most jewellery forms, including fittings for earrings. The only limitation is the physical strength of silver, so brooch pins or springs will usually be made in steel or white gold, which retain their form better.

**STERLING SILVER**
**Composition:** 92.5% silver, 7.5% copper
**Melting Range:** 805°C–950°C (1480°F–1740°F)
The alloy most commonly used for jewellery, since it is harder than fine silver, although tarnishes more quickly. Metal quickly becomes work-hardened and needs to be softened by annealing. Silver plating can cover firestain.

**BRITANNIA SILVER**
**Composition:** 95.83% silver
**Melting Range:** 900°C–940°C (1650°F–1725°F)
An historical alloy that is still commercially available, and being less susceptible to firestain, it is used for processes such as enamelling, where firestain under the surface of the metal is impossible to remove.

**FINE SILVER**
**Composition:** 99% silver
**Melting Point:** 961°C (1762°F)
Used where a softer metal may be appropriate – settings for fragile stones, for instance. Electroforming and precious-metal clay techniques produce pieces made of fine silver.

ANNEALING
Heat the silver with a torch until it is dull red. This shade is easier to see at low light levels, and will occur at 599°C–649°C (1110°F–1200°F). Allow to cool before quenching in cold water. Clean the metal in a heated pickling solution until all the oxides are removed.

SOLDERING
Silver solders of hallmarking quality are available with a number of melting points. Easy and medium solders have a lower melting point than those of hard or enamelling solders. These solders are sold as strips or wires, which should be used with borax as a flux, and are also available ready-mixed with flux in a syringe for easy application.

59
SILVER AND GOLD

THE IMPORTANCE OF WASTED TIME
BY KELLY McCALLUM
*The intricately pierced silver case of this locket opens to reveal a tiny plant displayed within.*

BUCKTHORN
BY SONJA SEIDL
*This wonderfully tactile bracelet was made using photoetching and soldering silver and gold.*

ROYAL EXCHANGE THEATRE RING
BY MELISSA HANSON
*An etched design decorates the oxidized domed silver form, with the stone setting surrounded by 18-carat gold granules.*

NECKLACE
BY REGINA ARADESIAN
*Plique-à-jour enamel was fired into the central element of this silver necklace, creating cells of colour that glow when held to the light.*

A quick reference to the possible uses for the material.

Further, technical detail about the various forms available.

## TECHNIQUES

*The main part of this book describes the techniques that can be applied to the materials and shows the effect once they have been put into practice.*

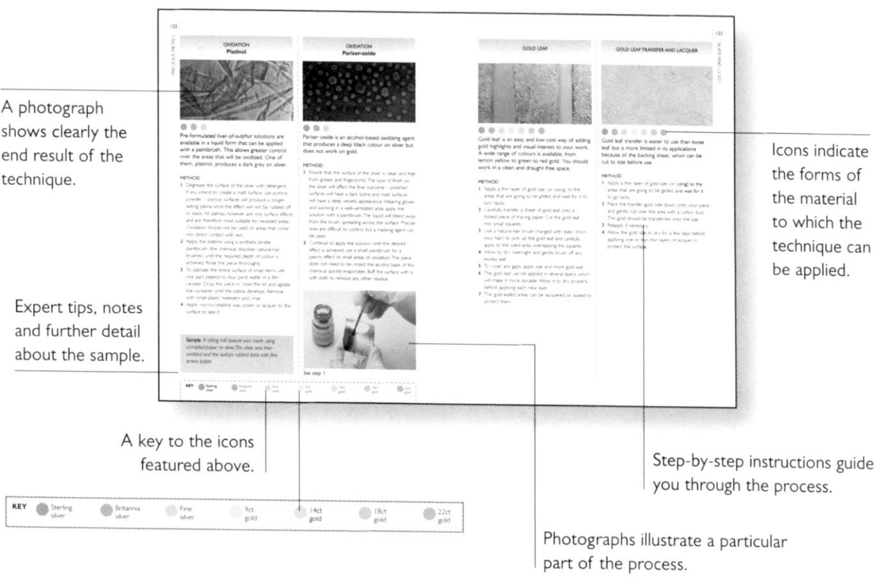


A photograph shows clearly the end result of the technique.

Expert tips, notes and further detail about the sample.

A key to the icons featured above.

Icons indicate the forms of the material to which the technique can be applied.

Step-by-step instructions guide you through the process.

Photographs illustrate a particular part of the process.

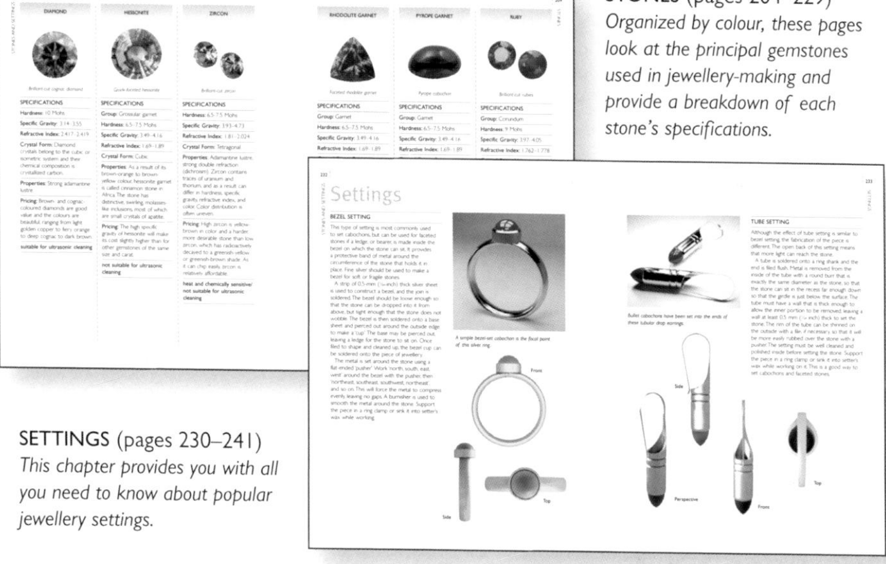

STONES (pages 204–229)

*Organized by colour, these pages look at the principal gemstones used in jewellery-making and provide a breakdown of each stone's specifications.*

SETTINGS (pages 230–241)

*This chapter provides you with all you need to know about popular jewellery settings.*

# Health and Safety

Jewellery-making is a surprisingly dusty and dirty occupation, and the use of bottled gases, flammable liquids and caustic solutions means you should exercise caution if you intend to work in a home environment. Jewellery-making is not in itself a dangerous hobby, but careless use of the equipment and materials could lead to accidents. Always make sure you have a first-aid kit handy in case of minor cuts and burns. Having a small fire extinguisher close by would also be prudent.

Follow these sensible precautions to avoid accidents:

- Always work in well-ventilated, well-lit conditions.
- When you have finished using a piece of equipment or a chemical, put it away.
- Keep children and animals well away from the workshop.
- Tie long hair back and avoid wearing loose clothing that can easily become caught on equipment.
- If you know you will be using a technique that has a high-risk factor, such as operating large machinery or using strong chemicals, make sure that somebody else is nearby – just in case.

## MACHINES

- Wear safety goggles when using high-speed polishing equipment and drills.
- Wear a dust mask when using polishing equipment and during any activity that generates airborne dust particles, such as using emery with a power tool.
- Never polish chain on a motor; use a barrel polisher.
- Never wear gloves while using a polishing motor. If finger protection is required, use leather finger guards.

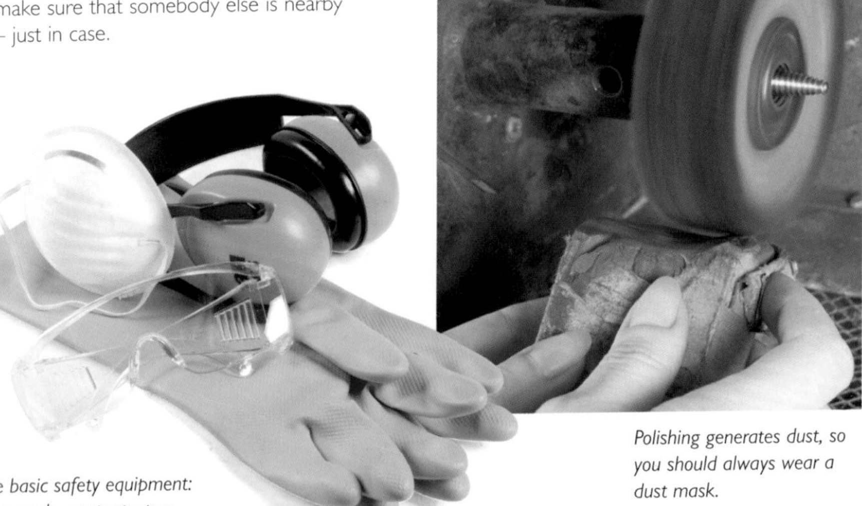

*The basic safety equipment: dust mask, ear protectors, goggles and gloves.*

*Polishing generates dust, so you should always wear a dust mask.*

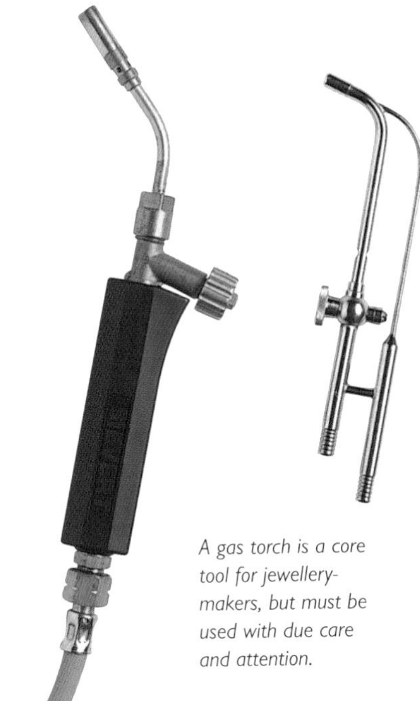

*A gas torch is a core tool for jewellery-makers, but must be used with due care and attention.*

## GAS TORCHES

- Turn off your gas torch at the bottle when you have finished using it to prevent leaks.
- To ignite the torch, hold the lighter close to the torch and slowly increase the gas.
- Lighters can explode when exposed to heat – once the torch is lit, put the lighter in a safe place away from heat.
- Never quench hot metal in the pickle bath – use cold water.

## KILNS

- Protect your eyes from infrared emitted by the kiln – wear dark safety goggles.
- Wear leather gauntlets to protect your hands from high temperatures.

## CHEMICALS

- Always wear protective gloves, goggles and a ventilator, and protect wooden surfaces from absorbing chemicals by working on a large plastic tray.
- Remember that you should always add acid to water. Never add water to acid, because it may bubble and foam rapidly in the container and even spill over the top.
- Pour baking soda on acid spills to neutralize the acid; clear up with newspaper and wash the area with plenty of water.
- Etching chemicals in the form of ferric chloride or ferric nitrate will stain clothing, benches and tabletops, so be sure to protect your clothes and surrounding work area.
- Always store bottles containing chemicals where they cannot accidentally be knocked over and, ideally, in a lockable metal cupboard. Make sure that all bottles are clearly labelled and well sealed.
- Work in a well-ventilated room or even outdoors as acids give off pungent fumes.
- Always follow manufacturers' directions when using chemicals, resins and caustic solutions.

*Acid and other chemicals require special treatment.*

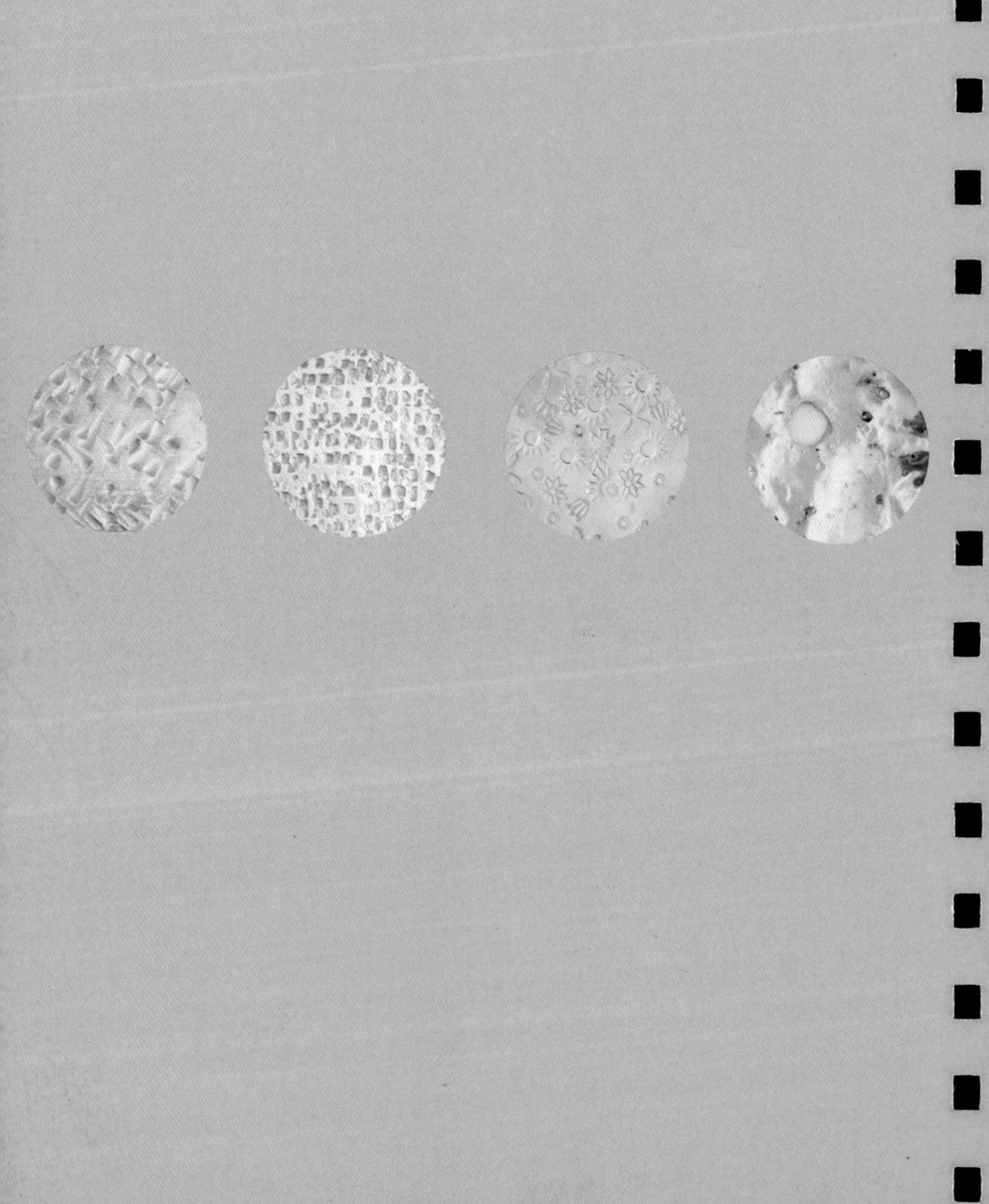

## MARRIAGE OF METALS

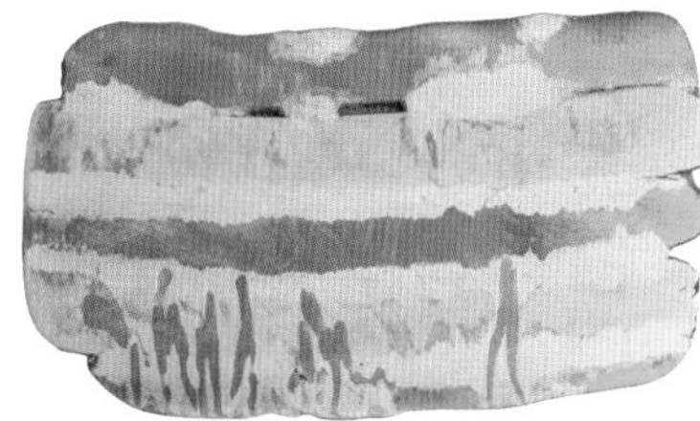

Different-coloured base metals can be soldered together to create pieces with a range of colour tones and that will include the silver solder used to join them. These 'married' metals can be used as component parts of a piece or rolled out to produce abstract designs on sheet metal.

### METHOD

1 Use binding wire to bind a bundle of different-coloured base metal wires together – the more strands you use, the more varied the pattern results will be. Sheets of base metal can be layered up and bound in a similar way, but be sure to flux the sheets before binding them.
2 Solder together the strands of wire or sheet using hard silver solder. Use plenty of solder to ensure a good bond between the component parts.
3 Pickle the piece, then rinse and dry it thoroughly.
4 Thin the piece in a rolling mill until a flat sheet is formed, taking care not to thin it too quickly. You will need to roll the wires lengthways, but as soon as is possible the wire should be rolled through the mill widthways so that the emerging sheet has a greater width.
5 If cracks begin to appear at the edges, solder them closed before continuing the rolling-down process.
6 Once an appropriate thickness has been achieved, carefully anneal and clean the metal.
7 Cold-joining can be used to construct jewellery, since it will not disrupt the structure of the sheet, which could happen with further soldering.

## INLAY
**Milled**

The effect of inlay can be created by soldering a pierced sheet of metal onto a base sheet of a different-coloured metal and then milling down the resulting piece until the surfaces are level. The pattern may be distorted by the milling, but this is a much quicker method of inlaying than fitting one shape inside another.

### METHOD

1 Trace the outline of your design onto a brass sheet, or apply the design with double-sided sticky tape.
2 Pierce out the shape and file the edges so that they are smooth and free of file marks.
3 Clean the reverse side of the sheet with emery paper and paint the surface with borax solution.
4 Place pallions of hard silver solder at regular intervals across the surface and heat the piece until the solder melts.
5 Flux one side of a clean piece of copper the same size as the brass sheet and place the brass sheet on top, with some solder on the inside. Secure the two pieces together with binding wire and heat until the solder melts and joins them.
6 Pickle the metal then use pumice powder and liquid soap and water to scrub it completely clean. Dry the piece thoroughly.
7 Use the rolling mill to thin the sheet until the base is level with the top surface of the pierced layer, and clean the inlaid sheet with emery or wet-and-dry paper.

INLAY
## Silver Solder

Recesses in the surface of metal can be flooded with silver solder to fill them, and filed back to leave clearly defined patterns. Large recesses may take several applications of solder to fill satisfactorily, but take care not to overheat the piece, especially if you are using brass.

METHOD

1. Texture the base metal sheet with pattern stamps, by etching it, or by putting it through a rolling mill.
2. Paint the recesses with borax solution, and place pallions of hard silver solder into the recesses with tweezers or a damp paintbrush. The amount of solder needed will depend upon the size and depth of the texture.
3. Heat the piece gently with a soft flame to dry out the borax so that the solder does not move out of position. Once the borax has bubbled up and settled down again, a more concentrated flame can be used to bring the piece up to soldering temperature, while heating the whole sheet evenly.
4. When the solder melts, remove the flame from the piece and check to see that the recesses are filled. If there are any gaps, pallions of hard solder can be positioned with tweezers, but dip the pallions into a borax solution first, so that they do not move when you start to heat the piece again.
5. Pickle the piece until it is clean and then file off any excess solder until the pattern is clearly defined.
6. Clean off the file marks with emery paper and apply an appropriate surface finish.
7. Any subsequent soldering should be done with easy silver solder, but as this will still run a risk of re-melting the hard solder, cold-joining techniques are more suitable for making the piece.

*See step 2 (applying solder)*

**KEY** Copper Brass Gilding metal

MOKUME GANE

## Wood-grain Effect

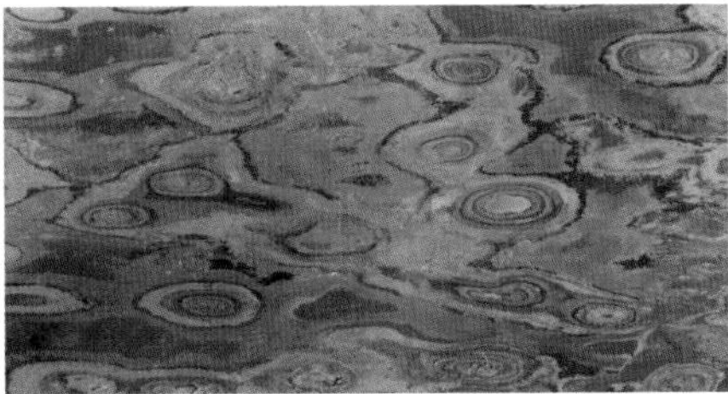

A wood-grain effect can be created on metal by layering up different-coloured sheets of metal and bonding them. The sheet is then distressed and the surface filed down to reveal the pattern. Mokume gane is time-consuming and therefore expensive to produce. It is often used as component parts for larger pieces of jewellery.

METHOD

1 Prepare small 2 x 3 cm (1 x 1¼ inch) sheets of different-coloured base metals by bevelling one edge and thoroughly pumicing both sides to remove all traces of grease.
2 Layer up the pieces with the bevelled edges all on one side, fluxing well with borax everywhere except the outside top and bottom surfaces. Bind the 'billet', or stack, tightly with binding wire.
3 Heat the billet with a gas torch. When it reaches soldering temperature, stick-feed hard silver solder along the bevelled edges. You will know if you have applied enough solder when it appears around all the edges. Do not quench or pickle the billet; set it to cool on a steel block.
4 Remove the binding wire and scrub the billet with pumice to remove the oxides that have formed from heating.
5 Use a rolling mill to thin the billet.
6 Cut the billet in half and flux, stack and bind the two pieces. Solder again with hard solder.
7 The more times this process is repeated, the better the final results will be – a minimum of 30 layers is suggested. After every round of soldering, thin the billet.
8 Textures can be applied to the sheet by chasing lines into the reverse of the piece and filing off the front to reveal layers, or by partly drilling holes, which are then randomly joined up with a burr.
9 These methods will achieve a wood-grain effect. Once the texture has been completed, mill the sheet until completely smooth; if it gets too thin, a back plate can be soldered on.
10 Cold-joining techniques are best used for fabricating jewellery that contains only sections of mokume gane. Soldering may disrupt the surface if the solder that is bonding the layers reaches the melting point.

△ POCKET WATCH
BY CHRIS HOWES
MOKUME GANE BY ALISTAIR MCCALLUM
*This watch features two different effects created with the mokume gane technique. Silver lines traverse the gilding metal face, while silver and nickel mokume gane has been used for the body of the piece.*

MOKUME GANE

## Concentric Circles

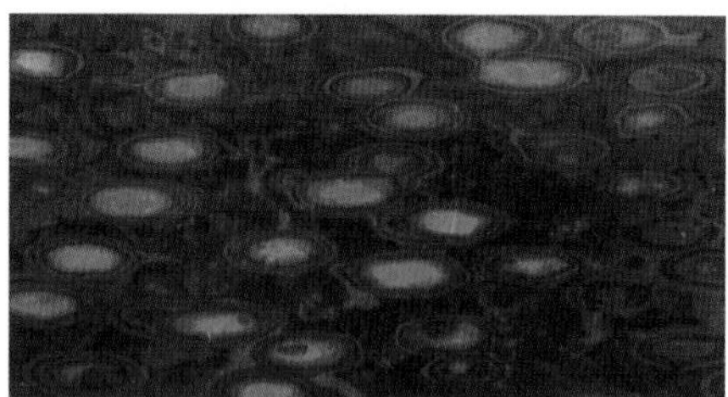

The particular texture applied to the billet will determine the pattern on the surface of the metal. Along with the traditional wood-grain effect, concentric circles or linear designs can be created. The final surface of the piece can be left as bare metal, or patinated using heat or chemicals to enhance the colour contrast.

### METHOD

1 Prepare the pieces of metal for the billet. Bind them and solder them together using hard silver solder.
2 Allow the billet to air-cool before scrubbing with pumice powder to remove any oxides that have formed during heating.
3 Cut the billet in half and solder the pieces together.
4 Once it has cooled and is clean, thin the billet in a rolling mill. Repeat the layering process until the required number of layers has been created.
5 Use a rounded punch to make dents in one side of the billet, then file material from the other side of the piece – this will create concentric circles. Grinding metal out of the front surface will create a similar effect. The piece must now be rolled down in a mill so that it is flat.
6 Patinate the piece to give greater contrast to the different metals – choose a chemical that will only affect copper and leave brass unchanged, for example. Heat patinas give less predictable results but are easily cleaned off in pickle.

## PRESS FORMING

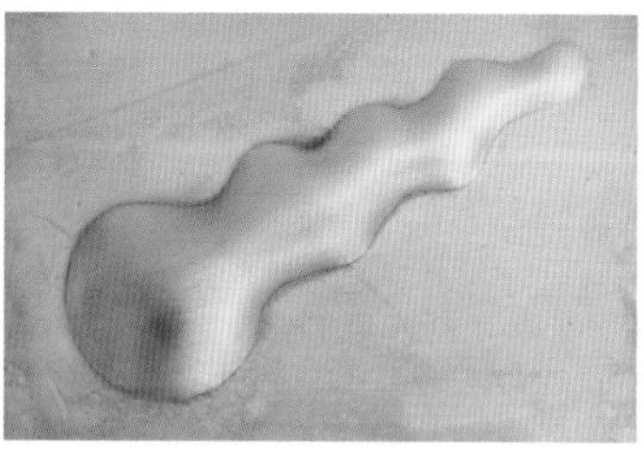

The malleable properties of copper allow it to be readily press formed into structurally robust forms that can then be soldered together, back to back, to create hollow forms. Take care when using sheet thinner than 1 mm (1⁄32 inch), since it can split easily under pressure.

### METHOD

1 Make the die for the press form by piercing a shape out of 10-mm (3⁄8-inch) thick acrylic sheet. Leave at least 10 mm (3⁄8 inch) between the edge of the acrylic and the outline of the shape.
2 File the inside edge of the pierced hole so that your press form will have a smooth outline.
3 The sheet used for the press form needs to have a 10 mm (3⁄8 inch) border around the shape, and should be annealed.
4 Tape the copper sheet onto the acrylic die and place several layers of rubber on top.
5 Position the pieces in the centre of the hydraulic press table and jack up the table until there is resistance. Release the pressure then jack the table up again. When you let the table down again and remove the pieces, you will see that the copper has sunk into the die.
6 Assess the thickness of the metal based on your end product: thick metal will make your piece heavy; thin will split more easily. Use 0.5 mm (1⁄64 inch) sheet for small shapes and sheet no thicker than 1 mm (1⁄32 inch) for large sizes.
7 Apply textures to the copper before press forming. Deep impressions are not suitable since they might cause the copper to split.

**KEY** Copper Brass Gilding metal

## ELECTROFORMING

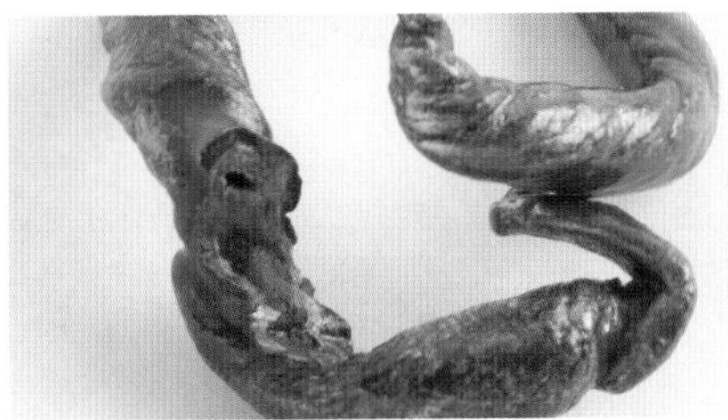

Electroforming is a commercially available process that will coat non-metallic objects or forms in a thin layer of copper or silver. This process is suitable for large forms that would be too heavy if constructed by other means.

### METHOD

1 Prepare the object to be electroformed by making sure it is clean and well finished if it is a wax form. Organic objects will need to be coated in a few thin layers of varnish so that they do not dissolve in the chemical baths. Ensure the object is sealed.
2 The surface is coated with a conductive copper paint; this will provide a base for the deposited metal to stick to.
3 The object is submerged in a tank and suspended from the wire that forms the cathode (negative pole) – your piece becomes the cathode. The anode (positive pole) is made of the metal – in this case, fine copper – that deposits onto your piece. When an electric current is applied, the copper dissolves and is deposited onto the object, creating a thin metal shell.
4 Once the coating is thick enough, the piece is removed from the solution and cleaned up. The original object can be burned out, leaving a hollow shell that can be cleaned up and even soldered onto, providing due care is taken.
5 The form is made entirely from thin, soft copper so treat it with care. Many techniques will not be possible – take this into consideration when designing your piece.

## ETCHING WITH NITRIC ACID

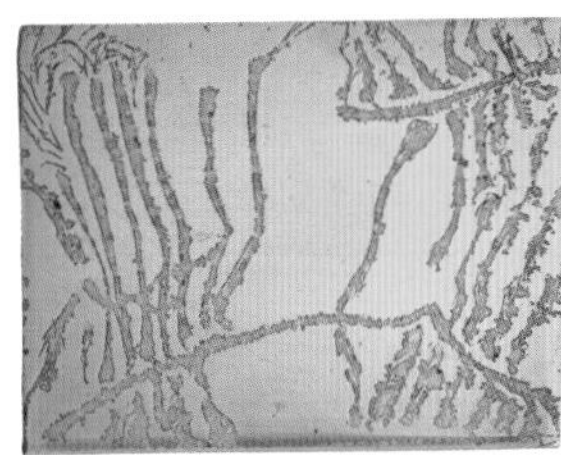

Etching is a method of chemically removing metal. Different resists can be used to create designs: use stop-out varnish or aquatint for painted effects; sticky-backed plastics for cut-outs; PNP paper for graphic designs. Stop-out varnish can also be painted on and scratched back to expose the metal, but lines need to be at least 1 mm (1⁄32 inch) wide.

### METHOD

1 Scrub the metal with pumice powder and liquid soap to degrease it.
2 Dry the metal and, while trying not to touch the surface, mask off the surface using either sticky-backed plastic, parcel tape or stop-out varnish. Cut a design through the tape, or scratch a pattern into the stop-out once it is dry.
3 Carefully slide the piece, design-side up, underneath the surface of the acid (see recipe on page 242). Check the progress of the etching every five or ten minutes, depending on the speed it is working at. A slower etch will be more accurate than a fast one but will take longer.
4 Once a satisfactory depth of etching has been achieved, remove the piece from the acid with plastic tweezers and wash off the acid. Stop-out varnish should be removed with a suitable solvent and the metal scrubbed thoroughly. Tape or sticky-backed plastic should be removed under running water since traces of acid are often trapped under the edges. Wash the metal with plenty of detergent and pumice if necessary.

## RIVETING

Joining together pieces of metal that have been heat-coloured or have had finishes applied that will be affected by heat can pose a problem, because you cannot use solder. Riveting is a cold-joining technique that utilizes metal pins or tubes to join sheets permanently, and will not affect surface patinas.

### METHOD

1 Layering up several different textures or colours of metal can be very effective, so prepare each sheet individually.

2 Mark, centre-punch and drill a hole on the piece of sheet that will lie at the front of the piece – this is where the rivets will be most visible and the shape of the sheet often determines where the rivets are positioned. The drilled hole needs to be exactly the same size as the wire that is being used for the rivets. Copper wire is too soft for making wire rivets; use brass wire instead.

3 To make the wire rivets, fix a piece of brass wire tightly in a vice, using protective pads or leather on the inside of the jaws so that the wire is not damaged. Only 2–3 mm (1/16 inch) of wire should protrude above the vice. File the end of the wire so it is flat, then use a ball-peen hammer to tap the top end of the wire so that it spreads evenly and forms a head. This will stop the wire from slipping through the hole.

4 Next, position the top sheet over the base sheet. Mark one hole, centre-punch and drill. The edges of the drilled holes need to be countersunk. Use a ball burr 0.5 mm (1/64 inch) larger than your drill hole size.

5 Push the first rivet through the hole. You can now mark through the other holes on the front sheet without the risk of the piece slipping and the holes moving out of alignment. Drill and countersink the rest of the holes.

6 Protect the front surface of the piece with masking tape and push the rivets through the remaining holes, from back to front. Working on a steel block, cut the rivet wire to about 1 mm (1/32 inch) above the surface of the sheet, file so that the top is flat and hammer to spread it. Be careful not to hit the sheet with the hammer since this will mark the metal. Turn the piece over and tap from the other side. The rivet heads should be slightly domed, but also make good contact with the surface of the sheet. Tap down or burnish any sharp edges.

**KEY** Copper Brass Gilding metal

## ENGRAVING

Shading tools (also known as 'lining gravers' or 'stitches') can be used to cut multiple fine lines into the surface of a metal. The lines will appear either darker or lighter against the uncut metal, depending on the angle from which the lines are viewed. For brass, it's best to use a high-speed steel graver, which copes with the harder metal.

### METHOD

1. Use a square graver, set in a handle at the correct length for your hand size, well sharpened on an oilstone, and polished on an Arkansas stone. Setting up the graver properly is crucial, including 'setting off' the underneath of the cutting edge so that the graver cuts at 5 degrees for flat work (see page 47).
2. Fix the sheet to be engraved onto a block of wood, using double-sided tape if it is large, or setter's wax if it is small. The metal must be no thinner than 1 mm (1/32 inch). Work on a leather sandbag and sit at a comfortable height with your elbows resting on the work surface.
3. Buff the metal with a wadding polish (Brasso) to remove grease marks and draw or trace your design onto the surface using a fine scribe.
4. Hold the square graver with the handle resting in the palm of your right hand, and your index and middle fingers resting along the graver. Your right thumb and left index finger should be touching and rest on the surface of the sheet, making a pivot; the remaining fingers of the left hand hold the block of wood so that it can be rotated on the sandbag.
5. Cut the outline of the design with a square graver. Use a stitch to fill in the shading; where the shading butts up against a curved line, the graver will need to be rolled slightly as it cuts in order to avoid cutting over the outline. Keep the cuts parallel to create uniform light-play.
6. Fine lines can also be cut with a square graver, but a disciplined rhythm is necessary to keep the lines parallel and even. Cut the outline of the design again to tidy up the overall effect, and rub out any slips with a steel burnisher.
7. Once the engraving has been completed, knock off any burrs on the surface of the metal with a steel blade. Polish the piece using soft rouge polish and a swansdown mop, which will not wear down the surface; traces of polish can be removed using lighter fluid and cotton wool.

## ENAMELLING

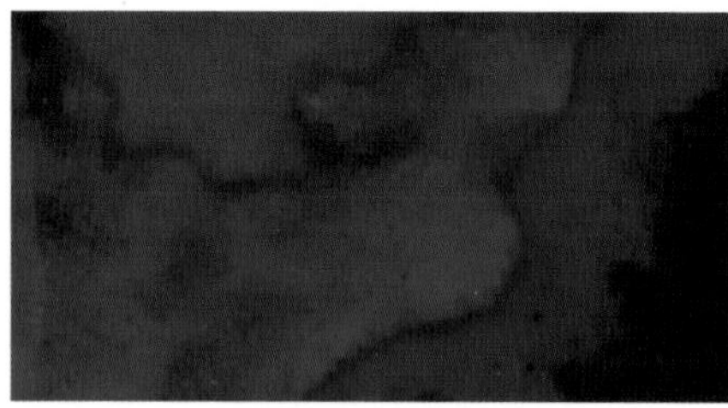

Enamel is coloured glass fused onto the surface of metal at a high temperature, and of the base metals, copper is the only one to which enamel can be applied. The colour of the copper will show through and affect the tones of transparent enamel, but a white opaque base layer of enamel will prevent colour distortions.

### METHOD

1 Prepare the powdered enamels by placing some enamel powder in a mortar, half filling it with water and grinding with the pestle until it feels smooth.

2 Tap the mortar with the pestle to settle the enamel, and carefully pour off the excess water. Use distilled water to wash the enamel, swirling it in the mortar and pouring away the excess water; repeat this until the water is clear, then transfer the enamel to a small, clean, sealable plastic container, making sure that the surface is covered by distilled water. Use this process for every colour you are going to use; the enamels can be stored in the containers for up to a month but may need washing again before use.

3 Anneal, pickle and scrub the metal you will be enamelling, which should be about 1 mm (1/32 inch) thick. Clean the metal with a glass brush under running water – the water should cover the surface of the sheet without pulling away from the edges. Do not touch the surface of the metal, and keep the metal underwater until you are ready to use it.

4 Heat the kiln to 870°C (1600°F). Counter-enamel is fired first onto the back of the piece, which will stop the sheet from warping. This is normally made up of scraps of different colours of enamels and is not thoroughly washed, since the surface quality is of little importance.

5 Apply enamel to the surface of the metal with a clean paintbrush; place the wet powder, methodically making rows and trying to keep the amount of enamel even, until the whole surface is covered.

6 Firmly tap the side of the sheet with the paintbrush to even out the enamel grains, and carefully use a tissue applied to the very edge of the sheet to draw out any water. There should be an even layer of enamel a few grains thick covering the whole surface. This technique is called 'wet packing'.

7 Place the sheet on a piece of wire mesh and set it on top of the kiln to dry completely.

8 Once dry, place the piece in the kiln using a spatula, and wait for the enamel to become shiny. This should take about a minute but will depend upon the size and thickness of your piece.

9 Remove the piece from the kiln and allow it to air-cool.

10 Once it is completely cool, pickle the copper sheet until clean; then use the glass brush under running water to prepare the front surface of the copper sheet for the enamel.

11 Subsequent layers of enamel can be applied in the same way. Use a diamond-grit pad under running water to grind down the surface until it is flat, and then return the piece to the kiln for a short time to restore the glossy surface of the enamel – this is known as 'flash firing'.

**KEY** Copper Brass Gilding metal

ENAMELLING
## Foil

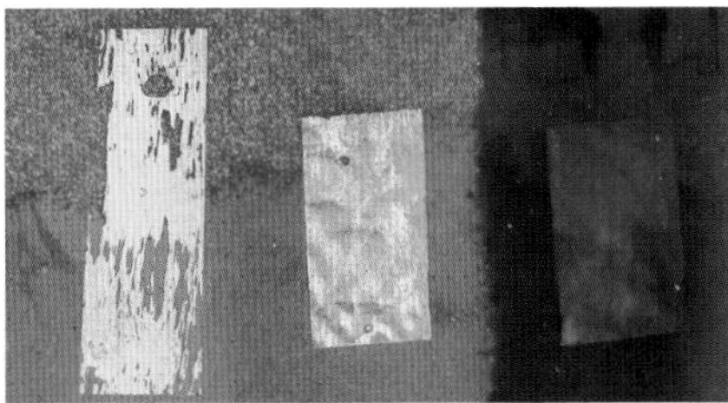

The colours of enamels can be greatly enhanced by firing a layer of gold or silver foil in between layers. This is especially effective when using warm tones such as reds and yellows. The gold foil stays bright and shiny under the enamel and provides an attractive contrast to the copper base sheet.

METHOD

1 Prepare the copper sheet for enamelling, and fire a layer of counter-enamel onto one side of the piece.
2 Pickle the sheet to remove the oxides and clean the front surface thoroughly with a glass brush under running water. Fire the sheet with a base layer of enamel, which can be opaque or transparent.
3 Clean the surface of the enamel with a glass brush and carefully dry the piece. Cut small pieces of 24-carat gold foil inside a folded piece of tracing paper with a craft knife, pick them up with a damp paintbrush and apply them to the enamel. Use a little water around the edges to seal the foil in place, making sure no air is trapped underneath. Do not touch the foil, since this will affect its adhesion.
4 Allow the foil to dry properly – ideally overnight. Use many small pieces of foil to cover larger areas, rather than one large piece of foil.
5 Fire the piece at 780°C (1450°F) for about 90 seconds and allow the piece to slowly air-cool on a heatproof surface, away from any draughts.
6 The gold foil will be bonded to the surface of the enamel and can be left as a surface finish, or further layers of transparent enamel can be fired over the surface of the piece.

*See step 5*

## ETCHING WITH FERRIC CHLORIDE

Ferric chloride gives a superbly clean etch, allowing a crisply defined design to be etched into the metal. 'Etching' pens that are used for electrical circuit boards are a versatile resist; permanent marker pens and nail varnish will also resist the ferric-chloride solution.

### METHOD

1. Prepare the metal in the same way as for etching with nitric acid (see page 23), then apply the resist. Allow the piece to dry thoroughly before etching.
2. Use a heated bubble-etch tank for the best results. This will prevent sediment from forming on the surface of the metal, which will inhibit the action of the ferric-chloride solution (see page 243). If a tank is not available, then the piece needs to be suspended upside down in a warmed bath of the solution. This solution gives a cleaner etch than nitric acid but may take longer.
3. Check regularly to ensure that the resist is not lifting off the metal. Rinse and dry the piece and reapply the resist if necessary. Water does not stop the action of ferric chloride, so once the etching is deep enough, remove the piece from the solution and scrub it with ammonia. Clean it thoroughly with water and detergent and remove the resist with a suitable solvent.

**Sample** *The etched design was filled carefully with cold enamel.*

## POLISHING

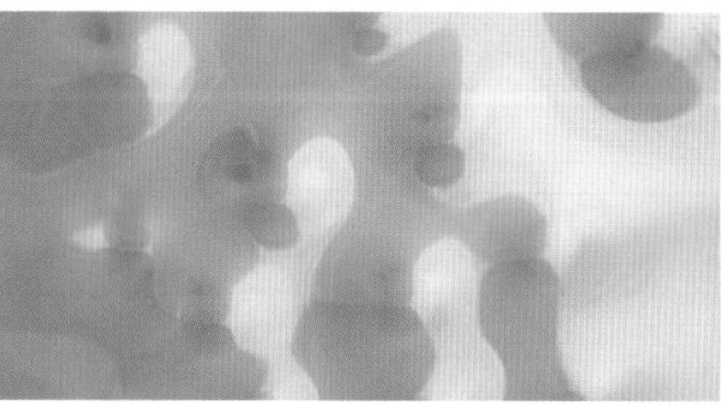

Polishing is often the final process, but it will depend on the individual piece of jewellery as to whether it can be polished in a barrelling machine or by hand on a polishing motor. Although barrel polishing is less work, it does take time and cannot be used for fragile pieces or those containing most gemstones.

### METHOD

1. Prepare the surface of the metal. It must be free from file marks and deep scratches, so use emery or wet-and-dry paper to clean it. Check to see that all deep scratches are initially removed with a rough grade of paper.
2. Use Tripoli applied to a cotton mop for the initial polishing. The polishing motor will cause the metal to become hot; keep the metal moving to minimize heat build-up. Apply more polish to the mop as necessary while the motor is running. Tripoli will remove any light scratches left by the emery paper.
3. Scrub the piece with a soft-bristled brush and plenty of detergent to remove all traces of polish from the piece and your fingers. Dry the piece.
4. The final polish is done with rouge polishing compound. Keep your Tripoli mops separate from the rouge mops to avoid contamination. Apply the rouge to the mop and polish the piece again. This will give the piece a bright shine.
5. Wash the piece to remove all traces of polish, or put it in an ultrasonic cleaner until the traces of polish have been removed.

**KEY**  Copper  Brass  Gilding metal

## MATT FINISH

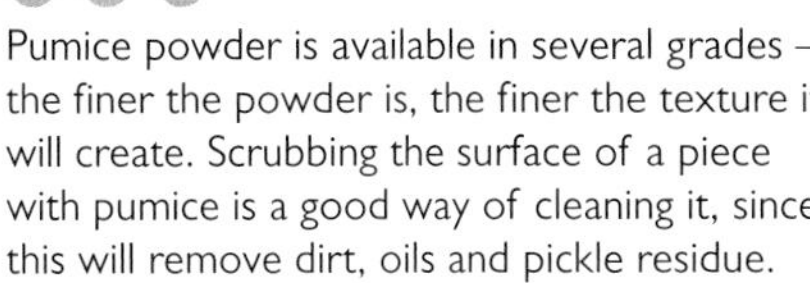

Pumice powder is available in several grades – the finer the powder is, the finer the texture it will create. Scrubbing the surface of a piece with pumice is a good way of cleaning it, since this will remove dirt, oils and pickle residue.

### METHOD

1 Prepare the surface of the metal by removing all scratches with emery paper, working through the grades. Use the first grade of emery in one direction only, and the next grade across the grain of the last; that way you will be able to see any scratches that run along the grain. Alternate the direction you are working in right up to the finest grade of paper. If any deep marks remain, you will have to file them out and work through the grades of paper again. The best matt results come from a well-prepared surface. Even though it might seem that scratches will be hidden or disguised, they will still be visible.

2 Use a stiff-bristle brush that will work up a lather on the surface of the piece, and water and liquid soap together with the pumice powder. It is advisable to work in a sink that will contain the spray produced by the brush. Work either from side to side, or in a circular motion, as you scrub the piece.

3 Rinse the metal under running water to check the progress, and apply more soap and pumice if required until the desired effect is achieved.

## SATIN FINISH

A satin finish gives a softly reflective surface to a piece rather than the bright, hard look of a high polish. A range of abrasive media can be used to create a satin finish, including emery paper, scouring pads and wire wool.

### METHOD

1 Remove any excess solder or blemishes from the piece with a file, then clean up the file marks using emery sticks or wet-and-dry paper, working through the grades until the finest paper has been used. Each grade of paper should be used across the grain of the previous paper, working backwards and forwards in one direction until all traces of the previous paper have been removed.

2 If a very fine satin surface is going to be produced, the piece can be polished with Tripoli at this stage, which will help make an even base for the texture. Use wire wool or fine emery paper, rubbed in one direction only to create the satin finish – be confident in the marks that you are making and try to keep the motion of the abrasive material parallel.

## FLICK WHEEL

Frosted surfaces can be created using flick wheels, which are made up of fine steel wires attached to a plastic wheel that is used on a polishing motor. It is easiest to create the finish on flat or convex surfaces – it can be difficult to apply the texture to enclosed spaces or dimensional intersections.

### METHOD

1 Clean up the surface with emery or wet-and-dry paper, ensuring that file marks and solder stains have been removed. The best results always come from a well-cleaned surface.

2 Screw the flick wheel onto the spindle of the polishing motor securely and, working in the bottom third of the wheel, switch on the motor and apply the piece. Hold the piece firmly, but be sure that your fingers are well clear of the path of the steel wires. A rough grade of flick wheel will produce a deep texture, but the force with which it hits the piece can distort the shape, so for thinner metal use a finer grade of wheel. Move the piece around so that all the required areas are textured.

## HEAT PATINA

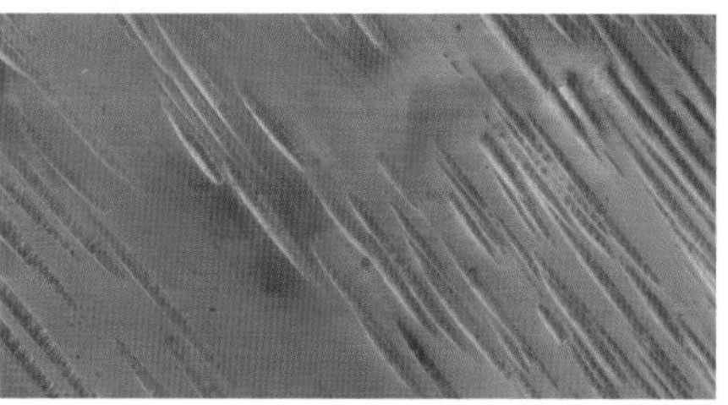

Mixed metal pieces can be enhanced with a heat patina – the metals will react slightly differently to the heat and produce contrasting colours. Unless the patina is applied to a finished piece, cold-joining techniques will need to be used for construction.

### METHOD

1 Polished, matt and textured metals will all produce slightly different surfaces when patinated with heat. Be sure the metal is clean and place it on a heatproof mat.

2 The colour of the metal will begin to change the instant it is heated, so apply the flame for a very short time and then lift it off, allowing the colours to develop. Repeat this process until a satisfactory patina is achieved.

3 Attractive fragments of refractory colours can be produced on copper. Experiment to see the range of effects you can make: try heating one area intensely, or placing heated pieces of steel on copper sheet.

4 As with all patinas, this is just a surface colour and will eventually rub off. Applying wax and lacquer can deaden colours, however, so test a small area first if you think it will be necessary to protect the surface.

**KEY** Copper Brass Gilding metal

## RED HEAT PATINA

Amazing shades of red can be produced on copper by heating it. Purplish reds are easiest to achieve, but brighter hues are also possible – try quenching the piece in hot water.

### METHOD

1 Ensure that the copper sheet is clean by rubbing the surface with a fine wet-and-dry paper. Paint a thin borax solution on one side of the sheet.

2 With the sheet of copper propped upright against a heatproof brick, heat the metal to annealing temperature and sustain this for a few seconds. Turn the metal over and repeat the process.

3 Once quenched, the surface will be a deep red colour, which can be buffed with microcrystalline wax. If you are not happy with the results, pickle the copper and make another attempt.

## BORAX

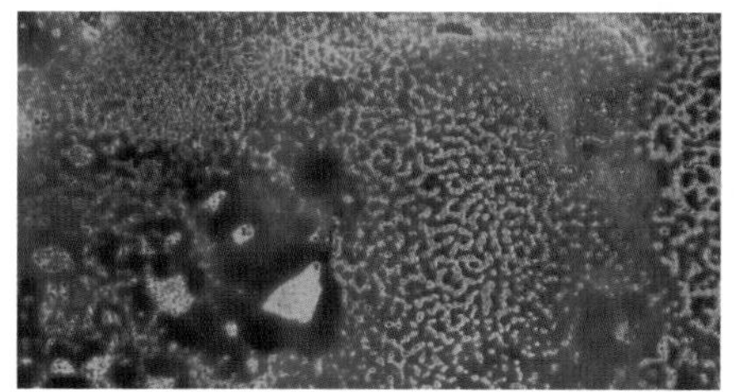

Although the results of this technique are rather brittle, stunning shades can be produced, especially on copper. Apply the borax to a finished piece or to sections that will be cold-joined together. Be aware that any flexing of the metal sheet can cause the borax to flake off.

### METHOD

1 Degrease your metal with pumice powder and liquid soap.

2 Paint the top surface of the metal with a reasonably thick borax solution.

3 Start heating the metal, as if you were soldering. The colours are formed during prolonged heating, which may take several minutes, and the metal must be kept at annealing temperature.

4 Allow the metal to cool slightly, which will reveal the colours. Continue heating if necessary, until the desired colour is achieved.

5 The borax has now formed a thin, glass-like layer on the surface of the metal, so any sharp shocks will cause it to fracture and fall off. This technique is best done on small, protected areas of thick metal. Do not pickle the piece as this will remove the borax.

## TOURMALINE-BLACK ANTIQUING FLUID

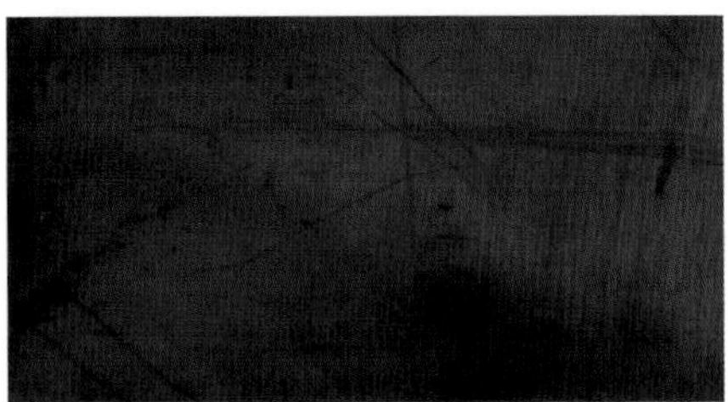

Oxidation artificially tarnishes the surface of metal and is often used to give high contrast to textured reliefs. The chemical must be used in a well-ventilated area or outdoors, because the fumes are toxic.

### METHOD

1 Prepare enough tourmaline-black solution in a deep glass dish to cover your piece, following the recipe on page 243.
2 Thoroughly clean the piece of metal with detergent and a soft brush to remove any grease marks.
3 Place the metal in the solution until it darkens, then wash it under running water with a soft brush. If the oxidation has not fully developed, return the piece to the solution again. Any fingerprints or streaks on the surface of the metal will need to be scrubbed with pumice powder to remove them before they are oxidized. To speed up the process, the piece of work can be heated in hot water before immersing it in the solution.
4 The finish on the surface of the metal will affect the intensity of the patina – matt surfaces will appear darker than those that are polished. Textures can be rubbed with fine emery paper to remove the patina from raised areas, producing a striking contrast.
5 Apply microcrystalline wax polish to protect the finish from wear; the wax polish will also darken the patina more.

## TOURMALINE-BROWN ANTIQUING FLUID

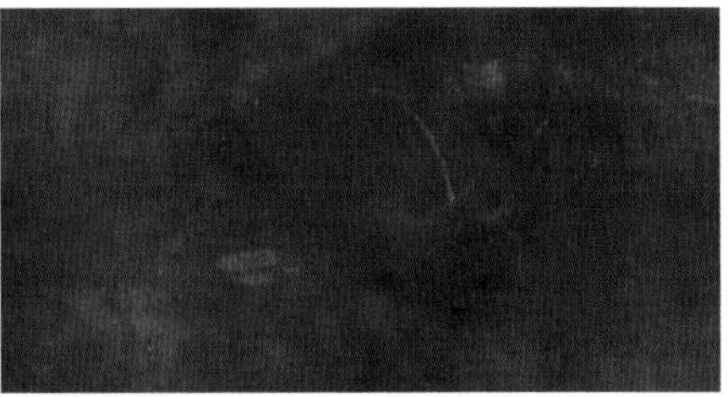

Warm, nut brown tones can be created on the surfaces of copper, brass and gilding metal by using tourmaline, a commercially available 'antiquing' fluid. The results produced will vary depending upon the metal used, since they each react differently to the chemical.

### METHOD

1 Prepare your metal, ensuring that it is grease-free – even fingerprints will inhibit the patination, so wear gloves to handle the metal.
2 Warm the piece of metal by immersing it in hot water and then place it into the diluted tourmaline solution (see page 243) with plastic tweezers.
3 Allow the colour to develop, then remove the piece. Use a soft brush to gently clean the surface under running water. A bloom usually covers the surface and should be cleaned off to reveal the true colour of the patination. If any areas have not changed colour, the whole surface of the metal should be lightly cleaned with pumice powder and the piece returned to the tourmaline solution, unless a mottled finish is desired.
4 The patination is only a surface effect and will eventually rub off. To protect the colour apply microcrystalline wax polish and buff the piece with a soft cloth.

**KEY** Copper Brass Gilding metal

## AMMONIA

Ammonia patinas are often applied using a 'bucket' patina in which the chemical is mixed with an absorbent material that transfers the chemical onto the surface of the metal. Cotton wool, sawdust and rolling tobacco are substrates commonly used for this purpose.

### METHOD

1 Prepare the bucket patina in a sealable plastic container.
2 Place a clean (textured) piece of brass into the container and close the lid firmly. The piece of metal can be buried within the absorbent substrate if the whole piece is going to be patinated.
3 The longer the piece is left in the bucket patina, the better the results, since the colours have more time to develop and the chemical crust can grow quite thick. The patina usually takes several days to develop, so check the piece every day until a satisfactory patina is reached.

## VERDIGRIS

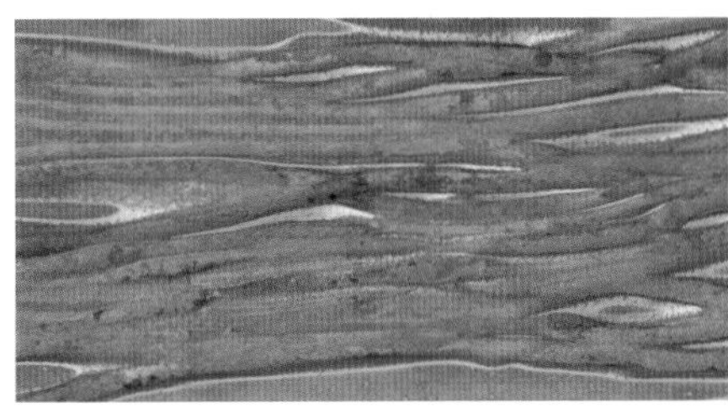

There is a range of ready-mixed patination fluids available on the market, namely for 'antiquing' base metals. These fluids are easy to use and often require no dilution and just a cold application, but the colours may take several days to develop.

### METHOD

1 Working in a well-ventilated area, use a synthetic-bristle paintbrush to apply the patina solution onto the surface of the metal. The colour will develop as the liquid evaporates. Further applications of the solution can be added if necessary.
2 Do not wash the piece as this will affect the patina.
3 These types of 'crusty' patinas are often ruined with the application of a wax polish and will be more durable if applied to a textured surface rather than a polished one.

## COPPER NITRATE

This technique produces a light-coloured verdigris, with or without a black background, on copper. This patina requires heating so should be performed in a well-ventilated area.

### METHOD

1 Position your piece on a heatproof mat and apply a small amount of copper-nitrate solution (see page 242) with a paintbrush or wire-bristle brush.
2 Gently heat the metal using a soft flame to evaporate the liquid and develop the colour. Dab more of the solution onto the metal while it is warm, and reheat until the desired colour is achieved.
3 To create a dark background, overheat the first application of copper-nitrate solution until it turns black. Allow the piece to cool slightly before applying more of the chemical and reheating the piece until green highlights appear. The formation of patterned green areas can be controlled by the application of the copper nitrate, dabbing it on for a blotchy effect or loading the brush with chemical solution for more dense areas.

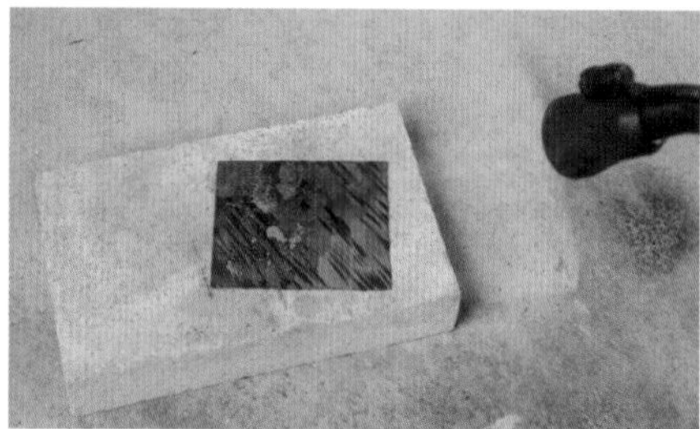

*See step 2*

## FERRIC NITRATE

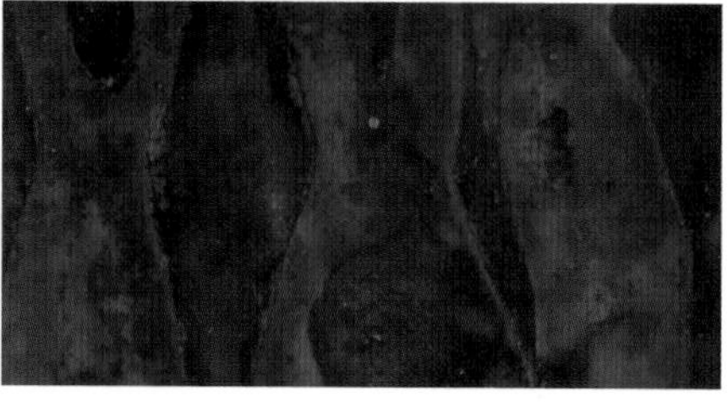

This is the same solution that is used for etching silver, so similar precautions must be taken. Due to the chemical residue left on the surface of the piece, it should be well sealed with wax or lacquer, or applied only to areas of a piece that will not come into contact with the skin.

### METHOD

1 Working on a well-ventilated hearth, place your piece of metal on a heatproof mat. Pour a small amount of ferric nitrate (see page 242) into a glass container and use a robust paintbrush or steel brush to apply the chemical to the upper surface of the metal.
2 Use a soft flame to gently heat the metal until the ferric nitrate has evaporated, leaving a warm brown residue. More of the ferric nitrate can be dabbed onto the metal with the brush while the metal is still warm, until a satisfactory colour is achieved.
3 Overheating will cause the patina to darken, but another application of the chemical and further gentle heating will bring back the brown colour.
4 Microcrystalline wax may be applied to the finish, but it will darken the colours.

**KEY** Copper — Brass — Gilding metal

## PICKLE PATINA

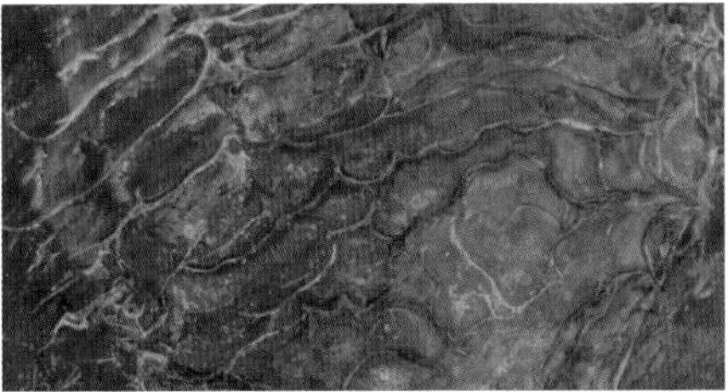

Pickle, as with any of the patination chemicals, will produce amazing landscapes and abstract patterns. The same results won't occur twice, and patience and dedicated experimentation are required – make notes of your experiments for future reference.

### METHOD

1. Layer up a few sheets of clean base metal and place them in a plastic container along with the chemical of your choice.
2. Add enough water so that the level of the liquid is high enough to allow it to leach in between the layers of metal. The evaporation of the chemicals causes the patterns to develop, so leave the container in a well-ventilated area for a few days. Do not seal the container as this will inhibit the evaporation process.
3. Wear gloves to check the development of the patina, and return the pieces to the container if the results are not satisfactory. More water can be added as required.
4. Try using pierced metal shapes within the layers as templates for the chemicals to pool around, which will leave residual marks.

## METAL LEAF

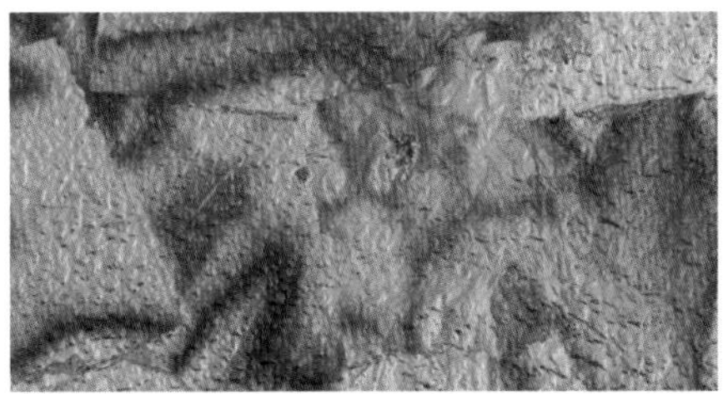

Metal leaf is available in many forms: from copper and aluminium leaf through platinum and palladium to the traditional base 'gilding leaf'. Heat-treated (abalone) and patchwork leafs are also available and will make an attractive feature on a piece.

### METHOD

1. Apply a thin layer of gold size to the areas that are going to be gilded, and wait for the areas to become tacky.
2. Carefully transfer a sheet of gilding leaf onto a folded piece of tracing paper. Cut into small squares.
3. Use a natural-hair brush charged with static (from your hair) to pick up the gilding leaf and carefully apply the leaf to the sized area. Overlap the squares as you go.
4. Allow to dry overnight and gently brush off any excess leaf.
5. To cover any gaps, apply size and more gilding leaf.
6. The leaf can be applied in several layers, which will make it more durable. Allow it to dry properly before applying each new layer.
7. Wax or lacquer can be applied to protect the gilded areas.

# Aluminium and Refractory Metals

Metals are called 'refractory' because of the range of colours that are produced when they are oxidized. Although aluminium is not in this group, the same effects are achieved once the metal has been anodized by applying dyes through printing or drawing.

**APPLICATIONS**
The physical limitations of this group of metals are made up for by the stunning colours that anodizing and applying heat patinas and dyes can produce. These metals can be combined with other base or precious metals with cold-joining techniques. The lightweight nature of aluminium and titanium makes these metals suitable for larger pieces of jewellery where weight would normally be an issue.

Aluminium is a lightweight, non-corrosive, silver-white metal that can be bought already anodized and dyed. The refractory metals are dull grey until worked on and are available in sheet, foil, rod and wire form. All of these should be purchased in an annealed state so that they will be easier to work. Separate tools should be kept for working with refractory metals – aluminium will contaminate precious metals because of its low melting point; titanium will blunt tools quickly.

## ALUMINIUM

**Composition:** 95–99% aluminium

**Melting Point:** 660°C (1220°F)

Aluminium is lightweight, corrosion-resistant and polishes well. Pure aluminium can be anodized and will give a brighter, more reflective effect than alloys containing magnesium and silicon. Anodizing produces a hard layer of oxide on the surface of the sheet. Brightly coloured aluminium powders can also be purchased.

## TITANIUM

**Composition:** 99% titanium

**Melting Point:** 1800°C (3272°F)

A lightweight, hard metal that is difficult to work, but which colours easily by applying heat or by anodizing to produce refractory colours.

## TANTALUM

**Composition:** 99% tantalum

**Melting Point:** 2996°C (5425°F)

Similar to gold in its working properties, a wider range of techniques can be applied to tantalum than to titanium, including dimensional forming, stone setting and also anodizing. Tantalum is the least reflective metal in this group.

## NIOBIUM

**Composition:** 99% niobium

**Melting Point:** 2468°C (4474°F)

Many techniques can be used on niobium, since it is the most malleable of these metals and work-hardens very slowly; but it is not as strong as other refractory metals. Vivid colours in a greater range than those of titanium form on the surface when niobium is anodized.

### ANNEALING

Aluminium can be annealed, but since there is no visible colour change it is very difficult to judge the temperature of the metal. Aluminium is also very easily melted. It is not possible to anneal refractory metals under normal conditions – above a certain temperature these metals absorb oxygen, and their surfaces become hard and difficult to work with.

### SOLDERING

These metals cannot be soldered but may be cold-joined to fabricate jewellery. It is possible to solder aluminium, but special solders and fluxes must be used, and the rapid formation of oxides inhibits the process. Aluminium can be TIG welded.

▷ PEOPLE BRACELET
BY ARTHUR HASH
*The outline of this narrative bracelet was cut with an abrasive waterjet. The low density of aluminium means that it is possible to use thicker metal without the piece being too heavy to wear comfortably.*

◁ RINGS
BY JENNI CALDWELL
*These titanium rings are set with rubies taken from a clockwork mechanism, giving a striking contrast between the colour of the stones and the matt titanium.*

▷ ANODIZED ALUMINIUM BANGLE
BY MELANIE EDDY
*Part of an exploration of colouring techniques on anodized aluminium, the printed image on this bracelet shows the fine detail that can be achieved.*

## BURRING AND GRINDING

Titanium is a hard metal and does not compress well, so the range of textures that can be applied are limited. Removing metal by mechanical means, however, does work effectively, and grinding titanium with a burr held in a pendant motor can produce a number of effects.

### METHOD

1 Use a permanent marker pen to mark out your design on the metal. Insert a small ball burr in the collet of the pendant motor: it should be less than 2 mm (1/16 inch) in diameter since larger burrs remove too much metal and are harder to control.

2 Hold the titanium tightly against the bench pin or stuck to a piece of wood and, with your fingers out of the path of the burr, start the motor. Lubricate the burr with a water-soluble cutting agent and apply it to the surface of the metal. Keeping the burr in the same position for a second or so will create a groove in the metal's surface. Use the burr to create an overlapping pitted surface and remember to lubricate it frequently – this will help the burr cut more efficiently, and it will stay sharp longer. If you are not confident using a pendant motor, practise on a scrap piece of metal first.

**Sample** *A burred texture was applied to tantalum sheet before it was anodized.*

## SCRAPED TEXTURE

Reflective lines can be cut into the surface of sheet metal, producing a surface that changes as it is moved. Anodized textures produce a greater colour range than anodized flat sheet and they can be incredibly effective.

### METHOD

1 The same files can be used on titanium as for precious metals, but you may wish to keep files for different metals separate. The deepest lines will be cut by a rough file, which will also remove the material much more quickly than a needle file.

2 Resting the piece against the bench pin, file across the surface with the edge of the file – the marks you make can be parallel or radial but will tend to be straight lines due to the nature of this technique. Deeper marks can be made in some areas, and this will add to the contrast of the finished piece – areas left unaffected will anodize to different colours than those of the freshly exposed metal.

**Sample** *Titanium sheet was scraped with a file before being anodized.*

**KEY** Aluminium Titanium Tantalum Niobium

## POLISHING

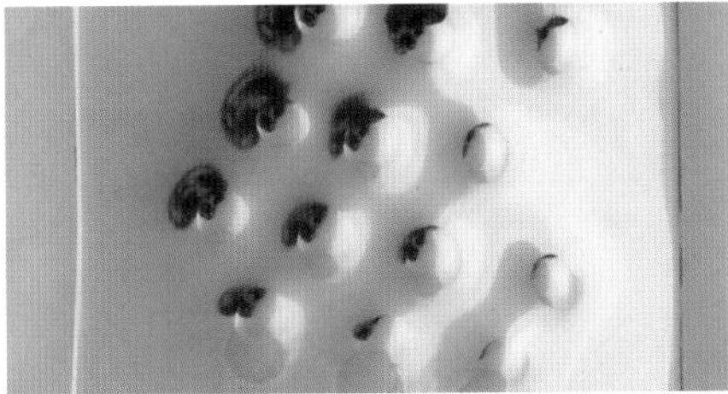

As a soft metal, aluminium must be polished carefully so that it does not scratch during the process. A polished finish is a necessity if glossy oxide colours are desired on the surface of the refractory metals. Tantalum and niobium can be polished in the usual way – titanium can be given a fine surface by use of successively finer abrasive wheels on a polishing motor.

### METHOD

1 Prepare the surface of the metal by removing all scratches with emery paper, by working through the grades, starting with the roughest. Use the first grade of emery in one direction only, and the next grade across the grain of the last; that way you will be able to see any scratches that run along the grain.
2 Apply a white polishing compound such as Hyfin to the polishing mop.
3 As you polish the piece, keep it moving and be careful not to round-off corners and edges too much. If you are using a pendant motor, keep the mop moving. Hold the piece firmly, and be aware that the piece will heat up.
4 Once the whole surface has been polished, wash the piece well with plenty of detergent and a soft brush. The surface of the metal should now be bright and very shiny.

## SANDBLASTING

Sandblasting will produce a sparkling, frosted surface that is very finely textured. During the process a small amount of metal is removed from the surface, effectively cleaning it. The effects of sandblasting will be more evident on aluminium than on titanium since the softer metal is abraded more easily.

### METHOD

1 Prepare the surface of the metal by creating an even finish with emery paper.
2 Position your piece inside the sandblasting machine, holding it a few centimetres (a couple of inches) below the nozzle.
3 Check to see that the pressure is at the optimum level; it is compressed air that fires the sand out of the nozzle at high speed.
4 Close the lid and fire the sand onto the surface, slowly moving the piece so that all areas are blasted. If the piece is angled down away from the nozzle on one side, the side nearest the nozzle will be blasted more intensely and a 'fading out' of the texture will occur. Tap off any sand that is left on the surface and handle the piece by the edges from now on.

## HEAT PATINA

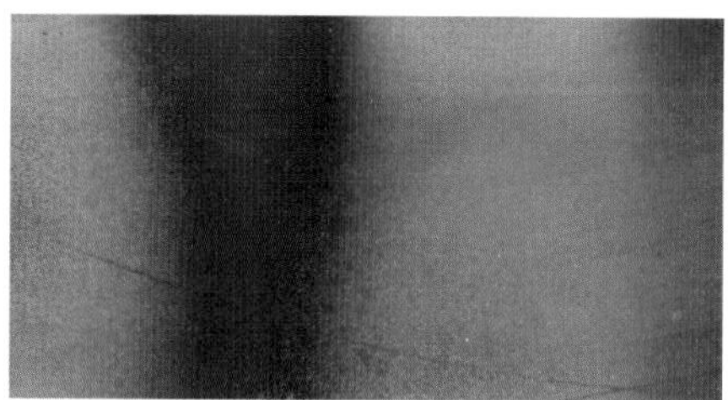

Brightly coloured oxides will form on the surface of titanium when it is heated. The oxide layer produced is relatively durable but, as with all surface patinas, will eventually rub away.

### METHOD

1 Polished, matt and textured metals will all produce slightly different surface effects when oxidized with heat. Ensure that the titanium is clean and place it on a heatproof mat.
2 The titanium needs to be heated with a torch, until it starts to glow red-hot, before the refractory colours will begin to appear. Allow the piece to cool slightly so that the colours are visible, before reapplying the flame to develop the colors further if necessary.
3 You will need to experiment with the length of time that the flame is applied in order to determine the colours that will be produced; the proximity of the flame to the metal will also have an effect. A flame applied close to the titanium and held still will produce tight, concentric bands of colour; if the piece is evenly heated, then the colours will be more evenly spread across the surface of the metal.
4 The coloured oxides can easily be removed with emery paper and the process repeated if the results are not satisfactory.

## ANODIZING

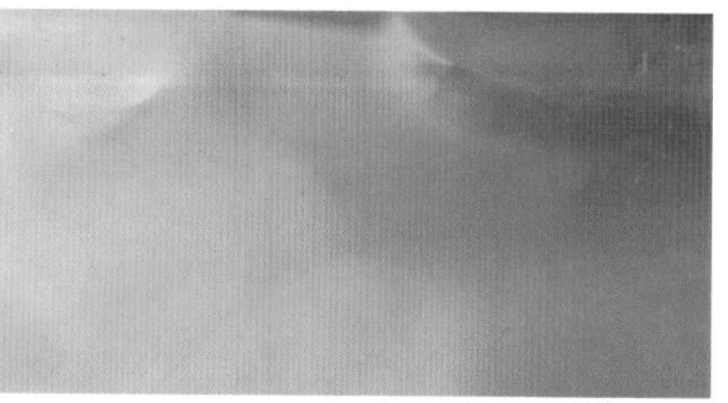

A layer of coloured oxide is formed on refractory metals by running an electric current through them when they are submerged in an electrolytic solution. Specific colours will appear on the metal at certain voltages. There are vendors who will anodize pieces for you.
A different process is used for aluminium.

### METHOD

1 Prepare the surface of the metal, creating a texture if desired, and ensuring that the piece is grease-free.
2 Drill a hole so that the piece can be suspended by a titanium wire hook – the hole must be a tight fit around the wire.
3 Suspend the piece in an electrolytic solution of one part ammonium sulphate to nine parts tap water, attaching the titanium wire to the anode of a variable transformer. The cathode must be put into the solution as well, but as far away from the anode as possible. Wear thick rubber gloves.
4 Switch on the transformer to apply the current to the piece and increase the voltage until the desired colour is achieved. Do not allow the piece to fizz for too long at higher voltages. It may take longer for the colours to appear on large pieces.

**TIP:** The variable transformer used in anodizing should be set up by a qualified electrician, since high voltages are potentially dangerous.

**Sample** *When anodized, niobium produces the brightest colours of all the refractory metals.*

**KEY** Aluminium Titanium Tantalum Niobium

## ANODIZING
### Resists

Masking off areas of the metal that is being anodized allows for two or more colours to be accurately applied to a piece. Apply the higher voltage colours first. The range of possible designs and effects deserves exploration.

METHOD

1. Prepare the piece as described in 'Anodizing' (see page 40), but mask off areas of the metal using sticky-backed plastic or masking tape, which can be cut to make designs.
2. Suspend the piece in the electrolytic solution and apply the current, gradually turning up the voltage so that a high-voltage colour develops.
3. Switch off the current and remove the piece. Some or all of the masking can be removed at this stage, exposing unanodized metal.
4. Return the dial on the transformer to 'zero' volts and anodize the piece again at a lower voltage than before – the colours produced by anodizing the first time will not be affected by the lower voltage, and a two-tone design will be produced.

## DYES

Anodized aluminium can be permanently dyed to produce luminous metallic colours. The dye is absorbed into the porous surface of the metal. Anodizing forms a tough layer of oxides on the aluminium, so form the metal beforehand to avoid disrupting the surface.

METHOD

1. Dyes for aluminium often come in powder form and must be mixed with water, but food colouring, ink and felt-tip pens will work as well.
2. Mix up the dye according to the manufacturer's instructions and apply it to the aluminium by dipping the piece in a dye bath until the colour develops.
3. Some dyes will make stronger or more vivid colours than others, but you can try leaving the piece in the dye bath for a longer length of time to obtain deeper colours. Overdyeing can be used to make new colours by submerging a piece that has already been dyed, or may be used to fill areas that were masked off while the first colour was being applied.
4. To fix the dye in the aluminium, place it in a pan of water that is just under boiling point for 10 to 20 minutes. This makes the effect permanent, but some dye will leach out into the water during the process.

## PRINTING

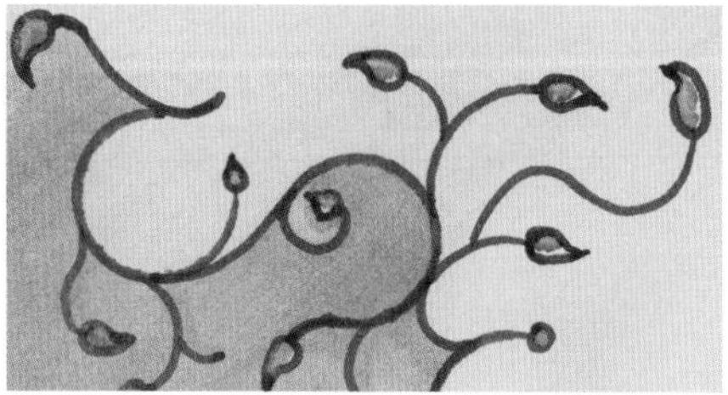

A number of different printing methods can be used to apply dye or ink to a receptive surface of anodized aluminium. You may need to test the compatibility of certain dyes before applying them to your final piece.

### METHOD

1 A receptive surface is needed so that the dye can be absorbed and held in the surface of the aluminium – this surface is created by anodizing the metal. Anodized aluminium must be handled very carefully since any grease marks will be permanent and inhibit the action of dyes.

2 Working on pre-anodized sheet, or a finished piece that has been anodized for you, apply the ink in a manner appropriate to your design.

3 Block printing or stencils will work well on a small scale, as will drawing with felt-tip or permanent marker pens; drawing ink can be used successfully.

4 Once dry, inks should be fixed in steam for one or two minutes, before placing the piece in a pan of water that is just under boiling point for 10 to 20 minutes to make the effect permanent.

5 Large pieces of anodized sheet aluminium can be screen printed, or even computer printed, if special professional manufacturing facilities can be located.

## IMAGE TRANSFER

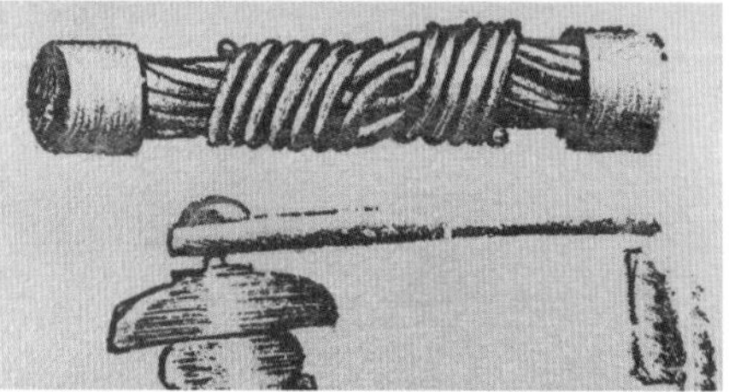

Photocopied images or text can easily be transferred onto the surface of anodized aluminium with acetone. Once sealed, the graphics will form a reasonably durable surface and can be put to a wide range of uses in jewellery. Both colour and black-and-white photocopies will work.

### METHOD

1 Ideally, the aluminium should be etched or anodized in order to take the image, since this creates a very porous surface on the metal. Anodizing aluminium causes a thick porous layer of oxides to form on the surface, which is then receptive to a number of techniques. It is possible to buy pre-anodized aluminium, or have pieces anodized once they have been fabricated. A sandblasted surface will also give satisfactory results.

2 Ensure that the surface of the metal is clean. Apply the photocopied image face down onto the metal. Wet the back of the photocopy with acetone or nail varnish remover and begin to rub the back of the paper. Do not rub too vigorously, otherwise the position of the image may slip. Apply a firm, even pressure with a burnisher or the rounded end of a pen, and work methodically across the surface. Carefully lift up the paper by one corner – if parts of the image have not transferred, apply more acetone and continue to rub the back of the paper.

**KEY** Aluminium Titanium Tantalum Niobium

## STAPLING

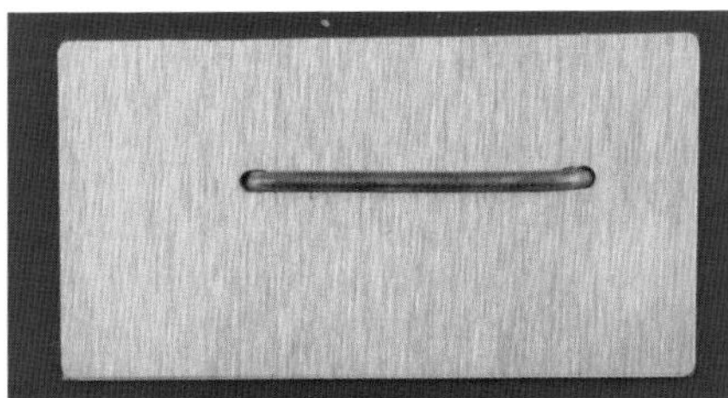

Staples, or pieces of wire that have been bent through a hole, can be used to secure elements of a piece together where soldering is not appropriate. As titanium wire will not easily form rivets, stapling is a good way of utilizing the coloured wire that anodizing or heat patination can produce.

### METHOD

1 Prepare all the elements of your piece: shape each section; use files and emery to clean; then patinate the pieces through heat or anodizing where desired, including the wire.
2 Drill two holes in position through the top layer of the piece, where the position of the staple will show.
3 Mark through these holes onto the layer below to place reference marks in the correct position to drill two more holes. The drill bit you use needs to be the same diameter as the wire you will be using for the staples. The distance between the two holes will determine the length of the staple.
4 Using parallel pliers, bend the wire into a 'U' shape so that the legs are exactly the same distance apart as the holes in the sheet.
5 Insert the staple into the holes, making sure it sits flat on the surface, and fold the legs flat underneath the piece, tapping with a mallet to sharpen the bend. If the legs of the staple are too long, trim them with end cutters.

## FOLDING

Metal foil can be folded into complex three-dimensional structures. Work out forms in paper first, and use these to make templates. Cold-joining techniques will need to be used to attach fittings and findings.

### METHOD

1 Prepare the surface of the foil by degreasing it thoroughly and applying the final finish.
2 Use the paper template you have made as a reference when bending the foil and use a ruler as a guide for long, straight folds. Folds can be left open to form three-dimensional forms, or can be flattened with a mallet to make a layered structure.
3 Fold the piece before anodizing it, since the process causes hard oxides to be formed on the surface; these may be damaged if the piece is worked, producing an uneven finish.
4 Anodize the piece to the desired colour and attach any fittings.

# Steel

Steel is an invaluable material in jewellery-making – most tools that jewellers use are made of steel. The techniques that can be applied to steel are limited because it is so hard, but a knowledge of tool-making will enhance every jeweller's expertise. Steel is also used to fabricate jewellery pieces.

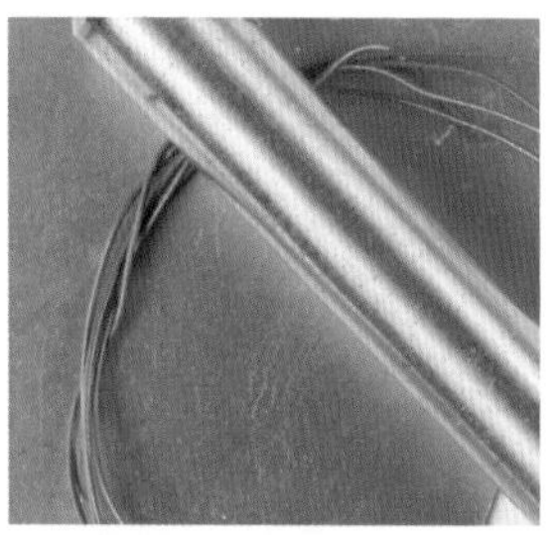

The hardness of a steel alloy is determined by its carbon content. High-speed steel, which has a high carbon content and is very hard, is often used to make cutting tools that will not blunt easily. The effects that can be created with steel are varied and durable. Steel is widely available in sheet, wire and rod form; and mesh, tube and pretextured sheet is also available.

**APPLICATIONS**
Stainless steel is mainly used in jewellery-making for pins and springs, since small, base-metal working parts are permitted under the Hallmarking Act of 1973, although the inert nature of stainless steel means that it can be used for earring fittings. Carbon steel is most commonly used for making tools.

### STAINLESS STEEL

**Composition:** Iron with 10–20% chromium

**Melting Point:** 1450°C (2642°F)

Very hard steel alloy that is corrosion-resistant and polishes well. Difficult to work and should be forged or bent while still red-hot.

### TOOL STEEL (SILVER OR CARBON STEEL)

**Composition:** Iron with 0.3–1.5% carbon

**Melting Range:** 1200°C–1400°C (2192°F–2552°F)

A robust alloy good for making tools, but it can be brittle and needs to be tempered before use. Must be forged while red-hot; grinding is the easiest way to remove metal from a piece. Will corrode.

### MILD STEEL

**Composition:** Iron with up to 0.25% carbon

**Melting Range:** 1300°C–1500°C (2372°F–2732°F)

A soft, low-carbon steel that is easier to work than other alloys but cannot be hardened and is prone to rusting.

#### ANNEALING

Heat the steel with a bushy flame until it is dull red. This shade of colour is easier to see at low light levels and will occur at 746°C–899°C (1375°F–1650°F). Quench in warm water or brine. Clean the metal with emery paper – steel cannot be pickled.

#### SOLDERING

Solder should have a high melting point and the flux should have a high temperature range – Tenacity 5 is usually used. Can be spot or TIG welded.

▽ TIN-PLATE CRAFT
BY TAKAFUMI INUZUKA
*Heat patinas have been cleverly used to create visual interest in this neckpiece, which was fabricated from tin-plated steel and copper.*

△ PERFECT FIT
BY SUZI TIBBETTS
*These threaded steel rings fit together, or can be worn separately.*

▷ CUFFLINKS
BY ERIK TIDÄNG
*Each cufflink has been ingeniously constructed from one folded piece of stainless steel sheet. A brushed satin finish has been applied.*

## PIERCING

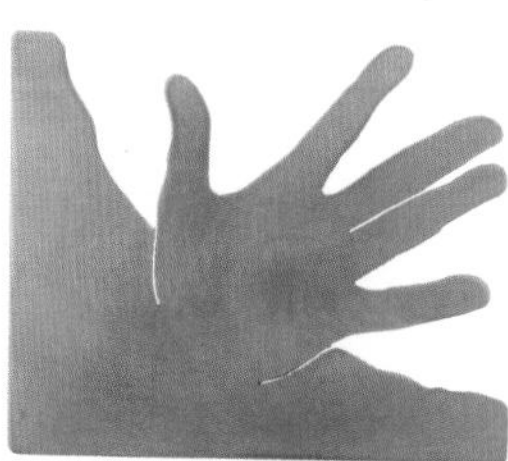

Detailed and durable templates can be created with steel, and it is very useful for making fretwork for embossing non-metal materials. Steel cannot be used for rolling mill textures since it may damage the rollers, which are also made of steel.

### METHOD

1 Work out your design on paper and transfer it to the metal with double-sided sticky tape.
2 Centre-punch a mark inside each section that needs to be pierced out, near the edge.
3 Drill a hole large enough for the saw blade to fit through. Use a 2/0 size blade, good for general-purpose cutting; for very thin metal or fine detail, use a 4/0 or 5/0 blade. Saw blades designed for use with platinum can also be used and should last longer since they are meant for cutting harder metal; a thin oil lubricant applied to the blade will also help.
4 Always pierce out inside areas first, starting with the smallest – it is easier to work on a large piece of metal.
5 With one end of the saw blade already secured in the saw frame (with the teeth pointing down), thread the other end through one of the drilled holes. Slide the steel right up to the top of the blade so that it won't pull on the blade as you tighten it, making sure you have good tension.
6 Lay the steel sheet down on your bench pin so that the area you are piercing is in the gap. Start cutting, using long, even strokes with the saw blade moving straight up and down. Cut a little inside the scribed line, rather than on it. If the saw wanders a bit, you won't go over the line.
7 To turn a corner, keep the blade moving on the spot as you incrementally turn the metal into the path of the blade, but try not to exert too much backward pressure on the blade. If the blade snaps at this point, it is probable that your blade was at a slight angle and couldn't easily turn the corner. Many saw blades will be broken when cutting steel, because they get blunt very quickly.
8 To pierce a curve, as you are moving the saw up and down, turn the metal into the path of the blade. The faster the metal is turned, the tighter the curve.
9 Pierce out the remaining areas. Use needle files to remove the saw marks and even out any areas. Clean up with emery paper.

**TIP:** In addition to creating detailed outlines, piercing can be used to cut out internal spaces and fine lines. The thickness of the saw blade will determine the width of the cuts.

**KEY** Stainless steel · Tool steel · Mild steel

## SHARPENING

Keeping your tools sharp and in good working condition is vital for the best results. This technique is suitable for engraving tools, chisels and scrapers on which a very sharp cutting edge should be maintained.

### METHOD

1 Apply some machine oil (such as 3-In-One) to a two-sided oilstone. Work on the smooth side – the rough side is rarely needed.

2 Butt the oilstone up against a fixed piece of wood so that you can use both hands to hold and balance the tool you are sharpening. Square gravers for engraving need to be 'backed off', that is, to have an angle ground onto both surfaces of the underside so that when cutting with the tool it does not dig into the metal too deeply.

3 Holding the tool at an angle of 5 degrees to the oilstone, rub one face of the graver backwards and forwards along the stone until there is a facet of about 2 mm (1⁄16 inch). Repeat for the other side of the underside so that it matches the first facet and the lower corner of the square section stays straight.

4 Once this stage has been completed, the oblique face of the tool can be sharpened. Hold the handle of the graver in your right hand, with the fingers supporting the shaft; the first two fingers of the left hand should rest just above the end of the tool where it touches the oilstone, ensuring that good contact is made.

5 Work the graver up and down the length of the oilstone, keeping it at its original angle. Test the sharpness of the graver by touching it on your thumbnail – if it catches, then it is sharp enough, but if it slips then more sharpening is required. Burrs created by the sharpening process can be knocked off by stabbing the tool into hard wood.

6 The cutting faces of the graver should be polished using a natural Arkansas stone in the same way as the oilstone. This stone is much finer and will refine the surfaces so that the point is less likely to chip.

7 For bright-cut engraving, the undersides of the graver must be polished. Use very fine emery paper on a flat surface to lightly smooth the back surfaces, pulling the tool towards you, handle first, so that the cutting edge is not dulled. The surfaces can then be polished by rubbing them on a piece of leather that has had steel polish applied to it.

**TIP:** Always keep your gravers sharp and store them with the cutting ends pressed into a piece of cork. All tools, including your rolling mill, pliers and flexshaft motor, should be cleaned and oiled every few months to prevent rust formation and keep their working parts moving smoothly.

## ETCHING

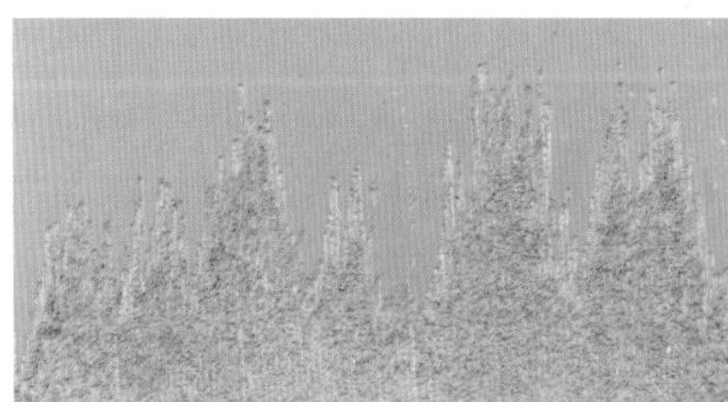

Elaborate designs can be produced on the surface of steel by removing areas with acid. Etching can also be used to create patterns on the ends of rods for use as punches; the recesses must be deep and the tools will need hardening and tempering before use.

### METHOD

1 Scrub the steel with pumice powder and liquid soap to degrease it. Dry the metal and, trying not to touch it, mask off the surface using sticky-backed plastic, parcel tape or stop-out varnish.
2 Cut a design through the tape, or scratch a pattern into the stop-out once it is dry.
3 Use plastic tweezers to carefully slide the piece, design-side up, under the surface of the nitric acid (see page 242).
4 Check the progress of the etching every five or 10 minutes, depending on the speed it is working at. Nitric acid works aggressively on steel, so use a feather to remove bubbles that form on the surface at regular intervals.
5 Once a satisfactory depth of etching is achieved, remove the piece from the acid with plastic tweezers and wash off the acid. Stop-out varnish should be removed with a suitable solvent, then scrubbed; remove tape or sticky-backed plastic under running water as traces of acid are often trapped under the edges. Wash the metal with plenty of detergent, and pumice if necessary.

## SOLDERING

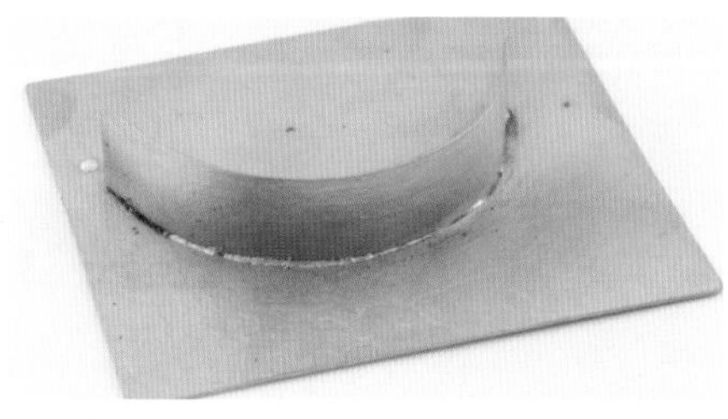

Although welding is commonly used to join steel pieces together, a jeweller might be more inclined to use soldering since the equipment is more likely to be at hand. The physical properties of steel make soldering a challenging process to achieve successfully.

### METHOD

1 Ensure that the join between pieces is a good match – you should not be able to see any light through the join, and the metal must be clean.
2 Position the piece on a heatproof mat and make a wall with firebricks around three sides to reflect heat in towards the piece. Place pieces one on top of another with tweezers to support them if necessary, so that you have both hands free. Spend time positioning pieces before you start heating rather than readjusting when everything is hot and has moved. Iron binding wire holds pieces in position.
3 Mix up some flux (Tenacity 5) in a dish with water to make a thin paste and apply it around the join with a fine paintbrush.
4 Apply cut pieces of hard silver solder (pallions) so that they butt up against both pieces of steel.
5 Begin heating around the piece, bringing it to temperature as quickly as possible to minimize oxides, which will inhibit the flow of solder. Stop heating the piece when the solder runs.
6 Allow the piece to cool before quenching in cold water; remove any binding wire; and place it in a cold pickling solution (such as Sparex #1).
7 Once clean and dry, the soldered join can be filed to remove any excess solder.

**KEY**  Stainless steel   Tool steel  Mild steel

## SPOT WELDING

This technique can be used to join rod or wire by fusing it through the application of pressure and an electric current. The fusion is limited to a small area, but many 'spots' may be welded to increase the strength of the join, especially on sheet steel.

### METHOD

1 Spot welding works best on low-carbon steel sheets or rods that are no thicker than 3 mm (⅛ inch). The parts being joined should be of a similar thickness and reasonably clean. Technical training will be necessary before attempting to work on any welding equipment, as every model of machine will vary.
2 Insert the two pieces of steel that will be welded, in the correct position relative to each other, in between the copper electrodes that will hold the pieces firmly in place. When the electric current is triggered, it travels through the copper contacts and creates enough heat to weld the steel in a localized spot. The weld itself will be between 3 and 12 mm (⅛ and ⅜ inch) in diameter, depending on the capacity of the machine used, the voltage and the length of time that the current is applied. Some spot welders have a timer and will allow greater control of the welding. This is a quick and easy way to fuse steel in order to make three-dimensional structures, especially in wire.

## HARDENING AND TEMPERING

Once shaped, steel tools must be treated so that they are of the correct hardness. Too soft, and they will lose their shape; too brittle, and they could shatter. Controlled heating and cooling will create the properties required for specific types of tool. Mild steel cannot be hardened sufficiently to be used for tools.

### METHOD

1 Coat the surface of the tool with soap or correction fluid to prevent scale from forming.
2 Working on a heatproof mat, start heating the tool at its centre point so that it glows red, and slowly move the flame down to the working end of the tool until it also glows red.
3 Quench the tool in tepid water, holding it vertically, and remove it from the water before it is cool.
4 Allow to air-cool before removing any oxides or scale with emery paper, and polish the tool.
5 Heat the centre of the tool with a gas torch and watch the colour bands as they travel towards the tip. Pale yellow will appear first, then straw yellow – the latter will give the hardest results and should be used for gravers, files and lathe tools. Dark straw or brown produces medium-hard steel, which is ideal for punches; chisels should be tempered to a light purple shade. When the correct colour reaches the tip, quench the piece in cold water.
6 Temper the tips of fine tools by touching them on a red-hot piece of steel until the required colour appears. Use a kiln to temper larger tools.
7 Polish the tool again – it is now ready for use.

## CARVING AND GRINDING

Steel is a relatively hard metal, and while it is possible to file forms to shape, grinding is a much faster method of removing material. Grinding wheels are made from bonded particles of aluminium oxide and are mounted on a motorized unit. It is also possible to sharpen tools such as chisels and punches on a grinder.

### METHOD

1 Wearing safety goggles, switch on the grinder. A medium-fine grinding wheel of 60–80 grit should be used for all steel tools, including those made from high-speed steel. You can judge the type of steel you are using from the sparks that are generated during grinding: mild steel produces a shower of long, white sparks; tool steel gives off a few red sparks; and stainless steel produces long, straight sparks.

2 Ensure that the clear plastic spark shield above the wheel is in position, and apply the tool to the flat edge of the wheel using the tool rest to support your hands.

*See step 2*

3 Hold the steel in both hands and rotate the piece for curved faces or angled tips. Use short bursts of grinding, and check the progress of the form frequently.

4 Keep a pot of water handy to cool the piece at regular intervals – the area you are grinding will quickly become hot from the friction of grinding. This will also prevent tools such as gravers from becoming tempered when they are ground, which would affect the performance of the tool.

5 Once the basic form has been ground from the steel rod, refine the form some more with files, then clean it up with emery paper. Tools must be hardened, polished and tempered before use – the exception is engraving tools that are sold correctly tempered and should not be heated at the tip.

**KEY**  Stainless steel  Tool steel Mild steel

## POLISHING

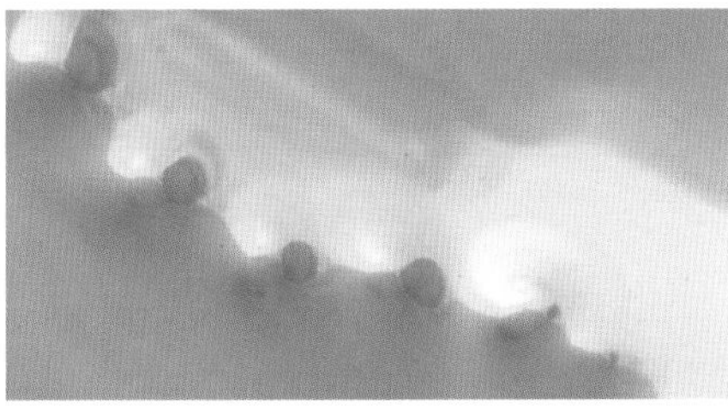

Polished tools will impart polished surfaces on the softer metals that they work on. Steel keeps its polish well, since it is so hard, but it does take time and much effort to gain a good finish.

### METHOD

1 Grind or file the form to shape. Use 400-grade wet-and-dry paper to begin removing the file marks – use rough paper to start with because steel wears out the paper more quickly than other metals.
2 Work up through the grades of paper, using each new grade at a 90-degree angle to the grain of the last. This will enable you to see scratches and ensure that any marks are removed before moving onto the next grade of paper.
3 When the scratches are fine enough to be polished out, apply a white polish such as Hyfin or Carborax onto a polishing mop reserved for steel, and apply the steel to the lower front quarter of the mop.
4 The polishing motor will cause the metal you are polishing to become hot – keep the metal moving to minimize heat build-up. Apply more polish to the mop while the motor is running, as necessary.
5 Scrub the piece with a soft-bristled brush and plenty of detergent to remove all traces of polish from the piece and your fingers. Dry the piece thoroughly.
6 If a high polish is required, apply Green Dialux polish to a clean mop and repeat the polishing process.

## MATT FINISH

Matt finishes on steel have less tendency to turn shiny with wear than silver or gold because the metal is much harder-wearing. Pumice powder used with liquid soap and water will give the surface of the metal a 'flat' look, because the reflective property of the metal is reduced. Use a steel burnisher to define the edges of a piece and create eye-catching highlights.

### METHOD

1 Prepare the surface of the metal by removing all scratches with emery paper, working through the grades. Use the first grade of emery in one direction only, and the next grade at 90 degrees to the grain of the last; that way you will be able to see any scratches that run along the grain.
2 Alternate the direction you are working in right up to the finest grade of paper. If any deep marks remain, you will have to file them out and work through the grades of paper again. The best matt results come from a well-prepared surface – even though it might seem that scratches will be hidden or disguised, they will still be visible.
3 Use a stiff-bristled brush to work up a lather on the surface of the piece, using water and liquid soap together with the pumice powder. It is advisable to work in a sink that will contain the spray produced by the brush. Work either from side to side, or in a circular motion, as you scrub the piece. Rinse the steel under running water to check the progress, and apply more soap and pumice if required until the desired effect is achieved.

## SATIN FINISH

A satin finish gives a softly reflective surface to a piece, rather than the bright, hard look of a high polish. A range of abrasive media can be used to create a satin finish, including emery paper, scouring pads and wire wool.

### METHOD

1 Remove any excess solder or blemishes from the piece with a file, then clean up the file marks with emery sticks or wet-and-dry paper, working through the grades to the finest paper.
2 Each grade of paper should be used across the grain of the previous paper, working backwards and forwards in one direction until all traces of the previous paper have been removed.
3 If a very fine satin surface is going to be produced, the piece can be polished with Hyfin at this stage, which will help make an even base for the texture. Use wire wool or fine emery paper, rubbed in one direction only to create the satin finish – be confident in the marks that you are making and try to keep the motion of the abrasive material parallel.

## HEAT PATINA
**Torch**

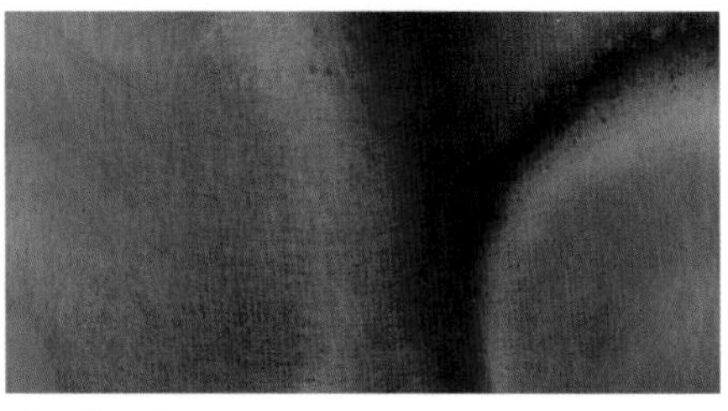

Refractory colours can be easily created on steel with the application of heat. Use cold-joining methods such as riveting in the construction of jewellery pieces with patinated elements, since the metal cannot be heated after colours have been applied.

### METHOD

1 Polished, matt and textured metals will all produce slightly different surfaces when patinated with heat. Ensure that the metal is clean and place it on a heatproof mat.
2 The colour of the metal will begin to change the instant it is heated, so watch carefully for the colour bands to develop – the colours will radiate out from the heated area. The proximity of the torch to the metal and the angle of application will affect the width of the bands, which may be circular or straight depending on how the metal is heated. Coloured spots can be made by holding the torch stationary, while the even heating of an edge will create a linear band across the steel. Repeat this process until a satisfactory patina has been achieved, and quench the piece in cold water.
3 The patina can easily be removed with emery paper and reapplied if necessary. As with all patinas, this is just a surface colour and will eventually rub off. However, wax and lacquer can deaden the colours if applied, so test a small area first if it is necessary to protect the surface in this way.

**KEY** Stainless steel · Tool steel · Mild steel

HEAT PATINA
## Oxyacetylene

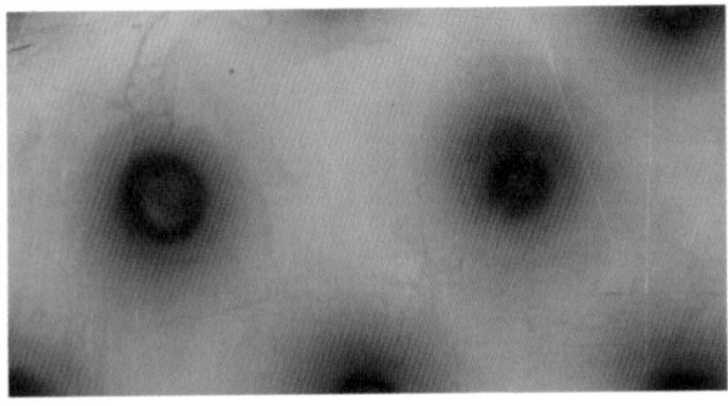

Although oxyacetylene torches are most commonly used for cutting and welding steel, a delicate application of the intense flame can be used to 'draw' on steel, producing the characteristic refractory colours on a smaller scale than is possible with the gas torches that jewellers normally use. Designs can be created on sheet that has already been heat-treated to produce some interesting effects.

### METHOD

1 Ensure you are aware of safe working practices concerning the use of oxyacetylene torches, including how to safely ignite the torch.
2 Adequate protective eye gear should be worn – welding goggles suitable for high-temperature work will filter out any harmful light frequencies.
3 Prepare your steel piece with a matt, satin or polished finish and place it on a heatproof mat.
4 Ignite the torch and carefully apply the flame – keep the flame moving; otherwise, you will make holes in the piece. The intense flame heats the metal quickly and will cause it to melt if care is not taken. Very fine designs can be applied by drawing with the flame, but it is difficult to be accurate.
5 Allow the piece to air-cool slightly before quenching it in cold water.

HEAT PATINA
## Kiln

This technique can be used as part of the tempering process, or purely for decorative effect. Heat colouring steel in a kiln means that an even temperature is applied, and the colours can be controlled more accurately and will form a shade that covers the whole piece uniformly.

### METHOD

1 Preheat the kiln to the correct temperature for the required colour. Temperatures in between the ones described below will give various shades of colour: yellow shades will become richer, before turning brown at around 260°C (500°F), and so on. Place the piece in the kiln and allow it to reach temperature, which can be judged by the colour of the steel.
2 When the colour is even throughout the surface of the steel, quench the piece in cold water. The surface finish of the steel will have a direct impact on the surface quality of the finished item – if you want a glossy blue effect, then you will need to polish your piece before patinating it.

| Colour | Temperature °C | Temperature °F |
|---|---|---|
| Yellow | 200–245 | 390–470 |
| Brown | 260 | 500 |
| Purple | 270–280 | 520–540 |
| Dark blue | 290 | 550 |
| Pale blue | 320 | 610 |

## BLACK PATINA
## **Hematite**

Steel can be chemically patinated to a deep metallic blue-black, which may be used to give high contrast to textured reliefs or simply to darken the whole surface of a piece. The chemical must be used in a well-ventilated area or outdoors because the fumes are toxic.

METHOD

1 Prepare enough hematite solution in a high-sided glass dish to cover your piece, following the recipe on page 243.
2 Clean the piece of metal with detergent and a soft brush to remove any grease marks.
3 Place the metal in the solution until it darkens; remove with plastic tweezers; then wash under running water with a soft brush. If the black oxidization rubs off too easily when drying the piece, or if the patina is streaky, scrub the piece with pumice powder and water and return it to the solution. Repeat as necessary until the desired effect is achieved.
4 Hematite can be painted onto the steel neatly, but will not produce an even effect.
5 The finish on the surface of the steel will affect the intensity of the patina – matt surfaces will appear darker than polished ones. Textures can be rubbed with fine emery paper to remove the patina from raised areas, which will give a striking contrast.
6 Apply microcrystalline wax polish to protect the finish from wear; the wax polish will also darken the patina some more but will dull any refractory colours that have developed on the surface.

## RUST

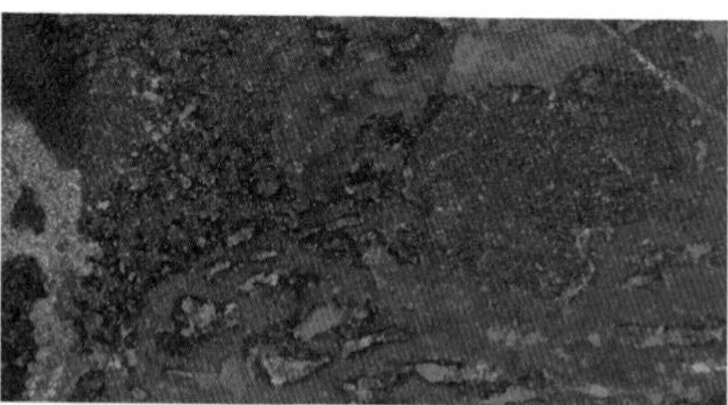

Rust can be an attractive surface texture and can provide colour contrast when combined with other colouring techniques or metals. It is possible to create rust on stainless and tool steel, but mild steel will work best.

METHOD

1 Mild steel will rust when exposed to water, but the process can be significantly speeded up by adding salt and an acid (vinegar works well) which will promote the chemical reaction. Mix up the solution using warm water, in a plastic container large enough to hold your piece.
2 Experiment with the concentration and temperature of the solution – the longer the piece is left exposed to the solution, the thicker the crust will become. Dirty or greasy metal will produce a random effect, so degrease the steel well using liquid detergent and an abrasive if you require even rusting.
3 It will take 24 to 48 hours for rust to develop, forming where the liquid evaporates off the surface. The process also requires oxygen to work well, so prop the steel against the side of the container and agitate the solution every few hours to wet the metal. The piece of steel can be left exposed to the solution for as long as is necessary; just add more water if the solution evaporates.
4 Waxes and oils can be used to darken and protect the layer of rust.

**KEY**  Stainless steel  Tool steel Mild steel

## RUST WITH MASK-OFF

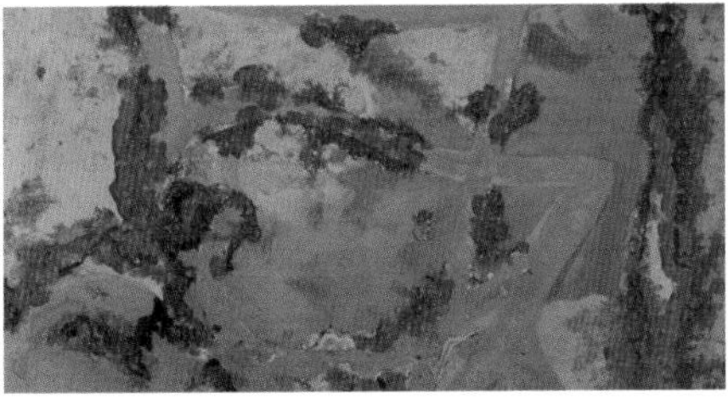

Patterns can be created in rust, by masking off areas of the steel so that they are not affected by the chemical solution and therefore do not rust. The steel can be heat patinated before the rusting process to provide added colours to your designs, which can be accurately executed using this technique.

### METHOD

1 Decide on the finish you would like to be contrasted with the rusted areas – whether polished or matt – and finish the surface to the required effect before continuing. Degrease the surface of the metal using liquid soap and a soft brush. Dry the steel and do not touch the surface – finger-marks will inhibit the adhesion of the resist.

2 Use permanent marker pen, stop-out varnish, lacquer or wax as a resist to mask off areas of the surface of the steel. The design can be painted, printed, drawn or scratched through the resist.

3 Once the resist is dry, stand the piece up in a solution of water, salt and vinegar. Check every few hours to see that the resist is not lifting off during the process as you agitate the solution, and reapply it if necessary – permanent marker pen ink will eventually dissolve into the solution, but this can give interesting results.

4 Rinse and dry the piece, and remove the resist with a suitable solvent.

△ HEIRLOOM 20–38P
BY SUZI TIBBETTS
*This die-formed steel locket has a tube rivet for the mechanism, and has been allowed to rust, giving an attractive, aged look.*

2

# Precious Metals

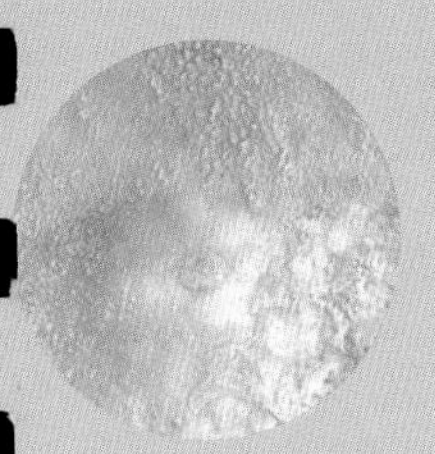

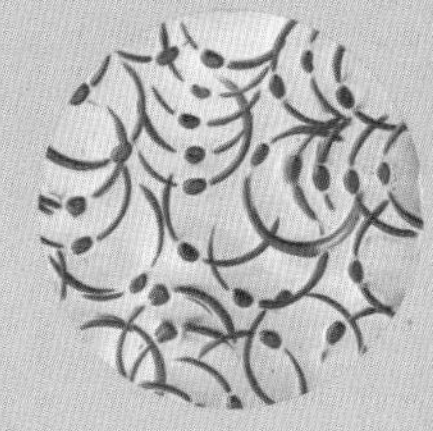

**Silver and Gold**

pages 58–125

Sterling silver, Britannia silver, fine silver, 9ct gold, 14ct gold, 18ct gold, 22ct gold

# Silver

Silver is the whitest of the precious metals – and also the most reflective. These properties, as well as its reasonable price, make it a popular choice of metal for making jewellery. Silver is also malleable, which means that a wide variety of techniques can be used to form and decorate it.

Silver is available in a variety of forms. Sheet, wire and tube are more expensive per gram than casting grain because they have higher processing costs. A supplier might cut silver to size, but buying either a large amount or remnants can be cheaper. Recently, tarnish-resistant alloys of silver have been developed. They are resistant to firestain and can be worked for longer periods before they need to be annealed. Precious metal clay, which will form fine silver once fired, is available in paste and sheet form.

### APPLICATIONS

Silver is suitable for most jewellery forms, including fittings for earrings. The only limitation is the physical strength of silver, so brooch pins or springs will usually be made in steel or white gold, which retain their form better.

### STERLING SILVER

**Composition:** 92.5% silver, 7.5% copper

**Melting Range:** 805°C–950°C (1480°F–1740°F)

The alloy most commonly used for jewellery, since it is harder than fine silver, although tarnishes more quickly. Metal quickly becomes work-hardened and needs to be softened by annealing. Silver-plating can cover firestain.

### BRITANNIA SILVER

**Composition:** 95.83% silver

**Melting Range:** 900°C–940°C (1650°F–1725°F)

An historical alloy that is still commercially available, and being less susceptible to firestain, it is used for processes such as enamelling, where firestain under the surface of the metal is impossible to remove.

### FINE SILVER

**Composition:** 99% silver

**Melting Point:** 961°C (1762°F)

Used where a softer metal may be appropriate – settings for fragile stones, for instance. Electroforming and precious-metal clay techniques produce pieces made of fine silver.

### ANNEALING

Heat the silver with a torch until it is dull red. This shade is easier to see at low light levels, and will occur at 599°C–649°C (1110°F–1200°F). Allow to cool before quenching in cold water. Clean the metal in a heated pickling solution until all the oxides are removed.

### SOLDERING

Silver solders of hallmarking quality are available with a number of melting points. Easy and medium solders have a lower melting point than those of hard or enamelling solders. These solders are sold as strips or wires, which should be used with borax as a flux, and are also available ready-mixed with flux in a syringe for easy application.

▽ THE IMPORTANCE OF WASTED TIME
BY KELLY McCALLUM
*The intricately pierced silver case of this locket opens to reveal a tiny plant displayed within.*

△ BUCKTHORN
BY SONJA SEIDL
*This wonderfully tactile bracelet was made using photoetching and soldering silver and gold.*

▽ ROYAL EXCHANGE THEATRE RING
BY MELISSA HANSOM
*An etched design decorates the oxidized domed silver form, with the stone setting surrounded by 18-carat gold granules.*

△ NECKLACE
BY REGINA ARADESIAN
*Plique-à-jour enamel was fired into the central element of this silver necklace, creating cells of colour that glow when held to the light.*

# Gold

Gold has been used in jewellery-making for at least 5,000 years – pure gold (24-carat) is incredibly malleable and resistant to tarnish, but it is too soft to be practical. Many gold alloys are available in a range of purities and colours that have better properties for making durable pieces.

Most jewellers do not now make up their own gold alloys since it is far more convenient to buy ready-made products such as sheet and wire. Gold has a greater density than silver, and so pieces will be heavier. Coloured alloys of gold include red, white and green and are dependent upon the proportion of other metals that the gold is alloyed with. White gold is either dull grey or slightly yellowish and is often rhodium-plated to give it a bright white finish. Gold-plating is often used to enhance pieces, especially where cost is an issue, and plating can be done in any colour and carat of gold, including black.

**APPLICATIONS**
Most processes and techniques can be used with gold, although some coloured alloys can be more difficult to work. The prohibitive cost of gold means that it is often used in small quantities to add detail to silver jewellery, which will increase the value of the piece.

### 9-CARAT YELLOW GOLD

**Composition:** 375 parts gold per 1,000

**Melting Range:** 879°C– 899°C (1615°–1650°F)

Mainly used in the United Kingdom, this is the lowest proportion of gold that can be used in an alloy before tarnishing will occur, and has the palest colour of all the yellow-gold alloys. The benefits of 9-carat gold are its hardness and comparatively cheap cost.

### 14-CARAT YELLOW GOLD

**Composition:** 585 parts gold per 1,000

**Melting Range:** 832°C–871°C (1530°F–1600°F)

A mid-tone yellow-gold alloy that can be used for most applications, but the low melting range may limit its use in certain applications.

### 18-CARAT YELLOW GOLD

**Composition:** 750 parts gold per 1,000

**Melting Range:** 904°C–960°C (1660°F–1760°F)

Has the best working properties and is the most durable of the high-carat gold alloys. It is malleable enough to take most techniques but hard enough to retain a high polish.

## 22-CARAT YELLOW GOLD

**Composition:** 916 parts gold per 1,000

**Melting Range:** 965°C–982°C (1770°F–1800°F)

This soft alloy has a high intrinsic value and a wonderfully rich colour. It is usually available in sheet and wire form but in a restricted range of gauges. Twenty-two-carat gold foil is useful for enamelling and fusing techniques. Precious metal clay is available in 22-carat gold, and also as a liquid that can be painted onto silver precious metal clay prior to firing.

### ANNEALING

Heat the gold with a torch until it is dull red. This shade of colour is easier to see at low light levels and will occur at 649°C– 760°C (1200°F–1400°F). Allow to cool slightly before quenching in cold water. Clean the metal in a heated pickling solution until all the oxides have been removed.

### SOLDERING

Each carat and colour of gold has its own specific hard, medium and easy solders. These are available in sheet or wire form and also as a paste ready-mixed with flux in a syringe. Use Auflux as a flux for best results when soldering.

▷ BLACK OPAL RING
BY BARBARA CHRISTIE
*This 18-carat yellow-gold ring has a large dark black opal as its main feature and a ruby set in a circular wire form to visually balance the piece.*

◁ BIRDWATCHING
BY HAYLEY FRIEL
*This piece is made from green gold with a green sapphire. Etched glass forms a stylish monocle.*

▷ FLOURISH BROOCH
BY NUTRE ARAYAVANISH
*Formed from gold-plated silver, freshwater pearls and wood sheets, this brooch was photoetched, pierced, soldered and laser-cut.*

## DRILLING

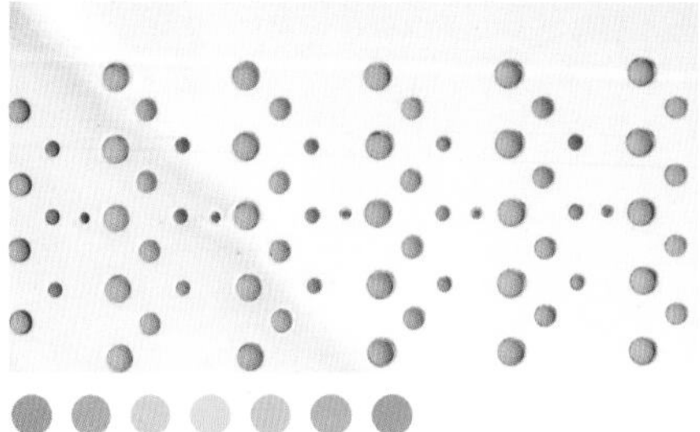

Drilled holes provide a starting point for a large number of techniques such as piercing or riveting, but can also be used as decoration.

### METHOD

**1** Working on a steel block, use a centre punch to mark where you want the drilled hole. This will give the drill bit purchase so that it does not skid around the surface of the metal sheet or break.

**2** Select a drill bit and secure it in the drill chuck. Good-quality high-speed steel drill bits work best and are a worthwhile investment. With proper care they will last a long time. It is always a good idea to use a lubricating agent, such as an organic cutting fluid or machine oil. For very large holes, you will need to clamp the metal sheet to the drill bed.

**3** Position your piece on the drill bed on top of a piece of scrap wood, having the centre punch mark directly under the drill bit. Holding the piece firmly at all times, turn the drill on and bring the drill bit down to make contact with the metal. Do not push too hard; the drill bit can break. You will feel the difference in resistance when the drill bit comes out of the other side of the metal. Turn off the drill.

**4** If necessary, clean up the edges of the drill hole using a ball burr held in a pin vice.

## DISC-CUTTER
**Hole Punch**

Disc-cutting is a faster and a less wasteful way to make holes in metal than drilling. The disc-cutter is a useful piece of equipment, and small, affordable ones are readily available and can be used either with a hammer or held in a vice. This method also cuts holes more accurately than piercing (see page 63).

### METHOD

**1** Anneal, pickle and dry your piece of metal.

**2** Select the size of punch you require and line up your metal sheet in the disc-cutter under the corresponding hole. Insert the punch.

**3** Use a hammer to force the punch through the metal. Alternatively, you can hold the whole disc-cutter sideways and, while being careful not to let your metal slip, place it in a vice and tighten the jaws. This will force the punch through the metal.

**TIP:** The thicker the metal, the more force it will take to make a hole. Metal thicker than 1 mm ($\frac{1}{32}$ inch) will be hard work!

**KEY**  Sterling silver  Britannia silver  Fine silver  9ct gold  14ct gold  18ct gold  22ct gold

PIERCING
## Straight Lines

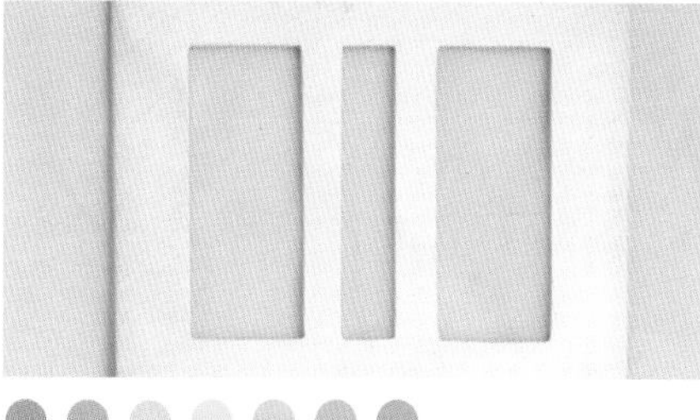

Once mastered, piercing is a versatile technique with which to enhance your jewellery-making. Straight lines are a challenge to begin with. Remember to relax and let your saw do the work.

### METHOD

1 Lay out your design on the reverse of the piece with dividers, or sketch it with a ruler or scribe.
2 Centre-punch a mark inside each section that needs to be pierced out, near the section edge. Drill a hole large enough for the saw blade to fit through.
3 With one end of the saw blade already secured in the frame (teeth pointing down), thread the other end of the blade through one of the drilled holes. Slide the silver sheet to the top of the blade so that it won't pull on the blade as you tighten it. Have good tension on the blade.
4 Lay the silver sheet down on your bench pin so that the area you are piercing is in the gap. Start cutting, using long, even strokes while moving the blade up and down. Cut inside the scribed line, rather than on it; if the saw wanders, you won't go over the line.
5 To turn a corner, keep the blade moving on the spot as you gradually turn the metal into its path – as if pulling backwards on the blade. If the blade snaps, it may have been tilted at an angle and couldn't easily turn the corner.
6 Pierce out the remaining sections. Use a flat needle file to remove the saw marks and even out any 'wobbly' areas.
7 Remove the file marks with an emery stick and polish if you wish.

PIERCING
## Curves

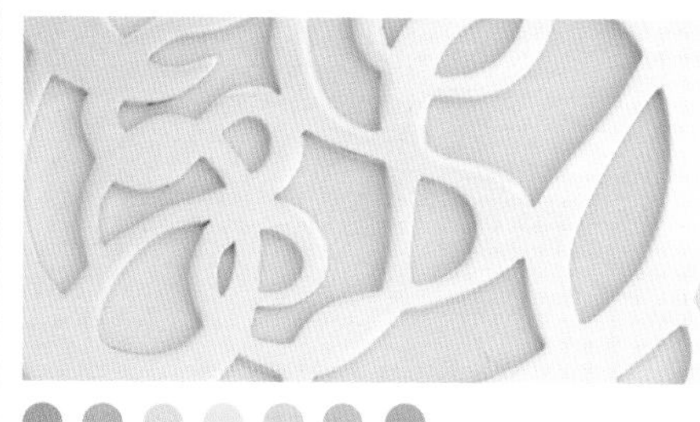

Piercing can create intricate patterns. When designing, consider the overall composition and the interplay of positive and negative spaces.

### METHOD

1 Plan your design on paper and transfer it to the silver sheet with double-sided sticky tape.
2 Centre-punch a mark inside each section that needs to be pierced out, near the section edge. Drill a hole large enough for the saw blade to fit through.
3 With one end of the blade already secured in the frame (teeth pointing down), thread the other end of the blade through one of the drilled holes. Slide the silver sheet to the top of the blade so that it won't pull on the blade as you tighten it. Be sure you have good tension on the blade.
4 Always pierce out inside areas first, starting with the smallest.
5 To pierce a curve, turn the metal into the path of the blade while you are moving the saw up and down. The faster the metal is turned, the tighter the curve will be.
6 After all the inner areas have been pierced, cut the outside areas of the shape.
7 Remove any saw marks with needle files. Try to match the profile of a curve with a file that is similar in shape – use a round file for tight curves and a half-round file for more open curves. File the outer surfaces of curves with a flat-faced file.
8 Clean up with emery paper and barrel-polish the piece if you wish.

ROLLING MILL TEXTURES
## Templates

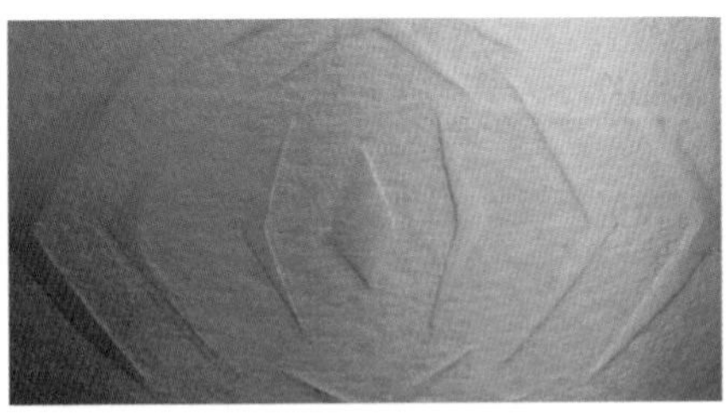

Almost any material with interesting shapes, such as leaves, feathers, paper, fabric or metal, can be used to create impressions on silver or gold in the rolling mill. The material you use must be dry.

METHOD

1 Anneal, pickle and dry two pieces of metal that are the same size; one can be a base metal (brass or gilding metal).
2 Cut out a design in a piece of watercolour paper with scissors or a craft knife; the areas that have been cut away will be raised on your final texture.
3 Sandwich the paper between the two pieces of metal and pass these assembled pieces through the rolling mill, with the rollers just far enough apart to allow the metal to pass through without needing to exert too much pressure. The paper will be compressed during the process.
4 The texture of the paper will now have been transferred onto the silver, with the cut-out areas slightly raised. If the effect isn't what you intended, then you will have to make a new template and try again. The closer the rollers are together, the deeper the impression will be. If too much pressure is used, however, then both the metal and the impression will be severely stretched and deformed. It is also possible to thin the metal too much.
5 Hand-polish the surface of the piece with fine wire wool to bring out the pattern.

ROLLING MILL TEXTURES
## Impressions

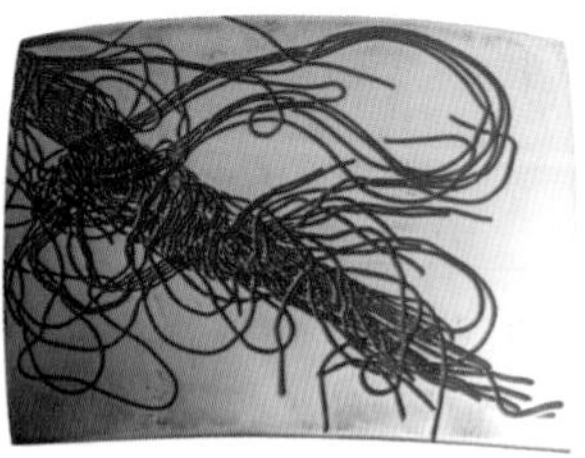

Materials used to make impressions do not have to be flat. Experiment with bulky forms such as tangled wires to see the effects that can be achieved. Be aware that impressed areas can become thin and may form weak points or even split; use thicker metal sheets to avoid mishaps.

METHOD

1 Choose an appropriate material with which to texture the metal sheet. Leaves, feathers and fine fabrics work best when passed through the mill along with only one sheet of metal. Adjust the rollers of the mill far enough apart so that the sheet will not stretch too much; otherwise, the impression will be distorted and indistinct.
2 Materials with greater thicknesses (which do not easily compress) should be sandwiched between two sheets of metal and rolled through the mill with more force.
3 Find some scrap pieces of metal with the same thickness as your final piece and experiment with changing the distance between the rollers to see how well your texture will impress – some texturing materials will compress more than others and may need to be rolled harder to force the texture further into the surface.
4 To flatten a piece of sheet metal that has become curved due to texturing, first anneal and clean it, then place it on a steel block with the corners of the sheet touching the block. Hit it with a rawhide mallet until it is flat.

**KEY**  Sterling silver  Britannia silver  Fine silver  9ct gold  14ct gold  18ct gold  22ct gold

ROLLING MILL TEXTURES
## Highly Textured

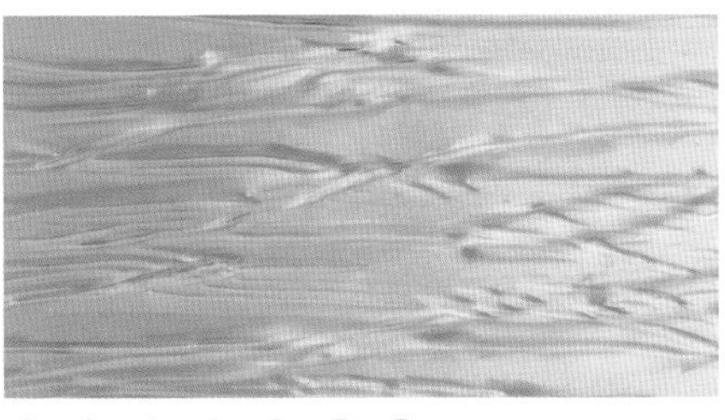

Textures applied to sheet metal need not be subtle. Large distortions can be created by sandwiching the metal sheet between suitable and interesting textures. Outer plates of base metal may be necessary to protect the rollers from being damaged.

### METHOD

1 Anneal, pickle, rinse and dry the sheet metal. Wrap thin, base-metal wire lengthways around the sheet until the sheet is almost covered. The results will be better if the wrapping is uneven and there are crossovers, as the sheet will be forced from both sides to fill any gaps in the outer wrapping.
2 Pass the wrapped metal through the rolling mill, squashing the wires into the surface of the sheet.
3 Adjust the rollers so that they are closer together and wind the piece through again. This will ensure that a deep impression is made – the wire should be almost flush with the surface of the sheet.
4 Anneal the whole piece to soften the wires, enabling them to be removed more easily.
5 Pickle and clean up the sheet.

ROLLING MILL TEXTURES
## On Wire

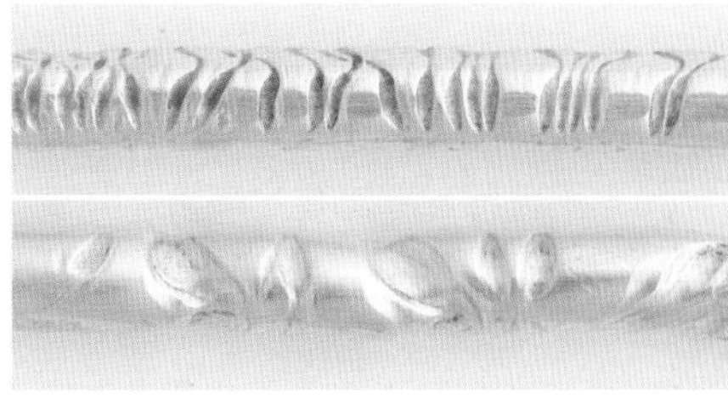

The rolling mill has special rollers for wire that are capable of doing more than tapering and thinning square wire. Interesting textures can also be applied to both thick rods and slender wires with a range of materials. Alternatively, with the wire rollers opened, sheet can be impressed with a linear texture.

### METHOD

1 The wire you want to texture can be sized from 1 mm (1/32 inch) in diameter and upwards and should be clean and annealed.
2 Wrap thin copper or nickel wire around the precious metal wire along its whole length. The neatness of the wrapping will have an effect on the final texture, and the thicker the wire used to wrap the rod, the larger and more distorted the resulting impression will be.
3 Ensure that the wire rollers are shut, so that there is no gap between them.
4 Start at the end of the rollers with the widest grooves and find the first smallest gap that the wire will not pass through simply by pushing it through. Wind the wire through the mill, then turn it 45 degrees before putting it through again – this is to stop the wire from taking on a square profile.
5 Find the next smallest gap and run the wire through the mill again. The wrapped wire should be almost flush with the surface of the precious metal, but you won't know the result until it is unwrapped.
6 To unwrap the piece, anneal it first, but do not pickle it. The wire will now be soft and can be easily cut away to reveal the texture.

HAMMER TEXTURES
## Cross-peen

This technique works best on flat sheet but can be applied to rings or bracelets that are formed on a mandrel. The metal will be stretched during the hammering process, so it's wise to take this into account when sizing your ring: start out by making it one or two sizes smaller.

METHOD

1 Anneal, pickle and dry your piece of metal.
2 Use a clean, flat steel surface – supported by a sandbag to reduce the noise – and begin hammering using the thin side of a cross-peen hammer. The width of the hammerhead will determine the size of the marks you make on the metal.
3 Holding the piece of metal flat on the block with one hand, evenly overlap the hammer marks to create a rippled effect; radial lines, cross-hatching and random marks are all equally effective.
4 The surface is now ready to be polished.

HAMMER TEXTURES
## Raising

There are numerous types of hammer, many of which are designed to perform specific techniques. Experiment to find out which marks can be made by which hammerheads.

METHOD

1 Anneal, pickle and dry your piece of metal.
2 Use a clean, flat, steel surface – supported by a sandbag to reduce the noise – and begin hammering using the thin side of a raising hammer. The width of the hammerhead will determine the size of the marks you make on the metal. Remember that any marks or pits on the face of the raising hammer will be transferred to the metal you are hammering.
3 Holding the piece of metal flat on the block with one hand, evenly overlap the hammer marks to create a rippled effect; radial lines, cross-hatching and random marks are all equally effective.
4 The surface is now ready to be polished.

**Sample** *A raising hammer was used to create this texture.*

**KEY**  Sterling silver  Britannia silver 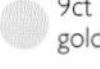 Fine silver  9ct gold  14ct gold  18ct gold  22ct gold

HAMMER TEXTURES
## Ball-peen

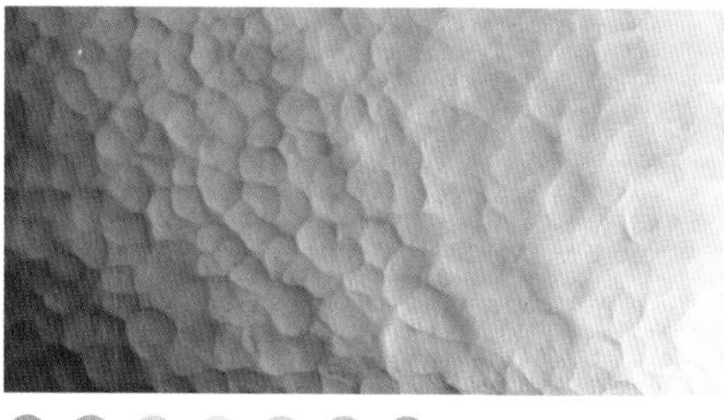

Hammer texturing is a versatile technique – the results of which are determined by the shape of the specific hammerhead. Good-quality hammers can be expensive, but less expensive ones will work just as well if you take good care of them.

METHOD

1 Anneal, pickle and dry your piece of metal.
2 Use a clean, flat steel surface – supported by a sandbag to reduce the noise – and begin hammering using the ball side of a ball-peen hammer. The size of the ball on the hammerhead will determine the size of the dimples you make in the metal – a repoussé hammer will leave much smaller marks than a jobbing hammer, for example.
3 Holding the piece of metal flat on the block with one hand, evenly overlap the hammer marks, covering the whole surface of the metal.
4 The surface is now ready to be polished.

HAMMER TEXTURES
## Planishing

Silversmiths often use planishing as a final finish on their pieces, but this technique is also useful for jewellers. Planishing hammers should be kept highly polished so that a polished finish will result on the piece. This hammer has a distinct advantage – small marks can be 'planished' out.

METHOD

1 Anneal, pickle and dry your piece of metal.
2 Use a clean, flat steel surface – supported by a sandbag to reduce noise – and begin hammering. The curved side of the planishing hammer is more appropriate for working on flat sheet, whereas the flat side of the hammer is best used for working on curved surfaces.
3 Overlap the hammer marks so that they form a uniform pattern. Pay particular attention to any areas that need marks to be hammered out, but be careful not to thin the metal too much.
4 The surface is now ready to be polished.

## STAMPS AND PUNCHES

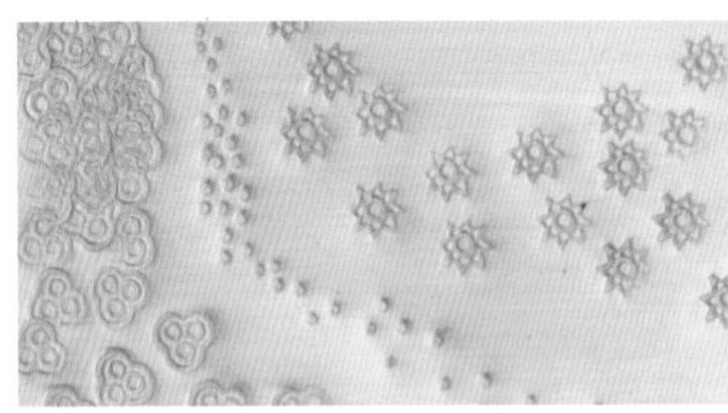

Metal stamps and pattern punches are useful for creating visual interest in a piece by allowing you to place details in textured areas. A range of ready-made punches is available, but you could make your own.

METHOD

1 This technique works best on flat sheet that has been annealed.
2 Fix your metal sheet onto a steel block with masking tape.
3 Hold the punch upright with one hand and strike it with a metal hammer with the other hand. One hard strike is better than several taps with the hammer, since the punch may move out of position. It is more difficult to make a clear impression with larger punches than it is with smaller ones. The harder you strike the punch, the deeper the impression will be.

**Sample** *Purchased pattern punches and a centre punch formed the design in this sample. The item was cleaned up afterwards with fine wire wool.*

## STAMPS AND PUNCHES
### Texturing

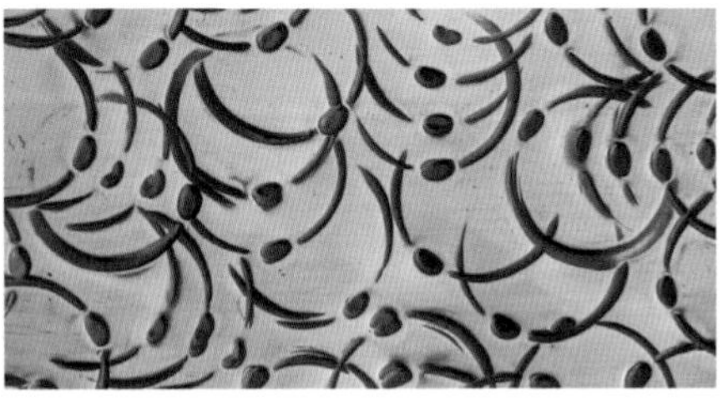

Create a field of texture by using a large pattern punch. It's best to use this technique to apply texture to metal before you begin any shaping processes, such as press forming or doming.

METHOD

1 This technique works best on flat sheet that has been annealed.
2 Fix your metal sheet onto a steel block with masking tape.
3 Hold the punch upright with one hand and strike it with a metal hammer with the other hand. One hard strike is better than several taps with the hammer, since the punch may move out of position.
4 It is more difficult to make a clear impression with a large punch than it is with smaller ones, so when using a larger punch, you should plan a design that will compensate for any imperfection by creating a random pattern. Also, try to keep a steady hand while holding the punch. Angle it slightly as you strike repeatedly, until the whole pattern has been stamped onto the surface of the metal. The harder you strike, the deeper the impression will be.
5 You can increase the visibility of the pattern by oxidizing it and gently rubbing the surface with fine emery paper.

**KEY**  Sterling silver  Britannia silver  Fine silver  9ct gold  14ct gold  18ct gold 22ct gold

STAMPS AND PUNCHES

## Letters and Numbers

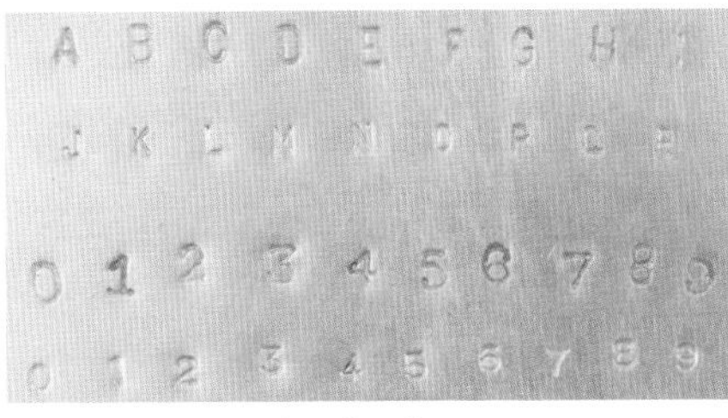

Letters and numbers are used to add an inscription to any piece, but you may simply want to use them for decoration. Punches of this type are available in a limited range of sizes. Swan-neck punches are used to inscribe the insides of rings.

METHOD

1 Anneal, pickle and dry your piece of metal.
2 Fix your metal onto a steel block with masking tape.
3 Hold the punch upright with one hand and strike it with a metal hammer with the other hand. One hard strike is better than several taps with the hammer, since the punch may move out of position. It is more difficult to make a clear impression with larger punches than it is with smaller ones. The harder you strike the punch, the deeper the impression will be.
4 Lining up letter punches to form a neat text may be difficult, so either allow for slight error in your design or align the punches against a straight piece of wood.

## RETICULATION

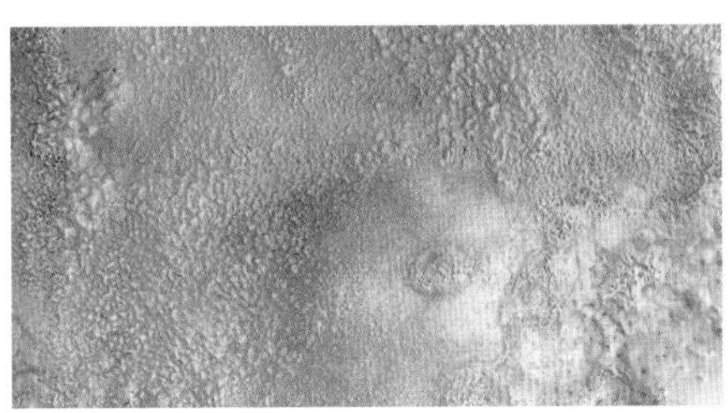

The effects of reticulation can be unpredictable, but this technique creates such interesting surfaces that it is well worth the risk. For the best results, work on sheet metal that is at least 1 mm (1⁄32 inch) thick.

METHOD

1 Anneal, pickle and dry your piece of metal.
2 Repeat the above process at least seven times. This will bring fine silver or gold up to the surface of the metal. There should be less oxidization of the metal during the heating process each time it is performed.
3 Working on a charcoal block, heat the metal with a torch beyond annealing temperature. The surface of the metal will turn liquid. Play the flame across the surface – the differences in temperature and stresses within the metal while it is being heated will create the best effect. Be careful not to overheat the metal, since only the surface needs to be liquefied.
4 Once the desired effect is achieved, allow the metal to cool slightly before quenching and then pickling.
5 Clean the metal with some pumice powder and liquid soap.
6 Be careful when forming pieces from reticulated sheet: the metal may be a bit brittle and will incorporate areas of different thicknesses.

## RETICULATION
### Pierced Sheet

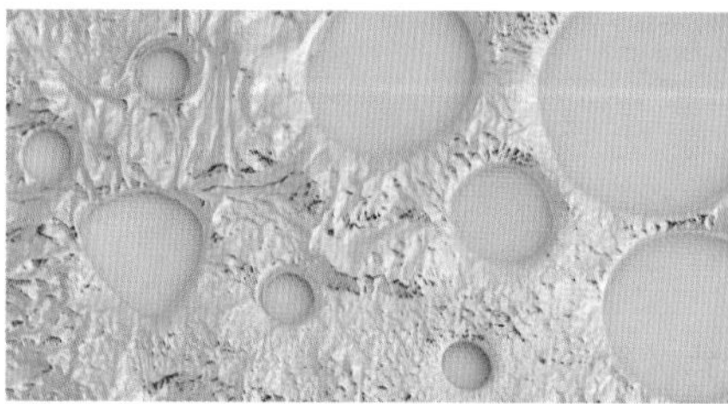

Reticulation creates evocative 'moonscapes', especially when used on a pierced sheet. Sterling silver usually yields the best results, but some gold alloys will work well too. Work on sheet that is 1 mm (1⁄32 inch) or thicker.

METHOD

1 Anneal, pickle and dry your piece of metal.
2 Repeat the above process at least seven times. This will bring fine silver or gold up to the surface of the metal. There should be less oxidation of the metal during the heating process each time it is performed.
3 Drill or stamp holes through the metal.
4 Working on a charcoal block, heat the metal with a torch beyond annealing temperature. The surface of the metal will turn liquid. Play the flame across the surface – the differences in temperature and stresses within the metal while it is being heated will create the best effect. Be careful not to overheat the metal, since only the surface needs to be liquefied.
5 Once the desired effect is achieved, allow the metal to cool slightly before quenching and then pickling.
6 Clean the metal sheet with pumice powder and liquid soap. The piece can be polished by hand or in a barrel polisher.

## FUSING
### Silver

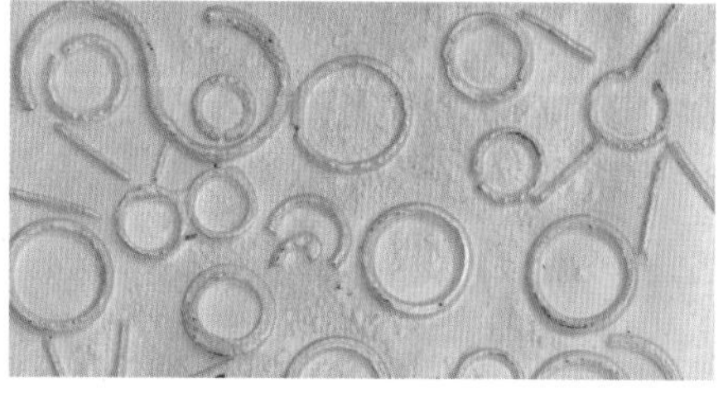

When heated to a sufficiently high temperature, pieces of silver can be permanently bonded without the use of solder. As the surface of the silver melts, elements that are touching will become fused. This technique also gives the silver a unique surface quality.

METHOD

1 Degrease the base silver sheet and flux its surface with borax.
2 Additional pieces of silver that will be applied also need to be clean and free of any solder, since this will eat into the silver when heated to the high temperature needed for fusing to occur. Dip each piece of silver into the borax solution before positioning it on the base sheet.
3 Heat the metal with a torch, playing the flame across the surface so that all the metal heats up at the same rate. The top surface of the sheet will glow brightly and turn into liquid. Watch for pooling around the edges of the applied pieces of silver and direct the flame at areas that need more heat, ensuring that areas don't overheat and melt.
4 Let the piece air-cool for a while before quenching. The silver will be brittle from the prolonged heating, so anneal and pickle it again.
5 Scrub the surface thoroughly with pumice powder and liquid soap; it will be slightly porous and may have trapped pickle residue. The raised areas can be highlighted with a steel burnisher to create contrast with the background.

**KEY**  Sterling silver  Britannia silver  Fine silver  9ct gold  14ct gold  18ct gold  22ct gold

FUSING
## Gold Foil

Fusing pure gold foil on to the surface of silver, or 'keum-boo', is a Korean decorative technique that fuses 22-carat gold foil with silver surfaces to add colour and contrast.

METHOD

1. Gold foil must be used, rather than gold leaf, which is too thin to withstand the heating required. Carefully place the gold foil in a folded piece of tracing paper so that it can be easily cut into small pieces, ideally no larger than 1 cm square (⅜ inch square). Try not to touch the foil at any stage.
2. Moisten the surface of the silver with saliva and transfer the gold foil pieces onto the silver sheet with a damp paintbrush.
3. With the silver resting on a charcoal block, apply a gas torch, being careful not to let the flame touch the gold foil since this will make it wrinkle up.
4. When the silver reaches annealing temperature and glows at the edges, rub a probe over the pieces of gold foil to help them bond to the silver. Burnish out any air bubbles trapped under the gold. Some gold foil will be lost in the initial heating, but if the piece is allowed to cool, then the process can be repeated.
5. Don't overheat the silver – the gold could sink below the surface. If that happens, reveal it by etching away the surface of the silver.
6. Pickle the piece to remove any oxides.
7. The fused metals can be put through the rolling mill along with any subtly textured material. As well as giving the surface a degree of continuity, this will also test how well the fusing worked.

FUSING
## Gold Dust

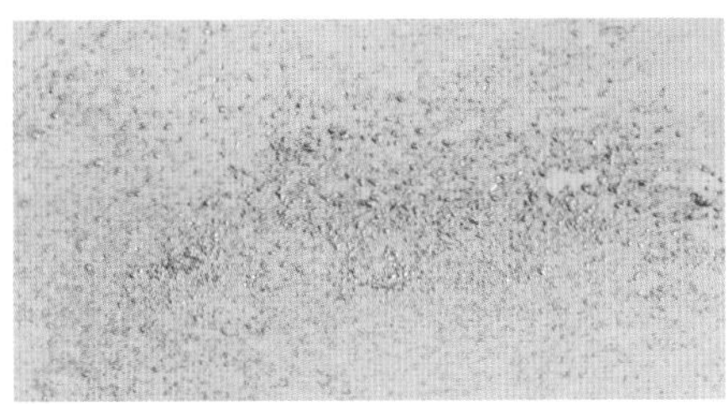

Gold dust can be fused onto the surface of silver to create a subtle texture and provide colour contrast. The intensity of the effect can be controlled by the amount of gold that is used; use a blunt object to scratch a pattern in the dust once it is laid down. Stencils can also outline the position of the dust.

METHOD

1. Degrease the surface of the silver and paint it with a borax solution.
2. Sprinkle gold dust on the surface. Gold that is 14-carat or higher will work best. Use a rough file to make dust if none is available.
3. Although gold has a much higher melting point than silver, the particles of gold are so small that they will quickly reach their melting point, so the silver must be heated from underneath to begin with.
4. After the silver reaches annealing temperature, bring the torch up onto the top surface and continue heating – as soon as the top surface of the silver reaches the melting point, the gold particles will also begin to melt and the two metals will fuse. Don't overheat the silver – the gold could sink below the surface. If that happens, reveal it by etching away the surface of the silver.
5. Pickle the piece and then scrub it with pumice to remove the pickle from the porous surface.
6. Brighten the surface with wire wool and highlight the gold by rubbing a steel burnisher across the surface. This will also smooth down any rough areas.

## SOLDERING

Soldering is one of the most useful techniques available to the jeweller since it allows metal to be joined permanently and, if done well, invisibly. As with all processes, it takes practice to master and gain confidence in the behaviour of the metal and other variables that may need to be taken into consideration.

### METHOD

1 Ensure that the join between pieces is a good match; you should not be able to see any light through the join, and the metal must be clean.

2 Position the piece on a heatproof mat with a heatproof block sitting upright behind it; this is to reflect heat back towards the piece. Always use gravity to your advantage: Rather than lie pieces on their sides, and using tweezers if necessary, place them one on top of the other so that you have both hands free. It is much easier to spend time accurately positioning pieces before you start heating than to readjust them when everything is hot and has moved. Iron binding wire can be used to help hold pieces in position.

3 Mix up some flux by grinding a borax cone in a dish with water to make a thin paste and apply it around the join with a fine paintbrush. Apply a cut piece of solder (a pallion) so that it sits over both sides of the join. The size of the pallion will depend on the join you are soldering.

4 Begin heating around the piece gently with a torch, allowing the borax to dry out without moving the solder. Once dry, you can start to heat the piece directly, but do not heat the join yet. Concentrate on heating up the surrounding metal until it starts to glow – the solder should melt quickly if the torch is applied directly now.

5 As soon as the solder has melted, remove the flame – there is a danger that the piece may melt. Quench the piece in cold water, remove any binding wire and place it in a heated pickle bath to clean off the oxides and borax.

6 Ensure that all the borax is removed, since once fired, it is hard enough to damage files. Once clean and dry, the soldered join can be filed to remove any excess solder.

7 Stick feeding is a method of soldering in which a stick of solder is applied to a join while it is being heated. This method is useful for larger joins, or where greater amounts of solder are needed, but it can be messy. Hold the stick of solder in insulated tweezers and apply one end to a fluxed join that has been heated to a dull red; continue to carefully heat the piece with the solder in contact, and the solder will be drawn along the seam.

8 Sweat soldering is a good way of joining forms together where there is no convenient external ledge to rest the solder on, such as pierced-out conforming press forms. Apply flux and plenty of solder pallions to the edges of one piece of metal, and heat it up to melt the solder. Pickle and clean the piece. Flux both parts of the form and bind them together with binding wire. When the piece is reheated to soldering temperature, the solder will melt, bonding the two parts. Remove the binding wire and pickle the piece.

**NOTE:** Sealed hollow forms must have a hole made in them if any subsequent heating is to be done – trapped air will expand when it is heated and can cause the piece to explode.

**KEY**  Sterling silver  Britannia silver  Fine silver  9ct gold  14ct gold  18ct gold 22ct gold

## INLAY
## Gold on Silver

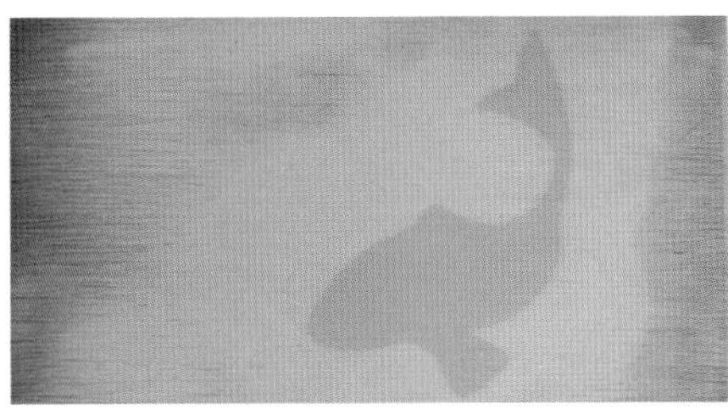

Different-coloured metals can be permanently joined together to make surfaces that are decorated with small areas of colour. The simplest form of inlay is designed by soldering gold wires into drilled holes in a silver sheet; the wires are then filed flush – they will look like dots on the sheet. For inlaying pierced shapes into a sheet, the metals used should be less than 1 mm (1⁄32 inch) thick and of equal thicknesses.

### METHOD

1 Trace the outline of your design onto the gold sheet, or apply the design with double-sided sticky tape. Don't design awkward grooves that may cause difficulties later.
2 Pierce out the shape and file the edges so that they are smooth and free of file marks.
3 Use double-sided tape to attach the gold shape onto the silver base sheet in the correct position, then trace the outline onto the silver using a fine scribe. Remove the gold piece and put it aside.
4 Centre-punch and drill a small hole inside the traced shape; thread a saw blade through the hole and pierce out the shape, keeping well within the line. Removing too much metal will leave holes, so make the cut-out hole smaller than the shape that will be fitted into it.
5 File the silver sheet until the gold piece fits snugly inside and ensure that it sits flush with the surface of the silver. The more complex your shape, the longer this will take. The pieces can be tapped with a mallet to even out any differences in surface height.
6 Flux around the join between the two pieces and use small pieces of hard silver solder to tack-solder them together. If the gold piece comes out of alignment at this stage, the small amount of solder used will allow it to be tapped back into position with a mallet.
7 Flux the join again and apply enough solder to flow around the whole outline.
8 Pickle, rinse and dry the piece.
9 At this stage, re-solder any large gaps that remain; small dents can be hammered out by working on them from the reverse of the piece using a hammer on a steel block.
10 The front surface will need to be finished with a file, an emery stick and polish.

INLAY

## Inlaying Wire

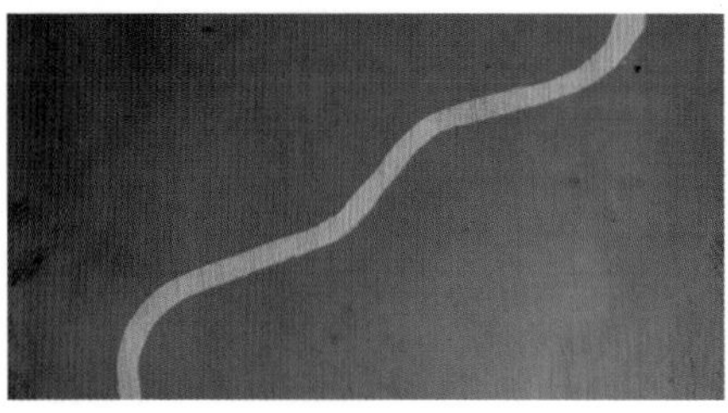

The traditional method of inlaying metal is to carve a groove into the base material that will receive the inlay. The two pieces are soldered together, and then various forming techniques are applied.

METHOD

1. Form your wire shape with pliers and tap it flat with a hammer on a steel block.
2. Scribe around the outline of the wire shape on the silver base sheet. The outline will be larger than the wire diameter, so work well inside the line.
3. Engrave, chisel or carve away the metal. The groove that you cut should have the same cross-sectional profile as the wire; any sections that are wider will result in a gap. The gold wire should fit snugly in the silver groove.
4. Tap one end of the wire into the silver sheet so that it stays there on its own; then tack-solder it in place with hard silver solder.
5. Use a hammer and punch to spread the soldered end of wire so that it fills the groove.
6. Tap down the next centimetre (half inch) or so of wire, and tack-solder it. Repeat this process until the length of the wire has been soldered.
7. Hammer the surface of the piece to make sure that any gaps are filled by spreading the wire; flux and use hard solder to fill any remaining gaps. The piece may need some light milling to even out the surfaces.
8. Clean up the surface and polish.

INLAY

## Gold Pieces

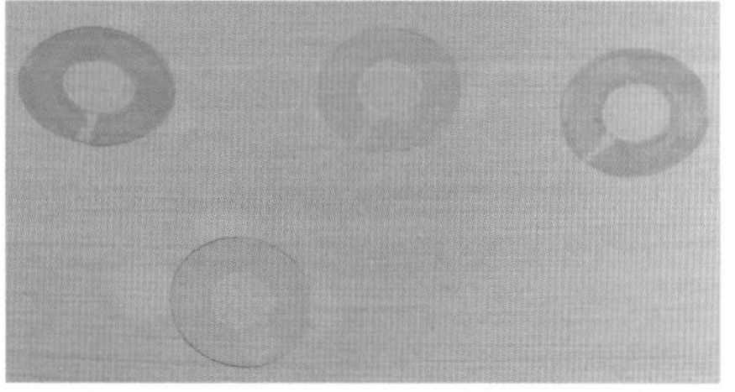

One way of inlaying gold in silver is to solder gold pieces onto the base sheet, using a rolling mill to thin the pieces until the surfaces are level. Nine-carat gold may melt into the silver if overheated, but other carat values work well.

METHOD

1. Form, cut and solder gold jump rings, using the appropriate-carat gold solder.
2. Pickle and clean the rings, removing excess solder.
3. Flatten the jump rings slightly with a hammer or in a rolling mill so that they will make better contact with the base sheet.
4. Flux the silver sheet and jump rings with borax, and use hard silver solder to join them. Heat from underneath to avoid overheating the gold rings.
5. Pickle, clean and dry the piece.
6. Use the rolling mill to thin the piece until the jump rings are level with the surface of the silver sheet. If the sheet is passed through the rolling mill solely along its length, the jump rings will become elongated and oval. To prevent this, rotate the sheet 90 degrees each time you pass it through the mill.
7. Clean up the sheet with a file if necessary, and emery paper.

**TIP:** Make a 'table' out of steel mesh for the piece to rest on while you do the soldering; this will enable easy access to the underside of the piece.

**Sample** *Red- and yellow-gold jump rings were inlaid into silver sheet.*

**KEY**  Sterling silver  Britannia silver  Fine silver  9ct gold  14ct gold  18ct gold  22ct gold 

## MARRIAGE OF METALS
### Gold Combinations

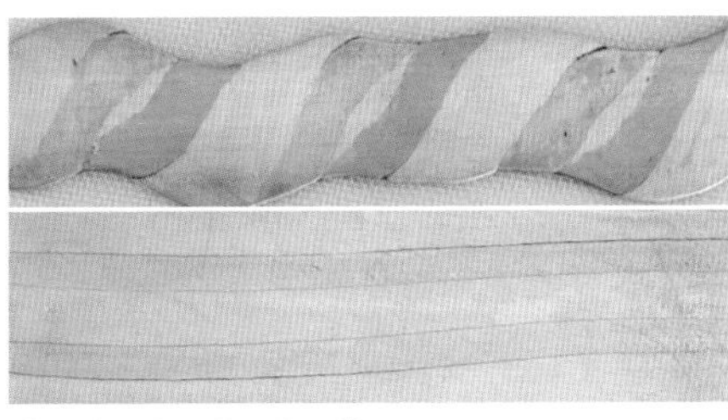

Wires can be twisted together, soldered and milled out to create interesting colour combinations and patterns. Try using gold of different colours and experimenting with the ways in which the wires are twisted together.

METHOD

1 Use binding wire to bind a tight bundle of wires together – the more strands you use, the more varied the resultant patterns will be.
2 Solder together strands of gold and silver wire in various colours with hard silver solder. The solder will flow along the wire once it has turned into a molten state. Use the flame to draw the solder down the wires (solder will travel towards heat). Do not use too much solder, since it may coat some of the gold and detract from the final finish.
3 Pickle the wires, rinse and dry thoroughly. The wires can be twisted at this stage, if you wish.
4 Thin the piece in a rolling mill until a flat sheet is formed, taking care not to thin it too quickly.
5 Eventually, you will need to roll the wires down their length, but initially roll them through the mill by their width as soon as is possible. The result will be a sheet that has a greater width and is not just a long ribbon of metal.
6 If cracks begin to appear at the edges, they will need to be soldered closed before you continue with the rolling down process.
7 Once an appropriate thickness has been achieved, carefully anneal and clean the metal before doing any further work on it.

## MOKUME GANE

Mokume gane, meaning 'wood-grain metal', is a Japanese metalworking technique. Sheets of different-coloured metal are layered and bonded, and then textured, filed and milled down, so that the colour layers produce a stunning surface.

METHOD

1 Prepare several 2 x 3 cm (1 x 1¼ inch) sheets of gold and silver by bevelling one side and pumicing to remove all traces of grease.
2 Flux both sides of each sheet and stack them up to form a billet, with the bevelled edges on one side.
3 Bind the billet tightly with binding wire.
4 Heat the billet with a gas-torch flame, and when it reaches soldering temperature, stick-feed hard solder along the bevelled edges until it appears around all the edges. Do not quench or pickle the billet; set it aside to cool on a steel block.
5 Remove the binding wire and scrub the billet with pumice to remove the oxides that have formed from heating. Use a rolling mill to thin the billet.
6 Cut the billet in half and then flux, stack and bind the two pieces. Solder again with hard solder – a minimum of 30 layers is suggested. After every soldering, thin the billet.
7 To apply texture, hammer up raised areas using a punch, and then file the surface to expose the layers of metal.
8 Once the texturing has been done, mill the sheet until it is smooth; if it gets too thin, a back plate can be soldered on.

## GRANULATION

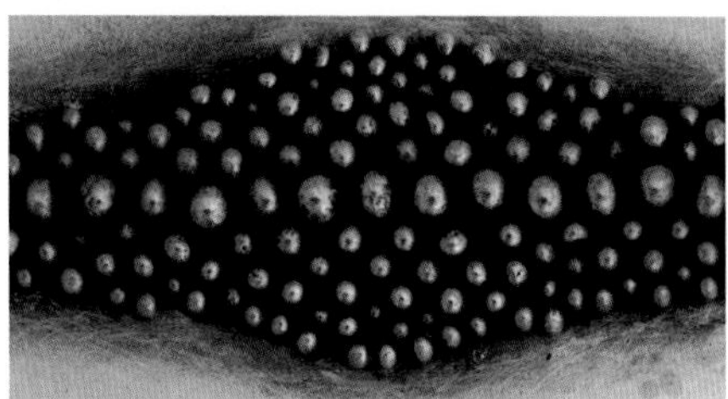

Granulation involves embellishing the surface of a base piece with tiny balls of metal. The granules are bonded on with solder. If you are using fine gold or silver, the elements can be fused rather than soldered.

### METHOD

1 Make dimples in a charcoal block, using a ball burr, to stop the granules from rolling away.
2 Cut small pieces of wire or, if granules of a uniform size are needed, use small jump rings. Dip the rings in a weak borax solution and place one in each dimple. Heat the wire until it melts and forms granules.
3 Carefully transfer the granules to the pickle in a glass dish. A small plastic sieve in the pickle will make it easier to remove and wash them.
4 Prepare your base sheet by using a centre punch to make depressions; one for each granule. The depression will hold them in position while you are soldering and also create more contact between the sheet and the granules so they will become more strongly bonded.
5 Flux the base sheet and use solder filings if you have a whole field of granules to be joined onto the base sheet, or use pallions of solder positioned alongside each granule if they are more spread out.
6 Heat the sheet from underneath to solder, gently to begin with to allow the borax to settle; and finally heat evenly, ensuring that all the solder has melted.

## BALLED WIRE

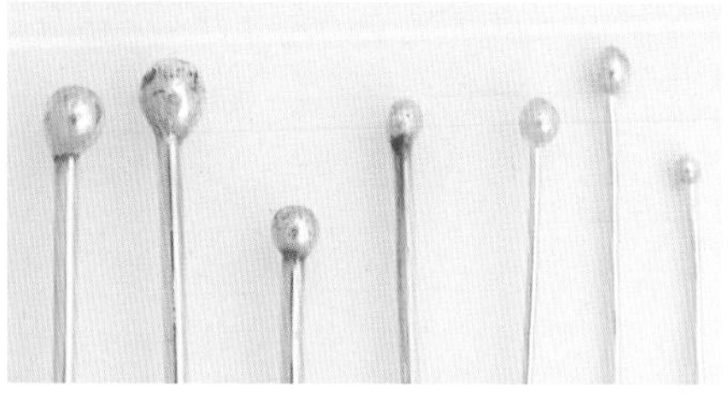

Using balled wire is an easy way to make head pins. Fine silver does not need to be treated with borax and will not tarnish during this process. For both sterling silver and fine silver, the process will work more successfully if you use wires thinner than 1 mm (1/32 inch). It is also possible to use an electric current to create balls, but you will need special equipment and that technique works best with gold.

### METHOD

1 Holding wire in insulated tweezers, dip one end in a borax solution.
2 Place the lower end of the wire in a flame, just in front of the pale blue cone (which is the hottest part of the flame).
3 The tip of the wire will start to melt and form a ball. The longer it is left in the flame, the larger the ball will be – if allowed to get too big, it will drop off.
4 Pickle, dry and buff the head pin.

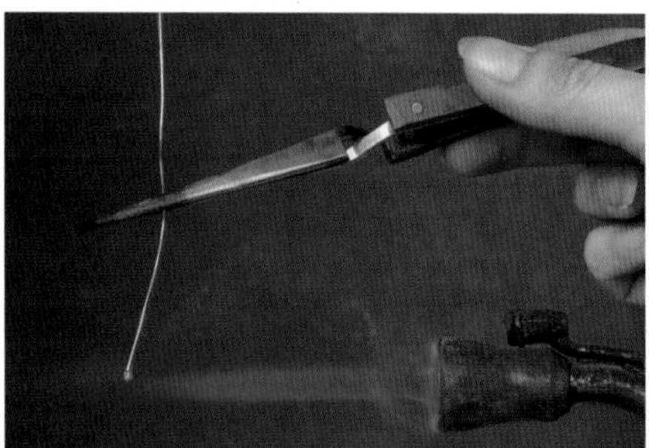

*See step 2*

**KEY**  Sterling silver  Britannia silver  Fine silver  9ct gold · 14ct gold · 18ct gold · 22ct gold

## JUMP RINGS

Although jump rings serve a variety of purposes, they are mainly used as the starting point for making chains and also as a way of joining or hanging pieces together.

METHOD

1 Anneal your wire to soften it.
2 Secure a steel former in a vise, trapping one end of your wire in the vise at the same time.
3 Wind the wire around the former, making a neat spiral with no gaps in between the turns. Take the spiral off the former.
4 Hold the spiral firmly against your bench pin, and start cutting at one end with a piercing saw. The saw should be angled slightly so that as you cut through one ring, the next one is also being cut. This will ensure that the ends of the rings will be neat and easy to close.
5 To close the jump rings, use two pairs of flat-nosed or parallel pliers and start by opening the rings sideways (to prevent the circles from becoming too deformed). Push the ends of each ring past each other slightly and then snap the ends back into position so that they are touching. There should be no gap between the ends. If there is, open the ring up sideways and try again. Once the jump rings are closed, they can be soldered shut if required.

## CHAIN

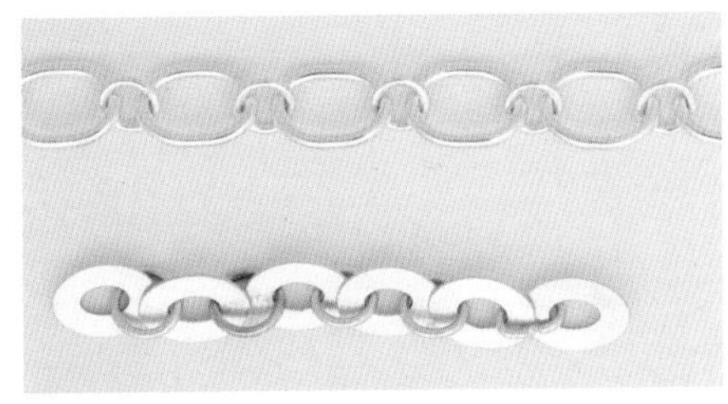

There are many ways to make chain interesting, for example: varying the shape and the thickness of the wire and the size and shape of the jump rings; flattening and texturing the jump rings; and how you join the jump rings together.

METHOD

1 Make the jump rings.
2 Close half of the jump rings and solder them shut using hard solder. You can lay out the rings in rows or in a grid formation to solder.
3 Pickle, dry and remove any excess solder.
4 At this stage you can flatten the jump rings in a rolling mill or hammer them.
5 Use an open jump ring to join two soldered ones, and close as before. Repeat until all the soldered jump rings have been used up.
6 Hold the two soldered jump rings in a pair of reverse-action tweezers, with the unsoldered one protruding. Use medium solder to close this jump ring – the other two should not heat up too much because they are insulated by the tweezers.
7 Join the groups of three into groups of seven, this time using easy solder. Repeat until the required length of chain is made.
8 To make sure that all the links are soldered, give the chain a good tug – any weak points will break.
9 To ensure that the links are even, you can pull the chain through a draw plate.
10 Polish in a barrel polisher – never polish chain on a motor or pendant motor.

## CHAIN-MAIL

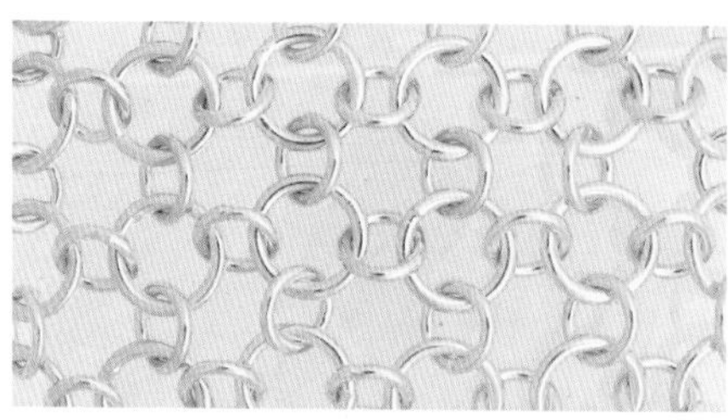

Chain-mail makes a beautifully fluid material that is incredibly tactile. You may want to calculate the number of jump rings you will need.

### METHOD

1 Solder all the large jump rings closed with hard solder. Pickle and clean them up.
2 Make a chain that equals the width you want the chain-mail to cover, using the small jump rings to join the larger ones together. Solder with medium solder.
3 Repeat until there are enough rows to cover the length of the piece you want to create.
4 Join the rows together with small jump rings and solder using easy solder.
5 Clean up and barrel-polish the chain-mail.

**Sample** *This sample was constructed using 6 mm (¼ inch) and 4 mm (⅛ inch) jump rings made from 1 mm (1/32 inch) wire.*

## CHAIN-MAIL
## Variations

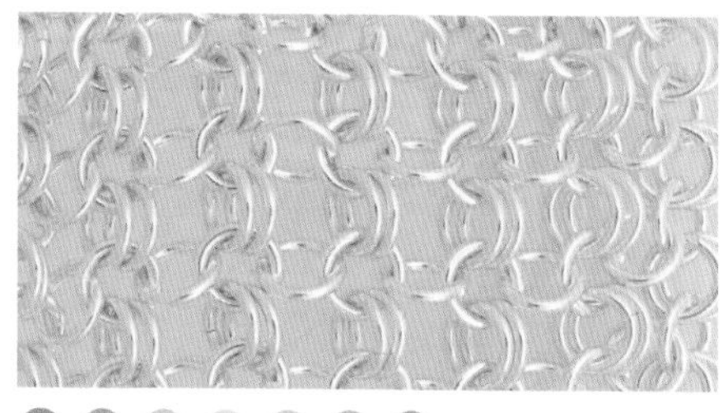

Jump rings can be joined together in many ways to make chain-mail: you can assemble many patterns; use gold jump rings with silver ones; and double-up jump rings to achieve a more compact effect.

### METHOD

1 Solder one-third of the jump rings closed with hard solder. Pickle and clean them up.
2 Make a chain that equals the width you want the chain-mail to cover, using the unsoldered jump rings to join the soldered ones together. Solder with medium solder.
3 Repeat until there are enough rows to cover the length of piece you want to create.
4 Join the rows together with two unsoldered jump rings per link and solder using easy solder.
5 Add an extra jump ring to every other link around the edge of the piece and solder closed, using easy solder.
6 Clean up and barrel-polish the chain-mail.

**Sample** *This sample was constructed using 4 mm (⅛ inch) jump rings made from 1 mm (1/32 inch) wire.*

**KEY**  Sterling silver  Britannia silver  Fine silver 9ct gold 14ct gold 18ct gold  22ct gold

## FILIGREE

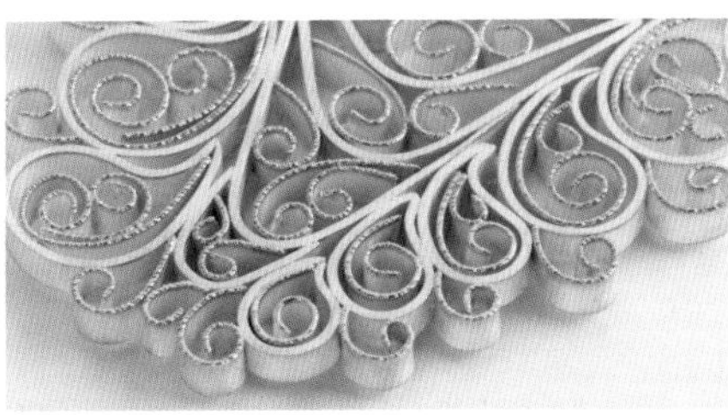

Filigree has been used in many cultures across the world for hundreds of years. Although labour-intensive, this technique creates a structure that is light, strong and uses a relatively small amount of metal.

### METHOD

1 Sketch your pattern on paper. Construct the frame first, using flattened wire or strips of sheet metal. Follow your design, making cells.
2 Solder each cell shut individually, clean up, then solder them together using hard solder. Tap gently with a mallet on a steel block to flatten the piece into alignment.
3 To texture the wire for the inner scrolls, use a die for screw threads along the length of the wire and then pass the wire through the rolling mill until the desired thickness is achieved. Your wire should be much finer than the frame, for contrast.
4 Form the scrolls and fit them snugly into the cells. Use plenty of easy solder to fix them in place, being careful not to overheat any sections.
5 Pickle and rinse thoroughly. Check to see that all the inner scrolls are soldered securely in place; re-solder if necessary.
6 Traditionally, only the very top surface is cleaned up, leaving the inside matt white. Use pumice powder and water on your fingers to rub over the surface of the piece. A burnisher can be used to highlight the textured wires some more, if you wish.

## KNITTING

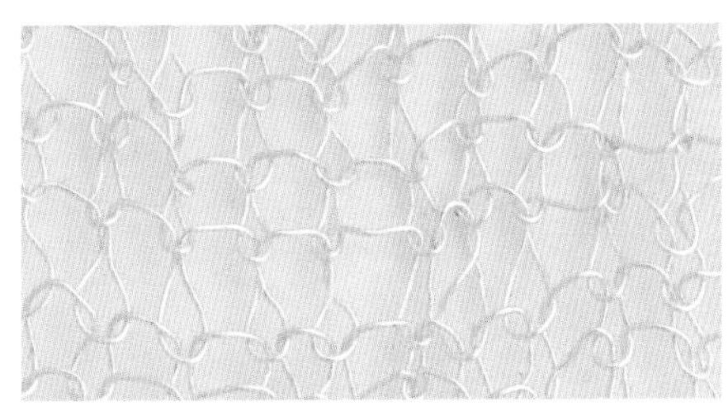

Knitting with wire is harder work than with wool, and fine silver or gold should be used because they are very pliable.

### METHOD

1 Using 0.4 mm ($\frac{1}{64}$ inch) fine silver wire and two 0.75 mm needles, make a loop at one end of the wire and slip it onto the left-hand needle. Insert the right-hand needle into the front of the loop, wrap the wire around the needle and use the needle to pull the stitch through so that you have a loop on each needle. Transfer the loop from the right-hand needle onto the left so that there are two stitches on it. Repeat until you have sufficient stitches for the length of your piece.
2 Insert the right-hand needle through the front of the first stitch on the left-hand needle, make a new stitch but keep it on the right-hand needle, allowing the stitch on the left to slip off. Make new stitches along the row, keeping them on the right needle. When you reach the end of the row, swap hands so that the knitting is in your left hand and repeat the process to make a new row.
3 Continue until your piece is the required length. To 'bind off', put the right-hand needle through two stitches, make a new stitch, allow the two stitches to slip off the left needle and put the new stitch on the left needle. Repeat until you reach the last stitch, threading the end of the wire through the loop to secure.
4 The piece of knitting can be pulled and stretched into shape – this will also neaten the overall effect.

## CROCHET

Crochet can be done free-form since there is only one point from which it can unravel – this allows great freedom of design.

METHOD

1 Working with 0.4 mm (1/64 inch) fine silver wire, make a loop at one end and twist it. Pass the tip of a 1.5 mm (1/16 inch) crochet hook through the loop, wrap the long end of the wire around the hook and pull it through the first loop. Wrap the wire around the hook and pull the hook through the second loop.
2 Continue until you have the required length, bearing in mind that the length of the chain will be reduced with each successive row, so make the first chain longer than is needed.
3 To add another row, push the tip of the hook through the last stitch you made so that there are two loops on the hook, wrap the wire around the hook and pull it through both of the loops so that there is one loop on the hook.
4 Continue picking up stitches until you reach the end of the row, and until your piece is the required size.
5 Free-form shapes can be easily constructed by making chains off the main form at various points and joining them back in again. Circular forms are made by connecting two ends of a chain.
6 To finish, cut the wire, leaving a long end to thread through the last loop, and pull it tight to stop your work unravelling.

## FRENCH KNITTING

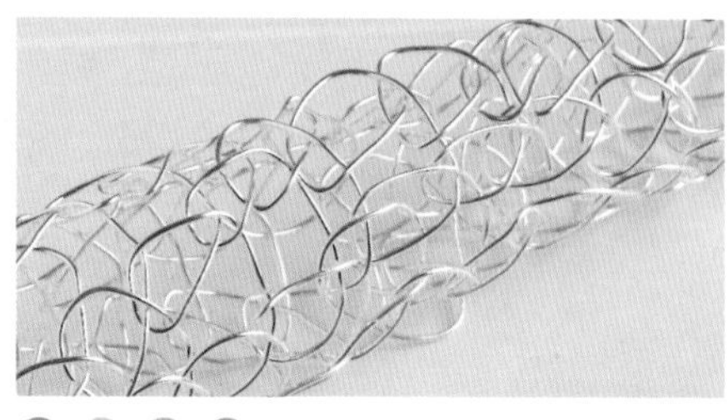

This is an easy way of crocheting tube on a frame and, when wire is used, a wonderfully tactile structure is created. Fine silver or gold are less liable to snap than alloys.

METHOD

1 You can use a store-bought knitting 'dolly', but since these usually only have four prongs, you may wish to make your own by gluing steel loops into an old cotton-thread spool. The more prongs, the denser the resulting form will be.
2 Thread one end of the wire through the central hole in the dolly from above. Hold the dolly in your left hand. Use your right hand to loop the wire around each metal prong so that it crosses at the back before looping around the next prong.
3 When a full turn has been made, make another loop on the first prong. Use a crochet hook to pull the first loop over the top of the prong so that it sits in the mouth of the hole. Loop the wire around the next prong and again, pull the first loop over the second one. The wire can be pulled from underneath to bring the wire structure through the dolly – do this regularly as you work.
4 When the chain reaches the required length, cut the wire, leaving a long end. Remove a loop from its prong and thread the end of the wire through it. Repeat with every loop – the ends of the tube can be woven together using the ends of wire left.

KEY  Sterling silver  Britannia silver  Fine silver  9ct gold  14ct gold  18ct gold 22ct gold

## TWISTED WIRE TUBE

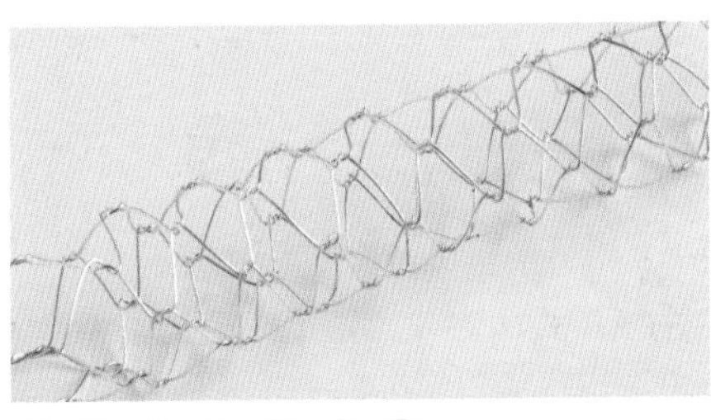

Light, flexible and structurally robust forms can be created from wire in a number of ways – twisting the wire around a former is a good basis for sections of and even entire pieces of jewellery. Employing different thicknesses of wire and formers and varying the method of twisting will affect the flexibility and also the visual weight of the forms created.

### METHOD

1 Cut two pieces of 0.4 mm (1⁄64 inch) wire long enough for the form you will make.

2 Twist the wires together so that they make a large cross. Use tape to secure the centre of the cross on the top surface of a 18 mm (3⁄4 inch) wooden former. Fix the other end of the former in a vice so that you have both hands free to work.

3 Take two of the wires, pull them so that they meet halfway and about 2.5 cm (1 inch) down the former, and twist twice, leaving the wires at an angle of 120 degrees apart. Repeat with the other two wires. This should give you twists at 'north' and 'south' – repeat the process for 'east' and 'west', and continue working in this way until your form is the required length, or you run out of wire.

4 The resulting form is surprisingly robust and flexible, considering the diameter of the wire, and should not be heated or annealed now that the wire is work-hardened.

## TWISTED WIRE

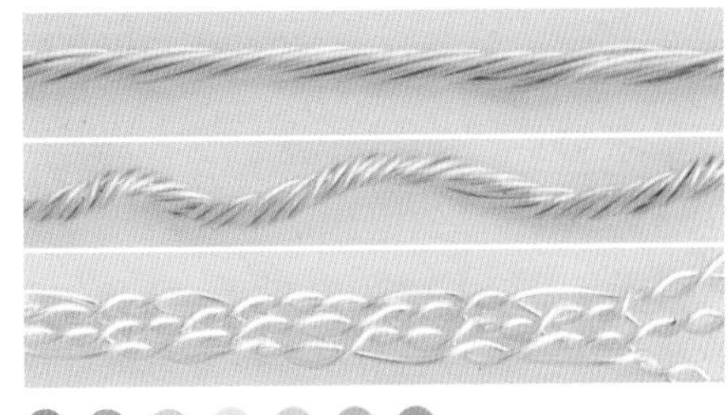

There are a number of methods of twisting wire, with the most consistent results being produced with a hand drill with a wire hook secured in its chuck. Wires twisted by hand will have a certain charm because each piece will have its own unique characteristics.

### METHOD

1 Anneal, pickle and rinse five pieces of 0.4 mm (1⁄64 inch) wire.

2 Dry the wires and fold each piece in half. Secure the loose ends in a vice and slip the loop at the other end of the wires over a hook that has been tightened in the chuck of a hand drill.

3 Wind the hand drill so that the wires twist until a satisfactory result has been achieved. Unhook the drill and remove the wires from the vice.

4 The wire will be work-hardened from twisting, so anneal, pickle and rinse the piece. The wire can be left at this stage, or folded in half and twisted in the same way as before. Interesting results are produced when the wire is untwisted again, giving an evenly undulating line.

5 When twisting wire by hand, it is necessary to secure the ends using either a vice or a clamp set on the edge of a table. Much greater freedom can be exerted in the number of strands that are twisted at once, the direction in which they are twisted and the choice of forms that can be created using this technique.

TWISTED WIRE
## Simple

Simple twisted wire can provide a starting point for a piece – the ways in which it can be used are incredibly versatile. Experiment with the thickness of the wire, the number of strands used and how many times they are twisted to generate ideas.

### METHOD

1 Anneal, pickle and rinse a piece of 1.2 mm (3/64 inch) wire. Dry the wire and fold it in half.

2 Secure the two loose ends in a vice and slip the loop at the other end of the wire over a hook that has been tightened in the chuck of a hand drill. Wind the hand drill so that the wire twists, until a satisfactory result has been achieved.

3 Unhook the drill and remove the wire from the vice. The wire will be work-hardened from twisting, so anneal, pickle and rinse it. The wire can be left at this stage, or folded in half and twisted in the same way as before.

4 The tighter the wire is twisted, the shorter the overall length of the piece becomes.

5 When soldering twisted wires, be aware that solder will want to travel along the wires and is likely to be pulled away from the join that you are trying to solder. To minimize this effect, use less water to mix up the borax so that it does not bleed along the wires, and use fine rouge powder mixed with water to paint a ring around the wires about 5 mm (1/4 inch) either side of the solder seam. Rouge prevents solder from flowing and makes an effective barrier but should be scrubbed off before the piece is pickled.

TWISTED WIRE
## Flattened

Any twisted wire can be passed through the rolling mill to flatten the form, changing the visual rhythm that the pattern of wires creates. Wires treated in this way can be used to make rings or bracelets, or form decorative borders around other elements in a piece.

### METHOD

1 Anneal a length of 1 mm (1/32 inch) wire. Pickle, rinse and dry the wire before bending it in half.

2 Secure the two loose ends in a vice and slip the loop at the other end of the wire over a hook that has been tightened in the chuck of a hand drill. Wind the hand drill so that the wire twists, until a satisfactory result has been achieved.

3 Unhook the drill and remove the wire from the vice. The wire will be work-hardened from twisting, so anneal, pickle and rinse it. Ensure that the wire is dry before rolling it through the rolling mill, with the rollers set at about 1 mm (1/32 inch) apart.

4 Tighten the rollers and run the wire through again if necessary, but take care not to flatten the form too much; otherwise the points where the wires intersect will become very thin and fragile. The intersections can have solder applied if further forming of the piece is required.

**KEY** Sterling silver  Britannia silver  Fine silver  9ct gold  14ct gold  18ct gold  22ct gold

## PLAITING

Plaiting can be used to create flat, linear wire structures. Intricate patterns can be made, as wire can be manipulated into shapes, perhaps on a pin board to hold pieces in place. Experiment with different-coloured wires to create patterns. If the wire is thick, 1 mm (1/32 inch) and above, it can be soldered with less risk of melting the wires.

### METHOD

1 A number of variations on the basic plait, which uses three strands of wire, can be used. Secure six strands of 0.5 mm (1/64 inch) fine wire at one end, either in a vice or by taping them to a board.

2 Split them into three groups of two wires. Pass the left-hand wires over the central wires so that they cross at the top. Reposition the central wires to the left. Bring the right-hand wires into the centre, across the top of the central wires, which will be pulled to the right.

3 Keep working in this way, taking wires from one side and then the other until the required length is reached. Secure the wires by wrapping one strand around the rest.

4 Any method of overlapping the wires to produce a rhythmic pattern can be used, and the pattern does not have to be the same for the whole length of the piece – intricate designs can be created, whether three-dimensional or flat. Try twisting the wires once or twice where they cross, and experiment with the patterns that can be made.

## WEAVING

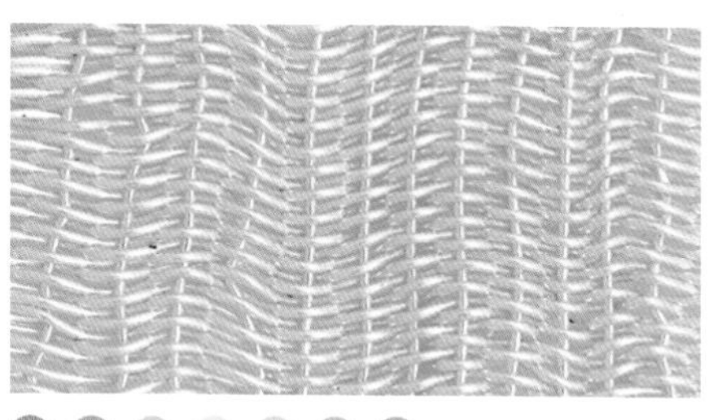

Although time-consuming and difficult to keep neat and even, weaving with wire can produce some beautiful results.

### METHOD

1 While a small loom makes weaving easier, it is possible to work on a home-made frame. The frame may be made of silver and form a structural part of your piece. The thinner the wire you use, the finer the texture and the more flexible the piece.

2 Drill evenly spaced holes or make pegs along two opposite sides of the frame; the woven piece will be dense if the pegs are close together and loosely woven if they are not.

3 Thread a piece of 0.5 mm (1/64 inch) fine silver or gold wire through the holes or around the pegs to make parallel lines of wire, leaving slack on each line.

4 Secure another strand of the same diameter wire on the top left corner of the frame. Weave this strand of wire from left to right over the first vertical wire and under the second, over the third and under the fourth, and so on, until the end of the row is reached.

5 After every row, force the wire back up against the last row – this will keep the edges neat and the tension even. The second row is worked from right to left, but where the wire passed over the top of a vertical wire in the first row, it must pass under it in the second. Continue weaving until the required length is reached.

6 Secure the end of the wire by weaving it back into the piece, welding it to the metal frame or riveting it through a small hole.

## DRAW PLATES

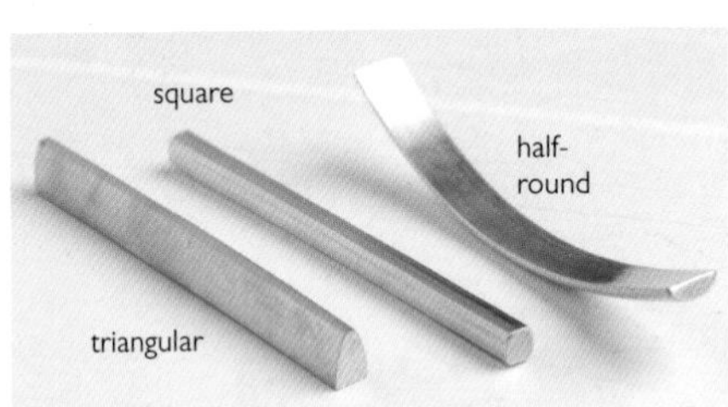


Draw plates are used to change the sections (or shapes) of wires. The most common sections are designed to be round, square or triangular, but custom draw plates to form shapes such as stars are also available. This is also a useful technique to use when you want to straighten or work-harden a wire.

### METHOD

1. Taper the end of the wire in the rolling mill, and file it round again.
2. Find the hole on the draw plate that is just smaller than the diameter of the wire and poke the tapered end through. Add a little lubricant.
3. Clamp the taper in the jaws of the draw tongs and begin to wind the handle of the draw bench, which will pull the wire through the draw plate.
4. Repeat, pulling the wire through the next smallest hole each time.
5. You will need to anneal the wire every so often, and may need to thin the taper too.
6. When designing with gold, it is common practice to solder a piece of silver or base metal onto the end that will be tapered to avoid wasting the precious metal.

## LATHE

The lathe is a versatile piece of machinery that can be used for carving, cleaning up and polishing items such as simple rings and rubbed-over stone settings in tubes, and for drilling centrally located holes in the ends of rods.

### METHOD

1. A watchmaker's lathe can be used for small pieces and is much less daunting than a full-size lathe. Secure your piece in the chuck of the lathe and remove the chuck key.
2. Use the compound and cross slides on the saddle of the lathe that holds the cutting tool to manoeuvre the tool into position before switching on the lathe and facing-off the rod to ensure it is true before starting to cut your design. The cutting tool should be at the same height as the centre of the piece.
3. Silver is sticky, so do not cut too much at once, and apply cutting oil as necessary.
4. When the cutting has been completed, remove the saddle from the lathe and replace it with a tool rest set at the correct height. Controlled use of files, emery sticks and a buffing stick can then be used to refine and clean up the form.

**KEY**  Sterling silver  Britannia silver  Fine silver  9ct gold  14ct gold  18ct gold  22ct gold

## DOMING

Doming is used when shaping sheet metals to give the finished design a three-dimensional form. Doming blocks contain hemispherical recesses of several sizes, with corresponding doming punches that fit exactly into the holes. Punches are available in steel and hardwoods.

### METHOD

1 Anneal the metal disc; then pickle, rinse and dry.
2 If the sheet is textured, protect it by sticking masking tape over the surface.
3 Place the disk in a recess in the doming block. Start in a large one and work your way down. When you stop depends on the degree of curve and depth needed.
4 Centre the disc in the bottom of the recess and place the correct punch for the size hole you are using above it. Strike firmly with a mallet.
5 Move the piece to the next-smallest size hole and use the appropriate punch and a mallet to shape the metal.

*See step 3*

## PRESS FORMING
### Die Matrix

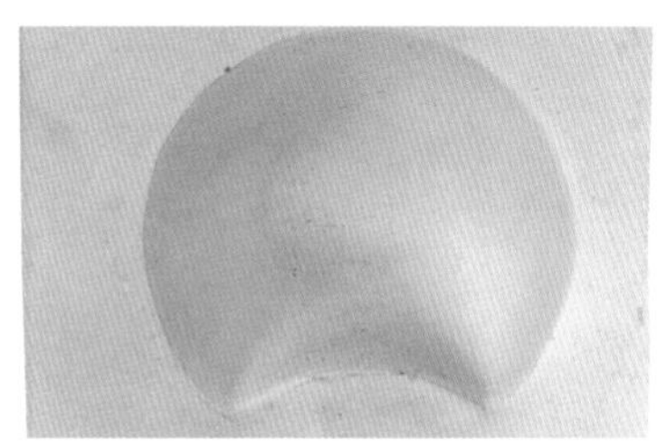

Symmetrical and irregular three-dimensional forms can be made in a hydraulic press and are ideal components for constructing hollow forms such as lockets.

### METHOD

1 Decide on the shape you want to cut in the die. Rounded edges and curves will produce better results than sharp angles and points.
2 Working on 1-cm (⅜-inch) thick acrylic sheet, drill holes around the inside of the design. Use a piercing saw with a waxed saw blade to cut the acrylic. The edge of the cut-out needs to be filed – hold the acrylic in a vice while doing this.
3 The piece of sheet used for the press form needs to have a 1 cm (⅜ inch) border all the way around the shape, and should be annealed.
4 Secure the sheet onto the acrylic die with masking tape and place several layers of rubber on top.
5 Position the pieces in the centre of the hydraulic press and jack up the table of the press until there is resistance. Release the pressure, then jack up the table again.
6 When you let the table down again and remove the pieces, you will see that the metal has sunk down into the die. If a greater depth is required, pickle and dry the metal and put it through the hydraulic press again. The thinner the metal is, the more quickly it will move, but it is also more likely to split under the pressure.

PRESS FORMING
## Die Matrix and Resist

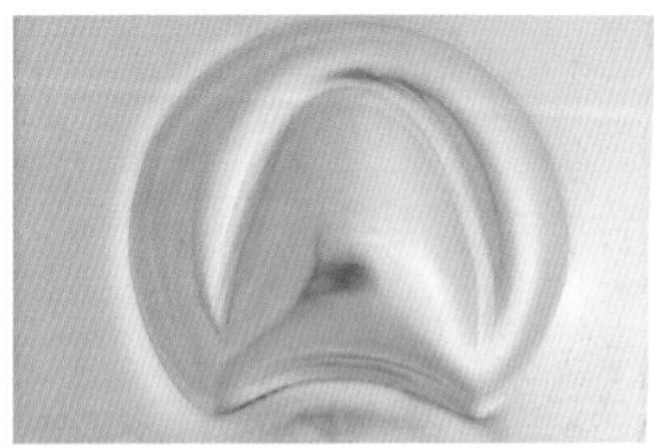

Using strips of metal underneath the die when you are press forming can produce dramatic three-dimensional effects by deeply indenting the surface of the form, allowing many design options. Avoid sharp angles, since they can cause the wire to split.

### METHOD

1 Prepare the die and silver sheet as described on page 85.

2 Before placing the die into the hydraulic press, insert a strip of brass under the sheet of silver, inside the die. The strip can be secured into position with a piece of masking tape across the bottom surface of the die. This strip should be similar in shape to the die as it will impress into the underside of the press form as it is pushed down in the hydraulic press.

3 Use a strip of brass, thicker than 8 mm (5⁄16 inch) and about half the depth of the die, and bend it into shape. Gentle curves will produce the best results. If the brass strip has sharp edges, they need to be filed so that they do not cause the silver form to split. Alternatively, pieces of rod or other objects can also be used inside the die matrix to produce interesting effects.

4 Anneal the press form after every pressing and continue pressing until a satisfactory depth is achieved. Use a thicker block for the die if a very deep form is required.

PRESS FORMING
## Die Matrix and Insert

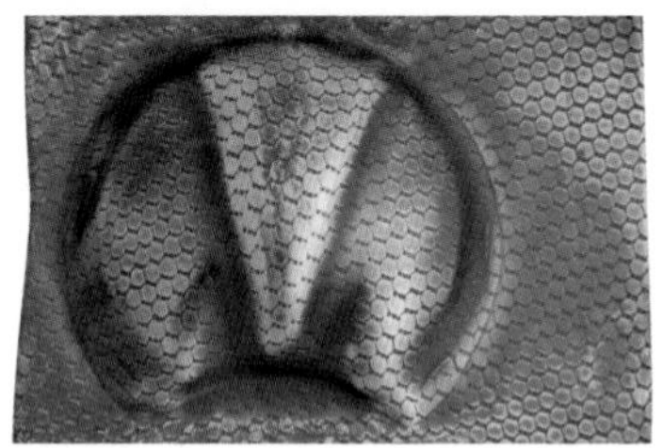

A special two-part tool can be constructed to form metal, giving greater definition to the profile of the press form. This technique is useful for making small batches of identically detailed components.

### METHOD

1 Make a die from 1 cm (3⁄8 inch) acrylic and retain the inside shape that is pierced out of the block. This will form the insert for the die matrix.

2 Carve the acrylic insert with a file: it needs to conform to the shape of the die matrix. Leave enough clearance for the thickness of the metal that you will be using. The insert should have rounded edges and no undercuts.

3 Clean up the form with 600-grade wet-and-dry paper and water.

4 Having annealed the silver, proceed as before, pressing the die with a rubber sheet in the hydraulic press once, without the insert.

5 Anneal the silver again and return it to the die, this time placing the insert face down in the depression already made and securing it with masking tape.

6 Place the layers of rubber sheet on top and put the stack in the hydraulic press. Jack up the table until there is resistance.

7 Anneal the sheet and press it a few times to get the insert flush with the top surface of the die matrix.

8 Anneal the silver sheet and press it once more, this time using just the acrylic insert. This will force the metal over the form and make any details crisper.

PRESS FORMING
## Punch

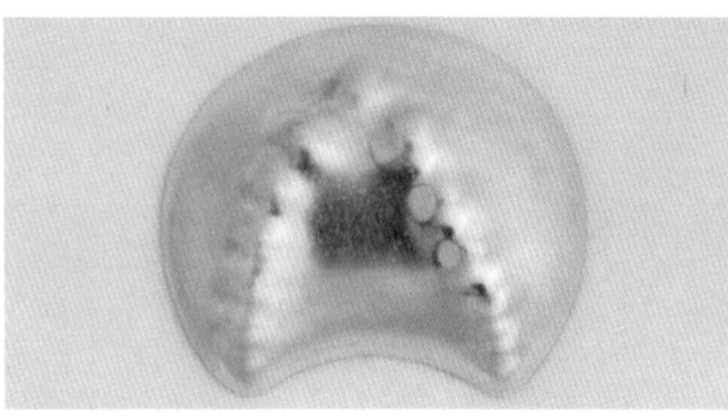

Punches can be used to distort press forms in a number of ways. The forms can be shaped more asymmetrically by distending them on one side, chasing lines and raising domes on the surface.

METHOD

1 Prepare the metal and die as described on page 85, and form the shape in the hydraulic press. The form does not need to be as deep because the punched marks will be raised above the surface.
2 Anneal and pickle the sheet and return it to the die, securing it in place with masking tape.
3 Working on a steel block supported by a sandbag, use doming punches or chasing tools with a hammer to punch a design into the sheet. You may wish to mark out the design with a permanent ink marker first.
4 The piece can be annealed and further distorted by punches, but take care that areas do not get too thin since they will be likely to split.
5 To solder two press forms together, ensure that the metal surrounding the press form is flat by tapping it with a mallet.
6 Use masking tape to secure the piece to a steel block and use a chasing tool to chase a line around the outline of the press form. This will ensure that the bottom surface of the press form is level.
7 Pierce out the press form, close to the edge.
8 Rub the bottom surface of the press form on rough emery paper so that there is at least a 1-mm ($\frac{1}{32}$-inch) flat ledge. The further it is rubbed down, the less filing needs to be done after it is soldered. Repeat with the second half.
9 Flux one half and melt large pieces of hard solder on the ledge of the underside.
10 Bind the two halves together with binding wire, making sure that the two halves match up perfectly, and reflux and reheat so that the solder melts.
11 Pickle the form. After pickling, it will need to be filed and refined with an emery stick.

**TIP:** Any subsequent heating of the piece will require a hole to be drilled so that expanding hot air can escape. This is very important.

PRESS FORMING
## Objects

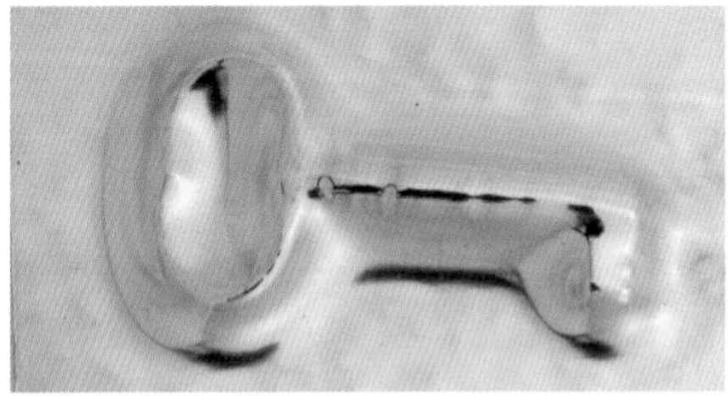

To form metals in a press, you need to choose a solid metal object that will not buckle under the forces of a hydraulic press. Keys, washers and other flat metal objects are ideal. Very fine details of objects will not be transferred, but a surprising amount of definition can be achieved. Forms carved from acrylic will also work well.

### METHOD

1 Anneal, pickle, and dry your metal, which should be 1 mm (1/32 inch) or thinner, and it should be big enough to leave at least a 1-cm (3/8-inch) border around the object.
2 Use masking tape on the underside of the metal to secure the object so that it doesn't move out of position during the process.
3 Position your piece in the centre of the table on the hydraulic press, with the object underneath the metal sheet.
4 Place a few layers of rubber over the top of the pieces and jack up the hydraulic pump until there is resistance. The rubber will force the metal sheet down over the form that lies underneath.
5 Release the pressure and allow the table on the press to drop enough for the piece to be removed.
6 The impression of the object may be satisfactory at this stage. If you need a deeper impression, the silver will need to be annealed first, since it will have become work-hardened.
7 There may be wrinkles around the edge of the sheet. They can be tapped down at this stage with a mallet while working on a steel block.
8 Put the object and the sheet back in the hydraulic press with the rubber, and press again.
9 The form of the object can now be pierced out of the sheet and soldered onto a base plate.
10 If the object is symmetrical, two pressed forms can be soldered together to make a hollow form.
11 Asymmetrical objects will need to be flipped over before the second pressing is done, so that a mirror image is produced. The two halves can then be soldered together.

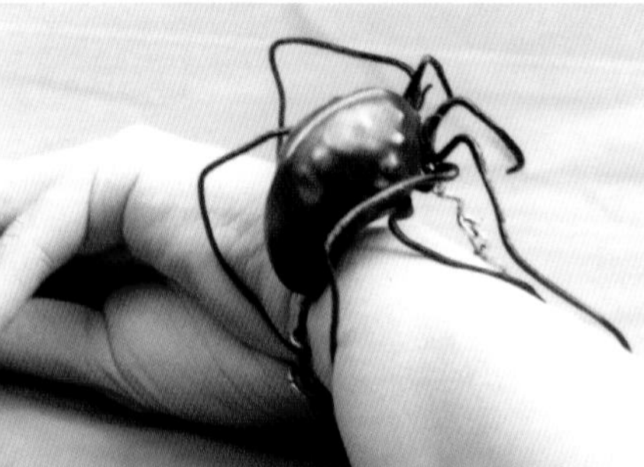

△ WRIST SPIDER
BY ANASTASIA YOUNG
*The main body of this piece is constructed from two pressed forms soldered together. The punched marks give the piece texture as well as increasing the depth of the pressed forms.*

**KEY**  Sterling silver  Britannia silver  Fine silver  9ct gold  14ct gold  18ct gold  22ct gold

## CHASING AND REPOUSSÉ

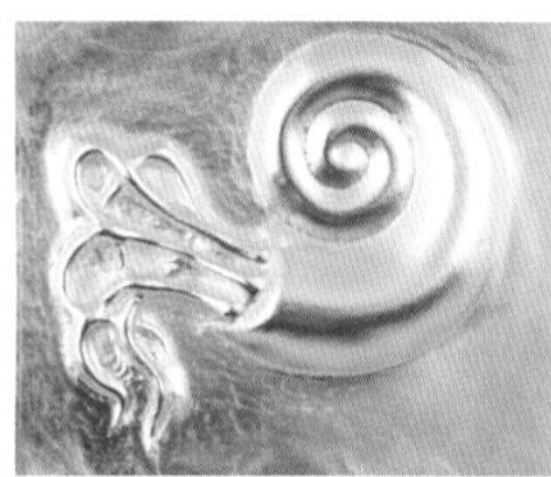

These two techniques are usually used in combination and involve embossing sheet metal with the use of steel punches. The metal is supported in pitch, which allows accurate detail to be applied to the sheet without distorting it. It is possible to create intricately worked hollow forms using this technique.

### METHOD

1 Anneal and pickle a sheet of 0.7 mm (1/35 inch) metal. Scrub it with a brass brush and liquid soap.

2 Dry the piece and mark out your design using a steel scribe.

3 Fold down two opposite corners of the sheet – this will prevent any movement while you are working.

4 Use a soft flame to warm the surface of the pitch in the pitch bowl, and place the sheet on it, making sure that the bent-over corners are pushed right down into the pitch.

5 The outline should be chased first – use a lining tool (one that comes to a flat taper), held in your left hand and a repoussé hammer in your right to tap it. Make overlapping marks along the scribed lines until they are all chased. The metal will feel different when it has become work-hardened and will not move very much.

6 Soften the pitch with a soft flame and pull out the sheet with a pair of tweezers. Clean off any pitch left on the piece with white spirit, and anneal the metal. The metal can be placed either way up in the softened pitch so that it can be worked from the back or the front depending on the desired effect, but as the form becomes three-dimensional, the underside needs to be filled with pitch before the piece is laid down into the pitch bowl. This will ensure that no air is trapped underneath.

7 Use rounded punches to create volume – special punches may need to be made for specific areas or details (see pages 49–50). Take care not to make areas too thin if they are being worked intensively, because although splits can be repaired with solder, the split will always be a weak point.

8 Flatten the metal surrounding your chased form before removing it from the pitch for the last time, and pierce around the outline.

## FOLD FORMS

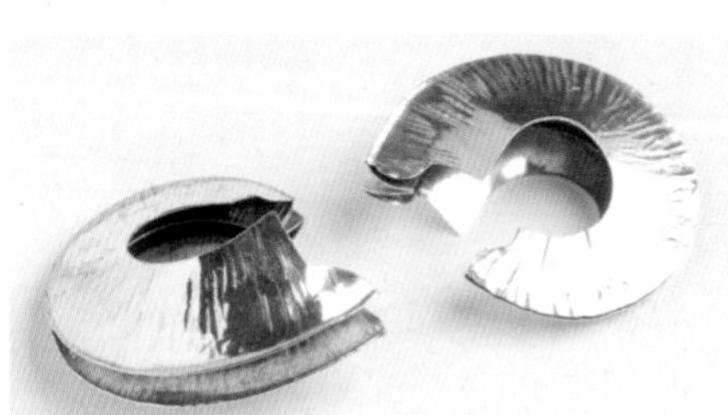

Fold-forming can be used to create sculptural three-dimensional forms from sheet metal. It offers a wide range of diversity. The shape of the metal you start with, the number of folds and the amount of hammering or milling will all affect the final outcome.

### METHOD

1 Anneal and rinse a 3 x 4 cm (1¼ x 1⅛ inch) piece of silver sheet that is 0.4 mm (1/64 inch) thick.
2 Fold the sheet in half lengthways and, working on a steel block, use a mallet to flatten the fold. Anneal the silver, but do not pickle it until the process has been completed, since the surfaces may fuse.
3 Using dividers, scribe a line approximately 4 mm (5/32 inch) up from the fold. Place the piece in the vice, pry open the sheet with a blunt knife and tap down the flaps with a mallet. Push the bottom edges together before tapping the form flat on a steel block – the side profile of the piece should now be an 'M' (with longer legs and shorter middle section). Anneal, but do not pickle the silver.
4 Use a creasing hammer to forge along the fold. Working at a 90-degree angle to the edge of the metal, and taking care not to hit the edge directly as this will cause it to split – work about 1 mm (1/32 inch) in from the folded edge. Hitting the piece in this way forces the side with the fold to stretch and makes the form curve.
5 Anneal the piece once you have worked along the fold once; then repeat the process on the other side of the form.
6 Continue rounds of hammering and regular annealing until a reasonable degree of curvature is achieved, but be careful not to thin the metal too much. Anneal the piece once more and carefully open the form with a blunt knife; the folds should open out into a robust three-dimensional form. The curve will become more pronounced as the form is opened. The piece can now be pickled to clean it.
7 Results can be varied by altering the number of folds or cutting the sheet into a gradual taper before hammering.

△ **FOLD-FORM BANGLE**
BY PAUL WELLS
*This bangle was made using a five-fold form. The enclosed folds have been oxidized, and the outer surfaces burnished to accentuate the design.*

**KEY**  Sterling silver  Britannia silver  Fine silver  9ct gold  14ct gold  18ct gold  22ct gold

## ANTICLASTIC RAISING

Thin gauge sheet can be used to create structurally strong, three-dimensional forms, using a sinusoidal stake and a wedge-shaped mallet. 'Anticlastic' curves are those where the curves on two axes of the piece are going in opposite directions; 'synclastic' curves work in the same direction, like the curves of a bowl.

### METHOD

1 The outline of the sheet that you use to begin with will directly affect the shape of the form that is made – a parallel strip of metal will give an even, symmetrical form. A 21 cm (8¼ inch) strip will form a medium-size bracelet, and can be from 10 mm (⅜ inch) to 6 cm (2¼ inch) wide for the best results.
2 Bend the strip of metal so that the ends meet, and file them to ensure a good join. Bind the piece with binding wire and solder the join.
3 When pickled and dry, lightly true up the circular form on a mandrel. It is not necessary to solder the form for the process to work, but it does need to be curved.
4 With a sinusoidal stake secured in a vice, start working in the largest curve of the stake and use a wedge-shaped nylon mallet. Hit the silver with the mallet just in from the edge, so that the metal is forced down into the curve of the stake a little, rotating the piece as you go so that a continuous line is followed.
5 Once the first round of hammering is complete, take the piece off the stake and turn it around so that the other edge of the silver can be worked in the same way.
6 True up the piece on a mandrel again, taking care not to open up the form too much. Anneal and pickle the piece. Several rounds of hammering and annealing will be needed on the largest curve of the stake before the silver sits evenly in the curve; the distance in from the edge can be incrementally increased with each round as more contact between the silver and the stake is achieved. The form can then be hammered in successively tighter curves, which will decrease the width of the silver strip and force it to curve more.
7 File the edges smooth and polish the piece, if desired.

*See step 4*

FORGING

## Tapering

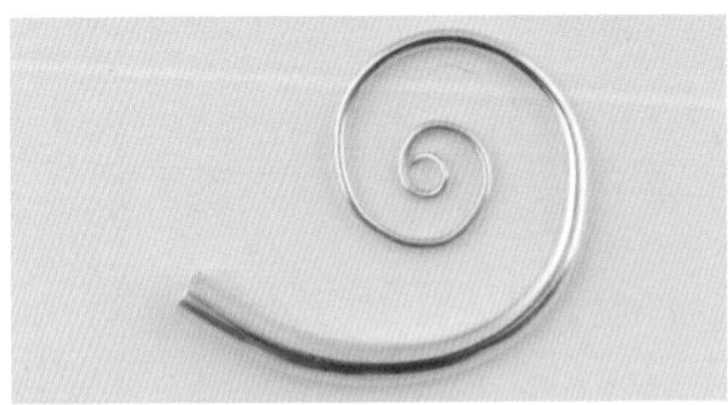

The shaping of metal through physical distortion, usually with a hammer, is known as 'forging'. The type of distortion depends upon the shape of the hammer and stake worked with. Tapering is a useful technique for a gradual reduction of diameter in rod or wire, and much faster than filing alone.

### METHOD

1 In order to facilitate the tapering process, first change the section of the rod from round section to square. Working on a flat steel stake, which should be roughly at the height of your elbow, use a raising hammer to flatten one side of the annealed rod, rotate the rod 90 degrees, and repeat to form a square cross-section. Hold the hammer at the end of the handle and use your elbow rather than your wrist to swing it.

2 Keeping the section square, continue hammering on each face, with greater concentration towards the tip so that it begins to taper. Anneal the piece regularly – a helpful sign for when to anneal is a high-pitched ringing sound when the hammer strikes the work-hardened metal.

3 It is common for the section to change into a rhombus; this must be corrected otherwise the taper will flatten. Anneal and hammer the rod along the longest axis of the section, forcing it back towards the centre of the rod. Repeat on the opposite side. Do the same along the most protruding edge from the section of this new facet. If any flaking of the metal has occurred, remove it with a file.

4 As the taper progresses, 'tubing' is likely to occur at the very end, and it will start to become hollow where the movement of the edges of the metal overtakes the centre – use end cutters to trim the end, or file it off.

5 Once the rod is sufficiently tapered it must be hammered back into a round section. Use a planishing hammer to flatten the corners of the square section so that it becomes an even, octagonal section. Flatten the corners of this form, and continue in this way until a round section has been achieved.

6 Hammer marks can be left on the rod, or it can be filed and made smooth with an emery stick.

△ POD BROOCH
BY PAUL WELLS
*Forged tapers protrude from a small raised pod and another taper forms the brooch pin of this oxidized silver piece.*

**KEY**  Sterling silver  Britannia silver  Fine silver  9ct gold  14ct gold  18ct gold  22ct gold

FORGING
## Spreading

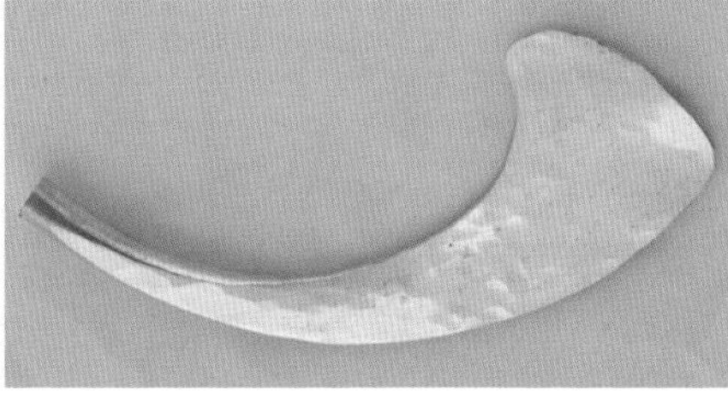

Spreading is a method of hammering a rod out so that it becomes flat and sheet-like. The direction of spread and shape of the resulting sheet can be controlled by accurate hammering.

### METHOD

1 Working on a slightly domed steel stake, use a flat-faced hammer to flatten the top surface of one end of a clean, annealed piece of rod.

**2** Use a raising hammer with its face in the same alignment as the length of the rod to start spreading the flattened area. The hammer should subtly hit the corner of the end first. Once the end has formed a wedge shape, hammer rows of overlapping marks, starting along the front edge. Each successive row must overlap the last.

**3** Anneal the rod and start hammering, again starting at the edge and working in. Regularly check the end face for protruding edges, called 'lips', and remove any with a file.

**4** If the edges are overthinned or the metal is not annealed regularly, cracks may appear. File out the crack, beyond its base, otherwise it will spread with continued hammering. Small fractures can be soldered to reinforce them.

**5** This spread end can be made to curve by hammering at right angles along one side only, causing it to lengthen around the unhammered side, which will compress and thicken.

**6** The face of the spread area can now be planished. Use overlapping marks of even pressure, applied with a planishing hammer. Clean up edges with a file and emery sticks before polishing.

FORGING
## Twisting

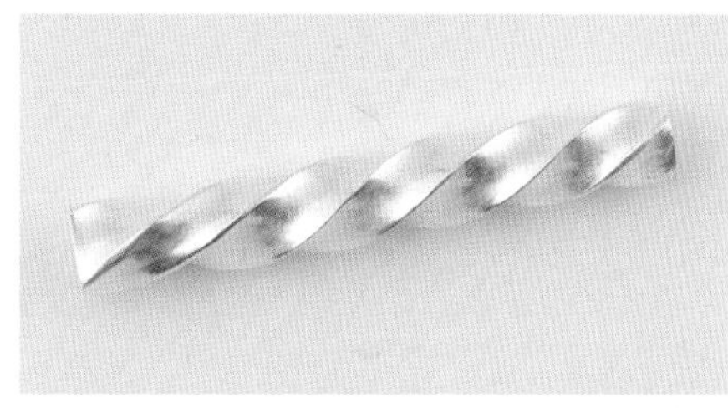

Square- or rectangular-section rods can be twisted to create a number of effects and can be used to add beautiful detail to forged pieces of jewellery. The twists can be applied loosely or tightly, and the rod can also be twisted clockwise and anticlockwise on the same piece.

### METHOD

1 Anneal, pickle, rinse and dry the piece of rod. Rectangular- or square-section rods with crisp edges will give the best effects. Oval wire will show subtle twisting; round section is unlikely to give any results unless it has been textured along its length. It is advisable to have a longer length of rod than needed since the ends are often damaged during the twisting process.

**2** Secure one end of the rod in between two pieces of softwood in a vice, leaving most of the rod standing straight up. Grip the top end of the rod with parallel pliers or an adjustable wrench. You may wish to wrap the jaws of the tool with masking tape to minimize damage.

**3** Begin to rotate the handle of the pliers using slow, even pressure. The rod will quickly start to work-harden and if much twisting is required, then anneal the rod before continuing. The rod may shear if too much twisting is applied.

**4** To create a change in direction, fix the rod in the vice with only half protruding and twist this portion clockwise. Then place the twisted section in the vice and twist the remaining half anticlockwise.

FORGING

## Upsetting

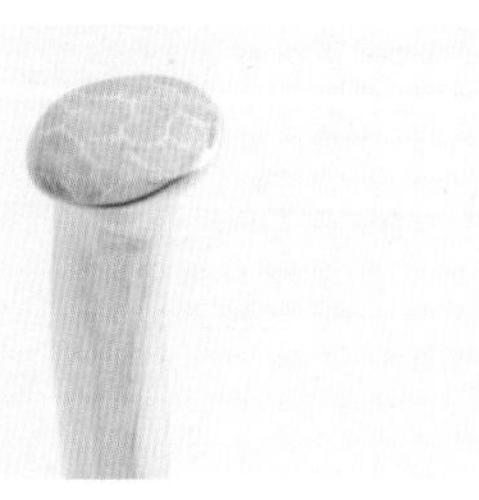

The edges of a piece of sheet or the end of a metal rod can be hammered in such a way that they will thicken. This can be a useful visual device, or may be a necessary part of the function of the piece you are making.

### METHOD

1 Anneal, pickle, rinse and dry the piece of metal you will be working on.
2 To thicken the end of a piece of rod, secure it in a vice that has fibre grips protecting the jaws, or ideally between two pieces of softwood. The vice must be tightened very firmly to prevent the rod from slipping.
3 Use a large, heavy hammer to spread the end of the rod. A flat-faced hammer will force the rod down into itself and make the end thicker in diameter. A round-faced hammer will encourage the end to spread by forcing the metal sideways in all directions and will give an effect like that of a nail head.
4 To thicken the edges of an object made from sheet, support the object on a sandbag, which will protect the underside from damage. Use a creasing hammer to make overlapping blows around the edge, working at 90 degrees to the edge and rotating the piece as you work.
5 Turn the piece over and repeat the hammering on the other side. This will force the metal to thicken at the edges and should not affect the overall shape of the piece. This process is known as 'caulking'.

ETCHING

## Stop-Out Varnish Resist

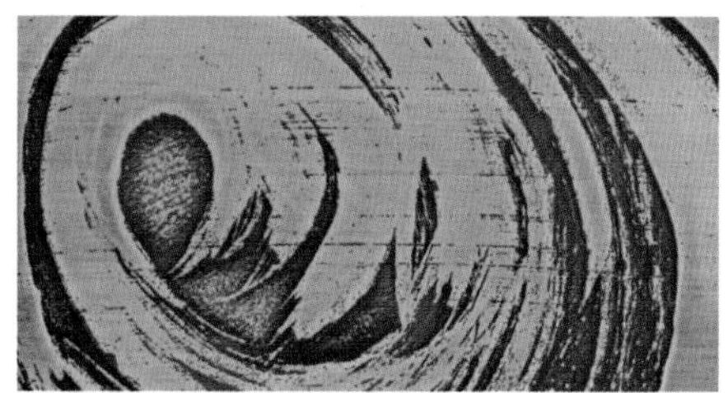

Etching utilizes the chemical effect of strong acids on metals. Areas exposed to the acid dissolve to create textures or designs. The process can be used for precise designs or oil-paint effects.

### METHOD

1 Degrease the metal using pumice powder, water and detergent.
2 Mask off the back of the sheet with stop-out varnish or parcel tape. Allow the varnish to dry.
3 Scribe a design on the front side of the silver sheet, and use stop-out varnish to paint on the design, leaving the areas you wish to be etched. For oil-paint effects, apply the varnish freehand, allowing brush marks to show. Let the varnish dry.
4 Wearing goggles and gloves, slip the metal into the acid solution (see page 242) with plastic tweezers. When bubbles form on the metal surface, brush them off with a feather. The tray containing the acid solution can also be agitated to disturb the bubbles.
5 Check the acid every 10 minutes and test the edge of an etched area with a pin, without damaging the varnish. If it begins to lift off the metal, rinse and dry the piece, reapplying varnish where needed.
6 When the required depth has been met, wear gloves and remove the silver from the acid. Rinse the piece in running water and clean off the varnish with white spirit (or acetone, depending on the varnish). Scrub with pumice powder, water and detergent to remove any traces of acid.

ETCHING

## Stop-out Varnish

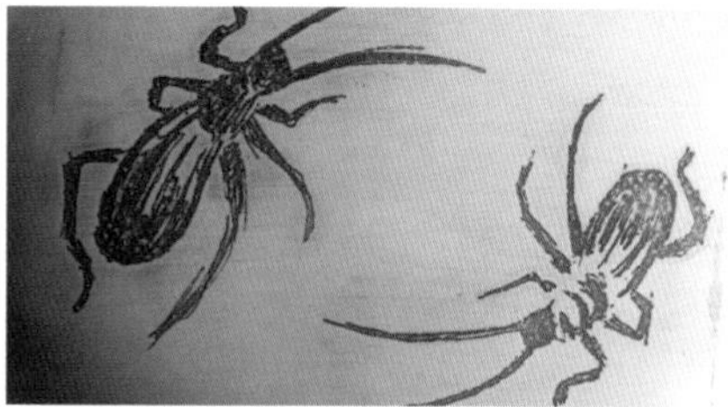

Hand-drawn designs can be etched into the surface of silver by scratching through the stop-out varnish once it has dried. Each design will be a unique artwork and imprints a personal creative expression onto your jewellery.

METHOD

1 Degrease the metal using pumice powder, water, and detergent. This will also 'key' the surface a little, helping the stop-out varnish to adhere better.
2 Mask off the back of the sheet and paint the front with stop-out varnish. Allow the varnish to dry.
3 Scratch through the varnish with a scribe or pointed tool – you are only scratching through, not marking the metal. For the acid to work best, the lines need to be at least 1 mm (1/32 inch) wide.
4 Slip the metal under the surface of the acid solution (see page 242) with plastic tweezers. If bubbles form on the surface of the metal, brush them off with a feather.
5 Check the progress of the acid every 10 minutes or so until the required depth is met. Weaker or older acid solutions will work more slowly, but the etch will be less aggressive – this is better for delicate hand-drawn designs that don't need to be etched too deeply.
6 Rinse the piece in plenty of running water and then clean off the stop-out varnish with white spirit (or acetone, depending on the varnish). Scrub with pumice powder, water and detergent to remove any traces of acid.

ETCHING

## PNP

'Press 'n' peel' (PNP) paper is an effective way to photoetch without any special equipment, as the resist is ironed onto the metal.

METHOD

1 Choose your design, which should be a high-contrast black-and-white image, and photocopy it onto the special blue PNP paper, on the matt side. Text or numbers will need to be reversed before photocopying.
2 Clean and dry your metal. Iron on the PNP, following the manufacturer's instructions.
3 Now you have choices: nitric-acid solution (see page 242) can be used to etch with PNP but may cause the PNP to lift off the surface of the metal before a satisfactory depth is met; ferric-nitrate solution (see page 242) is a more suitable etching agent but needs to be used in a bubble-etch tank, since a sediment forms that inhibits etching if it settles on the surface of the metal. If no tank is available, the metal can be suspended upside down in a normal bath to stop sediment from settling.
4 Allow the etching to reach the desired depth, then rinse and clean off the PNP resist with acetone or a suitable solvent.
5 Water alone will not stop the chemical action, so scrub the piece with ammonia then plenty of pumice powder and detergent.

ETCHING
## Aquatint

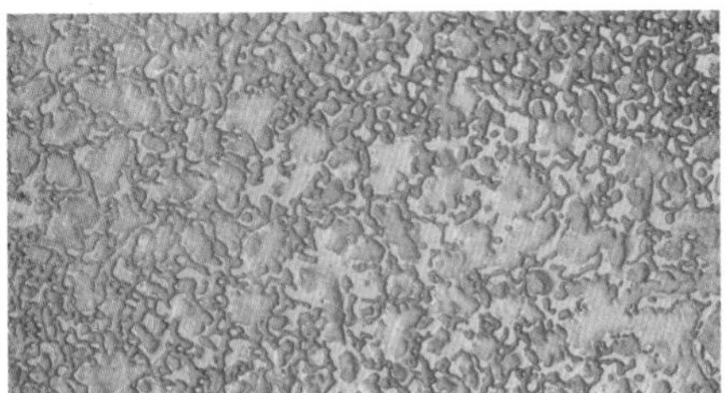

Aquatint is an incredibly effective texture on silver, with beautiful effects etched to cover a whole surface, or just used for details in designs.

METHOD

1 Prepare your metal. Sprinkle a little aquatint (powdered natural resin) onto the surface.
2 Gently heat the metal from underneath; it will not take much heat for the resin to melt. The longer the heat is applied, the more liquid the aquatint will become and the further it will spread. Allow it to cool, then mask off the back surface and edges with either stop-out varnish or parcel tape.
3 Etch the piece in nitric acid (see page 242) to the required depth.
4 Remove the aquatint resin with a suitable solvent; the resin is usually brittle when it comes out of the acid and can sometimes be flaked off with the aid of a scouring pad.

NOTE: For etching gold, use the Aqua Regia recipe on page 243.

ETCHING
## Sticky-backed Plastic

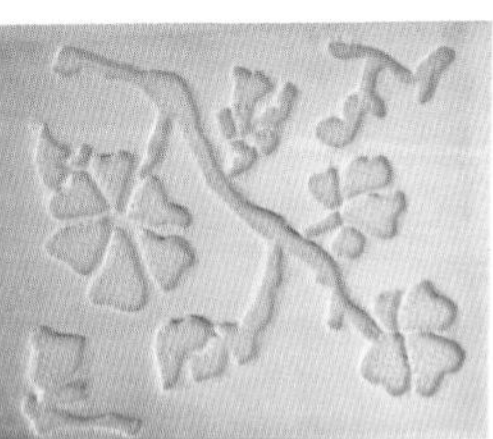

Sticky-backed plastic makes an effective resist and can be cut into intricate, stencil-like designs. It is easier to achieve geometric or angular designs than flowing curves, but anything is possible with a little patience.

METHOD

1 Degrease the silver using pumice powder, liquid soap and a scouring pad. Dry the metal.
2 Cut a piece of sticky-backed plastic twice the length of your piece of silver and allow for a 2 cm (¾ inch) border.
3 Remove the backing from the plastic and place the silver towards one end. Fold the plastic over so that the silver is enclosed, pushing out any air bubbles before the plastic is sealed. Rub over the plastic to make sure that the contact with the metal is strong.
4 Draw your design on one side of the sheet with a permanent ink marker and use a craft knife or scalpel to cut along the lines.
5 Remove the plastic sections by lifting up a corner with the tip of a blade and then peeling it off. Thinner sections of plastic can lift up and allow the acid (see page 242) to etch underneath, so try to avoid them in order for pieces to be deeply etched.
6 Ensure that the edges of the plastic are well rubbed down before putting the piece into the acid.
7 When etching is complete, peel off the plastic under running water – check to be sure no acid is trapped underneath– and scrub the silver clean.

**KEY**  Sterling silver   Britannia silver  Fine silver   9ct gold  14ct gold  18ct gold  22ct gold

## PHOTOETCHING

Photoetching is a process that is normally done commercially, since the process can handle large batches of identical components to be etched simultaneously. Consider whether the time you would save by having a batch produced commercially makes it financially justifiable.

### METHOD

1 Supply the photoetching company with an electronic file containing your design. The design should be created in a vector-based software program such as Adobe® Illustrator®, which will make it easier for the etching company's computer to translate; otherwise, you will be charged for the time it takes to convert other file types or hand-drawn original artwork into the correct format.
2 When designing, scale your design to at least twice the size you want the final result to be, and then shrink the image to the correct size before sending it; this will result in a much crisper final design.
3 Photoetching is so accurate that it allows a sheet of metal to be simultaneously etched from both sides – so outlines can be 'pierced'. Leave tabs, so that the shape is still connected within the sheet.
4 A design can be etched onto one side of the metal at the same time; by the time the acid has etched the outline from both sides, the design should be etched to about half the thickness of the sheet.
5 Clip the pieces from the sheet, file the edges and polish the pieces.

## ENGINE TURNING

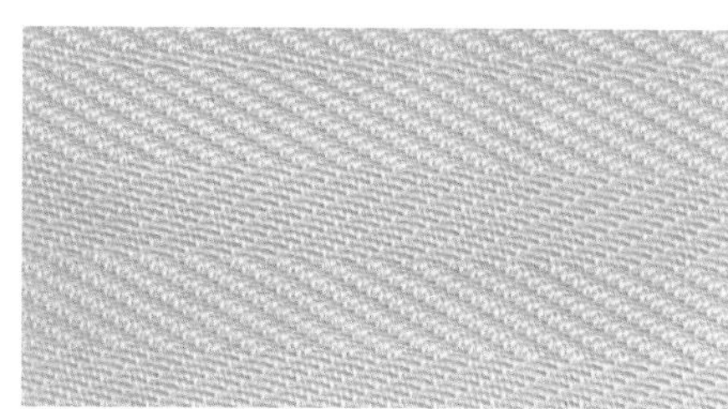

Engine turning produces bright-cut, overlapping, concentric patterns on the surface of metal, often used under basse-taille enamelling. The radial patterns catch the light in a way that creates movement in the texture, and different cuts produce different light-catching effects.

### METHOD

Due to the complex processes involved in setting up milling machines to accomplish varieties of this technique, it is impossible to explain it here either adequately or with enough detail to allow you to produce it effectively or provide for your safety. If you do decide to proceed, however, you will need special equipment and directions to produce engine turning.

Engine turning is also available as a commercial process, as is computer-assisted engine turning, which is a much more versatile process but may only be cost-effective if you plan to produce a large batch. Thanks to recent technological advances, most three-dimensional forms can be engine turned, although some forms may require special tooling, and this will therefore cost a lot more.

The effects are no longer restricted to the radial zigzags that were so popular in the nineteenth century – any hand-drawn or computer-generated image can be adapted and applied in a low-relief bright cut to the surface of metal.

## ENGRAVING

Hand-engraving is a wonderfully versatile technique, but a difficult one to master. Slivers of metal are removed from the surface of a metal piece with a steel graver. A skilled engraver can control an engraving up to the finest degree of detail. Only through lengthy practice with this technique will it become easy to execute a flawless engraving.

### METHOD

1 Select a square graver set in a handle that suits your hand size. It is crucial to set the graver up properly, so be sure to sharpen it well on an oilstone (see page 47) and polish it on an Arkansas stone – otherwise the cutting will be hard work and the results uneven.

2 Fix the sheet of metal that will be engraved onto a block of wood. Use double-sided tape if it is a large piece of metal, or setter's wax if it is small. The metal must be no thinner than 6 mm (¼ inch).

3 Buff the metal with a silver cloth to remove grease marks before drawing or tracing your design onto the surface with a fine scribe.

4 Work on a leather sandbag and sit at a comfortable height with your elbows resting on the work surface. Hold the square graver with the handle resting in the palm of your right hand, let your index and middle fingers rest along the side of the graver. The right thumb and left index finger should be touching and rest on the sheet, making a pivot; the remaining fingers of the left hand will hold the block of wood so that it rotates easily on the sandbag.

5 It is important to maintain the proper angle at which the graver will cut the metal. If the angle is too shallow, the graver will slip; if the graver is held too high, it will try to cut too deeply into the metal.

6 To cut curves, turn the silver clockwise into the path of the graver: for a tight curve, turn the metal at a greater speed than for an open curve. When you reach the end of a line, use the graver to flick out the sliver of metal. Cutting straight lines will require pressure from the ball of your right hand and controlling the graver with your fingers. It is difficult to cut long straight lines, so they are often cut by making many small cuts.

7 Any slips can be rubbed away with a burnisher, if they are not too deep.

8 Once all the traced lines have been cut, knock off any burrs on the surface of the metal with a steel blade. Polish the piece using soft rouge polish and a swansdown mop, which will not wear down the surface. Traces of polish can be removed with cotton wool soaked in lighter fluid.

△ ENGRAVED PENDANT
BY ANASTASIA YOUNG
*The heavily engraved panel has been secured in a spectacle setting to form a pendant. The piece was oxidized to accentuate the texture of the engraving.*

**KEY**  Sterling silver  Britannia silver  Fine silver  9ct gold  14ct gold 18ct gold  22ct gold

ENGRAVING
## Lettering

Lettering is notoriously difficult to cut evenly, especially on the insides of rings. You may wish to take your piece to a professional engraver if it's perfection you're seeking.

METHOD

1 If you are a beginner, you may find that handwriting script is much easier to reproduce than printed letters, which can take years to master.
2 Set up the metal on top of a block of wood placed on a sandbag.
3 Scribe on the complete lettering design; dividers help with making light reference lines.
4 Use a polished square graver for 'bright-cut' lettering styles. This type stands out well on silver with a satin surface.
5 First cut the 'line of beauty' for each letter; this is the longest, thickest part of the letter and will determine its visual flow. This cut can be thickened by 'threading' – cutting along the right-hand side of the first cut, while overlapping slightly so that you are widening the cut.
6 As the graver moves along the cut, angle it to the right to make the line swell, or roll the graver back to the centre position to reduce the thickness of the line. Repeat the appropriate technique wherever the line needs to be thicker.
7 Use thinner cuts to form other parts of letters, taking care not to slip where lines overlap.
8 De-burr and polish the surface. If you wish, rub fine pumice over the surface of the metal to dull it so that the lettering stands out more.

ENGRAVING
## Textures

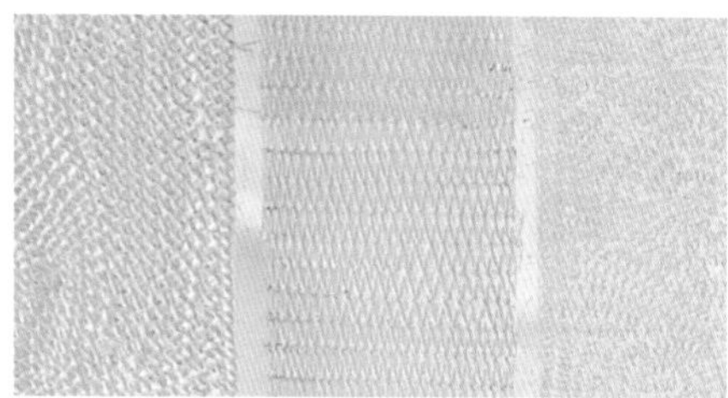

Engraving is an effective technique to produce textures. Traditionally, it has been used for shading in text and pictorial engraving. Almost any shape of graver can be used – the wider the blade, the bigger the zigzag it will produce.

METHOD

1 Fix your piece of metal on a block of wood and place it on a sandbag.
2 To produce 'wriggling' in your design, rock the graver from side to side as you push it forwards across the surface of the metal. The depth of the wriggled lines is determined by the angle at which you hold the graver and the amount of pressure that you apply. Random curves are easier to achieve than perfectly straight lines, which will show any discrepancies clearly.
3 Work over the surface of the metal in a methodical manner, stopping every so often to flick the metal that is being engraved from the surface. Do not rub your fingers over the surface, since raised burrs can be extremely sharp.
4 Scrape over the surface with a steel blade to detach any remaining burrs, then lightly burnish it.

**Sample** *Three different gravers have been used to produce these textures (from left to right: scorper, flat graver and stitch).*

## ENAMELLING

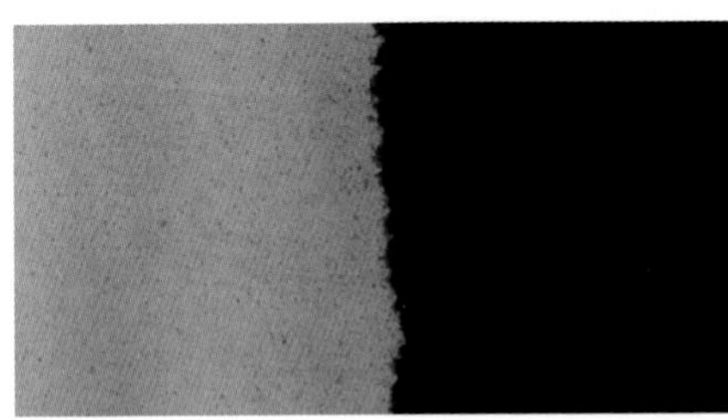

Enamel is coloured glass that has been fused to the surface of a metal at a high temperature. Enamelling is a time-consuming process, but the results can be stunning, since it adds colour, detail and a unique style element to your jewellery. Enamels are available in opaque, transparent, translucent and opalescent varieties, and come in a phenomenal range of colours. The colours are usually available in powder form, but they can come as glass chips, which require grinding before they can be used. Try to find lead-free enamels, since these are less toxic.

### METHOD

1. Heat the kiln to 870°C (1600°F).
2. Place some enamel powder in a mortar, fill the mortar halfway up with water, then grind the enamel with the pestle until it feels smooth.
3. Tap the mortar with the pestle to settle the enamel, and carefully pour off the excess water.
4. Use distilled water to wash the enamel, swirling it in the mortar, and pouring away the excess, leaving some to cover the surface of the enamel.
5. Wash the enamel until the water is clear.
6. Transfer the enamel to a small, clean plastic container that can be sealed, making sure that the surface of the enamel is covered by distilled water.
7. Follow this process for every colour you are using; the enamels can be stored in the containers for up to a month but may need washing again before use.
8. Anneal, pickle and scrub the metal where you will be applying enamel; the sheet should be about 1 mm (1/32 inch) thick. Clean the metal with a glass brush under running water; the water should cover the surface of the sheet without pulling away from the edges. Do not touch the surface of the metal.
9. Apply enamel to the surface of the metal with a clean paintbrush, making rows and trying to keep the amount of enamel even until the whole surface is covered.
10. Firmly tap the side of the sheet with the paintbrush to even out the enamel and carefully use a tissue applied to the edge of the metal sheet to draw out excess water. Your goal is to have an even layer of enamel a few grains thick covering the surface. This technique is called 'wet-packing'.
11. Place the metal sheet on a piece of wire mesh and then on top of the kiln to dry.
12. Place the piece inside the kiln using a spatula, and wait for the enamel to turn shiny. This should take about a minute, depending on the size and thickness of the piece.
13. Remove the piece from the kiln and allow to air-cool slowly. Subsequent layers of enamel can be applied in the same way.
14. To grind down the surface of the enamel until it is flat, use a diamond-grit pad under running water. Return the piece to the kiln for a short time; this will restore the glossy surface of the enamel – a technique known as 'flash-firing'.

**KEY**  Sterling silver  Britannia silver  Fine silver  9ct gold  14ct gold  18ct gold  22ct gold

ENAMELLING

## Plique-à-Jour

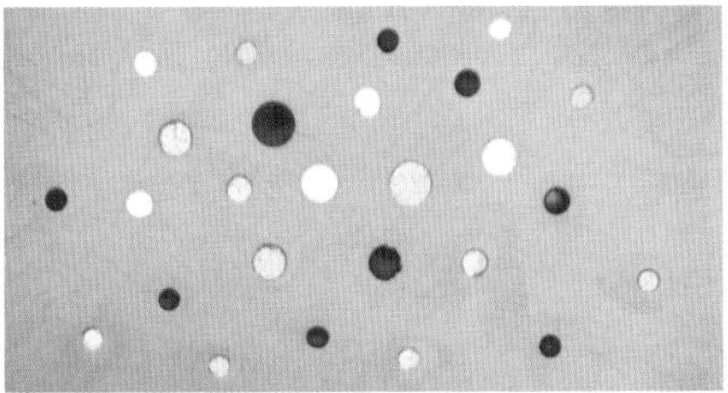

Plique-à-jour enamel allows the light to shine through and requires an open framework in metal, such as holes in sheet or wire structures. When designing, consider how the piece will be worn and whether it will show off the enamelling to its best advantage.

### METHOD

1. Prepare the enamels as previously described; transparent enamels should be used for this technique and lighter shades will show their colours better, especially if small areas are being enamelled.
2. Drill holes, or pierce shapes into 1 mm (1⁄32 inch) silver sheet, and ensure that the metal is clean.
3. Pack the holes with enamel and draw off the water.
4. Place the silver on a sheet of mica, which is a heat-resistant film, and dry the piece on top of the kiln.
5. Transfer the piece very carefully into the kiln and fire it – the mica should prevent the enamel from falling out of the holes.
6. Allow the piece to air-cool in a draught-free area.
7. Several layers of enamel will need to be fired into the holes to fill them completely.
8. Sand the piece with a diamond-grit pad under running water so that no enamel remains on the surface of either side of the sheet, and use wet-and-dry paper under running water to clean up the surface of the metal, finishing with a glass brush.
9. Return the piece to the kiln for a flash-firing.

ENAMELLING

## Champlevé

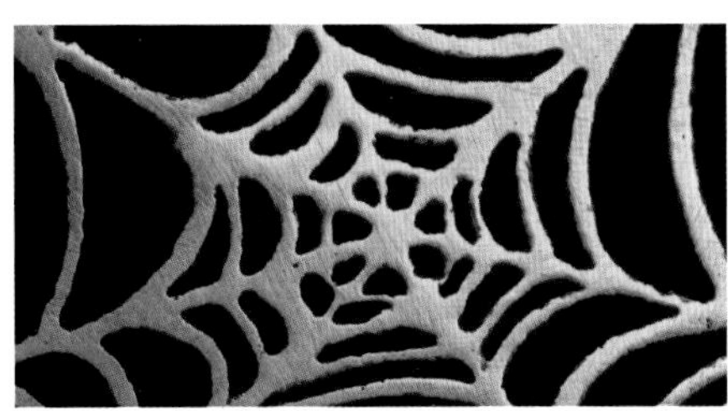

Traditional champlevé designs are composed of engraved or chiselled-away recesses in the surface of the metal, which are then filled with enamel while leaving a silver border. Etching is commonly used as a preparatory process. Since the recessed areas need to be deep, use 1 mm (1⁄32 inch) sheet or thicker, and etch to at least half the thickness.

### METHOD

1. Heat the kiln to 870°C (1600°F) and prepare the enamels as previously described.
2. Clean the metal. Applying a layer of counter-enamel to the back of the piece will stop the metal from warping, especially if it is thin.
3. Pickle the silver once the counter-enamel has been fired, and use a glass brush to clean the front surface and remove any traces of pickle; check to see that the recesses are free from dirt and grease.
4. Wet-pack the enamel into the recesses. Tap the sheet to level the enamel, and draw off the excess water. Allow to dry on top of the kiln before firing.
5. When the piece is cool, apply more layers of enamel until the enamel is level to or just projecting over the surface of the silver. Use a diamond-grit pad under running water to rub down the top surface until the enamel is flush with the silver – any dents or bubbles in the enamel will require another application and firing. Rub the surface down again, using a diamond-grit pad if necessary, then wet-and-dry paper to refine the surface of the metal.
6. Return the piece to the kiln for a flash-firing.

ENAMELLING
## Cloisonné

Small cells of fine silver or gold wire, or 'cloisons', define areas of enamels in different colours, which allows detailed designs to be applied with accurate colour separation. Foil fired inside the cloisons gives greater contrast.

### METHOD

1 Heat the kiln to 870°C (1600°F). Fire a layer of counter-enamel onto the back of the piece to stop it from warping.
2 Clean the front surface of the metal and apply a layer of clear flux enamel, using the wet-packing method. Fire until the surface turns shiny and allow the piece to air-cool.
3 Sketch your design on paper. Prepare the cloisonné wire by making small shapes that have a curve or an angle so they can stand on their own. Keep the wires short, and use flowing curves to build the design. The wires need to touch at intersections so that the enamel colours do not bleed.
4 Pour a thin layer of organic binder into a dish, and dip each piece of wire into it so that the bottom edge is coated. Position on the enamelled surface. Allow the binder to dry, then move it to the kiln and fire at 820°C (1500°F) for 90 seconds. The wires will bond to the surface.
5 Once cooled, the cloisons can be filled with different colours of enamel and fired at 870°C (1600°F). Build the enamel up by wet-packing. Do not fire any enamel grains onto the top edge of the wire.
6 Once you are satisfied with the depth of colour, grind down the surface of the enamel so that it is smooth and give it a final flash-firing.

ENAMELLING
## Basse-taille

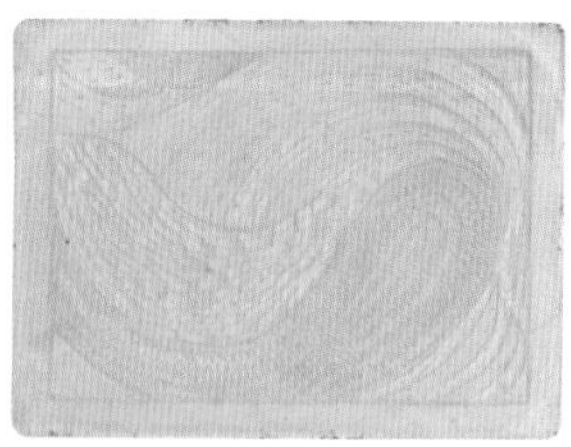

This enamelling technique utilizes the properties of transparent enamels by firing them on top of a textured surface so that the underlying design can still be seen. Most texturing techniques are suitable, whether etched, stamped or rolling mill textures. Britannia silver is often used as a base, as it has a lower copper content and is less prone to firestain.

### METHOD

1 Heat the kiln to 870°C (1600°F) and prepare the enamel using a transparent colour or flux.
2 Clean the metal with a glass brush, paying attention to the textured areas.
3 Apply the enamel using the wet-packing method. Sifting dry enamel through a fine mesh is fast, but proper safety precautions have to be observed. Enamel is a toxic substance and sifting it through a wire mesh will release minute particles into the air. Work inside a special ventilated structure.
4 Fire the enamel, cool and apply as many layers as necessary for the depth of colour required. The thicker the enamel is on a surface, the more intense it will be; deeper areas will therefore appear more intensely coloured than raised areas. Between each firing, clean the edges of the silver sheet; the oxides that form on the exposed metal can 'ping' off in the kiln and contaminate the transparent enamel. Any blemishes must be ground out.
5 Once firing is complete, allow the piece to air-cool, then grind down the enamel surface until it is flat and even, dry the piece and give it a final flash-firing.

**KEY**  Sterling silver  Britannia silver  Fine silver  9ct gold  14ct gold  18ct gold  22ct gold

ENAMELLING

## Gold Foil

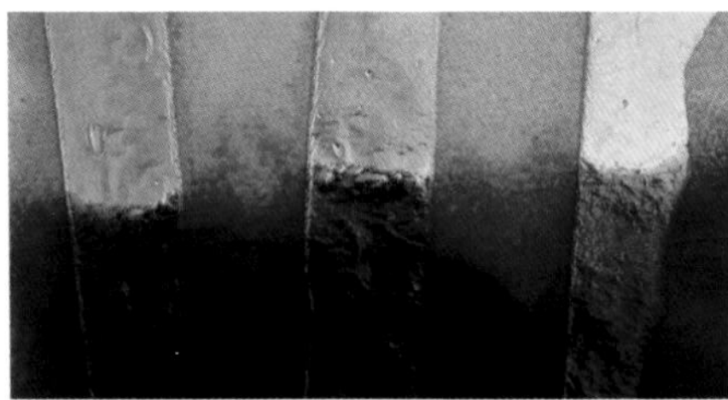

Twenty-two-carat gold foil can be applied to the surface of the enamel as a decoration or laid under a layer of transparent enamel to give it a deep lustre.

### METHOD

1 Fire the piece of sheet with a base layer of enamel, which can be opaque or transparent.
2 Clean the surface of the enamel with a glass brush and carefully dry the piece.
3 Cut small pieces of 22-carat gold foil inside a folded piece of tracing paper with a craft knife, then pick them up with a damp paintbrush and apply them to the enamel. Use small pieces of foil to cover larger areas, rather than one large piece of foil. Apply a little water around the edges to seal the foil in place, making sure no air is trapped underneath; do not touch the foil as this will affect its adhesion.
4 Allow the foil to dry properly, ideally overnight.
5 Fire the piece at 780°C (1450°F) for about 90 seconds and allow the piece to slowly air-cool on a heatproof surface.
6 The gold foil will be bonded to the surface of the enamel and can be left as a surface finish, or further layers of transparent enamel can be fired over the surface of the piece.

**Sample** *The gold foil under this sea-green transparent enamel makes the colour appear even more vivid.*

## WAX CARVING

Jeweller's wax is hard but slightly flexible, which will allow you to apply intricate details to potentially complex forms. When silver or gold are cast using the lost-wax method, an identical replica is produced.

### METHOD

1 Work out your design on paper first, or make a rough model in plasticine so that you have a three-dimensional reference to work from. Consider the way in which the molten metal will flow into the form: a piece with two bulky areas joined by a thin section is less likely to cast successfully.
2 Carve the outside form of your piece first, using a rasping or wax file to remove large areas of wax.
3 Smooth the form by rubbing it with coarse wire wool to erase the file marks; fine wire wool can be used to refine the surface.
4 Use carving tools to create details on the wax form. If you wish to create a relief design, trace the outline onto the wax and then carve the background away to a suitable level. The raised areas can then be perfected. Engraving tools cut wax effectively and can create textures and incisions as well. Thin patches should be carved last to avoid breakage.
5 Clean up the surface using fine wire wool.

**TIP:** It takes less time to carve details accurately in wax than it does when the form is in metal, so be thorough. Use a flame to 'lick' raised areas to make them shiny, but do not overheat the wax since it melts easily. Finally, cast the piece.

WAX CARVING
## Rings

Forms made by the lost-wax casting process have a tendency to be heavy, and it is nearly always necessary to hollow the piece out from the inside while the model is in its wax form. This will decrease the weight of the piece but retain its visual volume. Use a professional casting service to ensure the best results.

METHOD

1. To carve a ring, first cut a section from a wax tube. Tubes with pre-drilled holes are available in a number of profiles.
2. Size the ring by using a wax ring stick to carve the inner surface to the correct size.
3. Mark your design on the top surface of the wax first, then carve it to shape with a wax file.
4. Turn the wax on its side and mark a profile around the circumference of the ring; file the wax accordingly then round-off the corners. Make any adjustments to the final form before cleaning up with wire wool.
5. To hollow out the inside surface of the ring, use an appropriate-size ball burr in a pendant motor to carefully remove wax. Keep the burr moving and do not apply too much pressure. Leave a border of about 1 mm (1/32 inch) intact on the top and bottom edges so that the actual ring size is not affected.
6. Check the depth by holding the piece up to the light – if the wax is almost white, it is thin enough.
7. Weigh the wax and use the following formulas to judge how much the ring will weigh when it is cast:
   wax weight (grams) × 10.6 = silver weight (grams)
   wax weight (grams) × 16.3 = 18-carat yellow gold weight (grams)
8. Every carat and color of gold has a different weight ratio. The weight of a ring is a matter of personal taste but aim for less than 10 g of metal. Thin the wax more if the weight is still too high. Items for casting in gold will require more thinning than those for silver in order to keep the cost down.
9. Carefully clean the inner surface of the form with a small piece of wire wool. It is now ready to be cast.

**TIP:** The thickness of the wax can be judged by the amount of light it lets through.

**KEY**  Sterling silver  Britannia silver  Fine silver  9ct gold  14ct gold 18ct gold  22ct gold

CASTING
## Soft Wax

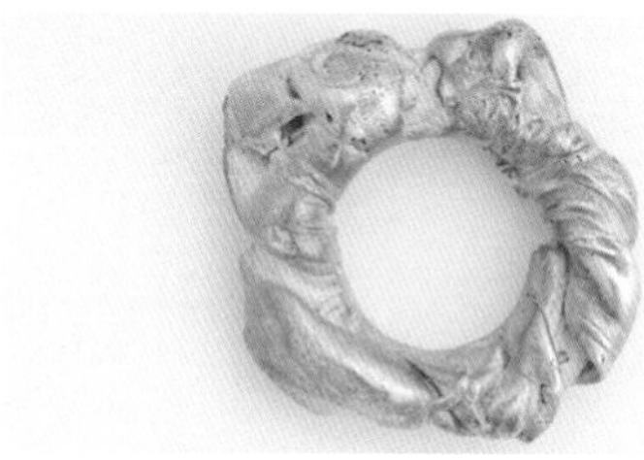

Experimenting with wax techniques can yield exciting and unexpected forms. Soft wax that is easily moulded by hand can be used to create beautiful sculptural forms, but check first with a professional caster that the wax is suitable.

METHOD

1 Use soft wax that can be modelled by hand. Form a long, flat ribbon, fold it in half, then twist it randomly.
2 Join the ends in a way that complements your form with a wax modelling tool.
3 Stamp out a circle of the size you need with a circular object. It is not possible to create refined, detailed forms in waxes that are softer than the jeweller's wax described previously. With soft waxes you have to allow the process to dictate the form and texture. Elegant, organic forms can be produced, for example. It is also more difficult to control the weight of the piece, but it is possible to burr out metal after the form has been cast.

CASTING
## Finishing

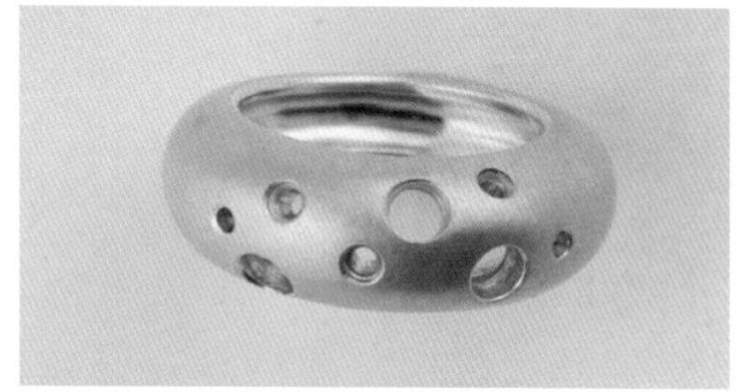

Cleaning up castings is a skilled procedure. Accurate filing and well-finished surfaces will enhance the overall quality of any piece. Cleaning in large amounts will teach you to work with speed and accuracy and will improve the rest of your bench skills.

METHOD

1 Use a piercing saw to cut the sprue off the piece, as close to the form as is possible.
2 Use a rough file to remove the rest of the sprue, so that the area is level with the surrounding metal.
3 You will probably need to file most surfaces. File the whole area with a half-round ring file. Use the curved side of the file on the inside of the ring and any inverted curves on its outside surface, and the flat side of the file for convex curves or flat areas. Use a needle file to refine rough file marks.
4 Use an emery stick or wet-and-dry paper to clean up all surfaces, starting with a rough grade and working up to a very fine grade.
5 You can speed this process up by using a split-pin mandrel with an emery paper insert in a pendant motor. Keep the hand piece of the pendant motor moving, otherwise it will make grooves in the surface of the metal. Small abrasive attachments for the pendant motor can be used to clean up the hollowed-out inner surface of the ring and polish it. Once the outside surface of the ring has been cleaned to your satisfaction, it can be polished on a polishing motor using Tripoli, then rouge. Any trapped polish can be removed in an ultrasonic cleaner.

CASTING
## With Moulds

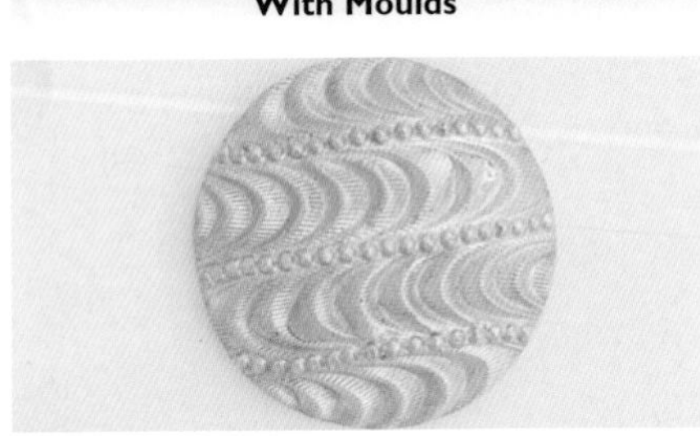

Jeweller's wax can be used to take impressions from a mould. Although the pieces will be textured on only one side, they can be applied to other pieces of wax or used with other metal elements to fabricate pieces of jewellery.

### METHOD

1. Make a silicone mould (see page 175), using the impression from an interestingly textured object, such as a button.
2. Melt some pink jeweller's wax (do not use a naked flame – molten wax is flammable) and pour it into the mould so that it is just less than half full.
3. Rotate the mould so that the wax coats the whole surface, and keep rotating the mould until the wax is set. A second coating may be necessary after the first one has cooled.
4. Once the mould and wax are completely cold, carefully flex the mould to release the wax. You can trim the edges with a craft knife at this stage, but wax is fragile, so take care.
5. Any air bubbles on the surface of the wax can be carefully filled either with molten pink wax, or with very soft wax pushed in with a fine tool.
6. The piece is now ready to be cast, using the lost-wax technique.
7. To clean up the silver casting, cut off the sprue with a piercing saw and file any surfaces or edges that need smoothing. File with an emery stick and then polish. Any textured areas can be cleaned with a brass brush and shouldn't need any filing.

CASTING
## Multiples

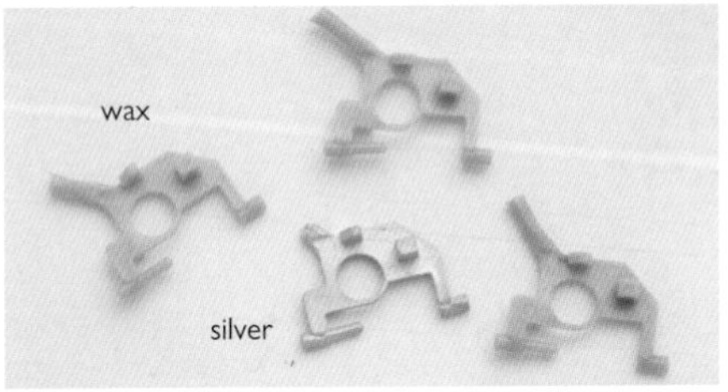


Casting is a good technique for producing large amounts of identical pieces, and is used on a massive scale in the jewellery industry.

### METHOD

1. Carve wax into the required form and have it cast, preferably in brass – this will be your 'master'. File, use an emery stick, and polish your master.
2. You will need to solder on a piece of 3/32 inch (3 mm) rod about 4 cm (1½ inches) long. Check with a professional caster where the best place to solder the rod might be, considering the flow of the molten metal into the form.
3. This rod will form the 'sprue' and is where the wax will flow into the mould. Use plenty of solder for a good join with no gaps.
4. The mould should be made by a professional caster, using vulcanized rubber heated in a press. The master is cut out of the mould, then molten wax is injected into it as required. These waxes will then be cast into the metal.

*See step 4*

**KEY**  Sterling silver  Britannia silver · Fine silver · 9ct gold · 14ct gold · 18ct gold · 22ct gold

## PRECIOUS METAL CLAY

Precious metal clay (PMC) consists of fine silver (or gold) combined with an organic binder that is driven off when the piece is fired. It handles the same way as clay and will take impressions well from silicone moulds, but can also be modelled and carved. The rate of shrinkage is an issue, but each successive generation of PMC has had a reduced percentage of shrinkage, so it is becoming less of a problem.

METHOD

1 Work on a clean surface and use olive oil to prevent the clay from sticking.
2 Keep the PMC moist while working on it.
3 Construct forms, either by rolling out the clay and impressing textures onto its surface or by pressing the clay into a mould.
4 Seal joins with a small amount of water smoothed over the surface.
5 You can create sculptural forms, but as with ceramic clay, raised hollow areas may need to be supported to prevent slumping when the piece is fired.
6 Allow the PMC to dry before firing it and, once dry, fine detail can be carved into the surface.
7 Fire the PMC in a kiln, or with a gas torch. Check the manufacturer's recommendations regarding temperatures and firing times.
8 Once fired, the piece can be cleaned up using files and emery paper, but you may wish to retain some of the surface qualities of the material by using a brass brush.

## ELECTROFORMING
### Fine Silver

Wax objects can be electroformed to make large, light, hollow forms. A thin layer of fine silver is deposited over the surface by passing a current of electricity through a special chemical bath. You will need to use a professional electroforming company, since the chemicals involved are toxic and the equipment is prohibitively expensive.

METHOD

1 Prepare the object by making sure it is clean, well finished and sealed; organic objects need a few thin layers of varnish so that they do not dissolve in the chemical baths.
2 A conductive silver paint is applied to the surface, providing a base for the deposited metal to stick to. The paint can be applied with a paintbrush, but the best results are achieved by airbrushing.
3 The object is submerged in a tank, suspended from the wire that forms the cathode (negative pole). The anode (positive pole) is made of the metal that will be deposited onto the cathode – in this case, fine silver. When an electric current is applied, the fine silver will dissolve and be deposited onto the object, creating a thin metal shell.
4 Once the coating is thick enough, the piece is removed from the solution and cleaned up.
5 The original object can be burned out, leaving a hollow shell that can be cleaned and even soldered onto, providing due care is taken.

**Sample** *A gold-plated silver electroform over wax.*

## CAD/CAM

Computer-aided design and computer-aided modelling (CAD/CAM) is generally taken to mean the rendering of a detailed blueprint for an object using a three-dimensional modelling computer program. A computer can use the information to facilitate the production of a three-dimensional model by a wax printer or similar device.

### METHOD

1 It does take time to master the software used for CAD, but if you can't do it yourself, then a skilled technician will be able to render a three-dimensional image from clear technical drawings of the object, usually in a three-dimensional computer software package such as Rhinocerous®, from which the technical specifications of the piece can easily be translated. The object can be constructed using a three-dimensional wax printer that transforms the information into a viable form that can then be cast, using the lost-wax method. There is a lack of interaction during the forming of the piece, and wax printouts are more effective for angular forms than organic ones, but as the technology improves, so will the results.
2 Forms can be created that would otherwise be incredibly labour-intensive to fabricate, but within the industry, CAD/CAM is used for producing masters for large batches of identical units, which makes the process cost-effective.

*CAD files can be used to render realistic representations of a piece for display or presentation purposes (above), or the information can be transferred to create a wax replica of the design, which can then be cast into metal. See Settings, pages 232–241, for further examples of CAD-generated work.*

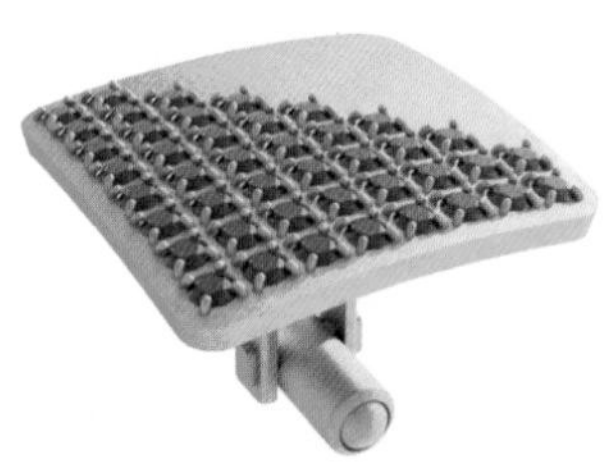

**KEY**  Sterling silver  Britannia silver  Fine silver  9ct gold  14ct gold  18ct gold  22ct gold

## RIVETING

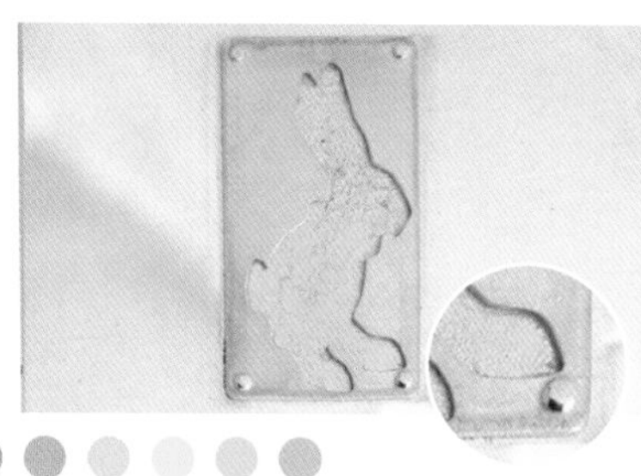

Riveting, a cold-joining technique, is very useful for joining pieces where soldering cannot be used. Stunning layered effects can be built up using thin sheets of metal. Riveting is particularly suitable if patinas or gold leaf on a piece would be damaged by heat, or if the mixed materials being used will not tolerate heat or chemicals.

### METHOD

1 Pieces should be in a finished state, since it is difficult to clean layers once they are riveted together. You may wish to vary the finishes on different layers.

2 Mark and drill a hole on the piece of sheet that will lie at the front of the piece; this is where the rivets will be most visible, and the shape of the sheet often determines where the rivets are positioned.

3 The drilled hole needs to be exactly the same size as the wire that is being used for the rivets: 1 mm (1/32 inch) is a good size. The wire for the rivets needs to be half hard. If your wire is soft, work-harden it in a draw plate.

4 To make the rivets, fix a piece of wire tightly in a vice, using protective pads or leather on the inside of the jaws so that the wire will not be damaged. Only 4 mm (1/8 inch) of wire should be protruding above the vice.

5 File the end of the wire so it is flat, then use a ball-peen hammer to tap the top end of the wire so that it spreads evenly and forms a head. This will stop the wire from slipping through the hole.

6 Position the top sheet over the base sheet, mark one hole and drill. The edges of the drilled holes will need to be countersunk, so use a ball burr 6 mm (1/4 inch) larger than your drill-hole size.

7 Push the first rivet through the hole. You can now mark through the other holes on the front sheet with less risk of having the piece slip; that would move the holes out of alignment.

8 Drill and countersink the rest of the holes and make enough rivets to use.

9 Protect the front surface of the piece with masking tape and push the rivets through the remaining holes, from back to front.

10 Working on a steel block, cut the rivet wire to about 1 mm (1/32 inch) above the surface of the sheet. File so that the top is flat, and hammer to spread it. Be careful not to hit the sheet with the hammer, since this will mark the metal.

11 Turn the piece over and tap from the other side. The rivet heads should be slightly domed but making good contact with the surface of the sheet. Tap down any sharp edges.

12 The rivets can be burnished to highlight them, or filed so that they are flush with the surface of the sheet; the countersink will prevent the rivets from dropping out, and will make an almost invisible join.

## TUBE RIVETS

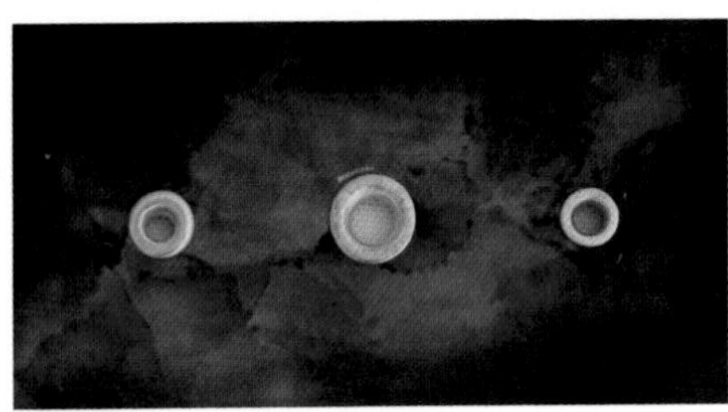

Making more of a statement than wire rivets, tube rivets can be cut with a saw, or filed so that they split in a controlled manner when riveted, forming petals.

### METHOD

1 Prepare the pieces of metal to be joined together. They should have their final textures or finishes already applied, since cleaning up once riveting is done will be difficult.
2 Centre-punch and drill a hole in both pieces the same size as the outside diameter of the tube.
3 Use a chenier vice to cut a length of tube that is 3 mm (1/8 inch) longer than the thicknesses of the two sheets to be riveted.
4 File the ends of the tube flat, or cut grooves in the top surface with a piercing saw and use a file to shape the sections. Smooth any sharp edges with emery paper.
5 Anneal, pickle and dry the tube – it needs to be soft in order to rivet successfully.
6 Place the sheets on a steel block and insert the tube into the holes. Use a doming punch that is 3 mm (1/8 inch) larger than the inner diameter of the tube. To open up the hole, tap the punch with a mallet just hard enough so that the top of the tube spreads. Turn the piece upside down and repeat the process on the other end of the tube.
7 Use progressively larger doming punches to open up the rivet until it is flush with the surface of the sheet, working from both sides. The rivet can be flattened with a hammer and if the inside edge has become misshapen, use a ball burr to clean it up.

## DECORATIVE RIVETS

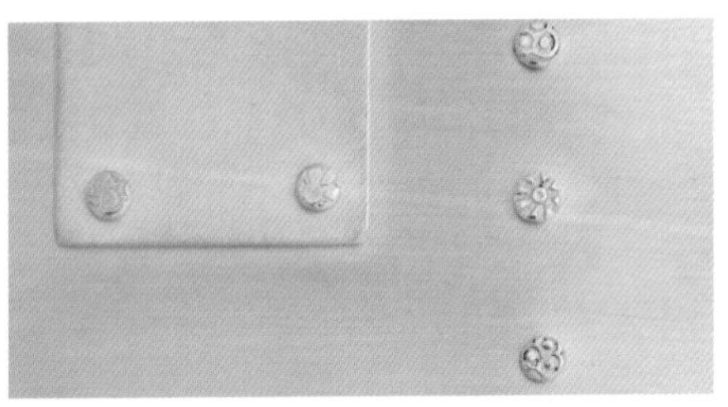

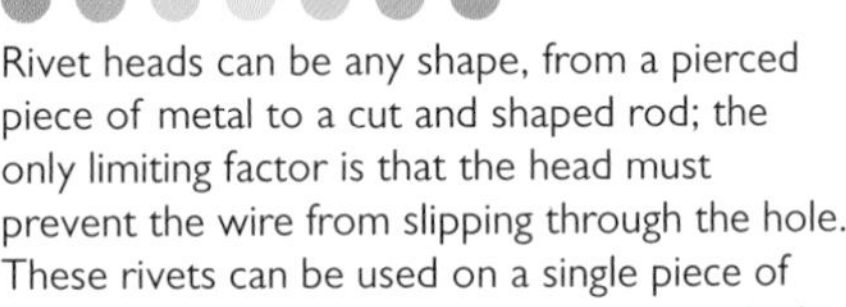

Rivet heads can be any shape, from a pierced piece of metal to a cut and shaped rod; the only limiting factor is that the head must prevent the wire from slipping through the hole. These rivets can be used on a single piece of sheet as a decorative device or to join multiple sheets together.

### METHOD

1 Prepare the metal that will be used as rivet heads: pierce out a shape or stamp discs, and texture.
2 File one end of a piece of 1 mm (1/32 inch) wire so that it is flat. The wire should be longer than is necessary for the rivet.
3 Place the rivet head face down on a soldering mat and position the wire so that it is in the centre of the piece, sticking straight up, and held in a pair of reverse-action soldering tweezers.
4 Flux, apply a pallion of hard solder and heat until the solder melts. Concentrate the flame on the rivet head – the wire is so thin it will heat up quickly.
5 Pickle, rinse and polish the rivet head.
6 Push the rivet through a 1 mm (1/32 inch) hole drilled into a piece of sheet and cut the end of the rivet wire so that it is protruding about 1.5 mm (1/16 inch) above the surface of the sheet. File the end of the wire flat.
7 Work on a steel block with a piece of leather under your work to prevent the decorative rivet head from becoming flattened, and use a hammer to spread the end of the wire and secure the rivet.

**KEY**  Sterling silver   Britannia silver  Fine silver  9ct gold   14ct gold  18ct gold  22ct gold

## SCREW THREADS

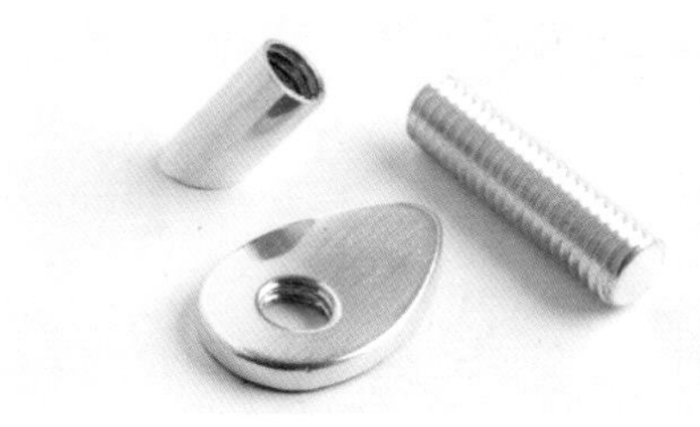

Screws are useful for 'cold-joining' pieces of metal and have the added advantage of not being permanent, which makes it easier to clean or reposition pieces. The lifespan of a precious metal screw will never be as long as that of a steel screw, because precious metal is so much softer. It's important to take this limitation into consideration when you design your piece.

### METHOD

1. You will need a tap and die set in order to cut the screw threads. These sets are available in metric and imperial sizes, and in standard sizes, including BA, UNF and UNC. Each type of set will require specific measurements in order to determine the appropriate diameter of rod, and the size of drilled hole with which you will need to work. Metric sets are a little easier to understand: an M6 die will cut a thread on a 6 mm (¼ inch) rod.
2. Ideally, the process should be done manually in a lathe, but it will work fine if done in a vice (there is just more room for error with the latter). To make a nut and screw that fit together, you must use a matching tap and a die of the same number.
3. Tighten the rod, which must be straight, in the vice. File the top flat and bevel the edge slightly.
4. Insert the correct-size die into the die holder and tighten the screws that hold it in place.
5. Place the die on the top end of the rod and begin to turn clockwise. Use plenty of lubricant.
6. Once the tap has purchase on the rod, you need to work as follows: one turn clockwise, then a half-turn anticlockwise; this clears the swarf from the die and stops it from getting clogged up. Work your way down the rod to the required length.
7. To make a nut you will need tubing that is thick enough to take a thread being cut, or a piece of sheet thicker than 1 mm (1⁄32 inch).
8. Fix the sheet in the vice horizontally, insert the tap into the tap holder, and start turning the tap clockwise. Again, use plenty of lubricant and work clockwise and anticlockwise to clear the swarf. Any wobbling in your movements will cause the thread to be cut wider, and the screw will have more room to move when it is inserted. If you are working with tubing in a vice, you will need to insert a piece of rod the exact size of the diameter of the hole in the tube so that it won't get squashed when you close the vice.

## WELDING

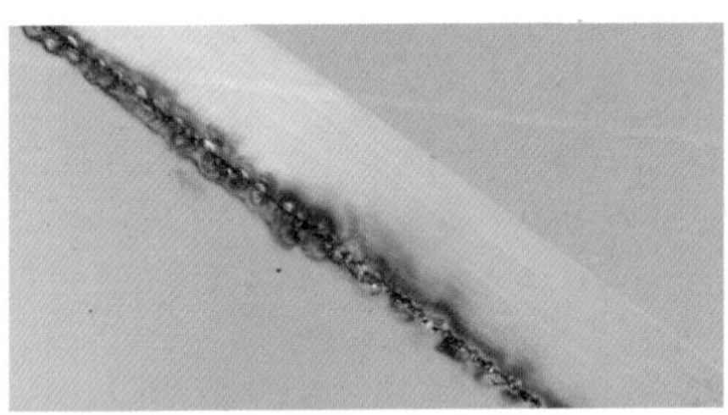

If elements need to be joined but cannot be soldered, and cold-joining methods will detract from the design, welding may be the answer. It is also good for tacking pieces of metal into position before soldering.

METHOD

1 Technical training is necessary before working with welding equipment, which often has built-in eye protection in the stereomicroscopic screen to magnify the work.
2 A PUK welder has a tungsten electrode in the hand piece that is applied to the area to be joined. Different shapes and sizes of tips will make joins of between 1–3 mm (1⁄32–3⁄32 inch).
3 As the current is applied through the tip, argon gas is blown over the surface, preventing contamination of the weld from atmospheric gases. Filler rod in the form of thin silver wire can also be applied to prevent pitting of the metal in the welding point, giving a neat, raised welt. Overlapping lines of weld points will form a stronger join than sparse dots. The pulse-arc system is good for continuous seams, and the low current ensures the pieces do not get too hot, and can be hand-held. The reflective nature of silver and gold mean that the technique works best when they are smeared lightly with plasticine.

TIP: This technique is very useful for tacking awkward-shaped pieces together before soldering so that they do not move, especially lugs of hinges.

## PENDANT MOTOR TEXTURES
### With Burrs

Burrs are normally used for removing areas of metal, particularly as part of the stone-setting process, but they can also be used to texture the surface of metal. Different-shaped burrs will produce different effects.

METHOD

1 Insert a flame burr into the pendant motor and tighten the collet. Apply some lubricant.
2 Depending on the size of the piece of metal being worked on and the area that needs to be covered, it might be a good idea to attach the metal to a piece of wood so that it can be more easily held and your fingers are less likely to come into contact with the burr. This can be done with nails or setter's wax to hold the metal in position.
3 The patchwork texture is created by 'scribbling' with the burr, across the surface of the metal in small areas. Work in small, overlapping patches, rotating the sheet a few degrees each time you start a new patch. Only the surface needs to be marked, so do not apply too much pressure.
4 The different directions of cuts applied by the burr will reflect light at different angles, so the more angles you have created, the greater the number of different 'shades' the metal will appear to have.

PENDANT MOTOR TEXTURES
## With Diamond Burrs

Diamond burrs have a thin coating of diamond particles over the surface and are available in a range of shapes. Although they are best used for cutting materials that are hard, such as glass and stone, diamond burrs cut metal a little less aggressively than steel burrs. They should be continuously lubricated, otherwise the diamond layer is worn down quickly.

### METHOD

1 Insert a diamond burr into the pendant motor and tighten the collet. Apply some lubricant; both cutting oil and wax burr lubricant work well. Reapply lubricant regularly throughout the process. When choosing the shape of your burr, consider the amount of contact the burr will make with the metal. A ball burr will make less contact than a cone-shaped burr held against the metal, and therefore smaller marks.
2 Be confident when making your marks. Hesitant marks will be obvious and look out of place. Move the burr in long, even strokes across the surface of the metal until you have created a uniform field of texture.
3 As this technique is removing a small amount of the surface of the metal, it can be used to remove excess solder marks or disguise fine scratches, but it is always advisable to start with a well-prepared surface to achieve the best results.

PENDANT MOTOR TEXTURES
## Silicone Points

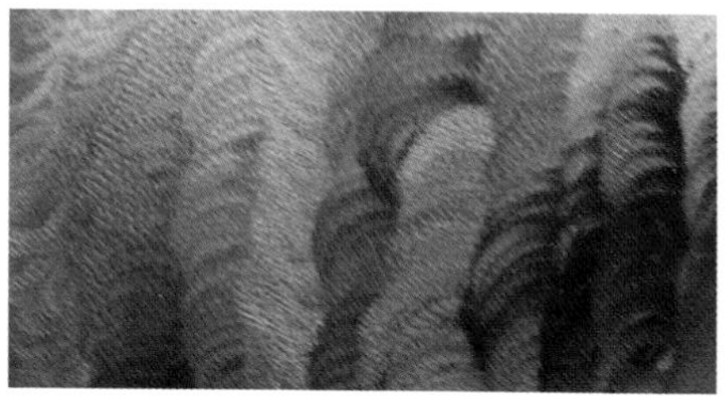

The amount of attachments available for pendant motors is bewildering; most are designed to aid the cleaning-up process and are abrasive in varying degrees. Impregnated silicone points can also create subtly reflective surface textures. Although they are useful for hard-to-reach corners and also labour-saving, silicone points are a more expensive way of working than using emery paper and sticks.

### METHOD

1 Insert the silicone point into the pendant motor and tighten the collet. It is not necessary to lubricate the rubber attachments since they are designed to wear down. Always wear a mask while using a pendant motor since a large amount of dust will be created. The grade of the rubber point will determine how deeply the metal is marked. Fine-grade points will leave a fine surface that is not as deeply cut as one made by a coarse-grade point.
2 Starting at one corner of the sheet of metal, rotate the handpiece of the pendant motor in a tight spiral motion as you move along the edge of the metal. Build up the texture in lines, having the edge of each new line overlap the edge of the last.

PENDANT MOTOR TEXTURES

## Deep Impressions

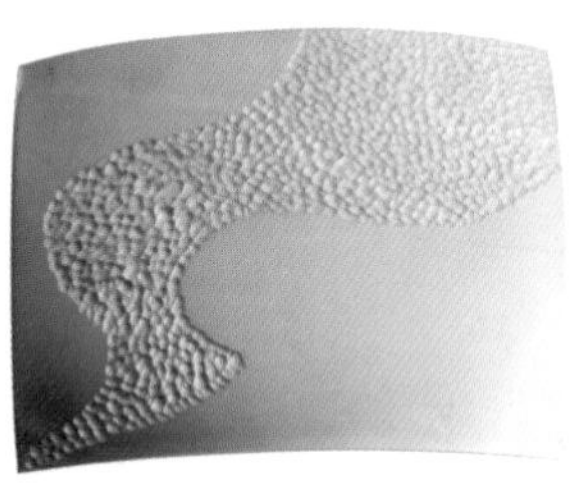

Using a burr to make deep impressions in the surface of gold or silver can be for purely decorative reasons, or to disguise surface areas that are impractical to polish. Experiment with different shapes of grooves that can be made by the various burrs.

### METHOD

1 Use a permanent ink marker to sketch your design on the metal.
2 Insert a small ball burr in the collet of the pendant motor; it should be less than 2 mm (1/16 inch) in diameter since larger burrs will remove too much metal and be more difficult to control.
3 Hold the silver tightly against the bench pin or stuck to a piece of wood and, with your fingers out of the path of the burr, start the motor, lubricate the burr and apply it to the surface of the metal.
4 Keep the burr in the same position for a second or so, using some pressure to make a groove in the metal's surface. Use it to create an overlapping pitted surface and remember to lubricate the burr frequently; this will make it cut more efficiently and it will stay sharp far longer.
5 Practise on a scrap piece of base metal first if you are not confident using a pendant motor. The marks you make must look intentional, and will have more of a uniform feel if you can establish a regular rhythm with the burr.

## POLISHING

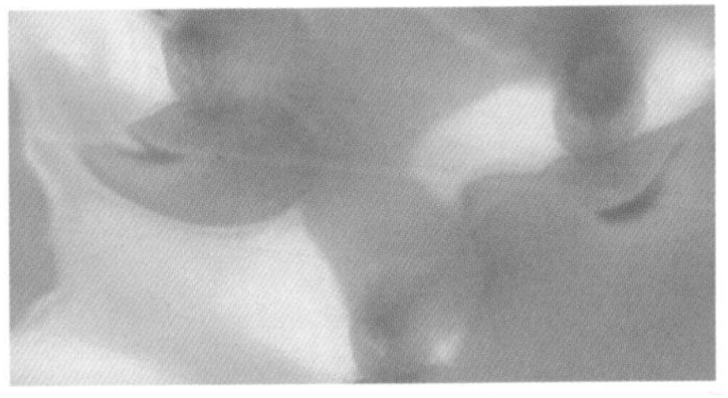

The finish of a piece is as important as the design, so try to use a sympathetic finishing technique, and consider how the form will be affected by light-play. A polished finish is suitable for areas on a piece of jewellery that will take a lot of wear, and although the surface will get scratched over time, the overall effect will not change much.

### METHOD

1 Prepare the surface of the metal by removing all scratches with emery paper, working through the grades. Alternate the direction you are working in right up to the finest grade of paper.
2 Initial polishing is done with Tripoli – this is a slightly abrasive compound that will remove fine scratches. Apply the compound to the polishing mop.
3 As you polish the piece, keep it moving and be careful not to round-off corners and edges too much. Hold the piece firmly, but not so firmly that you can't let go if the mop 'grabs' the piece, and be aware that the piece will heat up. If you are using a pendant motor, keep the mop moving.
4 Once the surface has been polished, wash the piece with detergent and a soft brush to remove the Tripoli.
5 Using a separate, softer mop, apply rouge polish and polish the piece again. The surface of the metal should now be bright and very shiny.
6 Remove any residual polish with a soft brush and detergent. Polish trapped in awkward places can be removed in an ultrasonic cleaner.

**KEY**  Sterling silver  Britannia silver  Fine silver   9ct gold  14ct gold  18ct gold  22ct gold

## MATT FINISH

Matt finishes give jewellery a soft look and are a good base for patinas; they also provide contrast with highly polished surfaces. Polish the piece first then mask off any areas you don't want to be matt, but bear in mind that any areas of the piece that are likely to get a lot of wear will eventually become shiny.

METHOD

1 Prepare the surface of the metal by removing scratches with emery paper, working through the grades. Go over the surface with the first grade of emery in one direction; choose the next grade to rub across the grain you just finished so you will be able to see any scratches that run along the grain. Alternate the direction you are working in right up to the finest grade of paper. If any deep marks remain, file them out and work through the grades of paper again.
2 Use a Scotch-Brite wheel on a polishing motor, or use a pendant motor with a screw-thread mandrel holding a cut piece of scouring pad. As you work the piece on the wheel, keep it moving; if you are using a pendant motor, keep the mop moving. Hold the piece firmly, but not so firmly that you can't let go if the mop 'grabs' the piece, and be aware that the piece may heat up.
3 The effect of the Scotch-Brite wheel will look better if its action is restricted to one direction – try to keep the strokes of the wheel parallel to the piece as you work.

## MATT FINISH
### Pumice Powder

Pumice powder used with liquid soap and water will give the surface of the metal a 'flat' appearance, since the reflective ability of the metal is reduced. Use a steel burnisher to define the edges of a piece – this will create eye-catching highlights. Cleaning with pumice powder degreases the metal to prepare it for other techniques.

METHOD

1 Prepare the surface of the metal by removing scratches with emery paper, working through the grades. Go over the surface with the first grade of emery in one direction; choose the next grade to rub across the grain you just finished so you will be able to see any scratches that run along the grain. Alternate the direction you are working in right up to the finest grade of paper. If any deep marks remain, file them out and work through the grades of paper again. The best results come from a well-prepared surface; pumice powder is a fine medium and abrades only the top surface of the metal.
2 Load a stiff-bristled brush with pumice powder and liquid soap. Work in a sink, as the brush will throw off some spray. Scrub the surface of the metal, building up a lather; you can work in a circular motion, or from side to side. Add more pumice powder to the brush as required and keep going until the surface has an even quality.
3 Rinse well to remove any residual powder, and dry.

## SATIN FINISH

Satin finishes scatter light in a uniform manner. Light scratches made by fine emery paper, whether running along the surface of the metal or scratched in a circular motion, will scatter reflections. Make confident marks with the emery paper because, as with polishing, any marks that are out of place or that throw light out at a different angle, will detract from the piece as a whole.

### METHOD

1. Prepare the surface of the metal by removing scratches with emery paper, working through the grades. Go over the surface with the first grade of emery in one direction; choose the next grade to rub across the grain you just finished – that way you will be able to see any scratches that run along the grain. Alternate the direction you are working in right up to the finest grade of paper. If any deep marks remain, file them out and work through the grades of paper again.
2. Lightly polish with Tripoli.
3. Select a fine-grade emery paper and firmly rub across the surface of the metal using either a circular motion or from side to side. Keep at an even speed and apply consistent pressure until the surface has an even quality. For flat surfaces, an emery stick can be used, which will allow you to apply more pressure.
4. Raised areas or edges of the piece can be burnished for a finishing touch.

## SATIN CIRCULAR FINISH

This technique scatters light in a seemingly random way, but this is the result of a carefully controlled application of an abrasive medium to the surface of the metal. The process makes the metal appear a little brighter than a matt finish can, and is also more durable.

### METHOD

1. Prepare the surface of the metal by removing scratches with emery paper, working through the grades. Go over the surface with the first grade of emery in one direction only; choose the next grade to rub across the grain you just finished – that way you will be able to see any scratches that run along the grain. Alternate the direction you are working in right up to the finest grade of paper. If any deep marks remain, you will have to file them out and work through the grades of paper again. Scratched surfaces will cover the finest of marks but will not disguise solder marks or remove firestain.
2. Use a medium-grade emery paper, abrasive rubber block or abrasive sponge in a circular motion, scratching the metal's surface. If your circles are too small, the effect can look messy, so use a regular sweeping movement and build up a rhythm. The rougher your abrasive is, the deeper the scratches will be and the more light will be reflected – finer emery papers will give a more delicate surface.

**KEY**

 Sterling silver
 Britannia silver
 Fine silver
 9ct gold
 14ct gold
 18ct gold
 22ct gold

POLISHING

## Semi-polished Finish

Brass brushes can be used to brighten the surface of gold and silver, particularly in deep textures or awkward places where polishing with a mop would wear down raised areas.

METHOD

1 Prepare the surface of the metal by removing scratches with emery paper, working through the grades. Go over the surface with the first grade of emery in one direction; choose the next grade to rub across the grain of the one you just finished – that way you will be able to see any scratches that run along the grain. Alternate the direction you are working in right up to the finest grade of paper. If any deep marks remain, file them out and work through the grades of paper again.

2 For large areas use a large brass-bristle wheel on a polishing motor to work evenly over the surface until a satisfactory result has been achieved. For small areas use a small brass-bristle attachment in a pendant motor; these are available in different shapes (cup, wheel and point) and will allow you to access areas where it may not be possible to use files or emery paper. In this way, deeply textured surfaces and recesses in castings can be cleaned quickly. In both of those processes, brass can be transferred from the bristles onto the surface of your piece and will discolour it. Avoid this by limiting the duration of the process.

## ABRASIVE BARRELLING MEDIA

A barrelling motor functions well for more than just polishing. Abrasive media, ranging from ceramic cones to grit-impregnated plastic chips, are available for use with it. Barrelling is good for softening the edges of complex shapes and forms and is therefore perfect as a pre-polishing stage for castings and pierced work.

METHOD

1 Prepare the surface of the metal by removing blemishes first with a file, then with emery paper, working through the grades. Go over the surface with the first grade of emery in one direction; choose the next grade to rub across the grain, so that you can see any scratches. Alternate the direction you are working in right up to the finest grade of paper. If deep marks remain, file them out and work through the grades of paper again.

2 Place your piece in the barrel of the machine with your abrasive medium and sufficient water. Cutting powders may be used to speed up the process. Close the lid and turn the motor on.

3 The process can take a couple of hours or, if a fine plastic medium is used, then a satisfactory result may be achieved only after one or two days, depending on the degree of barrelling needed. Use a more abrasive medium first, followed by a finer one before you barrel-polish the piece. The abrasive effect of the barrelling media will affect raised and protruding parts more than recessed areas, so take care when barrelling delicate textures or pieces with thin parts, such as wires.

## FLICK WHEEL

'Frosting' wheels are available in several grades from extra fine to coarse, and there are smaller versions for pendant motors. This process is not suitable for delicate or fragile work, work made from thin sheet or pieces too small to allow you to use the wheel without having it touch your fingers. This type of wheel is made with steel pins that flick over the surface of the metal at great speed.

### METHOD

1 This finishing technique is one where surface preparation is less crucial since minor blemishes can be disguised. Some marks, however, such as solder marks and bad firestain, will still show through and should be removed with emery paper.

2 Attach the flick wheel to a polishing motor. A fine wheel will give a light frosting; a coarse one will produce a deeper texture. The direction of application should not have any effect on the finish, so you can move the piece to get into corners.

*See step 2*

## SANDBLASTING
**Silver**

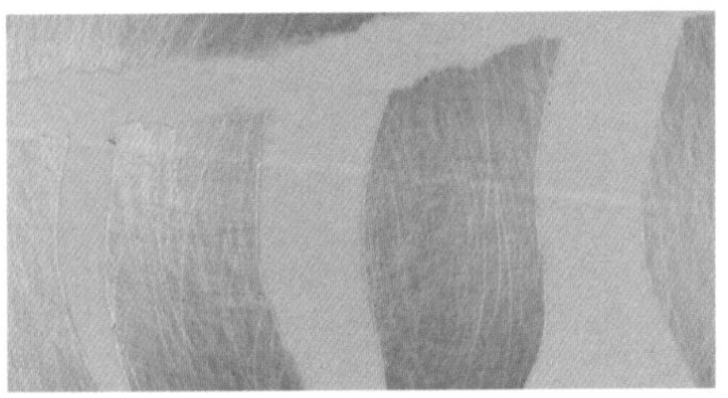

Sandblasting produces a sparkling, frosted surface that will add striking visual impact to your jewellery. However, since the surface effect is very finely textured, it easily picks up dirt and grease, so shouldn't be used in any areas that come into contact with skin.

### METHOD

1 Prepare the surface of the metal by creating the finish you want to contrast with the sandblasting, whether it is polished, satin or textured. Scrub the metal with a soft brush and liquid soap to remove any grease, and dry thoroughly.

2 Mask off any areas that you don't want to be sandblasted: masking tape, sticky-backed plastic and stickers all work well. Ensure the mask is well stuck; any areas that lift up during sandblasting will cause 'bleeding' and definition will be lost.

3 Position your piece inside the sandblasting machine, holding it a few centimetres (a couple of inches) below the nozzle. Check that the pressure is at the optimum level (compressed air is what fires the sand out of the nozzle). Close the lid and fire the sand onto the surface, slowly moving the piece so that all areas are blasted. If the piece is angled down away from the nozzle on one side, the side nearest the nozzle will be blasted more intensely and a fading-out of the texture will occur.

4 Tap off any sand left on the surface and remove the masking tape. Use lighter fluid applied with cotton wool to remove any residue.

**KEY**   Sterling silver 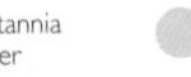 Britannia silver · Fine silver · 9ct gold · 14ct gold · 18ct gold ·  22ct gold

## SANDBLASTING
### Gold

If you don't have access to a sandblasting machine, perhaps you can borrow one. Some professional plating and jewellery workshops provide the service, as well as plastics suppliers and sign painters.

METHOD

1 Use emery paper to give your piece of metal a satin finish, then scrub the surface with a soft brush and liquid soap to remove any grease; dry.
2 Mask off any areas that you don't want to be sandblasted: masking tape, sticky-backed plastic and stickers will all work well. Stickers are available in a variety of interesting shapes and can also be cut or torn. Ensure that the mask is well stuck down, as any areas that lift up during the sandblasting process will cause 'bleeding' and definition will be lost.
3 Position your piece inside the sandblasting machine, holding it a few centimetres (a couple of inches) below the nozzle. Check to see that the pressure is at the optimum level (compressed air is what that fires the sand out of the nozzle). Close the lid and fire the sand onto the surface, slowly moving the piece so that all areas are blasted at an even level.
4 Tap off any sand left on the surface and carefully remove the stickers. Use lighter fluid applied with cotton wool to remove any residue.

## HEAT PATINA

Subtle colours are produced on the surface of the metal using a torch. Patina can be applied to both gold and silver, but the effect will depend on the starting texture of the metal. Cold-joining techniques are usually used to piece together metal shapes that already have had a heat patina applied.

METHOD

1 Heat patinas work best on clean metal and will work well on any 'finish', such as polished or matt.
2 Heat the piece of metal. The colour will start to change almost instantly. The first colour to appear will be straw yellow. Heating for longer will cause other colours to develop: magenta, blue, and finally a dull brown. The trick is to remove the flame at just the right moment.
3 To create colour 'banding', apply the flame to one edge of the metal only, so that the heat travels along the metal.
4 You cannot now heat, solder or pickle your piece of metal, since this will destroy the patina. As with all patinas, it is just a surface colour and will eventually rub off. If you think it will be necessary to protect the surface, test a small area first before applying wax or a lacquer, since they can deaden colours. If an even colour is required, heat the piece in a kiln. First, you will need to experiment with temperatures to obtain the exact colour you wish.

## BORAX

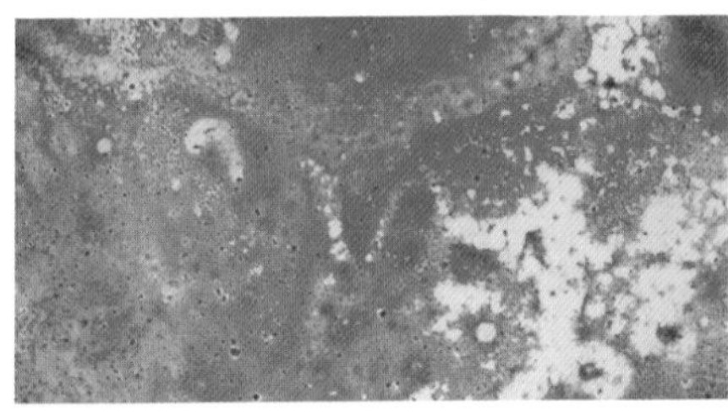

This technique of using borax is limited in its applications but can yield some amazing colours, ranging from yellows and pinks to vibrant blues and violets.

### METHOD

1. Degrease your metal with pumice power and liquid soap.
2. Paint the top surface of the metal with a thick borax solution.
3. Start heating the metal, as if you were soldering. The colours are formed during prolonged heating, which may take several minutes. The metal must be kept at its annealing temperature, but be careful not to melt any areas.
4. Allow the metal to cool slightly. This will reveal the colours. Continue heating if necessary, until the desired colour is achieved.
5. The borax has now formed a thin glasslike layer on the surface of the silver, so any flexing or sharp shocks will cause the borax to fracture and fall off. This technique is best for small protected areas of thick metal.
6. If you are not happy with the results, the piece can be pickled to remove the borax.

## COPPER PLATE

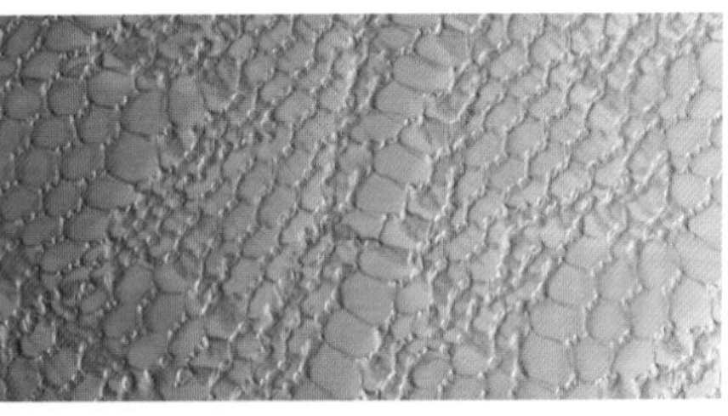

Usually, copper-plating a metal is an inadvertent and unwanted effect – an accident caused when binding wire contaminates pickle. It can be used deliberately, however, to create contrast on silver and also to apply dark copper patinas onto gold when they would not normally work.

### METHOD

1. Wrap your piece loosely in fresh iron binding wire.
2. Place the piece in warm pickle. You may want to use a plastic dish in your pickle tank to avoid contamination: residue often forms during this process, and any other pieces that are in the pickle will also be plated with copper. The pickle should not plate copper once the binding wire is removed.
3. The longer you leave the piece in the pickle, the thicker the copper plate will become. Ten minutes may be enough, but it will depend on the copper content of your pickle (you can judge this by how blue the solution is – the bluer it is, the higher the copper content).
4. If the colour is not particularly even, scrub the piece with pumice powder and return it to the pickle with binding wire.
5. Use emery paper to rub back the copper from raised areas of your texture. This will expose the underlying metal and give a stunning contrast.
6. Copper oxidizes quickly, so to preserve the colour apply a microcrystalline wax polish or a lacquer.

**KEY**  Sterling silver  Britannia silver  Fine silver  9ct gold  14ct gold  18ct gold  22ct gold

## IRIDESCENT PATINA

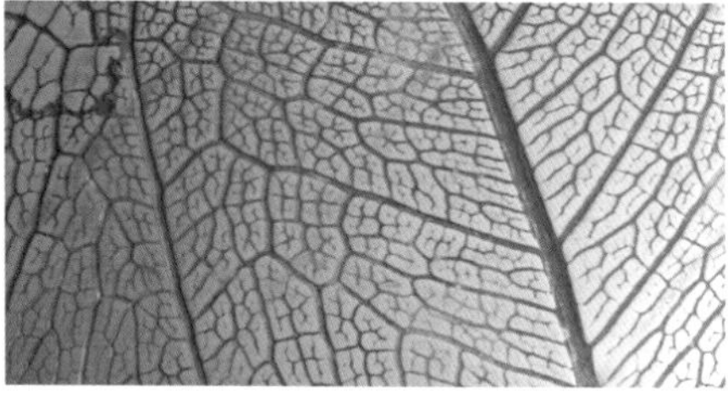

This technique produces iridescent colours on silver, but the final effects are random. Do not expect to get the same results twice.

### METHOD

1 Warm the clean piece of metal in hot water for a minute or so, to speed up the chemical process.
2 Immerse the metal in undiluted liver-of-sulphur solution (see page 243). Wear gloves and work in a well-ventilated area or outdoors.
3 Allow the colours to develop to the desired degree then rinse in plenty of water. The colours may continue to develop for a little while.
4 Rub back the surface of the metal with fine emery paper and apply microcrystalline wax polish to preserve the surface.

## OXIDATION
## Liver of Sulphur

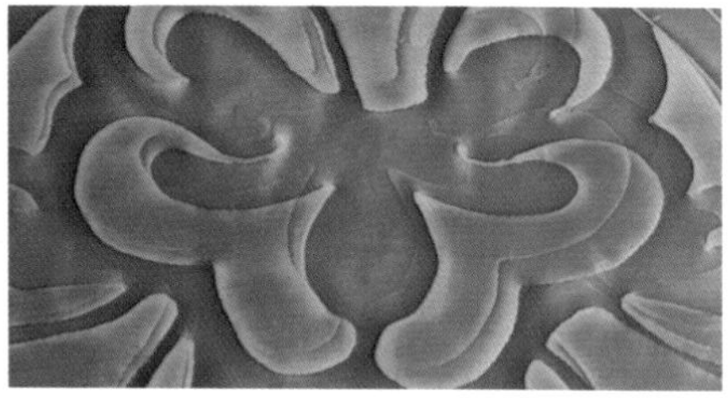

Oxidation is a chemical treatment that artificially tarnishes the surface of silver. It gives high contrast to textured reliefs. The chemical must be used in a well-ventilated area or outdoors because not only are the fumes toxic, they smell bad too.

### METHOD

1 Prepare some liver-of-sulphur solution in a tall glass dish, following the recipe on page 243.
2 Wearing gloves, clean the silver with detergent and a soft brush to remove any grease.
3 Suspend the piece of work with wire in the solution for 10–20 seconds, then rinse it under running water. If the oxidation has not fully developed, return the piece to the solution. Any fingerprints or streaks on the surface of the silver will need to be scrubbed with pumice powder to remove them before the liver of sulphur will oxidize them. To speed up the process, run the piece under hot water before immersing it in the solution.
4 The finish on the surface of the silver will affect the intensity of the patina: matt surfaces will appear darker than those that are polished; and liver of sulphur usually produces a dark steel-grey, rather than a true black. Buff the surface of the metal with a silver-polishing cloth to lighten the raised parts of a texture and apply microcrystalline wax polish to protect the finish from wear. The wax polish will also darken the patina some more.

OXIDATION

## Platinol

Pre-formulated liver-of-sulphur solutions are available in a liquid form that can be applied with a paintbrush. This allows greater control over the areas that will be oxidized. One of them, platinol, produces a dark grey on silver.

METHOD

1 Degrease the surface of the silver with detergent. If you intend to create a matt surface, use pumice powder – porous surfaces will produce a longer-lasting patina since the effect will not be rubbed off so easily. All patinas, however, are only surface effects and are therefore most suitable for recessed areas. Oxidation should not be used on areas that come into direct contact with skin.
2 Apply the platinol using a synthetic-bristle paintbrush (the chemical dissolves natural-hair brushes) until the required depth of colour is achieved. Rinse the piece thoroughly.
3 To patinate the entire surface of small items, use one part platinol to four parts water in a film canister. Drop the piece in, close the lid, and agitate the container until the patina develops. Remove with small plastic tweezers and rinse.
4 Apply microcrystalline wax polish or lacquer to the surface to seal it.

**Sample** *A rolling mill texture was made using crumpled paper on silver. The silver was then oxidized and the surface rubbed back with fine emery paper.*

OXIDATION

## Pariser-oxide

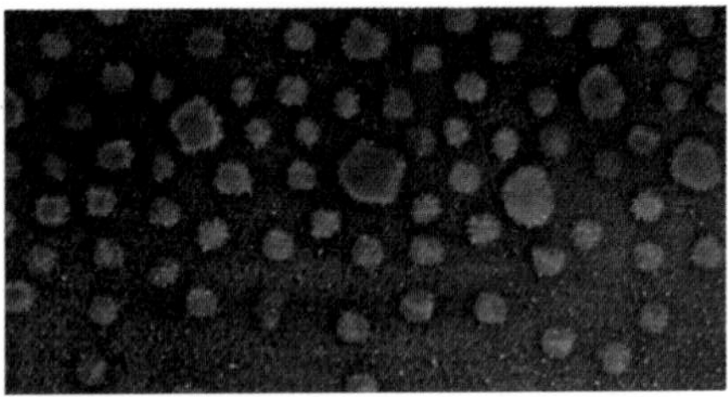

Pariser-oxide is an alcohol-based oxidizing agent that produces a deep black colour on silver but does not work on gold.

METHOD

1 Ensure that the surface of the silver is clean and free from grease and fingerprints. The type of finish on the silver will affect the final outcome – polished surfaces will have a dark lustre and matt surfaces will have a deep velvety appearance. Wearing gloves and working in a well-ventilated area, apply the solution with a paintbrush. The liquid will bleed away from the brush, spreading across the surface. Precise lines are difficult to control, but a masking agent can be used.
2 Continue to apply the solution until the desired effect is achieved; use a small paintbrush for a patchy effect or small areas of oxidation. The piece does not need to be rinsed; the alcohol base of this chemical quickly evaporates. Buff the surface with a soft cloth to remove any other residue.

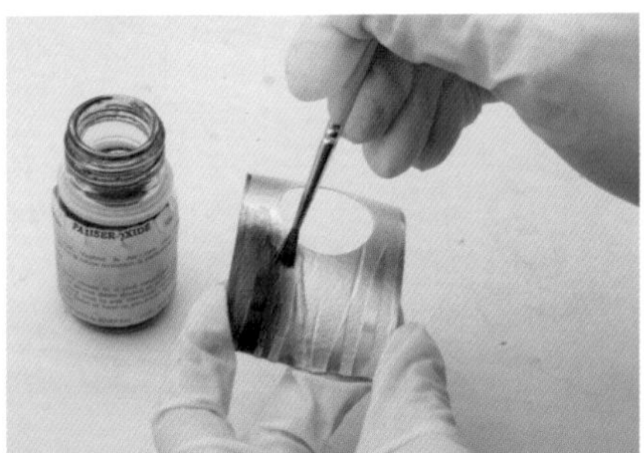

*See step 1*

**KEY**  Sterling silver   Britannia silver  Fine silver  9ct gold 14ct gold 18ct gold 22ct gold

## GOLD LEAF

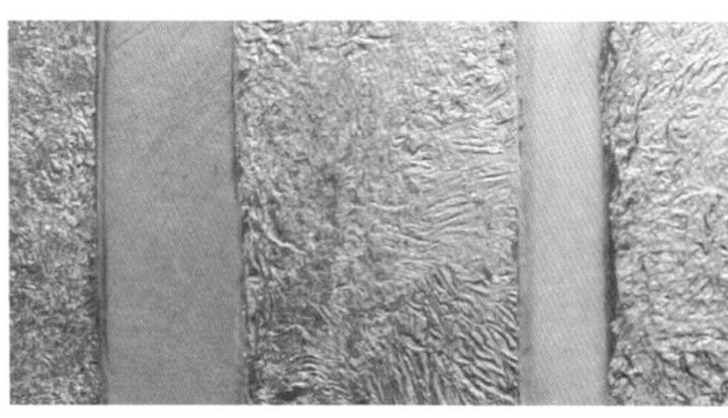

Gold leaf is an easy and low-cost way of adding gold highlights and visual interest to your work. A wide range of colours is available, from lemon yellow to green to red gold. You should work in a clean and draught-free space.

### METHOD

1. Apply a thin layer of gold size (or sizing) to the areas that are going to be gilded, and wait for it to turn tacky.
2. Carefully transfer a sheet of gold leaf onto a folded piece of tracing paper. Cut the gold leaf into small squares.
3. Use a natural-hair brush charged with static (from your hair) to pick up the gold leaf and carefully apply to the sized area, overlapping the squares.
4. Allow to dry overnight and gently brush off any excess leaf.
5. To cover any gaps, apply size and more gold leaf.
6. The gold leaf can be applied in several layers, which will make it more durable. Allow it to dry properly before applying each new layer.
7. The gold-leafed areas can be lacquered or waxed to protect them.

## GOLD LEAF TRANSFER AND LACQUER

Gold leaf transfer is easier to use than loose leaf but is more limited in its applications because of the backing sheet, which can be cut to size before use.

### METHOD

1. Apply a thin layer of gold size (or sizing) to the areas that are going to be gilded, and wait for it to go tacky.
2. Place the transfer, gold side down, onto your piece and gently rub over the area with a cotton bud. The gold should be transferred onto the size.
3. Reapply if necessary.
4. Allow the gold size to dry for a few days before applying one or two thin layers of lacquer to protect the surface.

## METALLIC POWDERS

This is a delicate surface finish that should be applied to recessed areas on pieces that will not receive a great amount of wear. Despite the limitations, spectacular results can be achieved.

### METHOD

1. Apply gold size (or sizing) to the areas you want to colour and wait for it to turn tacky.
2. Working on a clean sheet of paper, apply the powders – either as blocks or merging areas of colour. If you are using blocks of different colours, ipaint the size in stages and apply the colours one by one to avoid cross contamination.
3. Allow to dry overnight.

**Sample** *A gradient of pink through white was applied to a radial recessed-etched pattern.*

## PLATING

Plating is possible on all precious metals and also on copper, brass and gilding metal. A thin layer of plate can be deposited on a piece using an electric current applied through an electrolytic solution with the piece suspended in it. The chemicals involved are toxic and corrosive, so it is best to have plating done professionally.

### METHOD

1. Finish your piece completely, including stone setting. An exception will be where organic materials are to be combined with metal, in which case finish the metal parts up to the point at which you are ready to assemble the pieces. Organic materials are likely to dissolve in the chemical baths used in the plating process. Some stones react badly, too.
2. You will need to be able to tell your plater the colour, thickness and finish required on your piece. Most platers will be able to plate in a range of shades of yellow gold, but not all will cover the full range of colours and metals.
3. A 'flash' plate is a very thin layer of deposited metal, used often to cover firestain on silver with silver plate. Where the piece will receive much wear, such as a ring, a thicker layer of plate can be applied, usually five microns thick, which will last much longer than a thin flash plate before it gets rubbed away in raised or exposed areas. Hard plate is much better for rings than soft plate, which will rub back much more quickly.
4. Plated pieces cannot be heated – the plate burns off because it is so thin.

**KEY**   Sterling silver  Britannia silver  Fine silver   9ct gold  14ct gold  18ct gold  22ct gold

PLATING
## Colour Contrasts

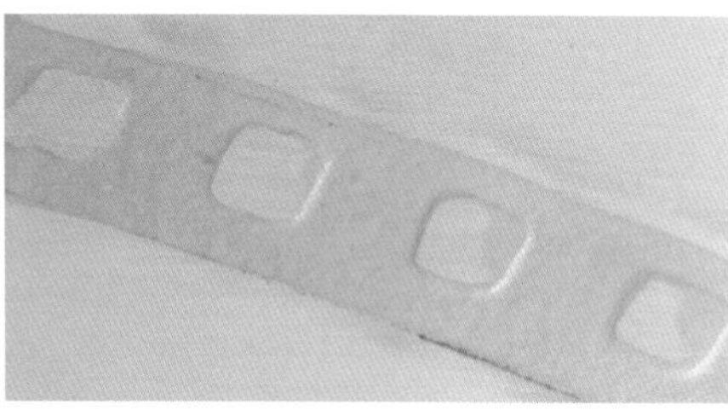

The final finish of your piece – whether polished, matt or satin – will have a direct effect on the visual quality of the plating. Many platers offer a range of finishes that they can apply. Several effects can be applied to pieces once they have been plated, including rubbing back areas with an abrasive.

### METHOD

1 Plate will take on the finish of the metal underneath, so a matt surface will remain a matt surface – the amount of metal being deposited is so small that it will not cover scratches. For this reason, the piece needs to be finished to a high quality before it is plated. Plate will cover differences in colour, such as firestain and solder in a cleaned join, but will not disguise file marks, pits or lumpy solder.
2 Most platers offer a polishing service as well and are skilled finishers. Sandblasting and matt or satin finishes can also be applied, but say so beforehand if you only want your piece to be plated.
3 It is possible for the plater to mask off areas of a piece with a special varnish that is not the same as stop-out, since this special varnish needs to cope with harsh chemicals that are used in plating solutions. This will allow some areas of a piece to be plated and not others, and may be used for contrasting effect.

**Sample** *Textured silver sheet was gold-plated and then rubbed back to reveal the silver on the raised areas.*

PLATING
## Rhodium

Plating is possible in a range of colours and metals, as well as gold and silver; rhodium is often used as a bright white plate to cover white gold and platinum. Most platers will have a range of samples displaying the different colours and surface finishes they can apply.

### METHOD

1 In the same way as coloured alloys are made, the proportion of certain metals in the plating material will determine the colour of the plating. It is possible to create red and green gold, as well as several shades of yellow gold, including colours that will match 9-, 18-, 22-, and 24-carat gold. Platers will often be able to match antique shades of gold.
2 Rhodium is an incredibly hard metal and, in terms of plating, is available in black and white. White rhodium plate is used to enhance platinum and white gold jewellery, where it provides a more reflective and brighter surface, especially useful for maximizing the optical effects of stones such as diamonds. Black rhodium plating is less commonly used; it gives a glossy, dark gunmetal finish that sets off black diamonds and other dark stones well.
3 Black gold plate is not as hard-wearing as rhodium, but produces an attractive finish with slightly yellow highlights.

**Sample** *Black rhodium plate over an etched texture can be very effective.*

3

# Natural Materials

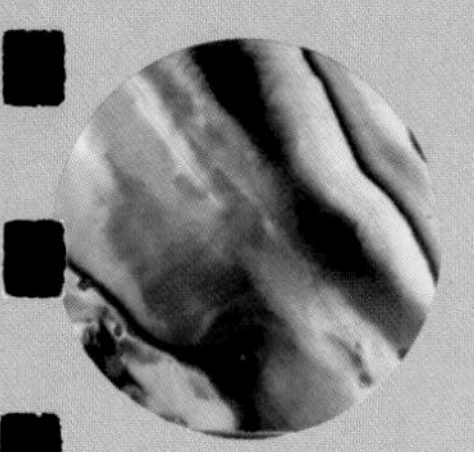

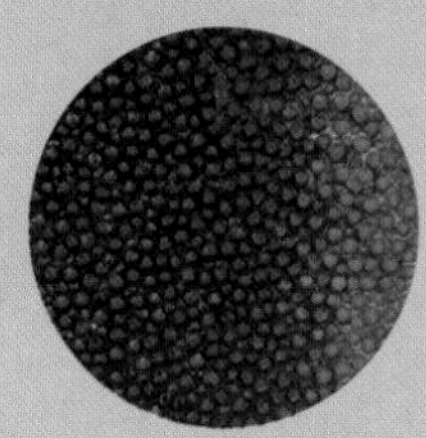

**Wood**
pages 128–139

**Bone, Ivory, Shell, Horn and Jet**
pages 140–149

**Leather**
pages 150–157

**Feathers, Hair and Quills**
pages 158–163

# Wood

An abundant natural material, wood can be worked with a wide variety of techniques that will take advantage of its structure and properties. All woods can be stained, waxed or varnished to deepen colours and protect surfaces once they have been refined.

**APPLICATIONS**
Wood is particularly suitable for large, sculptural pieces if a light wood is used. Denser woods are heavier and will need to be used in smaller quantities. Other materials such as metals are often combined with wood and used in the form of findings.

'Hardwood' and 'softwood' refer to the types of tree, rather than the properties of an individual wood – many hard softwoods are harder than soft hardwoods. The most useful part of the tree is the innermost, darker heartwood, which is dense and resistant to decay. Wood from protected species such as ebony and mahogany can be obtained from reclaimed or antique sources, and synthetic alternatives are available.

## HARDWOODS

**Source:** Mainly deciduous trees

Trees that produce close-grained hardwood suitable for fine carving include boxwood, holly, hornbeam, walnut (both the black and white species), maple, sycamore, sandalwood, oak and beech.

Fruitwood, from cherry and pear trees, is also suitable. Although balsa is technically a hardwood, it is the softest of all woods and is useful for making light jewellery.

## SOFTWOODS

**Source:** Mainly conifers

Pine is the most typical softwood – it is light in weight and has a wide grain. Hard softwoods include cedar, Douglas fir, larch and yew.

## OTHER USEFUL WOODS

**Driftwood:** May come from any tree species; most notable for the interesting forms it takes and can be found washed up on beaches.

**Bamboo:** Hollow, cylindrical wood that is very hard; it can be steamed and flattened.

**Coconut:** Technically, the husk from the shell of the coconut; a hard, dark wood with attractive white flecks.

**Engineered wood:** Plywood and medium-density fibreboard (MDF); used mainly in building construction, where cheaper materials can be used as a base for veneers.

◁ MUSIC BOX RINGS
BY ANASTASIA YOUNG
*Reclaimed ebony piano keys have been riveted into these intricate 18-carat yellow-gold rings, which are set with rubies and sapphires.*

▷ TOP OF TREE RING
BY METTE T JENSEN
*Cherry wood was steamed and coiled before being set into a fabricated silver collar to make this sculptural ring.*

◁ BROOCH
BY MARTIN HOPTON
*The ebony in this brooch was carved and polished. It is set into a silver frame to protect the hard yet vulnerable wooden structure.*

## DRILLING

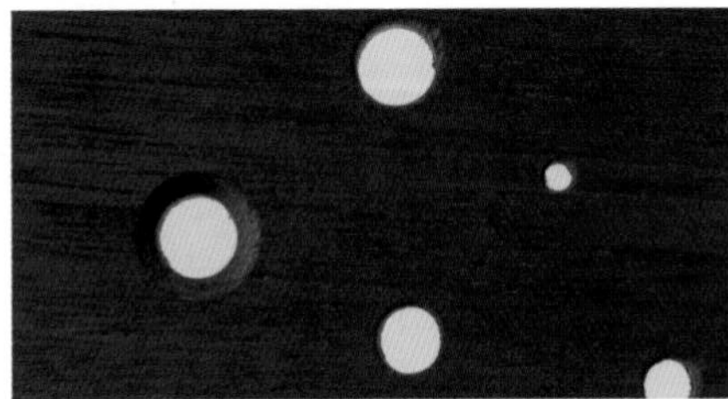

A drilled hole in wood is useful for a number of purposes. Pegs can be inserted into half-drilled holes, materials can be threaded through fully pierced holes and metal rivets or screws can be used to join different layers or materials together.

### METHOD

1 Wood drill bits are designed not to get clogged, but metal drill bits may also be used with wood and will give a cleaner hole. Use a bench drill to make straight holes in woods thicker than 2 mm (1⁄16 inch). The precision of drilled holes often has a bearing on the accurate construction of a piece, and holes drilled by hand or with a pendant motor will often be at a slight angle, which will be more pronounced in thicker materials. When drilling large holes, clamp the piece to the drill bed.
2 Drill slowly and allow the swarf to clear, especially when drilling small holes in hardwoods – they can easily overheat and begin to burn.
3 Clean up exit holes using a ball burr.

**TIP:** Softwoods have a tendency to tear when drilled, so take extra care.

## PIERCING

Pierced fretwork can be effective for creating large pieces that are lightweight, but the limitations of the material must be taken into consideration. Choose a wood with a tight grain that is not too brittle, and refine designs to eliminate weak points.

### METHOD

1 Lay out the design on the surface of the wood.
2 Drill holes large enough for the saw blade to fit through. A waxed saw blade will work faster than a metal one, but the results will be less accurate.
3 Some types of wood are more brittle than others. Take the direction of the grain into account so that it is travelling down, rather than across, any thinner sections of the fretwork. Make some test samples before you start on the final piece so that you are aware of the limitations of the particular type of wood you are working with.
4 Use needle files to tidy up the edges of fretwork; cut 1 or 0 needle files may work more effectively than the cut 2 needle files that are usually used for metal, since these will clog up with dust very quickly.
5 Use emery or glass paper to sand out the file marks, and seal with varnish or wax, if you like.
6 For large amounts of piercing in thin sheet, you may wish to consider having the piece laser-cut.

## CARVING

Wood is a versatile material. Softwoods will allow large, three-dimensional forms to be constructed and are also relatively lightweight. Hardwoods are denser and will therefore be heavier, but you will be able to achieve a much greater level of detail. Choose your material with these factors in mind.

### METHOD

1 For reference, make a detailed sketch or a model of the design in plasticine. Cut your piece of wood to roughly the right size and mark out the design on the surface with a soft pencil. If you are working on a very small piece, it will be easier to work on a larger piece of wood and then cut off the carved section once it is almost complete.

2 Remove as much material as possible with a chisel and mallet, supporting the work in a vice or clamped to a stable surface. Wood files or a scraper can be used to tidy up chisel marks and refine the form. Carve fine detail into the surface of the piece with a burr in a pendant motor; engraving tools can also be used.

3 Smooth the surface of the carving with glasspaper or rough emery until a satisfactory finish has been achieved, making sure that all areas are of the same quality. The carving can now be painted, stained or varnished.

## TURNING

In jewellery terms, wood-turning on a lathe is often used to make tools such as punches or formers, but the lathe can also be used to drill centrally orientated holes in rings and bracelets.

### METHOD

1 Secure and centre your piece in the chuck of the lathe. It is safer to work on short pieces of wood, but this is not usually applicable in a jewellery context. Always true up the piece you are working on before cutting the final shape. The outside of the wood can be turned with lathe tools, files and emery sticks. It is also a good idea to have a drawing of the design handy, or a card cut-out of the profile of the piece to work against.

2 To drill a hole down the centre of the piece, use a 'centre drill' in the tailstock to make a mark in the end of the wood; then use a drill bit of the required size in the tailstock and drill to the necessary depth.

**NOTE:** Never use a lathe unsupervised unless you are entirely confident working on that particular machine and have plenty of experience doing so. Rotary machines can be dangerous.

*See step 1*

## INLAY

Metal pieces can be inlaid into the surface of wood to create decorative designs. The ends of pins can be hammered directly in or tapped lengthways into a groove that has already been cut in the wood. Traditionally, ivory and mother-of-pearl have also been inlaid into wood.

### METHOD

1 Pierce out some small metal components and file the edges to smooth the lines. If being inlaid into a softwood, short metal pins can be soldered onto the back of the form. These metal pieces can be hammered into the wood until they are flush with the surface since the wood will compress when the piece of metal is tapped down into it.
2 Hardwoods will need to be recessed to allow the metal to be embedded so that the surfaces are flush. Trace around the metal shape on the wood and use a burr in a pendant motor, or an engraving tool, to remove a portion of the surface of the wood. The metal should fit snugly into the wood with no gaps. Use a glue such as a two-part epoxy resin suitable for bonding a metal inlay in wood.
3 Once the glue has dried, the surface can be sanded smooth. Use a cork or rubber sanding block to keep the emery paper flat – wood will be worn away much more quickly than metal.
4 Wax the surface of the piece to seal it.

## VENEERS

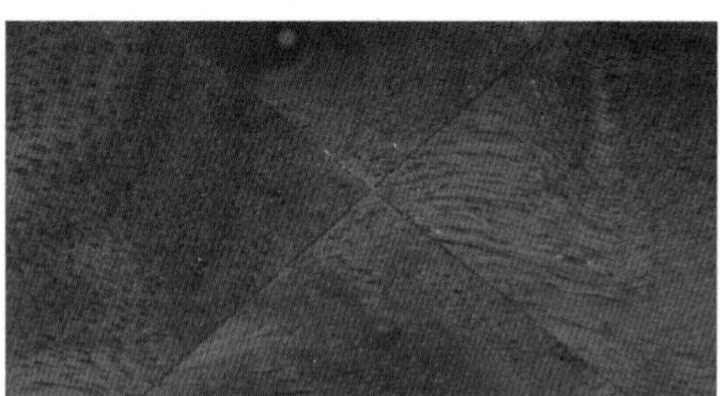

Veneer (thin sheets of wood) can be applied to a wooden ground to improve the quality of a piece. This enables the body of the work to be made from cheap wood and then veneered with an outer layer of expensive wood, such as satinwood or burr walnut. Several layers of varnish will make the veneer appear deeper.

### METHOD

1 Veneers are most easily applied to flat or gently curved surfaces.
2 Ensure that the surfaces of your form (to which veneer will be applied) are free of dust and grease.
3 Some interesting effects can be achieved by cutting the veneer into sections, some of which are rotated 90 or 180 degrees, or flipped over. This will either create geometric designs or an attractive light-play, depending upon the type of veneer used.
4 Cut the veneer with a craft knife and steel ruler and work on a self-healing cutting mat; the veneer should be cut slightly larger than necessary around the edges.
5 Apply PVA wood glue to one section and stick it onto the base, pressing out any excess glue before applying the next piece. If possible, place a heavy weight on top of the piece and allow it to dry for 24 hours.
6 Trim off any excess veneer from around the edges of the piece with a sharp craft knife before lightly sanding, then wax or varnish the piece.

## LASER CUTTING
### Marquetry

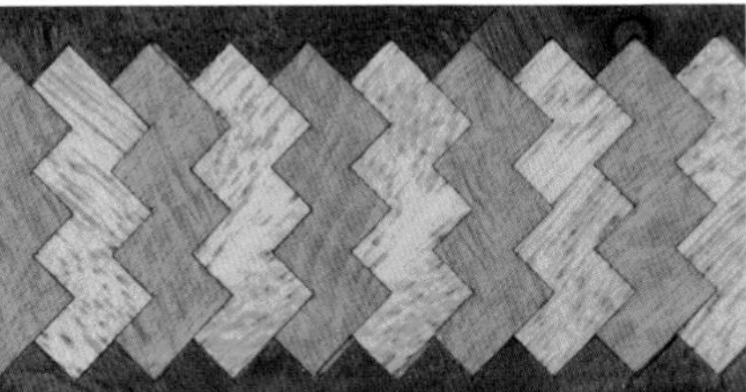

Marquetry uses cut pieces of different-coloured veneers to create images or patterns, usually on a wood ground. Laser-cut veneer elements can be used in the same way and may be much more intricately designed than was possible in the past. Be aware, however, that the laser may scorch the edges of the wood as it cuts.

METHOD

1 The design must be produced in a computer program that uses vector lines, such as CorelDraw® or AutoCAD®. When designing, you will need to allow for the width of the cut made by the laser if you want the pieces to match up exactly: usually about 0.26 mm (0.01 inch). The laser cuts along the centre of the vector line. This will ensure accurate adjustments in your design so that various elements will fit together perfectly.
2 Once the pieces have been cut, it will be like putting a jigsaw puzzle together. Starting at one side, lay out all the pieces in the correct positions and glue them to the base one at a time. Use PVA glue, applied with a brush in a thin layer. Press each piece of veneer down firmly into position and wipe off any excess glue with a damp cloth.
3 Once the pieces are all glued down and firmly in position, put a large, flat, heavy object on top of the piece and let it dry for 24 hours.
4 Sand the surface of the veneers with a sanding block to smooth any raised areas.
5 Apply several thin coats of transparent varnish to protect the surface.

## LAMINATING

Laminating is the process of joining different layers of a material together. When wood is laminated, it is often to make use of the wonderful range of natural colours available. This technique is also useful for constructing large forms made up of multiple components.

METHOD

1 Prepare pieces of wood that will be laminated, so that they are free of dust and grease. Apply a thin layer of glue to one side of each sheet and sandwich the wood into a stack, in the order you want.
2 Clamp the pieces tightly together with a vice or G-clamps – use scrap pieces of wood on the top and bottom surfaces of your piece to stop it from becoming marked – and remove any excess glue with a damp cloth.
3 Allow the piece to dry properly for at least 24 hours. Use a linisher or glasspaper and a sanding block to remove material and shape the piece – the wood can be cut at an angle to expose larger amounts of each stripe.

## BENDING

Stunning three-dimensional forms can be created by steaming wood until it becomes flexible, then bending and clamping it so that it sets and will hold the altered form. This technique will work best on particular types of wood, such as beech, hickory, elm and walnut; softwoods rarely produce good results.

### METHOD

1. Cut and file the wood to the correct shape and sand it to the point of finishing. It is more difficult to work on complicated forms than flat, straight ones, so preparation now will save time later. If your design requires the end tips to be curved, the wood may need to be longer than the length of the final form – it is difficult to get leverage on short lengths.
2. Timing is crucial. Place the wood in a steam cabinet; it needs to be steamed for one hour for every 2.5 cm (1 inch) of thickness. Smaller pieces may also be boiled, or even wrapped in a damp cloth and microwaved for a few seconds. It is possible to steam the wood too much, so watch for wrinkling. Wear gloves to protect yourself from scalding.
3. Take the wood out of the steam box and clamp it as quickly as possible. Leave it clamped until it has cooled, longer if possible. When the wood is unclamped, it may spring back a little. It is difficult to achieve tight curves, and you should over-compensate in the design of the jig if necessary, but be aware that the tighter the curve, the more likely the wood is to crack or split.

**NOTE:** The clamp or jig that the wood will be shaped on needs to be set up in advance.

## RIVETING

Making jewellery with mixed materials can cause construction problems when it comes to soldering certain parts. Clever use of rivets enables pieces to be joined securely.

### METHOD

1. Only the hardest woods are suitable for small-headed wire rivets, but even they may be bruised during riveting. Soldered-on rivet heads or metal washers are advisable for hardwoods and necessary for softwoods. Metal screws can also be used to cold-join wood with other materials.
2. If using wire rivets to make an invisible join, sandwich the wood between two layers of metal. Centre-punch and drill the top sheet with a drill bit of the same diameter as the rivet wire.
3. Make a mark on the wood through this hole so that you know the position of the next drill hole. It is important that this hole is straight, so use a bench drill rather than a pendant motor or pin chuck. Make a mark through the hole in the wood onto the sheet of metal underneath, and drill.
4. Make up enough rivets for the project, and countersink the outside surfaces of the metal with a ball burr before inserting the first rivet. Further holes for rivets can now be marked without the pieces slipping, but holes should be drilled separately in each layer to avoid trapped dust holding the pieces apart once they are joined.
5. Once all the holes are drilled, insert the rivets and hammer them so that they make good contact with the metal. The rivet heads can be filed flush with the surface of the metal sheet and cleaned up using wet-and-dry paper.

## GLUE CONSTRUCTION

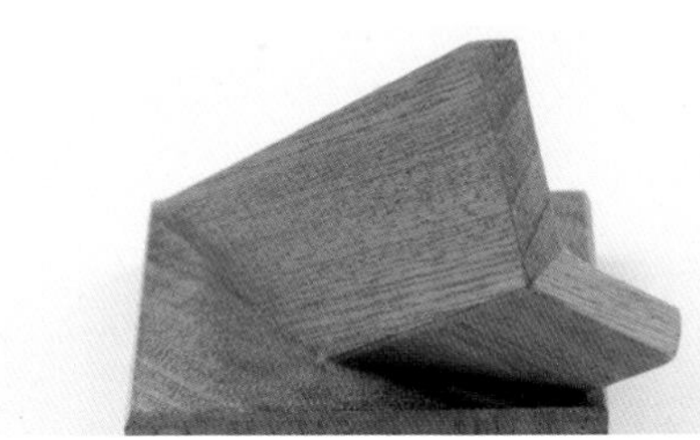

Pieces of wood can be permanently bonded together with glue, but the components need to fit well and be clean for best results. Wooden frames are a useful and lightweight starting point for pieces using a range of media and can be constructed reasonably easily.

### METHOD

1 Cut and shape the pieces of wood that you will be joining. It is a good idea to make a model from card before you begin, so that you have a pattern to work against.
2 The pieces of wood can be held together with masking tape while the form is being fine-tuned. Ensure that the surfaces you will be joining have good contact and are free from dust and grease.
3 Apply a thin layer of PVA glue to one of the surfaces and join the pieces immediately. If possible, clamp the pieces in position and let the glue set for several hours. The glue will be completely set after 24 hours, after which time the wood can be sanded, stained and waxed.
4 PVA wood glue is incredibly strong – it is often the wood that breaks first. Some forms may need extra reinforcement if there are points of stress where there is a join. In these cases, drill a hole through both parts and use a small screw as well as glue to secure the join. The screw head should sit lower than the surface of the wood so that the hole can first be filled with wood filler and then sanded flush with the surface.

## SANDBLASTING

Sandblasting on wood produces quite a different effect from sandblasting on metal, because the softer parts of the wood are worn away, leaving the harder parts raised. This gives the wood-grain physical as well as visual depth. Choose a wood that has well-defined grain.

### METHOD

1 Mask off any areas of the piece that you do not want to be sandblasted with several layers of masking tape or a heavy-duty, plastic-coated fabric tape. The tape needs to be able to withstand the sandblasting, and it may take some time to wear the wood down.
2 Position the piece of wood under the nozzle of the sandblaster, close the lid and fire the sand. Softwoods will be affected much more quickly than hardwoods. You may have to apply a greater degree of pressure to fire the sand with more force or use a rougher grade of sand on hardwoods.
3 Continue the process until the desired effect has been achieved.

## STAMPS AND PUNCHES

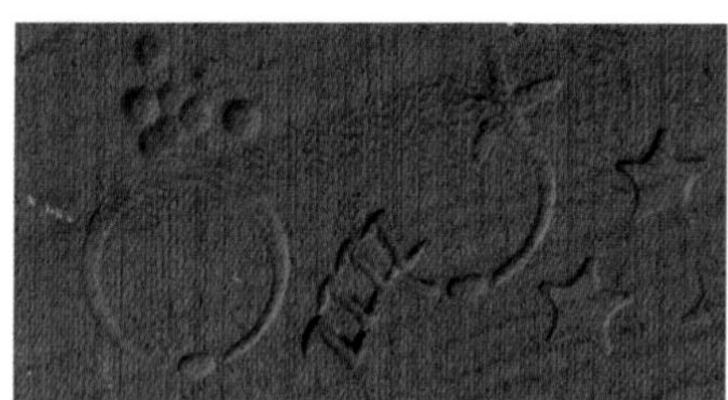

Impressions can be made in wood with punches and a hammer. Softwoods will mark more easily but may lack the precise definition that is possible in hardwoods. Attention must be paid to the direction of the grain of the wood since one wrong blow can cause the piece to split.

### METHOD

1 You may wish to perform this technique before completing the final stages of your piece, since some bruising of the wood is likely to occur, and it will need cleaning up afterwards. Patterns made with punches are most easily accomplished on flat sheets of wood.
2 Secure the piece of wood on a steel block with masking tape so that it does not move out of position while you are working on it.
3 Use a metal hammer to strike the pattern punch once, firmly, so that it leaves an impression in the wood. Small punches have a tendency to sink in too deeply, especially on softwoods; either hit the punch with less force or use a rawhide mallet instead of a hammer. Large punches make clearer marks in wood than small ones, and the punches transfer design areas much more easily on wood than when used with metal. The polished face of a punch will leave a shiny depression in the wood, and makes an interesting contrast to a matt surface.

## ENGRAVING

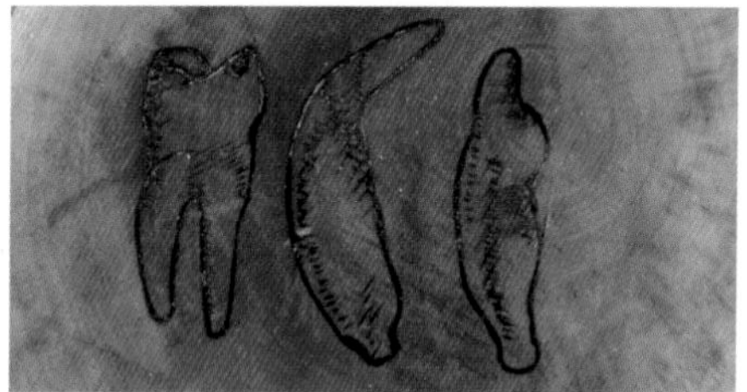

Wood engraving has traditionally been used for cutting designs on wood blocks from which to print. Similar to engraving on metal, wood engraving is a decorative technique used in making jewellery because of the small scale at which it can be used and the need for attention to detail.

### METHOD

1 This technique works best on hardwoods such as box, holly or hornbeam that have been cut across the grain. Ensure that the surface of the wood is sanded smooth before transferring your design with a soft pencil. Large pieces of wood resting on a sandbag can be worked on directly, but smaller pieces may need to be backed with another piece of wood to make them easier to hold during engraving.
2 The process of wood engraving is much the same as for metals: use a square graver to cut the outline first. The nature of the wood means that deeper cuts will be possible than with metal, but be careful not to cut too deeply, too quickly. A fine degree of detail is possible on these hardwoods, so much so that you can create low-relief carvings with engraving tools.
3 Explore mark-making with different shapes of gravers to give your designs a greater range of visual possibility.
4 Engraved wood can be stained, dyed and sealed.

## PYROGRAPHY

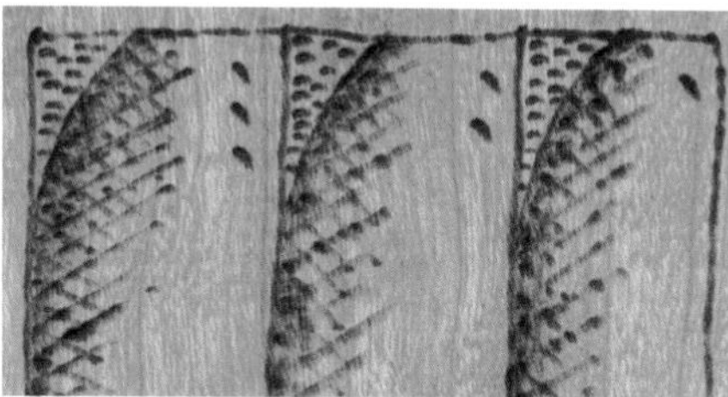

The results of this technique will be most striking on light-coloured woods, but you may wish to create more subtle patterns by using it on dark woods. A heated point, such as a soldering iron, is used to write or draw on the wood, and intricate designs can be executed to great effect.

### METHOD

1 Preheat a soldering iron. Various metal tips in a range of shapes and sizes are available for soldering irons. If you require very fine definition, then one of these tips may be necessary.
2 Finish your piece up to the point where just the surface finish needs refining.
3 You may wish to draw or trace your design on the surface of the wood with a soft pencil before you apply the soldering iron to it.
4 Use the tip of the soldering iron to write or draw on the wood. In effect, the surface of the wood is being burnt. Experimentation will tell you how much pressure to use and how slowly to move the point around in order to achieve the results that you require.
5 A transparent stain can be applied at this stage, if you like, before waxing or varnishing the piece to preserve the colours.

## HEAT COLOURING

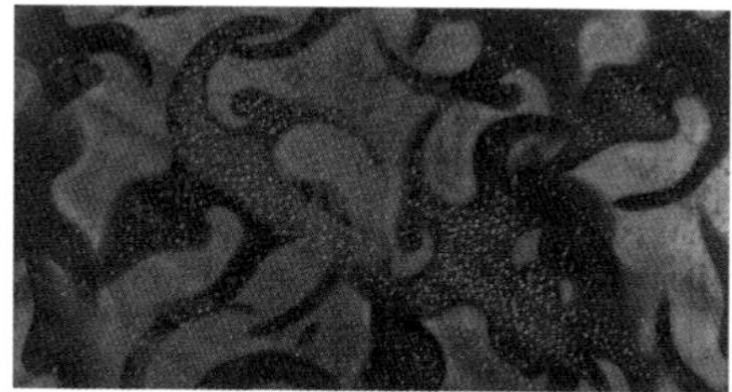

Heated pieces of metal can be used to burn or darken the surface of the wood. Repeat patterns can be built up in this way, and the effect of the scorching can be varied by the temperature of the metal tool and the duration of its contact with the wood.

### METHOD

1 Make a heat branding tool from brass or steel – a pierced-out shape with a rod soldered onto the back will be easiest to use. Heat, rather than pressure, will mark the wood, so the tool does not need to be incredibly robust, but it must be able to withstand repeated heating.
2 Prepare the wood up to the point where it is almost finished.
3 Heat the branding tool with a gas torch to a dull red colour. Allow the tool to cool slightly to black-hot before applying it to the wood. If your tool has a large face, be sure all of it is applied parallel to the surface of the wood; otherwise not all of the pattern will be transferred.
4 Repeat as necessary and finish the surface of the wood with a light sanding and an application of wax.

*See step 3*

## DYES

Wood dyes in colours designed to imitate other types of wood are the ones that are most commonly available, but it is possible to find more vivid shades. Oil-based artists' paints will also be effectively absorbed into the wood, as will fabric dyes. Ensure that there is no chance of chemical transfer from a piece by sealing the surface with wax or varnish.

### METHOD

1 Prepare the wood, making sure it is free from dust and oils by wiping it with white spirit on a soft cloth. Be sure to work in a well-ventilated area and wear protective gloves when handling chemicals.
2 For an even finish, apply the dye or stain using a paintbrush or cloth to spread it over the surface of the wood. The stain will be more visible on lighter areas in the wood that will absorb the dye more readily; these lighter areas can also expand slightly.
3 It may be necessary to give the surface a light sanding before applying wax or varnish if a perfectly smooth finish is required.
4 Oil paints may need to be thinned before they are properly absorbed into the wood, but they provide a much greater range of colours and effects. Allow the paint to dry before sealing the surface – drying time will depend upon the thinness of the paint and the absorbency of the wood.

## WAX RESIST WITH DYES

Designs can be stencilled, painted or dripped onto the wood with wax or varnish. These will act as a resist to water-based dyes, such as those used for fabric, and thereby create a contrast between the natural colour of the wood and the applied dye.

### METHOD

1 Lightly sand the surface of the wood so that it is clean and receptive to water-based dyes. Remove dust from the surface with a damp cloth.
2 Once the wood is completely dry, the wax or varnish can be applied.
3 Apply the varnish with a paintbrush and let it dry before applying the dye to the wood. The areas of the wood covered by the varnish will resist the dye and retain their natural colour. Fine lines may be less successful than thick ones, since the dye has a tendency to bleed underneath the outside edges of masked areas.
4 Molten wax will be absorbed into wood much more readily than if it is applied while solid. This can be done in a way similar to batik-dyeing techniques used for fabrics.
5 The piece must be dry before a sealing coat of wax or varnish is applied.

## POLISHING

Hardwoods will take polishing much more readily than softwoods, which are best treated with several layers of gloss varnish if a high shine is required. A beautiful natural lustre can be created by treating hardwoods in much the same way as you would plastics (see page 186).

### METHOD

1 Remove all file, burr and chisel marks from your wooden form with glasspaper. A rough grade of paper, such as 120-grit, is a good one to start with and will quickly remove blemishes and help to shape the piece, rounding off edges if required.
2 To retain flat surfaces, wrap the glasspaper around a sanding block, or use the paper on a flat surface to rub down the areas on the face of the piece. Sanding is usually done along the grain, but this is less important for hardwoods because the grain is so dense that there is little risk of tearing the wood.
3 Emery and wet-and-dry papers can also be used on wood – work up through the grades until you reach the finest. Wood dust will clog finer-grade papers, but make sure the piece is well prepared if you want to achieve a high shine.
4 A light-coloured, grease-free polish such as Vonax is ideal for polishing wood but must be used on a clean mop that has not been used for polishing metal. If the piece is too fragile or too small to be polished on a motor, use a felt buffing stick with some polish rubbed onto it to buff the piece.

**Sample** *Coconut shell has an attractive, warm tone with white flecks, only revealed once it has been sanded and polished.*

## VARNISH, WAX AND OIL

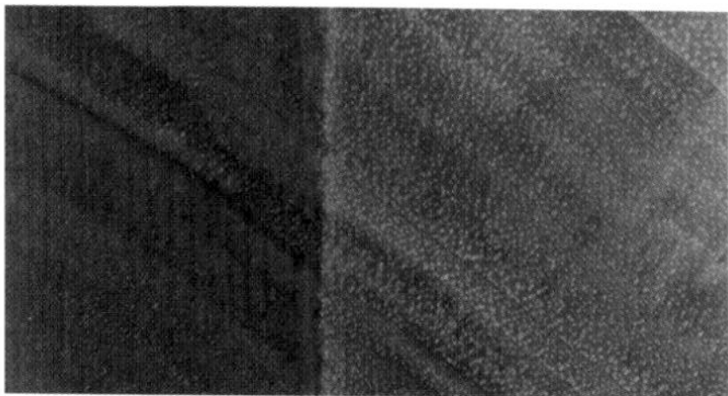

Treatments often improve the natural colour of wood and give greater depth to tonal qualities. It is advisable to seal wood so that it does not pick up oil from the skin and discolour.

### METHOD

1 Bare wood should be cleaned with white spirit on a soft cloth; ensure that treated or stained wood is dust-free. Do not use white spirit on finished pieces.
2 Apply varnish using a paintbrush, in several thin coats. Brush along the grain of the wood and ensure that no drips are left around the edges. The penultimate layer should be sanded lightly to improve the finish of the last coat, which should be smooth and free of brush marks. Aerosol varnishes are also available from artists' suppliers, in matt, satin and gloss finishes; these should only be used outside or in a well-ventilated area.
3 Waxes are applied with a cloth or a stiff brush and need to dry before being buffed with a soft cloth. The type of wax you use will determine the length of drying time needed – microcrystalline wax can be buffed almost immediately, but some beeswax mixtures need to rest for a couple of days. Coloured waxes darken tone and seal the wood. Gilding creams in metallics give an antique finish.
4 Finishing oils such as Danish oil also seal wood; they produce a more natural-looking finish. Apply either with a stiff brush or a cloth and allow to dry. The surface may need a light sanding to remove any raised areas; a second coat can then be applied and the piece buffed again when dry.

# Bone, Ivory, Shell, Horn and Jet

Natural materials provide a world of possibilities for the jeweller, since they are easy to work with and available in a range of colours and textures. Many of the animals used as a source for these materials are endangered species, so responsible acquisition is paramount.

Many of these materials are subject to the Convention on International Trade in Endangered Species of Wild Fauna and Flora (CITES), and care must be taken not to break the law when importing any natural products. Responsible suppliers will be able to supply the relevant information on request. Synthetic alternatives are available for all of the materials described in this section, and unless the natural material is reclaimed or found, it is generally preferable to use a synthetic product. Synthetics are also available in larger sizes.

**APPLICATIONS**
Often combined with precious metals, synthetic materials are much more durable and less chemically susceptible than their natural counterparts. The light weight of many of these materials makes them suitable for large pieces of jewellery.

△ EYE BROOCH
BY ANASTASIA YOUNG
*A buffalo-horn collar holds a glass eye, with a riveted bezel of oxidized silver.*

## BONE

**Composition:** Calcium phosphate

Bone is easy to work, but can be heavier and more brittle than ivory and has a more open structure. Bone from a fresh source must first be properly cleaned to dissolve out the natural oils, and then bleached to whiten it. Bone that has been buried will not require much cleaning, but it will have a patina.

## IVORY

**Composition:** Dentine

Ivory is mainly obtained from elephant tusks but can come from walrus and narwhal tusks or sperm whale teeth. Ivory trade is strictly regulated, but legally antique material can be found, mainly in the form of veneer on old piano keys. Synthetic ivory is cheap, easily available, and does not have the same stigma; it is also more easily worked, since it is made of polyester resin. Vegetable ivory from certain nuts is also a useful material, but limited in size.

## TORTOISESHELL

**Composition:** Keratin

From the carapace of the hawksbill turtle (now an endangered species); plates are welded together to make flat sheet material. A range of synthetic alternatives is available in either celluloid or polyester resin.

Horn and most types of shell are covered by fewer trade restrictions than the materials described on the opposite page, but common sense should still be used when obtaining materials. Jet is increasingly difficult to find in large-size pieces, but broken antique jewellery items provide an inexpensive and interesting starting point.

**APPLICATIONS**
Soft, and prone to chemical damage, these natural materials are not suitable for rings. They are often combined with precious-metal findings; set in a bezel for protection; or used as inlays to add contrasting detail to precious-metal jewellery.

△ BLUE SHELL RIVER
BY TAKAFUMI INUZUKA
*A disc of imitation tortoiseshell inlaid with blue shell has been set on top of a ring shank.*

## HORN

**Composition:** Keratin

Usually sourced from male cows, buffalo and sheep. Its composition means that specific techniques such as moulding and bending can be used. Warm to the touch, lightweight, easy to work and polishes well – often with a slight translucent lustre.

## JET

**Composition:** Lignite, sometimes with pyrite inclusions

Jet is formed from fossilized wood that has been subjected to high pressures underground over a long period of time. The best quality jet originates from Whitby, England. Popular in Victorian jewellery, jet can be intricately carved and polishes to an excellent finish.

## SHELL AND MOTHER-OF-PEARL

**Composition:** Aragonite (calcium carbonate) layered with chitin and lustrin

Nacreous shell (mother-of-pearl) is an attractive material with a pearly lustre that is easily cut and polished. Dyed sheet products are available. Other types of shell are also suitable for use in jewellery and can be carved, etched and engraved with very fine detail.

▽ RINGS
BY MARTIN HOPTON
*These two rings are made from faceted jet and imitation ivory, and are set with gold-plated silver bezels.*

## PIERCING

Horn is the most suitable of the natural materials for piercing, as it is the least brittle. Delicate fretwork made in other materials can also be very beautiful, so consider how it could be protected within a piece if you are thinking of using this technique.

### METHOD

1 Mark out the design on the surface of your piece.
2 Drill holes large enough for the saw blade to fit in any areas that cannot be accessed from the edge. A metal saw blade should be used in the saw frame for thin sheet or delicate material, but thick sheet and material such as horn will be cut faster with a wax saw blade. Ivory, bone and shell can be brittle, so take the direction of the grain into account so that it is travelling down rather than across any thinner sections of the fretwork.
3 Make some test samples up before starting on the final piece so that you are aware of the limitations of the particular type of material you are working with. Wear a mask when piercing these materials since a very fine dust is created.
4 Cut the piece slowly, using long, even strokes of the saw blade, and always cut thin sections last to prevent breakages.
5 Use needle files to tidy up the edges of fretwork; cut 1 or 0 may work more effectively than the cut 2 needle files that are usually used for metal; these will clog up with dust very quickly.
6 Before polishing, use emery or glasspaper to sand out the file marks.

## LASER CUTTING

Laser cutting is a versatile technique that can be applied to many materials. You may wish to produce a batch of elements that interlock with slots and tabs, or multiple pieces that will be inlaid into another material.

### METHOD

1 You will need to provide a digital file with the image that you would like to be laser-cut. The design must be produced in a computer software package that uses vector lines, such as Abode® Illustrator®, CorelDRAW® or AutoCAD®. Most companies will accept original artwork but will charge a fee for converting it into a digital format.
2 The laser cuts along the centre of the vector line, with the width of cut usually about 0.26 mm (0.01 inch), but some materials react differently to the process and the cut may be wider. The intensity of the laser can be accurately controlled – a more intense beam may be required to cut through some materials – and slight scorching around the edges of the cuts can occur. This will be more visible on light-coloured materials.
3 Once the designs have been cut, the edges of the pieces can be cleaned up with wet-and-dry paper and water and can then be polished.

**Sample** *Capiz shell discs were laser cut to produce geometric components.*

**KEY** Ivory Bone Horn Jet Shell Synthetics

## CARVING

All of these materials can be carved on a small scale and to a very fine level of detail. Keep the weight of the material in mind – heavy or large pieces may be limiting in terms of the type of jewellery they can be used for.

### METHOD

1 Make a detailed sketch or a model of the design in plasticine for reference.
2 Cut your material to roughly the right size and mark out the design on the surface with a soft pencil. If you are working on a very small piece, it will be easier to work it while it is still part of a larger piece of material, then you can cut off the carved section once it is almost complete.
3 Remove material with a burr in a pendant motor, a rough file or engraving tools and fine chisels.
4 Once the form is carved, the surface can be refined. Smooth the surface with wet-and-dry paper until a satisfactory finish has been achieved. The piece can now be polished or have textures applied.

**Sample** *Tagua nut, also known as vegetable ivory, has been used for this carved piece.*

*See step 3*

## ENGRAVING

It is possible to create delicate designs on sheet material by engraving. Ivory and bone are difficult to engrave well because of their grain, which often causes the graver to chip the surface of the material as it is cut. Synthetic materials do not suffer from this problem.

### METHOD

1 Separate gravers should be kept for engraving ivory, since the faces need to be angled differently from those that are used for metal. The graver should be backed off at 15 degrees and the face should be acute, between 15 and 20 degrees.
2 To cut successfully, the graver needs to be kept very sharp. Use a fine Arkansas stone lubricated with olive oil on all faces of the tool.
3 Fix the ivory to a piece of wood, so that you can hold it more easily while working on it. The surface of the ivory should be darkened to avoid eye-strain – spread printing ink across the surface and scratch the design back through the ink.
4 The lines of the design can be scored first to break up fibres in the grain of the ivory, and where possible, work along the grain rather than across it. Begin engraving the ivory, cutting quickly to minimize chipping and using a light touch for fine detail.
5 Engraved ivory is traditionally blackened to accentuate the cuts, but this will also make any chips or slips appear more obvious.

## INLAY

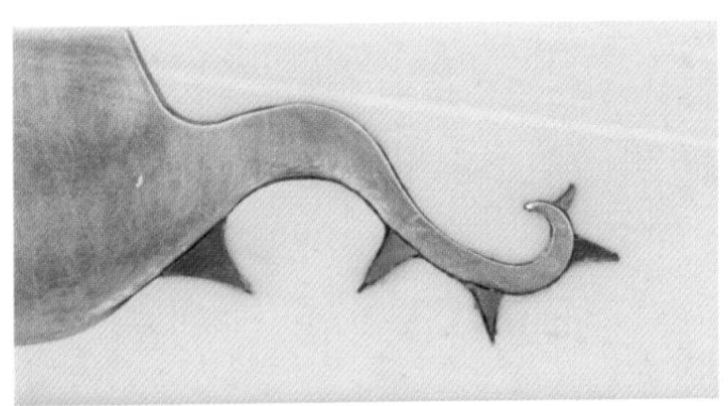

These materials can all be inlaid into one another, or inlaid with metal. The inlay can be set into carved recesses or raised bevels. Small segments of the sheet material may be cut so that they can be applied to a curve smoothly. Inlay should not be used in areas of a piece that will receive a lot of wear.

### METHOD

1 Pierce out some small components in your chosen material and file the edges to smooth them.
2 Trace around the shape with a scribe onto the material in which it will be inlaid – if the two materials are of a similar thickness, use a piercing saw to cut just inside the scribed line and then carefully file up to the line. Thick materials will need to be recessed to take the inlay, so use a burr in a pendant motor or an engraving tool to remove a portion of the surface of the material down to the required depth. The inlay should fit snugly into the base with no gaps.
3 Use a glue suitable for the materials you are using – such as a two-part epoxy resin – to bond the inlay, and place a heavy object on top of the pieces to prevent warping.
4 Once the glue has dried, the surface can be sanded smooth – use wet-and-dry paper on a flat surface and work up through the grades. Wax the surface of the piece to seal it.

**Sample** *Silver and shell were inlaid into an ivory ground.*

## PIQUÉ WORK (WIRE INLAY)

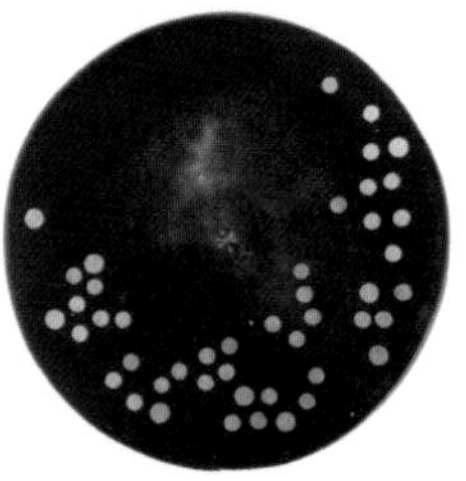

Wire that has been inlaid end-on is used to make a pattern of dots in the surface of a contrasting material. Different colours and sizes of wire can be used to add interest.

### METHOD

1 Mark out your design, working either on paper or directly onto the material you will be using.
2 Drill holes, the same diameter as the wire you will be using, into the piece to a depth of about 4 mm (⅛ inch). File the end of a wire to a slight point and insert it into a hole firmly. Cut the wire with end cutters, leaving about 2 mm (1/16 inch) sticking out.
3 Tap the end of the wire with a metal hammer to secure it in the hole. Repeat the process to fill the remaining holes.
4 File the wires flush, but take care not to scratch the surface of the piece. Use wet-and-dry paper on a flat surface to rub down the face of the piece so that the wires are completely level with the surface.
5 The piece can be polished on a motor using a clean mop and Vonax polishing compound. Metals will discolour the polishing mop and taint light-coloured materials, so give the piece a light buffing only.

**KEY** Ivory Bone Horn  Jet  Shell  Synthetics

## ETCHING

Shell, bone and ivory can both be chemically etched in a similar way to metal, by using a resist to mask off areas. It is particularly effective on shell when a light top layer is etched away in a design, exposing a darker layer underneath, as is the case with shell cameos.

### METHOD

1 The final finish should be applied to the piece before etching. Most resists used for metal will stain the material, so use melted rosin varnish and apply it with a brush to all areas of the piece. Scratch back through the resist with a wooden point to expose the areas that will be etched.
2 For the acid to work best, the lines need to be at least 1 mm (1/32 inch) wide. Nitric acid works aggressively on these materials, but the lines can be refined with a graver once the etching is complete.
3 Gently slip the piece under the surface of the acid solution (see page 242) with plastic tweezers. Check the progress of the acid regularly until the required depth is met.
4 Rinse the piece in plenty of running water and then clean off the resist with alcohol or acetone.

## STAMPS AND PUNCHES

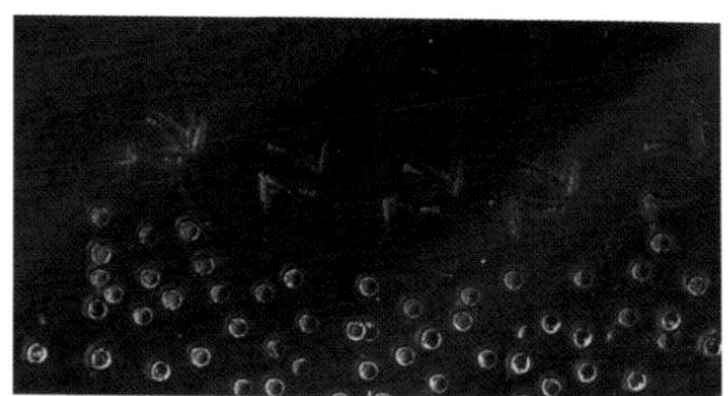

Steel pattern punches can be used to impress textures into horn, which will compress to take the pattern. Larger stamps may be more clearly visible, but it is more difficult to get a good impression. Natural materials other than horn are too brittle to withstand hammering.

### METHOD

1 Working on a steel block, use masking tape to hold the piece of horn in position. Hold the punch upright with one hand and strike it firmly with a metal hammer with the other hand. One good hard strike is better than several taps with the hammer because the punch may move out of position. It is more difficult to get larger punches to make a clear impression than it is for smaller ones, but on horn the larger stamps will be more visible.
2 The harder you strike the punch, the deeper the impression will be, so do a test piece to check the pressure required for a good result. Handmade or shop-bought punches can be used, and intricate patterns can be built up using this technique.

## TURNING

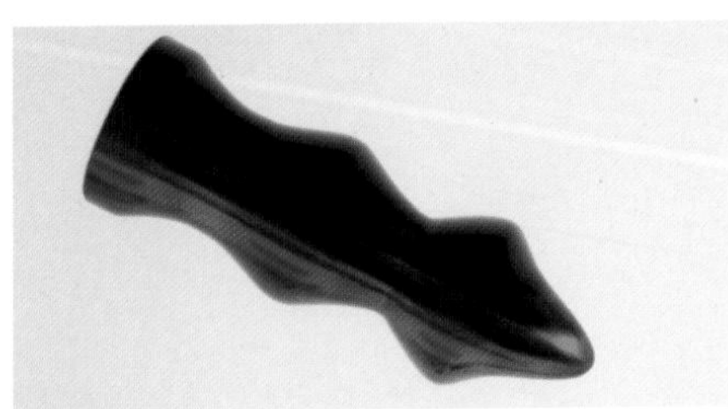

Turning is most suitable for synthetic materials, which have a regular consistency and no grain. However, small pieces of natural material turned at a slow speed on a watchmaker's lathe can produce satisfactory results – but be aware of the direction of the grain.

### METHOD

1 Secure your piece in the chuck of the lathe, making sure it is centred. It is safer to work on short pieces of material where there will be less vibration.

2 Always true up the piece you are working on before cutting the final shape. The outside of the piece can be turned using lathe tools, files and emery sticks, and it is a good idea to have a drawing of the design handy, or a card cut-out of the profile of the piece to work against.

3 To drill a hole down the centre of the piece, use a 'centre drill' in the tailstock to make a mark in the end of the wood, before using a drill bit of the required size in the tailstock and drilling to the necessary depth.

**NOTE:** Never use a lathe unsupervised unless you are entirely confident working on that particular machine and have plenty of experience doing so. Rotary machines can be dangerous.

## BENDING

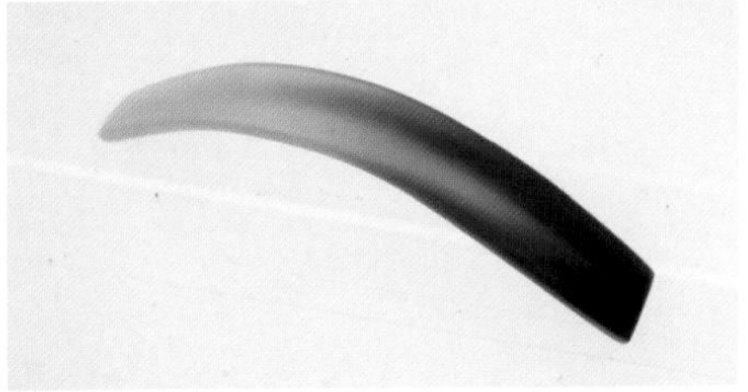

Horn will go soft when boiled in water, enabling it to be bent or pressed into a mould. Once it sets, the new form is permanently retained. Great design potential is possible with horn when this technique is used.

### METHOD

1 Cut and shape your piece of horn, using wet-and-dry paper to refine the surface before polishing it.

2 Place the piece in a pan of boiling water large enough to contain it and boil until it is soft.

3 Remove the piece with tongs and quickly clamp it into the desired shape. The clamps must be left in position until the piece is cool and hard again. The shape can be refined by cutting and filing if necessary. Thin pieces of horn can be steamed to soften them before clamping.

4 When soft, horn can be pressed into a mould that is clamped shut. The mould is returned to the boiling water for 30 minutes and the clamps tightened, forcing the horn to take fine detail from the mould.

5 The clamps can be removed once the piece has set, and the edges of the piece trimmed and polished.

**KEY** Ivory Bone Horn Jet Shell Synthetics

## FACETING

Faceting is usually used in stone-cutting to allow internal reflections of light, but can be effective when applied to opaque materials. Polished facets will catch the light at different angles – the more facets there are, the more 'glittering' the piece will be when it moves.

### METHOD

1 If the piece is too small to hold comfortably, attach it to a wooden stick with setter's wax. Facets can be made following a design, or in a way that is suggested by the form itself.
2 Rough out the basic shape of the piece before breaking up the surface with smaller facets. Use a flat file to form each facet – the trick is to keep each facet absolutely flat so that it gives a well-defined reflection when light hits it. Accurate filing of this type is not easy, but will improve with practice. Clean up file marks with an emery stick so that the facets stay flat and ensure that all scratches are removed.
3 Carefully polish the piece without rounding-off any edges, using Vonax on a hard felt mop.

**Sample** *Faceted jet.*

## RIVETING

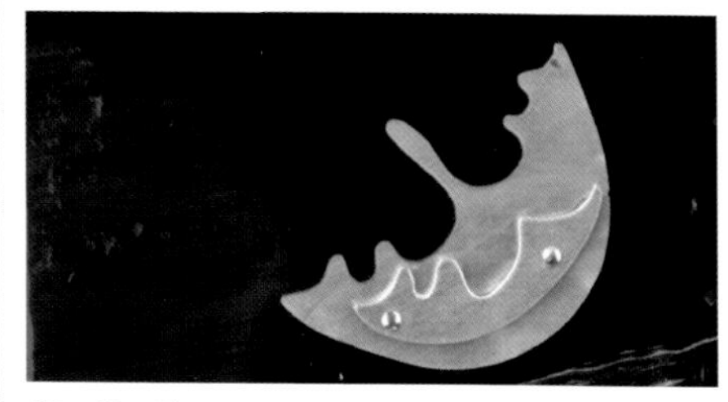

Riveting is useful for joining layers together when using mixed materials, or purely for decoration. Silver or gold rivets provide a good colour contrast to natural materials.

### METHOD

1 Mark and drill a hole in a piece of sheet material – the hole needs to be the same size as the rivet wire. Use a small ball burr to countersink the hole.
2 To make the rivets, place protective pads or leather on the inside of the vice jaws and fix a piece of half-hard wire tightly in the vice with only a small amount protruding.
3 File the top end of the wire flat, and use a ball-peen hammer to spread the end so that it forms a head.
4 Push the rivet through the hole as far as it will go. Working on a steel block, cut the rivet wire to 1 mm ($\frac{1}{32}$ inch) above the surface of the sheet material. File the top flat, and hammer to spread.
5 Turn the piece over and tap from the other side. The rivet heads should be domed and can be burnished to highlight them or filed flush with the surface of the sheet.

*See step 3*

## BEZEL SETTING

One way to include natural materials in a piece so they are protected is to use a bezel setting. Setting a carved piece will not compromise the integrity of the form like other methods, such as drilled holes, would.

### METHOD

1 Construct a fine-silver wall that fits snugly around the form you have made; circular forms are the easiest to make bezels for. The silver strip should be 0.4 mm (1⁄64 inch) thick and high enough to securely hold the piece once it is set.
2 Solder the ends of the strip shut, pickle and file the join smooth.
3 Check that the bezel still fits around the shell and make adjustments, if necessary, before soldering the bezel onto a base sheet of 0.6-mm (1⁄64-inch) thick sterling silver.
4 Pierce around the outside edge of the bezel and file it flush. The bezel can be soldered onto a ring shank, or have fittings or findings attached to it.
5 Polish the metal and insert the piece of natural or synthetic material, which should sit flat against the inside of the base. The fine silver is soft and can be set with a plastic pusher to avoid damaging delicate natural material.
6 Push the bezel around the form, working 'north, south, east, west' – repeat this motion so there are 16 points flush with the material then push in any gaps that remain.
7 Use a burnisher to smooth the fine silver against the material, taking care not to scratch it.

## DYES AND STAINS

Dyes will give more vivid colours if used on pale materials such as bone or blonde horn. Commercially available dyes suitable for use with these materials are generally toxic, so take precautions when using them. Tea can produce an antique effect on bone and ivory.

### METHOD

1 Dyes and stains will be absorbed more easily if applied before a piece is polished. Ensure that your piece is free of dust and grease.
2 Stains are applied with a brush and will not be as deeply absorbed into the material as dyes.
3 Dye baths should be prepared according to the manufacturer's instructions – experiment with different dyes, such as those for fabric, to find suitable results for the effect you are trying to achieve. Submerge your piece in the dye bath for the recommended amount of time, or until the colour has sufficiently developed. Remove the piece from the dye bath and place it in a container filled with cold water to allow any dye that has not been bound into the material to leach out. Allow the piece to dry out thoroughly.
4 The dye may disrupt the surface by causing some areas to expand more than others. This will mean that the surface needs to be lightly sanded before the piece is given a final polish.

**KEY**  Ivory  Bone  Horn  Jet  Shell  Synthetics

## POLISHING

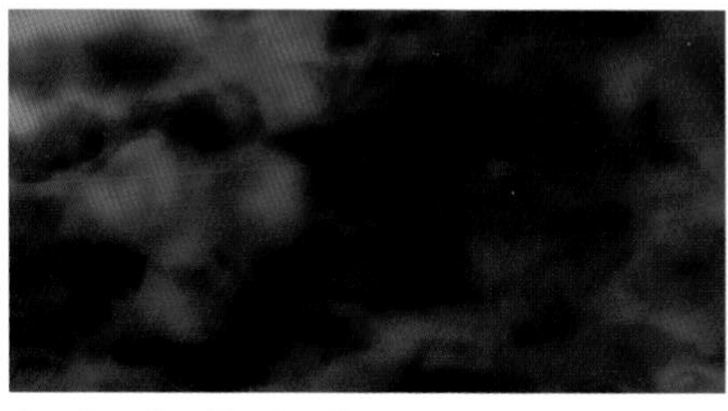

A high-gloss shine can be achieved on these materials when polished on a motor. Use polish to buff the piece by hand for a less glossy finish. Synthetic materials can generally be polished in the same way as plastics (see page 186).

METHOD

1 Use wet-and-dry paper with plenty of water to stop any dust from being released into the air. Work up through the grades of paper, starting at 400-grit and going up to 1200-grit, while rinsing the piece well in between each grade. It may be necessary to allow the piece to dry out if it has absorbed a lot of water, and it may then need a light sanding if the surface has distorted or the grain has risen up.
2 Use a grease-free, light-coloured polish such as Vonax applied to a clean mop on a polishing motor.
3 Polish the piece, keeping it moving at all times so that it does not overheat. For pieces that are too small or fragile to be polished on a motor, apply some Vonax to a felt or light-coloured leather buffing stick and rub the surface of the piece. The result will not be as glossy as if it had been polished on a motor, but will look more natural.

**Sample** *Polished synthetic tortoiseshell.*

## VARNISH, WAX AND OIL

These materials are all prone to water damage and should not be used in pieces that will receive a lot of wear. They are also prone to drying out; if your material is fresh, then account for some warping or shrinkage over time. Wax and varnish will prevent water loss from the material and also enhance natural lustre and colours.

METHOD

1 Finish your piece and apply the final surface finish to it. Ensure that the surface is free of dust and grease before sealing it with wax or varnish.
2 To apply microcrystalline wax, use a small amount of wax on a cloth to wipe the surface of the piece, then buff with a soft cloth. Several coats may be applied.
3 To apply varnish, use a brush to paint on several thin coats, allowing the varnish to dry between coats. Brush along the grain of the material and ensure that no drips of varnish are left around edges. The penultimate layer of varnish should be sanded lightly once dry, to improve the finish of the last coat, which must be smooth and free of brush marks.
4 Special finishing oils can be used to seal these materials and will not interfere with the surface quality; they produce a more natural-looking finish. Apply the oil with a stiff brush or a cloth, wipe away any excess and allow the piece to dry.

**Sample** *Gold leaf was applied to the surface of a piece of shell, and a matt aerosol varnish was used to seal the piece.*

# Leather

Animal skin or hide is a strong, flexible material that can have many techniques applied to it. These range from dyeing, embossing patterns and applying gold leaf to methods for creating three-dimensional forms by boiling, vacuum-forming and stretching.

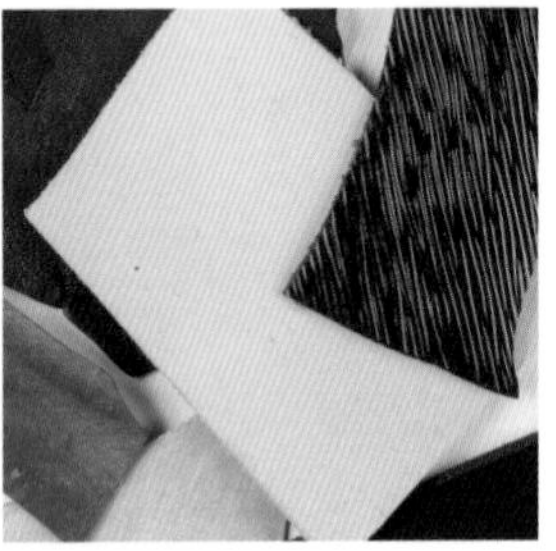

Leather-working is a craft in its own right, so look to tradespeople such as bookbinders and crafters who work in leather for inspiration. Animals are farmed for their exotic leathers: stingray (for shagreen), ostriches and fish – but are still subject to Convention on International Trade in Endangered Species of Wild Fauna and Flora (CITES) restrictions. Leather is usually sold as hides, which are the whole animal skins, but scraps and remnants are easy enough to find and will work out much cheaper, especially if only small amounts of leather are required.

**APPLICATIONS**
Used as a sheet material or to form structural elements, leather is often used to make bracelets, cuffs and collars and can be combined with metal fixings and findings. Due to the chemicals used in tanning, some types of leather will cause silver to tarnish quickly.

### VEGETABLE-TANNED

Leather tanned with vegetable-based chemicals containing tannin. It will discolour in contact with water, and has less of a color range than chemically tanned leather, but is more suitable for boiling and carving than other types of leather.

### CHEMICALLY TANNED

Salts of chromium and other chemicals are used to treat and preserve the hide, producing a pliable leather with greater colour ranges than vegetable-tanned leather.

### FULL GRAIN

Only the hair is removed from the leather, leaving the natural grain of the animal's skin still visible. A thick and very hard-wearing material.

### TOP GRAIN

Usually made from low-quality hide that has been sanded smooth and often given an artificial grain. The thickness of the material will vary. Most leather is top grain.

### SUEDE

The natural grain of the leather has been completely removed or the hide has been split to reveal the soft inner surface. Thin and very pliable.

### VELLUM

Very thin, semi-translucent sheet material made from stretched and dried calfskin. It is not tanned and can go mouldy if stored in the damp. Vellum does not tear easily. A good source of vellum is old legal documents.

▷ ARMOUR FINN CUFFS
BY WILLIAM VINICOMBE
*A pierced template was used to emboss a pattern onto the dyed rawhide before the final construction of these leather cuffs. The inner surfaces have had gold leaf applied, and gold-plated silver studs set with peridots form the closures.*

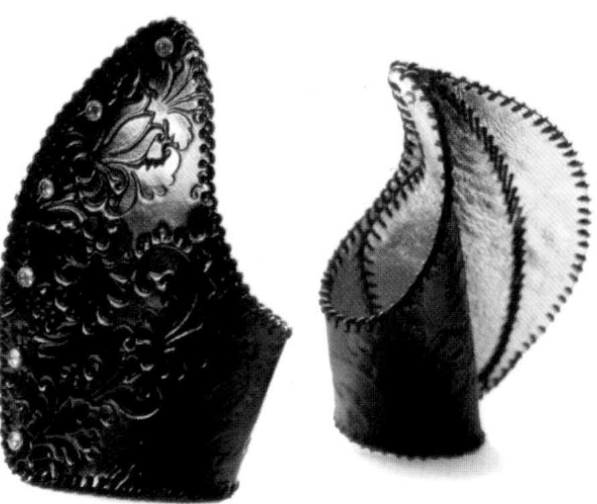

△ MADAME DU BARRY NECKLACE
BY WILLIAM VINICOMBE
*Leather was hand-moulded over machined wooden forms to upholster them, and the forms trimmed with a fine black plait. Oxidized silver fittings link the elements.*

▽ CHESTERFIELD HUNTERS BANGLE
BY TOMASZ DONOCIK
*The luxurious quilted leather of this bracelet has been studded with sapphires, and is backed with a gold-plated electroformed silver liner, which echoes the form of the leather.*

## CUTTING

It will be necessary to cut leather for most applications, whether with scissors to trim a piece to a manageable size, or with a template as a guide for specific shapes. It is not easy to cut leather accurately by hand, but careful practice will eventually improve the results.

### METHOD

1 Work on a self-healing cutting mat. To cut straight lines, use a steel ruler as a guide and cut the leather with a sharp craft knife with firm, even pressure. Thick leather may need more than one stroke from the knife, so take care to cut in the same place and at the same angle so that the edge does not become ragged.

2 Templates should be made for curved cuts, preferably from metal sheet. Secure the leather in place so that it does not slip while it is being cut. Position the template and use a pointed craft knife to follow the template.

3 Take care when cutting corners or where lines intersect one another, since slips of the knife will show. If the cut-out corner does not come away easily, carefully cut into the corner again, with the cutting edge of the blade absolutely perpendicular to the leather.

4 Cut edges can be sealed using a professional leather sealant, then sanded to clean up the lines and remove any 'whiskers'.

## STAMPING

This technique is used to cut complex or multiple shapes out from leather. A steel tool with a sharp cutting edge is used to shear the leather.

### METHOD

1 Draw a diagram of your template to scale, and use this as a guide to make a steel tool from a 10-mm (3⁄8-inch) wide strip of steel sheet. The strip of steel must have parallel edges otherwise it will not cut evenly.

2 Solder or weld the ends closed, and file the cutting edge so that it is sharp. Alternatively, a small biscuit cutter can be used – the cutting edge can be sharpened with an oilstone if necessary.

3 Place the leather on top of a piece of wood, with the steel tool in position on top. Use either a vice, hydraulic press or, as a last resort, a hammer to force the tool through the leather. The best results will come from an even application of pressure. The result should be a neat, clean cut that requires little or no cleaning up.

4 Laser cutting is also a good method of creating multiple cut-outs of complicated shapes, but may char the edges of the leather slightly, which will be more obvious on light-coloured material.

## SEWING

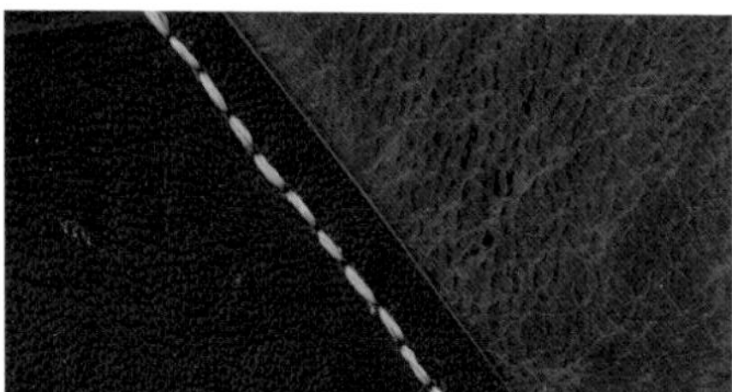

Stitched seams are a very effective way of joining pieces of leather together and creating strong intersections that can form three-dimensional structures. Special leather needles, which are flattened steel tapers, make the job easier, whether you are using a sewing machine or stitching by hand.

### METHOD

1 Thin leathers may be stitched using a sewing machine with a leather needle. Thick leathers will require an industrial sewing machine specially designed to handle the stresses produced when stitching such a thick and resistant material.
2 For hand-stitching thin leather, first make marks at regular intervals where the stitches will go.
3 Pierce holes along the line, but only do a few at a time because the holes will quickly close. Use strong thread and a leather needle to stitch along the seam. If a very strong seam is required, two needles can be used to stitch at the same time – the double thread will give long seams extra strength. Hand-stitching thick leather is more of a challenge. Leather-workers use a special wooden clamp to hold a piece while it is being stitched.

## DYEING

For the best results when dyeing leather, use professional leather dyes and ensure your leather has not been sealed or waterproofed since this will inhibit the effects. Some fabric and hair dyes will work but will not have the same permanency, effectiveness or range of colours as those specifically designed for leather. Always make a test sample first.

### METHOD

1 Apply the dye to the surface of the leather with a cloth or sponge; wipe the dye across the leather. Dye can also be applied with a brush, or with a spray gun, which will produce the most even effect.
2 Allow the dye to dry thoroughly before applying any finishes or waxes to the leather.
3 Experiment with the effects that can be achieved – scoring or sanding the surface of the leather will allow the dye to be absorbed more readily, and these areas will appear darker.
4 The cut edges of leather will often be a different colour from the surface, but the edges can be dyed to either match or contrast with the surface before sealing and polishing the edges.

**Sample** *Dyed vellum.*

## POLISHING

The sealed edges of leather can be sanded and burnished to add the finishing touch to a piece. The extra time spent perfecting the edges will make a great difference to the quality of the leather, giving it a professionally finished appearance. Polish can be applied to the top surface of leather to deepen colours and help protect finishes from wear.

### METHOD

1 Seal the cut edges of your leather piece using a product designed specifically for this purpose. The edges can then be sanded and burnished with a polished-agate burnisher.
2 The surface of leather can be polished with waxes such as shoe polish, or special waterproofing agents. These products should be applied with a brush or a soft cloth and buffed to a shine.

## FORMING

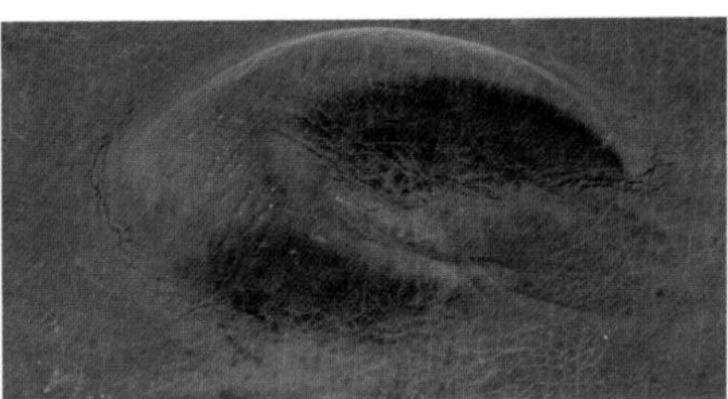

Three-dimensional leather forms can be easily made with a vacuum former, but similar effects can be created in a hydraulic press or by tooling the leather over a form by hand. The form can be carved from wood or acrylic and should not have deep undercuts.

### METHOD

1 The material used to construct the solid form over which the leather will be formed must be resilient enough to cope with the degree of pressure created during the vacuum-forming process – solid acrylic is perfect. Place your dampened leather over the form, with a sheet of thermoplastic over the top, so that the vacuum will work with the porous leather.
2 Switch on the machine. The thermoplastic will pull the leather tightly down over the form. Switch off the machine and remove the pieces. You may wish to keep the leather sandwiched between the two plastic layers until you are certain that it is dry.
3 The three-dimensional form can be cut out of the leather or stitched onto a back piece. Leave the former inside if you wish to prevent the leather from deforming, or if you require a solid object.

## BOILING

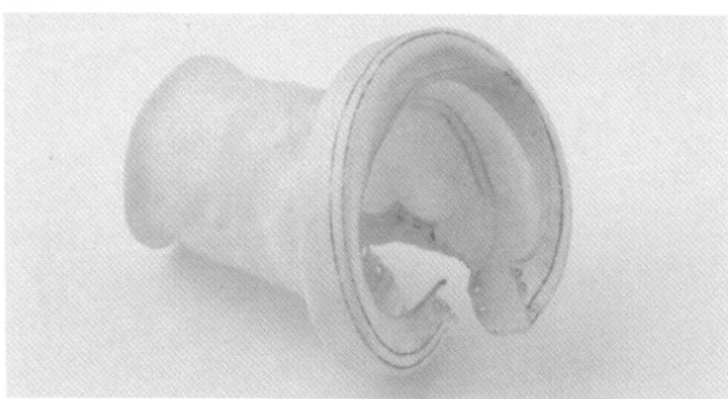

Leather can be stiffened or made entirely rigid by dipping it in boiling water. This technique can be used on finished pieces or on the raw material, changing its physical properties so that a greater range of techniques such as carving and drilling can be applied. Boiling is also useful for shrinking leather around a form.

METHOD

1 Cut your leather to shape. Pieces can also be wrapped around a form that will survive boiling water – wax is not suitable – or the leather can be attached to a frame so that it shrinks to fit.
2 Set a pan of water on a hotplate and allow it to come to boiling point; the pan must be large enough to fit your piece in.
3 Dip the leather in the boiling water for up to one minute. When the leather has cooled and dried, it will be more rigid than before. The results will depend on the type and thickness of leather used and the length of time it remains in the water – do plenty of experiments before attempting your final piece. If the leather is left in the water for too long, it will shrivel, but this can also be an interesting effect.

**Sample** *Boiled vellum.*

## SANDING

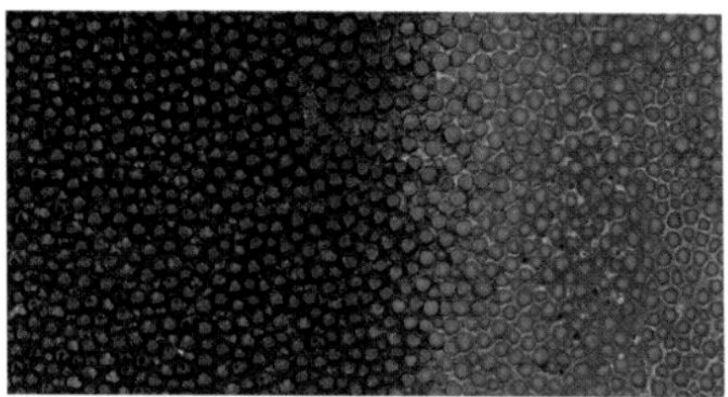

Sanding the surface of leather will change its properties by roughening the texture and exposing more absorbent material. Dyed shagreen (stingray hide) is often sanded to create characteristic 'spots', but unsanded shagreen is a wonderful material with which to experiment.

METHOD

1 Work on a larger piece of leather than is required so that it can be tacked down onto a piece of wood without damaging the area that you will be using.
2 Wrap a piece of glasspaper around a sanding block and begin to rub down the surface of the leather. Shagreen is covered with tough, shiny granules and should be sanded with a rough paper, such as 200-grit. Once the granules have been sanded flat, successively finer grades of wet-and-dry or emery papers can be used to refine the surface quality.
3 The edges of thick leather pieces can be sanded to smooth them but must be sealed first; otherwise a ragged effect will be produced. Use a sealant specially designed for leather to obtain the best results, and wrap the emery paper around a wooden stick so that you have better control.

## EMBOSSING

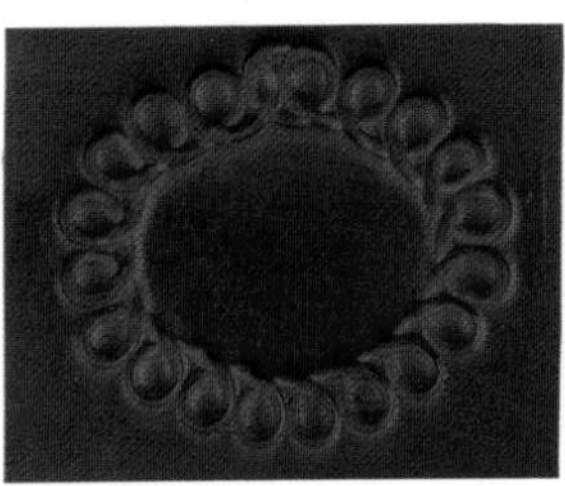

Designs can be imprinted into leather using pierced, etched or embossed metal templates to create low-level relief with very fine detail. The leather should be embossed before it is formed into a piece, since it is much easier to work on the flat.

### METHOD

1 Use water to wet the leather – it will compress much more easily when damp.

2 Place the template in position on the leather, and place them both on the bed of a press that can be tightened. A vice will work, but care must be taken so that the template does not slip. Metal sheets can be placed either side of the leather and template for protection.

3 Tighten the press so that the template is forced into the surface of the leather, and leave it in the press overnight to ensure a lasting result.

4 Heated tools applied with a degree of pressure to leather will also emboss patterns or text into the surface, but the tool must not be so hot that it scorches the leather.

*See step 2*

## RIVETS, STUDS AND EYELETS

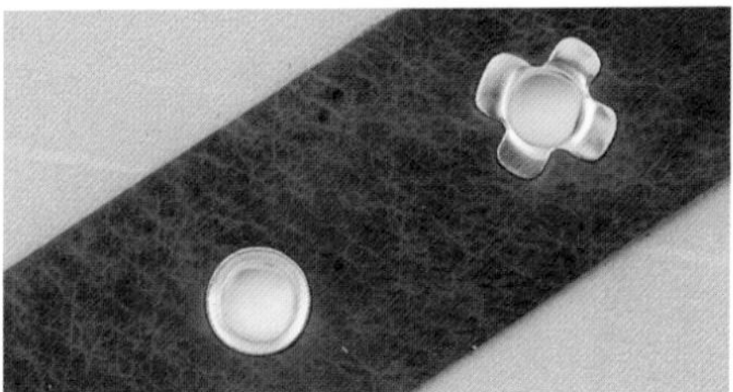

Metal components can be attached to leather either as a way of joining sections together or for purely decorative reasons. These metal parts can take many forms, including stone settings, but must be suitable for being secured into the leather without the use of heat.

### METHOD

1 Rivets for use with leather must have a large head at one end and be secured with a washer on the underside. This is to allow for any stretching of the leather so that the rivet heads will not just slip through. For the same reason, studs usually have a large, decorative head on one end and are fixed through the leather with a back piece that secures the stud when hammered shut.

2 Eyelets are made from pieces of tubing with one end flared out at 90 degrees and with cuts in the other end, so that when it is opened it will split and spread evenly, holding the leather firmly.

3 Make a hole in the leather slightly smaller than the diameter of your fixture, using a leather hole punch.

4 Push the fixture through the hole so that its head is touching the top surface of the leather. Protect this surface with masking tape, and if the fitting contains a stone setting or is in any way fragile, work on a piece of wood rather than a steel block.

5 Rivets made from wire should be at least 1 mm (1/32 inch) in diameter, and hammered to spread the end of the wire into a countersunk hole in the washer. Eyelets can be closed with a special tool that will open out the underside, or spread using doming punches, and finally tapped flat with a mallet.

## PYROGRAPHY AND BRANDING

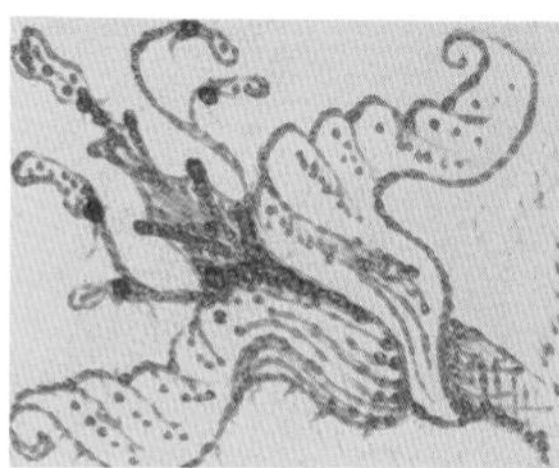

A heated point, such as a soldering iron, is used to write or draw onto the leather. Intricate designs can be executed to great effect. The results of this technique will be most striking on light-coloured leathers, but you may wish to create more subtle patterns by using it on darker materials. Heated pattern punches can also be used to scorch designs into the leather.

### METHOD

1 Preheat a soldering iron. Various metal tips are available for soldering irons in a range of shapes and sizes; if you require very fine definition, then one of these tips may be a necessity.
2 Work on raw material rather than a finished piece so that any distortions or mistakes can be rectified before fabrication of the final piece. Tape or tack the leather to a flat surface, such as a piece of wood.
3 Use the tip of the soldering iron to write or draw on the leather. Experimentation will tell you how much pressure to use and how slowly to move the point around in order to achieve the results that you require. Very light shading can be achieved with a light touch and constant movement of the tip of the soldering iron.
4 Thin leather will warp from this process, since the heated areas will contract. This can be used to good effect, but if the piece needs to be flattened, dampen it with water and leave it under a heavy book overnight.
5 Once completely dry, seal the surface of the leather with a transparent wax, which will also help to condition the 'burnt' areas.

## GOLD LEAF AND POWDERS

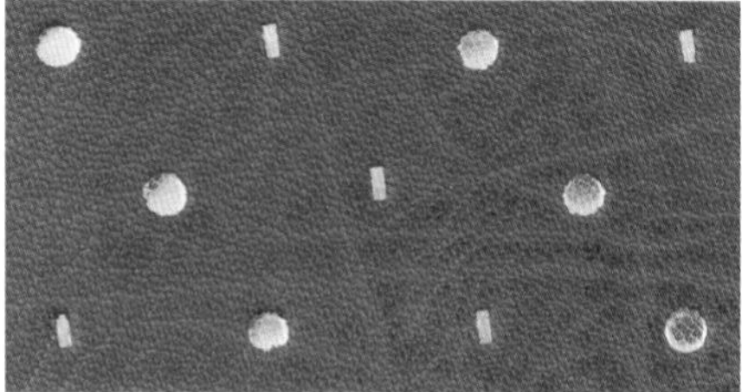

A technique more commonly found in bookbinding, gold leaf or powders can be applied to the surface of the leather with a special glue, which is activated during the application of heated steel tools that will emboss the leather during the process.

### METHOD

1 Paint the whole surface of the leather with glair, a special glue used by bookbinders for gilding, and leave to dry for 24 hours. Apply a thin coat of petroleum jelly over the surface of the leather and place a sheet of gold leaf on top.
2 Use cotton wool to gently smooth down the gold leaf, ensuring that no pockets of air are trapped underneath.
3 Heat the metal tools you will be using to around 120°C (250°F) in an oven. Wearing heatproof gloves, apply the face of a tool to the gold leaf for about two seconds, using some pressure, and ensuring that the whole face of the tool comes into contact with the gold. The heat from the tool will activate the glue and also emboss the leather. Remove excess leaf with white spirit and cotton wool, wiping the surface gently – the gold leaf should remain only in the embossed areas.
4 The surface can be varnished with shellac to protect it from wear.

# Feathers, Hair and Quills

Materials produced naturally by birds and animals, from peacock feathers to porcupine quills, have been used by most cultures throughout history as decorative elements. These materials provide colourful, lightweight and structural components that can be easily incorporated into jewellery.

These materials are naturally shed by animals, and can be found in the wild. When buying feathers, check the source – many bird species are on the CITES list and the feathers can only be traded under certain conditions. Fishing-tackle suppliers have a range of attractive feathers used for fly-tying, but they are usually sold in small quantities.

**APPLICATIONS**
Suitable for most types of jewellery, but some feathers are particularly delicate and will require careful application and storage. Sensitive to heat, chemicals and water; these materials shouldn't be used in pieces that will receive excessive wear.

## FEATHERS

**Composition:** Keratin

Flexible, strong and lightweight, feathers can be found in an amazing range of colours, shapes, sizes and forms. Whether used by birds for flight or insulation, feathers generally have a central quill with a 'web' on either side that is made up of linear 'barbs'. Feathers can be bought loose, in bundles or strung on a cord, and are often dyed with vivid colours.

## HAIR

**Composition:** Keratin

Using hair in jewellery-making is often associated with Victorian mourning mementos or sentimental rings and brooches that contain human hair – which is either woven or made into images – and necklaces that are made entirely from woven hair, often with gold caps. Elephant hair used in jewellery-making has been replaced by giraffe hair, which is also thick and strong. Horsehair can be used, as can synthetic hair fibres, and both have the benefit of long length, which makes them suitable for weaving and braiding.

## QUILLS

**Composition:** Keratin

A quill is either the central shaft of a feather, sometimes shaved of all the barbs, or a spine from any of the various species of porcupine. Both provide lightweight, structural material that can be dyed, softened in hot water, set in metal, pierced or bound. Porcupine quills should be handled with care since the points are sharp and covered with tiny barbs, making them difficult to remove if they pierce the skin.

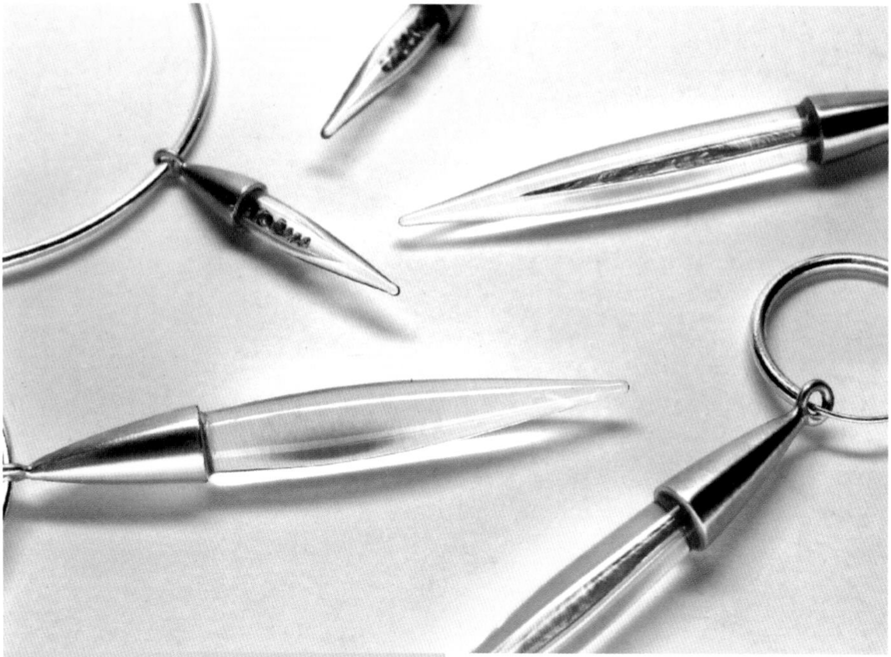

△ SPINEL EARRINGS
BY TRACY FURLONG
*Enclosed glass forms containing vivid pink feathers and spinels have been set into silver collars to make striking ear pendants.*

▷ HORSEHAIR BRACELET
BY ANASTASIA YOUNG
*Horsehair was plaited in such a way that it became elasticized, and was set into an engraved silver panel.*

COMBINING MATERIALS
## Setting

Feathers can be fixed into curved metal forms and will form radiating spikes. Because no heat can be applied to fix the feather in place, tension settings or cold-joining techniques must be used.

### METHOD

1 Use a soft metal such as copper or fine silver to create a form into which the feather can be inserted.
2 Apply some epoxy-resin glue into the recess that the feather will sit in, and place the feather inside with the shaft running along the seam. Allow the glue to dry.
3 Tap the edges of the metal lightly to force the seam to close over the feather, but not so tightly that the barbs of the feather are severed.
4 Use a burnisher to continue pushing down the metal on both sides of the form until it is neatly closed. Gently pull at the feather with your fingers to arrange the barbs.
5 Feathers can also be set in between two pieces of metal that are fixed together using riveting.

COMBINING MATERIALS
## Tube Setting

The simplest way to combine feathers with metal elements is to use glue to secure the shaft of the feather into a piece of tubing. The arrangement of the tubes will directly affect the way in which the feathers protrude from the form.

### METHOD

1 Construct and clean up the metal form in which the feathers will be set – this could be as simple as soldering an earring post onto the tube to make a stud earring.
2 You may wish to solder caps onto the ends of the tubes to seal them and prevent the ends of the feathers from being visible. Dip the end of a feather into some mixed epoxy-resin glue and carefully insert it into the tube, trying not to get glue further up the feather.
3 More than one feather can be inserted into each tube, depending on the diameter of the tube and the shaft of the feather. Arrange the position of the feathers before the glue sets.

**KEY** Feathers Hair Quills

## COMBINING MATERIALS
### Collets

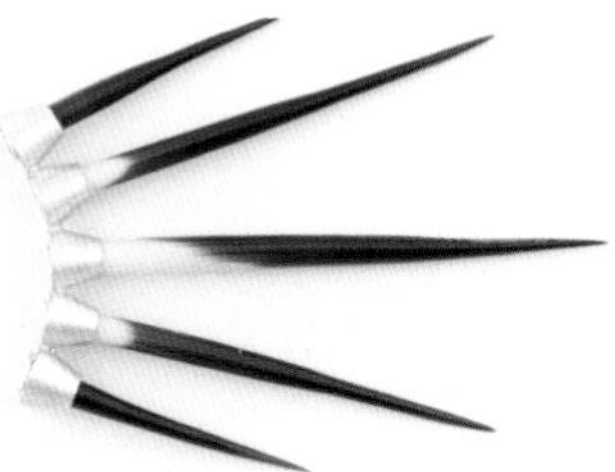

Angled collets or settings echo the taper of a quill. The quill can be inserted from behind the setting, and glue will hold it. Take care when working with sharp, pointed quills – and consider the safety of the wearer too.

METHOD

1 Cut enough pieces of tube for your design with a chenier vice. The vice can be set so that equal lengths of tube are cut.
2 Anneal, pickle, rinse and dry the pieces of tube.
3 Place one tube into a collet block in a suitable-size hole and tap inside the tube with a collet punch. This will open out one end of the tube so that a cone is formed. Take care that the smaller-diameter end stays open enough to expose a reasonable amount of the quill when it is pushed through.
4 Clean up the top and bottom surfaces of the silver tube with emery paper, and remove any sharp edges.
5 Solder the conical tubes together to form a suitable piece, with the narrow ends pointing outwards.
6 Clean up and finish the metal form.
7 Push a quill through the back of one of the tubes as far as it will go. It may need to be cut shorter, so mark where you need to cut and remove the quill. A straight saw blade in a piercing saw frame can be used to cut the quill. Insert the quill into the tube again and apply some glue to the lower edge, ensuring it is pulled tightly into the cone.
8 Repeat with the other quills and allow the glue to dry thoroughly.

## OVERLAY

Forms can be covered with overlapping feathers to give them a wonderfully soft and tactile surface. Keep the overlaid form simple, but be creative with the incorporation of this technique into your jewellery designs.

METHOD

1 The selection of feathers for this technique is crucial. The curve of the feathers needs to be as similar in shape as possible to the curve of the form where the feathers will be applied, especially if a smooth overlay is required.
2 Small feathers should be used to create a uniform texture and may need to be trimmed at the base so that they will lie flat.
3 Draw evenly spaced lines in pencil on your form, and use these as a guide for making rows of feathers.
4 Apply glue to the form in a thin line, stick down the ends of the shafts, and allow one row to dry completely before repeating the process to add another. Continue the process until the whole surface is adequately covered.

## BINDING

To secure loose strands of hair or other fibrous material into a form such as a tube, it is first necessary to bind the hair so that it can be easily inserted.

### METHOD

1 Secure one end of a 30 cm (12 inch) piece of waxed cotton thread in a vice. The lock of hair can be held together with masking tape. Hold the thread taut and place the hair across it, about 4 cm (1½ inches) from the vice.
2 Wrap the thread tightly around the hair, making a neat coil, trapping the end held in the vice under the coil as you go.
3 Make the coil as long as possible within the constraints of your design. If the hair is being fixed in a tube, then the coil must be short enough so that it is not seen.
4 Knot the two ends of thread together at the top of the coil; seal the knot with glue or clear nail varnish; and cut the thread as close to the knot as possible. Glue the lock of hair into position.

## PLAITING

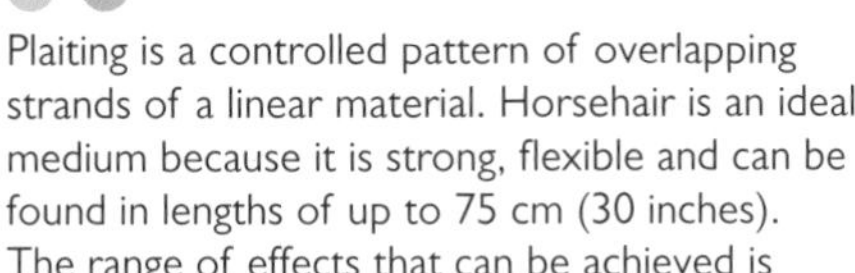

Plaiting is a controlled pattern of overlapping strands of a linear material. Horsehair is an ideal medium because it is strong, flexible and can be found in lengths of up to 75 cm (30 inches). The range of effects that can be achieved is wide and includes macramé techniques.

### METHOD

1 Bind a lock of hair at one end so that it is held securely. Split the lock into three equal sections and smooth down the hair so that it will plait evenly, pulling out any hairs that are too short or that will stick out.
2 Pass the left-hand section over the central section so that they cross at the top. Reposition the central section to the left. Bring the right-hand section into the centre, across the top of the central section, which will be pulled to the right.
3 Keep working in this way, taking a hair section from one side and then the other until the required length is reached. Secure the end by wrapping thread around it.
4 Any method of overlapping the hair sections to produce a rhythmic pattern can be used, and the pattern does not have to be the same for the whole length of the piece.

**TIP:** Long-stem, split-shaft feathers can be plaited to create interesting effects and can be bound in a similar way to hair. Feathers are more fragile than hair and need to be handled carefully.

**KEY** Feathers Hair Quills

## DYES

Vivid colours can be produced on feathers, hair and quills using fabric or hair dyes, but subtle colours and beautiful effects can also be achieved with vegetable dyes. Experiment with pre-dyed feathers to create colour combinations.

### METHOD

1 Results will vary when this process is attempted in the workshop, so if even colours are desired it may be worth sourcing pre-dyed feathers. Horsehair is easily treated with hair dyes, but the colours are limited and the hair may require bleaching first so that it takes the colour better.
2 Commercially available textile dyes will produce good effects – follow the manufacturer's instructions since some of the chemicals involved are toxic.
3 Paint the dye onto the feather, hair or quill with a paintbrush and leave it to develop for the required length of time before rinsing the piece with water. Run your fingers over the piece from the end to the tip to restore its shape and allow it to dry.

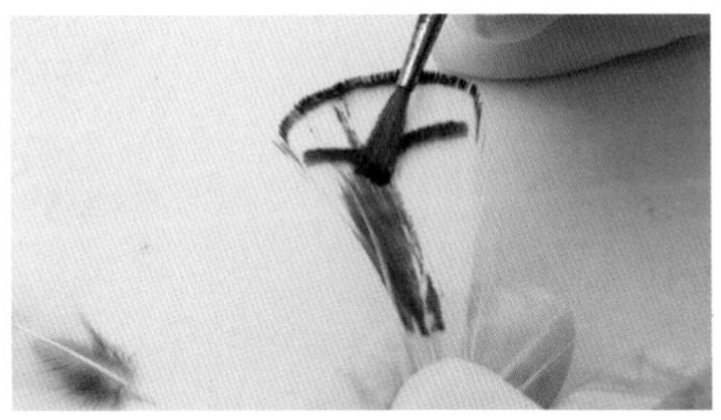

*See step 3*

## BLEACHING

The natural colours of hair and feathers can be altered by applying hair bleach. The bleach strips the colour from the material and is capable of producing a range of colours from rich browns to dark brassy yellows to off-white.

### METHOD

1 Secure the material you will be bleaching at one end to a plastic bag with masking tape. Mix up equal amounts of bleach powder and 9 per cent (30 vol) hydrogen peroxide solution, available from most pharmacists.
2 Paint the mixture onto the material in a thick layer and leave until the required colour has been achieved. Horsehair is very thick and may require bleaching for several hours to achieve lighter shades, or even a second application. Delicate feathers may not withstand the chemicals, so do some test samples before working on your final piece.
3 Wash away the bleach with plenty of water – shampoo and conditioner can also be used and will help to restore lustre lost through chemical damage.

4

# Plastics and Rubber

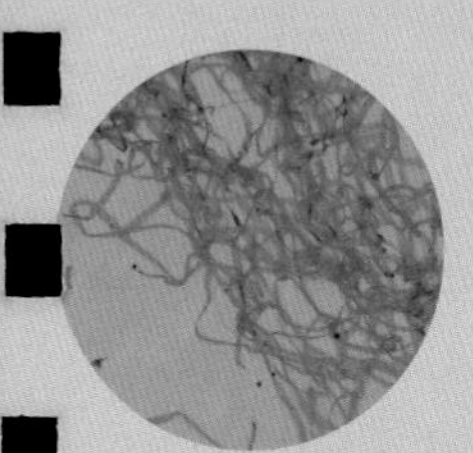
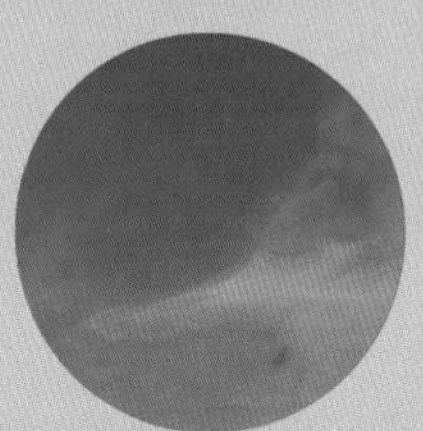

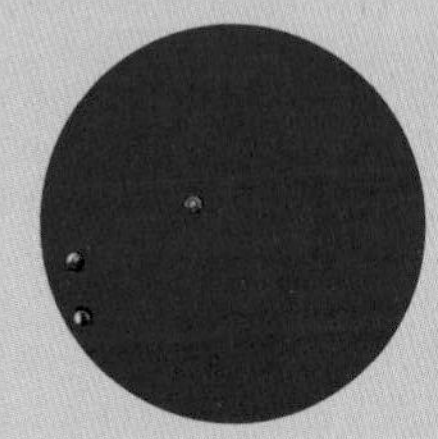

**Plastics and Rubber**
pages 166–187
Acrylic, polypropylene, nylon, resin, silicone, neoprene, polyurethane, thermoplastic polymer

# Plastics

Colourful, lightweight and easy to work, plastics provide many opportunities to explore form, colour and light-play within jewellery objects. Plastics are grouped into two main types: thermoplastics and thermosetting plastics.

'Thermoplastics' are pre-made plastic products that will soften when gently heated. They can be formed and textured while still soft, then set aside to harden once cooled. 'Thermosetting plastics' are usually viscous liquids that require being mixed with a chemical catalyst to make them solid, but are also available as ready-made products. Thermosetting plastics should not be heated. Plastics are mainly manufactured from petrochemical sources, but vegetable-based and biodegradable plastics are being developed to produce less environmentally harmful products.

### APPLICATIONS

Most jewellery forms can be made with plastics, which are generally non-reactive once solid. This makes them suitable for wearing next to the skin. Findings and mechanical parts of plastic jewellery will often be made of metal, as will protective frames or inserts. Plastic surfaces can scratch easily.

### ACRYLIC (brand names include PERSPEX, PLEXIGLASS and LUCITE)

**Composition:** Synthetic polymer

Cast thermoplastic that can be manipulated when heated. Available in rod, tube and sheet form in a wide variety of colours and gauges. Cuts and polishes well, and can be dyed.

### POLYESTER RESINS

**Composition:** Synthetic polymer

Thermosetting plastic that can be mixed with dyes and fillers and can have objects embedded in it. Dries with a tacky surface and shrinks. Best cast in thin layers. Gives off toxic fumes in liquid form.

### EPOXY RESIN

**Composition:** Synthetic polymer

Low-temperature, exothermic, thermosetting plastic. Dries tack-free with little or no shrinkage and is suitable for use with dyes. Often used as a high-gloss coating but can be cast into moulds. Also available as a two-part adhesive useful for joining mixed materials with a strong bond.

### POLYURETHANE

**Composition:** Various synthetic polymers

Manufactured into foam, paints and hard plastics. Available as a liquid resin that, once cured, is less brittle than other types of resins; is usually opaque but can be dyed.

## POLYPROPYLENE

**Composition:** Synthetic polymer

Manufactured in high-density and low-density forms (HDPE, LDPE) as a rigid plastic. Often used in packaging. Most useful to jewellers in its flexible sheet form; can be opaque or translucent.

## NYLON

**Composition:** Synthetic polymer

Most useful to jewellers as a fibre or mesh. Nylon fishing line is incredibly strong and can be dyed, woven and easily combined with other materials.

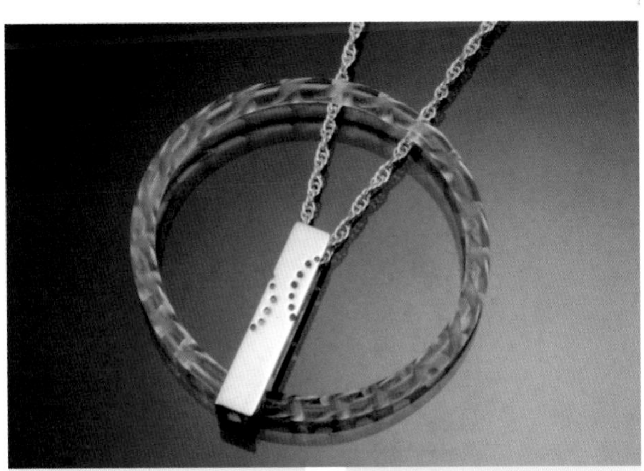

△ BUILDING OF RAINBOW
TAKAFUMI INUZUKA
*Drilling, heat-bending and carving with a pendant drill were all used to make this silver and acrylic pendant.*

▽ WATER DROPS
BY JANA REINHARDT
*These pieces were made from acrylic on a lathe and are designed to be worn between two fingers.*

◁ DOUBLE CHERRY NECKLACE
BY TINA LILENTHAL
*This necklace uses polished cast forms in both silver and resin.*

# Rubber

Rubber is used for making moulds, allowing easy duplication of cast elements. Flexible, colourful elements of silicone have become more prevalent in jewellery pieces as small-batch casting is a straightforward process, and the materials are not prohibitively expensive.

**APPLICATIONS**
Silicone rubber and neoprene are suitable for most types of jewellery forms and are often combined with metal findings. Latex and vulcanized rubber are more suitable for making moulds than jewellery forms since they discolour and degrade quickly.

Due to advances in technology, a greater range of rubber products with specific working properties is available, and it is possible to find materials that are either soft and flexible or dense with little give. Ask your supplier about the suitability of a particular product for your project. Familiarize yourself with the data sheet of the product, to identify any health and safety issues.

### LATEX

**Composition:** Natural or synthetic polymer

Viscous liquid or paste often used in making moulds; can be dyed. Discolours and degrades with age and exposure to some substances. Can cause allergic reactions.

### VULCANIZED RUBBER

**Composition:** Natural or synthetic polymer

Rubber heated in the presence of sulphur becomes very strong and durable, which allows greater manufacturing capabilities. Available in a range of colours but most often used by jewellers for making moulds suitable for wax injection as part of the casting process. Will eventually degrade.

### SILICONE RUBBER

**Composition:** Polysiloxane

Room-temperature vulcanized (RTV) rubber is treated with chemicals rather than heat. Silicone rubber is very durable and chemically resistant. A range of liquid products is available – the resulting rubber can either be soft and flexible or rigid, depending on the type of silicone used.

### NEOPRENE

**Composition:** Synthetic polymer

The first mass-produced synthetic rubber to be developed; neoprene is a slightly spongy sheet material available in a range of colours.

▷ BLACK HOOP EARRINGS
BY MIN-JI-CHO
*Even the most domestic of materials can be used innovatively to make jewellery, like these earrings, for which black rubber gloves were cut up and folded intricately.*

▽ KNUCKLEDUSTER
BY FRIEDA MUNRO
*The main body of the piece was pierced from thick black rubber, and black pearls were strung on a brass wire so that they move when the piece is worn.*

△ THE GLOVE'S DREAM
BY MIN-JI-CHO
*This pink necklace is made from pearls and the textured tips of household rubber gloves.*

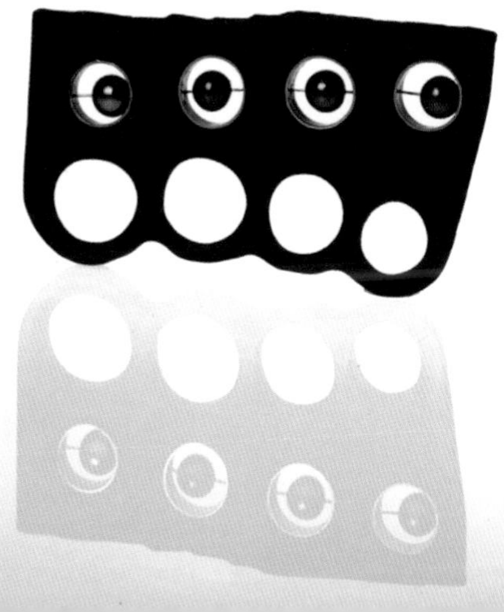

## DRILLING

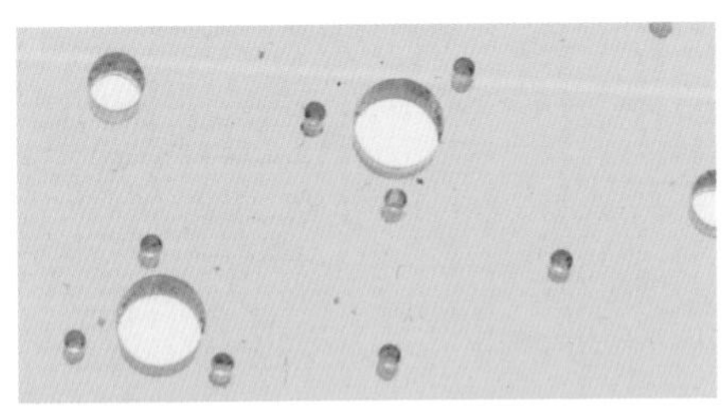

The harder the plastic, the more suitable it is for drilling; however, resin and acrylic can be brittle and may shatter if not drilled carefully. Use a hole punch in softer plastics and rubbers such as neoprene, nylon or silicone sheet.

### METHOD

1. Plastics do not need centre-punching. Make a mark with a permanent marker pen where the drill holes will be; if using acrylic, keep the protective plastic on the sheet for as long as possible – this will stop it from getting scratched.
2. Hold the piece firmly in place on a wooden block on the drill bed. Switch on the drill and do not apply too much pressure while drilling; allow the swarf to clear by lifting the drill out every so often. Remove the swarf from the drill bit regularly, to stop it melting onto the drill bit.
3. When drilling large holes, ensure that the underside of the sheet is fully supported by the wood to prevent the drill bit from chipping the plastic as it exits the hole. The drill bit will exert more force on the sheet, so hold it tightly in position. A ball burr can be used in a pin vice to tidy up the edges of the hole if necessary.
4. For large holes such as the insides of rings, the plastic will need to be clamped to the drill bed in between two sheets of wood to prevent cracking; do not work too close to the edge of the acrylic sheet and remove the swarf after every hole has been drilled. The drill should be set to the slowest speed to reduce heat build-up.

## PIERCING

Transparent acrylic is more brittle than opaque and may crack if thin areas are created within a pierced design. Large pieces of acrylic can be cut down to more manageable sizes with a band saw or hacksaw.

### METHOD

1. Work out your design on paper first. It can be transferred to the acrylic with double-sided sticky tape or by drawing it onto the protective plastic covering with a permanent marker pen.
2. Drill small holes in any areas that need to be pierced out and cannot be accessed from the outside edge.
3. Acrylic can be pierced with a jeweller's saw using a blade designed for metal or wax. Metal blades cut more accurately but can get stuck in the sheet due to heat from friction, so work slowly. Wax blades cut faster, but are less accurate and cut a wider path.
4. Pierce out any inside areas first. Thread the saw blade through the drill holes and tighten the blade, keeping the acrylic at one end.
5. Keep the saw blade vertical. When cutting curves, turn the work into the path of the saw blade and do not push too hard. Use a rough file to remove saw marks.
6. Smooth the edges with wet-and-dry paper, starting with 500-grade paper and working up to 1200 before polishing. Water must be used with this paper so that no dust is created, and the piece must be rinsed well between each filing grade.

**KEY** Acrylic · Polypropylene · Nylon · Resin · Silicone · Neoprene · Polyurethane · Thermoplastic polymer

## INLAY

The optical properties of acrylic can be put to good use in inlaid designs – try combining transparent and opaque colours. Inlaid sheet will withstand thermoforming to a degree – test pieces first to ensure that your design is suitable. The glue used in this technique is not suitable for bonding flat sheets together.

### METHOD

1 Drill holes in the sheet that are exactly the same size in diameter as the acrylic rod you will be using to inlay. Push the rod through the hole – it needs to be a tight fit.
2 Using a fine paintbrush, apply a small amount of a professional glue (such as Plastiweld) to both sides of the sheet around the protruding rod. The glue will move inside the join by capillary action, and will chemically 'melt' the two surfaces together. Leave the piece for about 10 minutes to allow the glue to evaporate and set properly.
3 Cut and file the rod so that it is flush with the acrylic sheet. Clean up with water and wet-and-dry paper, starting with 500-grade and working up to 1200, then polish.

## TURNING

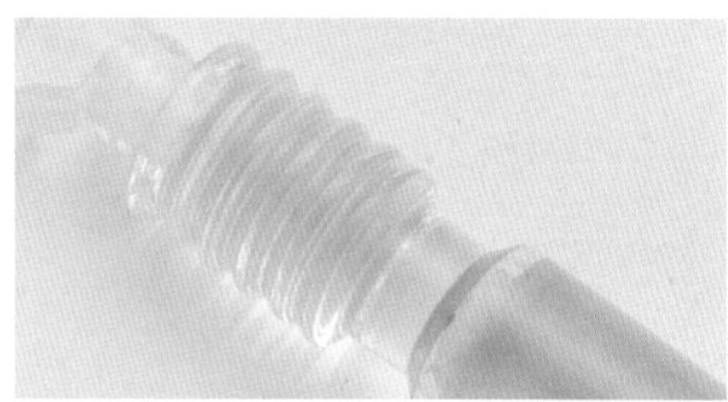

Acrylic rod and cast resin can be turned on a lathe, either to create new shapes or to make cleaning up and polishing a less time-consuming process. The plastic pieces should be cylindrical to begin with, since their brittle nature means any sudden force will cause fractures.

### METHOD

1 Make a card template of one edge of the profile of your design – this can be used to check the progress of the cutting. Short, thick sections of plastic will give the best results, since there is less likelihood of movement from vibration.
2 Secure the piece of plastic in the chuck of the vice and position the cutting tool. Be sure that it is at the correct angle. Set the lathe to a slow speed and switch it on.
3 Manoeuvre the cutting tool so that it is removing a small amount of material on each pass, working backwards and forwards until the required depth is met. Leave any thin sections until last, since this will minimize the risk of breaking the piece.
4 An emery stick can be used to clean up the piece while it is rotating on the lathe, but you should wear a mask because it is not possible to use water with the paper.
5 To buff the piece, use a felt stick that has had plastic polish applied.
6 Switch off the lathe and remove the piece of work from the chuck.

## LAMINATING

Sheets of acrylic can be permanently bonded by heating them and then clamping them under pressure until they are set. Once bonded, further techniques can be applied, such as thermoforming or carving, to expose the different-coloured layers.

### METHOD

1. Heat an oven or kiln to 180°C (355°F). Remove the protective plastic covers from the sheets of acrylic and layer them up, without touching the surfaces.
2. Place the stack into the kiln and close the door. The piece will take a couple of minutes to get hot; the more layers of acrylic sheet, the longer the piece will take to reach the right temperature. Keep checking – overheated acrylic becomes riddled with internal bubbles that are impossible to remove.
3. Once you are sure that the stack is heated right to the centre, remove it from the kiln (wearing thick gloves) and place it in between two steel plates. Acrylic sets in about 90 seconds, and the steel will draw heat out of the stack, so you must work quickly: apply a heavy weight on top of the stack, or use a G-clamp tightened around the steel sheets to create enough pressure for the acrylic to bond while it is still hot.
4. Allow the piece to reach room temperature before releasing it, and check to see that the layers have bonded – returning the piece to the kiln if necessary.
5. The piece can be cut, carved, cleaned, polished and thermoformed in exactly the same way as unlaminated acrylic.

## LAMINATING
## With Inclusions

Objects, textures and metal leaf can be included within a laminated piece of acrylic. Objects with a substantial thickness may cause air to be trapped between the layers of acrylic, but this can also look interesting. Choose a material that will not be adversely affected by the heating process.

### METHOD

1. Layer up the pieces of acrylic with the material that is going to be embedded within it, having removed the protective plastic coating and degreased the acrylic if necessary. Place the stack on a clean piece of aluminium foil in an oven or kiln heated to 180°C (355°F).
2. Allow the acrylic to reach the temperature to the centre of the stack and, while wearing thick gloves, remove the piece from the kiln and quickly clamp it in between two steel sheets and apply pressure until it cools. The thicker the inclusion or texture, the more pressure you should apply in order to avoid leaving air gaps. It is not always possible to remove trapped air, and textures will not always work as well as you might like, but acrylic is an inexpensive material and you can learn from your mistakes.
3. Clean up and polish the laminated piece. It may be possible to heat and bend the piece, but this will depend on the inclusions.

**KEY**  Acrylic  Polypropylene  Nylon  Resin  Silicone  Neoprene  Polyurethane  Thermoplastic polymer

## THERMOFORMING

The thermoforming properties of acrylic make it a very versatile material – it can be bent around formers, pressed into heatproof moulds, or formed freehand. Kiln heating will give the best results for large pieces, but local heating with a heat gun or gas torch (carefully) can produce effective results on small areas.

### METHOD

1. Prepare your acrylic sheet by cutting it to the right shape, cleaning it up with wet-and-dry paper and polishing it, since this is much easier to do when the piece is flat.
2. Heat the acrylic in an oven or kiln set at 180°C (355°F) until it is soft, which will take two to five minutes, depending on the size of the piece and the efficiency of the oven. Use a clean piece of aluminium foil to support the piece while it is being heated and to stop it from becoming contaminated.
3. Remove the acrylic from the kiln once it has become fully flexible and, while wearing thick gloves, bend it freehand or around a former. The soft acrylic can also be pressed into a mould at this stage.
4. The plastic will set in about 90 seconds, so work quickly and hold the shape securely in position until the acrylic has set. The piece can be run under cold water to cool it down.
5. If you are not happy with the results, return the piece to the oven and heat it again – the acrylic will flatten itself and you can try to form it again once it is soft. After four or five heatings, however, the plastic begins to lose its ability to bend.
6. Final polishing may be needed to remove marks or scratches that occurred during the heating process.

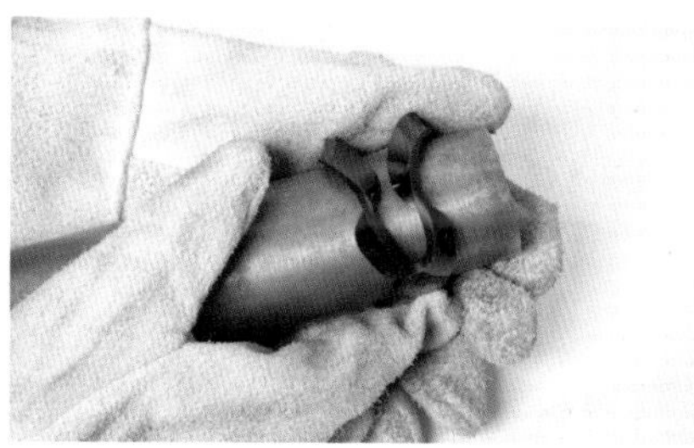

*See step 3*

△ BLACK BANGLE
BY ANASTASIA YOUNG
*To make this bangle, an acrylic shape was pierced out and then decorated with drilled holes of different sizes before being thermoformed.*

## THERMOFORMING
### Acrylic Rod

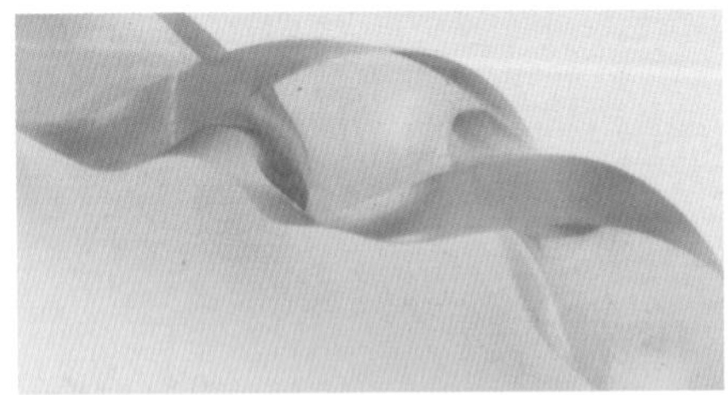

Acrylic rod is available in a variety of diameters and colours, both transparent and opaque, and can be thermoformed in exactly the same way as acrylic sheet. Square rod or strips of acrylic sheet can be twisted and formed while soft to create a strong visual impact – try using different finishes on different edges for contrast.

METHOD

1 Prepare the rod by cleaning and polishing the cut ends if necessary. You may, for example, be using silver tube to cap the ends, in which case cleaning is optional.
2 Heat an oven or kiln to 180°C (355°F). Place the piece of rod on a clean piece of aluminium foil in the kiln and allow it to reach a high enough temperature for it to become soft – check regularly during the heating process to see that no bubbles have formed due to overheating.
3 When soft, remove the acrylic from the kiln and bend it around a former – the rod is incredibly flexible but does need to be held firmly in position until it has set.
4 Try tying knots or making coils and if the results don't go according to plan, then return the piece to the kiln where it will flatten out as it softens, and try again.

## HEAT TEXTURING

Impressions can be made in acrylic while it is still soft from heating by using a range of textures. Bent strips of metal will make bold, deep indentations, and leaves and feathers can be used to create subtle surface decoration. Experiment with the textures you use – the possibilities are infinite.

METHOD

1 Heat the acrylic in a kiln or oven set at 180°C (355°F) until it is soft.
2 Remove the piece from the kiln using a spatula and place it on a wooden board; put the texture on top of the acrylic and apply a heavy steel weight to force the texture down into the softened sheet (you can stand on it too!). The pieces can also be squashed in a press, or clamped to the work surface. The plastic cools quickly once it has left the kiln, so the quicker it is clamped, the softer the plastic will be, and the deeper the impression.
3 Allow the piece to cool for a minute and then run it under cold water. If the plastic is reheated now, the pattern will disappear because the acrylic has a memory and will return to its original shape.

## HEAT TEXTURING
### Raised

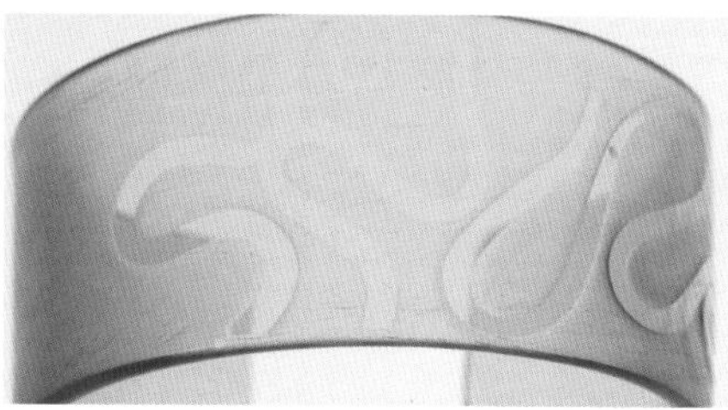

This versatile technique allows textures to be used in conjunction with thermoforming the acrylic into a three-dimensional shape. The contrast between matt and shiny surfaces is very effective on transparent acrylic.

METHOD

1 Soften the acrylic in a kiln or oven heated to 180°C (355°F). Impress a texture into the surface of the plastic sheet, using a heavy steel weight. If heated now, the pattern will disappear and the acrylic will return to a flat sheet. To prevent this from happening, and to create a raised texture, a portion of the surface of the sheet must be removed.
2 Rub the surface with 320-grade and then 600 wet-and-dry paper, using plenty of water and rinsing in between grades; you can continue on up through the grades of paper to the finest and then polish, if you like. The more surface that is taken off before reheating, the further the pattern will stand out.
3 Now reheat the acrylic – the indented areas will rise up to their original position because the plastic has a memory, and they should be shiny since they were not touched by the abrasive paper. This second heating can also be used to shape the acrylic.

## MOULD-MAKING
### Impression

Flat-backed objects or textures with no undercuts can be used to make simple open moulds. There are different types of two-part silicone putty available, some mix at a ratio of one-to-one, others at one-to-twenty, so make sure you check before starting to mix.

METHOD

1 Mix up a suitable amount of silicone to make a 1 mm ($\frac{1}{32}$ inch) layer over the surface of the object. Manipulate the putty in your hands until it has an even colour and consistency.
2 Ensure that the object is clean and lay it face up on a smooth surface. Press the putty over the surface of the object, ensuring that it makes good contact. After about 10 minutes the silicone will set and the object can be removed from the mould.
3 The mould is now ready to be cast into using wax, plaster, speciality resins or low-melting metals. The application of a release agent to the mould before casting will often make it easier to remove the cast object from the mould. (See pages 106–108.)

MOULD-MAKING
## Silicone

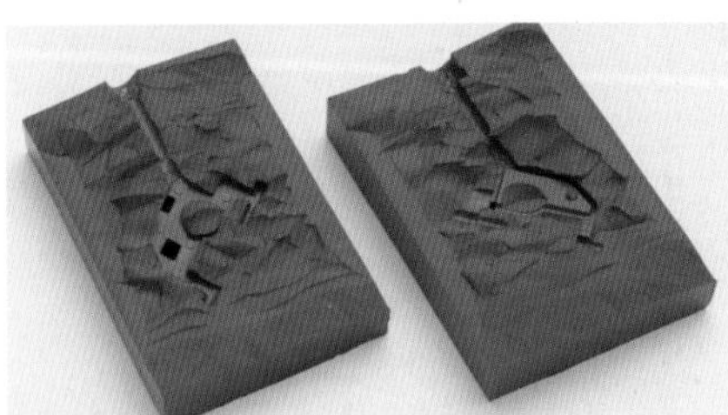

Silicone is an ideal material for cold-formed moulds and is flexible enough to allow for undercuts and complex three-dimensional objects. Casts can be easily taken from organic objects such as fresh plant material, but it is necessary to consider how easily the resulting cast can be removed from the mould.

### METHOD

1 Select the appropriate type of silicone for the object you are taking a cast from – an object with large undercuts and deep detail will need a mould made from very flexible silicone so that the casts can be easily removed; a simple shape with little or no surface decoration will be easier to remove from a mould, and so a less flexible rubber can be used to make the mould.

2 Prepare the object you are taking the cast from by applying a sprue to one end, made either from wax or plasticine.

3 Make a frame with dimensions large enough to contain the object, but not so big that an unnecessary amount of silicone will be used. The frame can be made from foam board (for small objects) or folded aluminium sheet sealed onto a base. Seal the mould thoroughly around every edge with molten wax – leaks are an expensive waste. Secure the sprue onto the base of the frame and spray the inner surfaces with a release agent.

4 Check the information sheet of the silicone for the percentage of catalyst that needs to be added (often five per cent by weight). Place an empty plastic cup on electronic scales, set the weight to zero and weigh out the required amount of silicone. Add the correct weight of catalyst for the amount of silicone and mix the two parts together until the colour of the mixture is even. At this stage, the mixture should be degassed in a vacuum chamber, which will remove air. If this is not possible, take greater care when mixing up the solution so as not to create air bubbles.

5 Pour the silicone mixture down one inside surface of the frame while tilting it – but not over the object. Allow the level of the silicone in the mould to rise up, covering the object as it goes, until it reaches the top of the frame. Tap the frame to release any air bubbles clinging to the object, and allow the silicone to cure for 24 hours.

6 Remove the frame from around the silicone and locate the sprue. Use a sharp craft knife to cut the silicone on opposite sides of the sprue, as if you were going to cut it in half, until you have cut deep enough to remove the object and the sprue. The mould is ready, and multiple casts can be taken.

MOULD-MAKING

## Polymorph

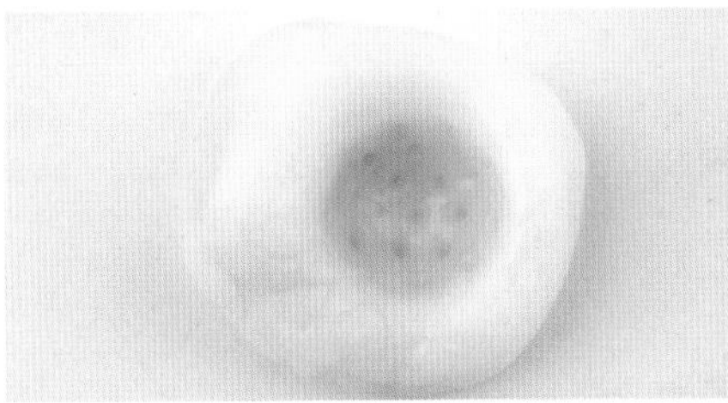

Many 'smart' materials that have been produced for industrial applications are well worth investigating. Polymorph is thermoplastic polymer that has a low melting point and can be moulded at room temperature. Its applications are not limited to making moulds, since useful components or models can be also made – but bear in mind polymorph's physical limitations.

### METHOD

1 Pour polymorph granules into a heatproof container and add hot water from a kettle. The granules change from white to clear at 62°C (143°F) and will begin to stick together.

2 Remove the polymorph mass from the hot water with plastic tongs, and squeeze it to force out any air or water trapped within. The putty-like polymorph can now be pressed over an object that doesn't have undercuts, and left to cool – the material will turn white again. Remove the object from the mould.

3 The mould is suitable for use with plaster, resins and silicone. If the resultant casting proves difficult to remove from the mould, then put the whole piece in hot water until the polymorph becomes flexible again and peel off the mould. The use of a release agent is also advised.

**TIP:** Polymorph can be reused many times.

CASTING

## Silicone

Silicone is an interesting material to use for jewellery but is limited by its material properties. Casting the material into an open or two-part mould will give the best results, since the only other way the rubber can be worked is by cutting it, but this often looks untidy on anything other than flat sheet.

### METHOD

1 Experiment with the materials you are casting the silicone into – most rigid plastics will work well, as will metal, though it may cause discoloration. Apply a release agent to the surface of the mould so that the cast can be removed easily.

2 Check the information sheet of the silicone for the percentage of catalyst that needs to be added (often five per cent by weight). Place an empty plastic cup on electronic scales, set the weight to zero, and weigh out the required amount of silicone. Add the correct amount of catalyst for the amount of silicone and mix the two parts together until the colour of the mixture is even. At this stage, the mixture should be degassed in a vacuum chamber, which will remove air. If this is not possible, take greater care when mixing up the solution so as not to create air bubbles.

3 Pour the silicone mixture slowly into the tilted mould, concentrating on one edge and allowing the silicone to cover the inside of the mould. Once the level of the silicone has reached the desired level, tap the mould firmly to release any air bubbles and allow the silicone to cure for 24 hours. The cast can then be removed from the mould.

CASTING
## Resin

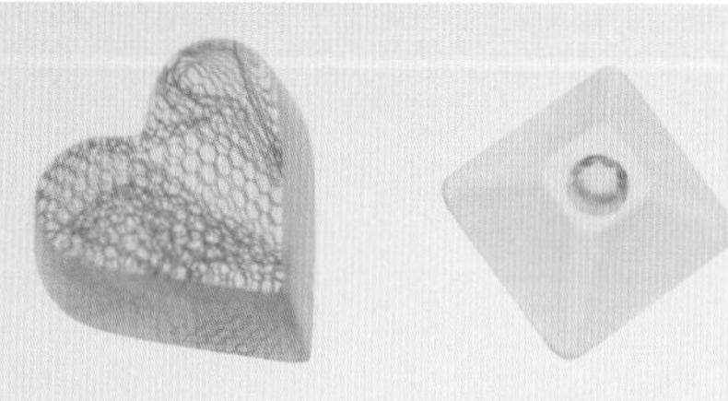

Polyester resin is available in a number of varieties, from general-purpose to clear-casting. The type of resin you choose will depend upon the results you want; for jewellery, clear-casting resin that is built up in thin layers is often the most suitable choice. Ice-cube trays make useful moulds for small pieces, but some types of plastic mould may react badly to the heat that is given off by the resin when it has been mixed with the catalyst. Not all types of resin are suitable for use with silicone moulds.

METHOD

1 Clear-casting polyester resin, which comes in liquid form, is mixed with two per cent MEPK catalyst; 100 ml (3.5 fluid ounces) of resin will need 2 ml (0.07 fluid ounces) of catalyst.
2 When the two liquids are mixed, they will start to solidify and will be jelly-like after about 15 minutes, but this will depend on the ambient temperature. Pour the required amount of resin into a plastic measuring cup and add the correct amount of catalyst with a pipette (or chemical dropper). Use a plastic spoon to mix the resin and catalyst slowly, trying not to create air bubbles. The mould needs to have a very thin layer of petroleum jelly or a release agent applied, which will allow the resin to be removed more easily once it has set.
3 Carefully pour the resin into the mould, with the aid of a plastic spoon or pipette if necessary. The layer should not be more than 15 mm (⅝ inch) thick; if a deeper cast is needed, the resin should be added in layers to minimize shrinking. Wait until the first layer has turned to jelly before you add the second. Layering is not always viable when making small objects, because it is difficult to mix small amounts of resin accurately, so prepare a number of moulds to cast into, or use a design where shrinkage won't affect the final outcome.
4 Tap the mould to release any trapped air bubbles – any bubbles sitting on the surface will need to be dragged out with a pin. The resin will be set after 24 hours; any air bubbles should be filled with more resin before cleaning up the piece. (See page 186.)

**Sample** *Resin forms made in an ice-cube tray.*

NOTE: Never be tempted to do resin work indoors without proper ventilation. For safety, always work in a well-ventilated area. It is possible to work outside, but you must wear a mask specifically designed for chemical fumes and vapours – dust masks will not protect you.

*See step 1*

**KEY**  Acrylic  Polypropylene  Nylon  Resin  Silicone  Neoprene Polyurethane  Thermoplastic polymer

CASTING
## Embedded Objects

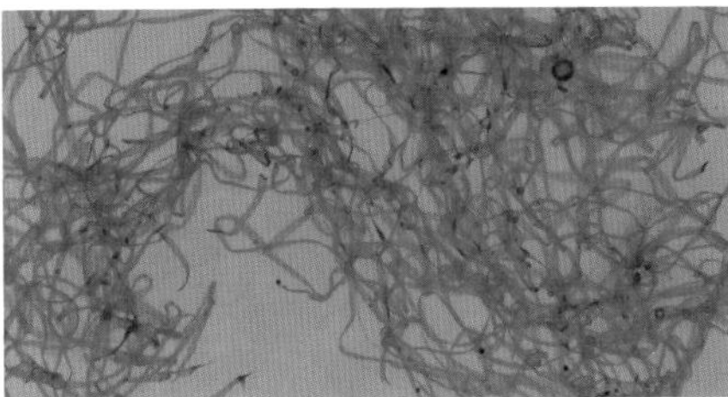

Clear-casting resin or crystal-clear resin will produce the best results when embedding objects. Dyes, powders and metal leaf can also be used with these types of resin, so different-coloured backgrounds or areas can be created within a design. Any organic objects you use should be dried, since fresh material can rot, even when encased in resin.

METHOD

1 Mix up enough resin for a thin layer on the base of the mould and pour it into the prepared mould. Allow it to set. Ensure that the mould you are using is large enough to hold the object you will be embedding without it protruding above the surface.

2 Resin affects materials in different ways. Some types of paper absorb the resin and become almost transparent, leaving the images looking as if they are floating. Highly textured objects can trap air around them and will look 'silvery' – this can be prevented by painting the object with clear varnish before embedding it in resin.

3 Place your object in position and add another layer of resin mixed with catalyst. If your object sinks, then the mould can be filled to the top and allowed to set – the object will be held in the middle. A floating object will be damaged during the cleaning-up process, so keep the second layer thin and wait for it to set before topping up the mould.

4 Let the piece set for 24 hours before removing it from the mould and cleaning it up.

CASTING
## Dyes

Special dyes for resin are available in both transparent and opaque forms and in a range of colours. Dyes can be mixed to create varying shades and subtle tones – the amount of dye used determines the intensity of the colour. Be aware that some resin dyes contain lead and therefore extra precautions must be taken when mixing the resin and when cleaning up the finished piece.

METHOD

1 Pour the required amount of resin into a plastic measuring cup and add the correct amount of catalyst with a pipette. Use a plastic spoon to mix the resin and catalyst slowly, trying not to create air bubbles.

2 At this stage the dye should be added; only a small amount needs to be used, since it is very concentrated. If more than five per cent of the mixture is dye, it will inhibit the setting process and the resin will take much longer to harden. Mix the dye into the resin with a plastic spoon, again taking care not to create air bubbles, until the dye is evenly distributed. If the colour is too weak, add more dye and mix until the liquid is a uniform shade.

3 Carefully pour the resin into the mould, with the aid of a plastic spoon or pipette if necessary, and allow it to set for more than 24 hours before removing it from the mould and cleaning it up.

CASTING
## Marbled Colours

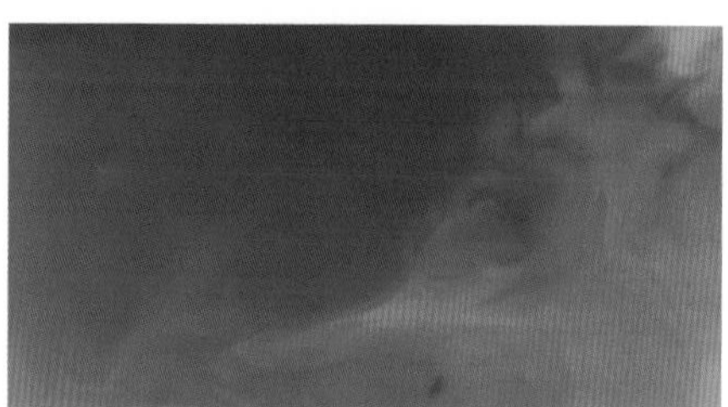

Subtle colour variations can be created within a piece by marbling dyed resins. You may need to experiment, since some colours have a tendency to bleed into others. Transparent and opaque dyes can be used within the same piece for stunning effect.

METHOD

1 Mix up a suitable amount of resin with catalyst, and pour half of it into a separate plastic container.

2 Add a different-coloured dye to each container and stir gently. The colours do not need to be mixed until uniform, since this will add visual interest to the effect, but you should ensure that no concentrated areas of dye are left.

3 Half fill the prepared mould with one colour of resin then add the second colour, swirling it into the first with a plastic spoon or cocktail stirrer. Coloured resins can also be mixed into clear resin, which can help to give depth to a piece of jewellery.

CASTING
## Metallic Powders

Glitter mixed with resin has a tendency to sink, but the tiny particles of metallic powders remain suspended in solution until the resin hardens, producing a subtly reflective material. Powders can be used to create solid blocks of colour, or 'highlight' powders can be used to make iridescent resin pieces. The powders can be combined with dyed resins for an even greater number of colour combinations.

METHOD

1 Mix an appropriate amount of resin for the size of mould you will be using (see page 178). Add a small amount of metallic powder to the liquid plastic with a plastic spoon.

2 Stir the mixture carefully – any lumps of powder are likely to contain air and will need to be broken up to ensure a uniform result. If the effect is not intense enough, more powder can be added, but it should not make up more than five per cent of the total mixture. Different colours of powders can be marbled together or layered up with clear resin to create different effects.

3 The addition of metallic powders may increase the time that it takes for the resin to set, but it should still be fully cured after 24 hours.

CASTING
## Metal Leaf

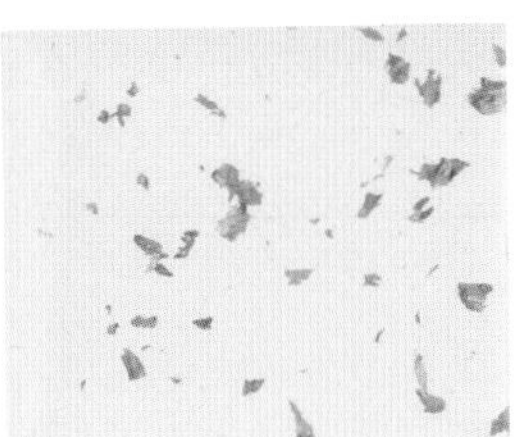

Gold leaf can be used to add glamour to resin, creating glints of precious metal within a non-precious material. Getting the fragile leaf into position in a viscous and sticky liquid can be a challenge, but the results are well worth it.

### METHOD

1. Mix the clear-casting resin with two per cent of catalyst by weight or volume in a plastic measuring cup. Pour the resin into a prepared mould, filling it to about one-third of its depth, then allow it to set.
2. Cut small pieces of metal leaf in a folded piece of tracing paper, or tear off bits of foil for a less uniform effect. Larger pieces of leaf can be used but have a tendency to trap air, which can cause problems when cleaning the piece. Silver leaf will become discoloured within the resin after a few months, but gold leaf and coloured aluminium leaf will not and are a better choice for this application.
3. The leaf can be applied to the resin either by sticking it to the tacky surface of the initial resin layer then adding an additional layer; or by adding another layer of resin and immediately adding the metal leaf, pushing it under the surface and positioning it with a cocktail stirrer.
4. A final layer of resin should be added once the second layer has set so that none of the leaf is damaged during the cleaning-up process.

CASTING
## Other Materials

Casting resin directly into metal frames is an effective way of combining precious and non-precious materials. Pins or internal devices may need to be soldered onto inside surfaces to hold the resin in position, but they can be hidden if opaque dye is used.

### METHOD

1. The frame to contain the resin should have a flat base so that it can be placed onto a backing sheet of acrylic that will be removed once the resin has cured. Use petroleum jelly to grease the acrylic before positioning the frame on the backing sheet. Seal the frame in position with plasticine, making sure that there are no gaps for the resin to leak out from. If you have made divisions within the frame for different-coloured areas, then seal off any sections that will not be filled with the first colour.
2. Fill the frame, using a plastic spoon to accurately pour the resin. Frames deeper than 5 mm (⅟32 inch) should be filled with two or more separate layers to minimize shrinkage and stop the resin from coming away from the frame sides. Fill the frame so that the resin is sitting above the top edge of it, without having the surface tension break and the resin spill out.
3. Let the first colour set before removing all traces of plasticine from the frame; reapply the frame to the acrylic base and seal it, then add subsequent colours of resin as required.
4. Let the piece cure for 24 hours before cleaning it.

## FOLDING AND SCORING

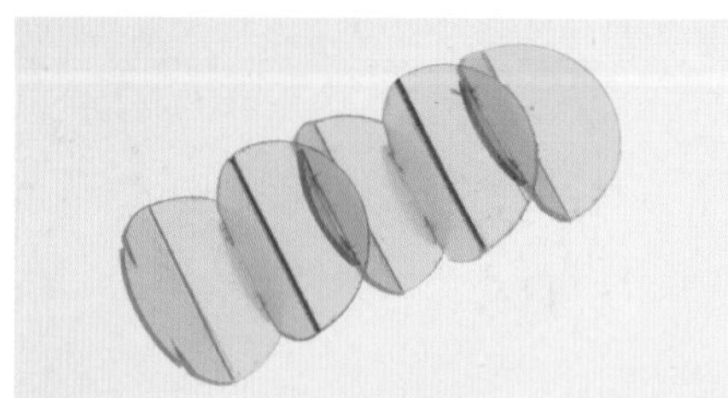

Polypropylene can be scored and folded in a similar way to card, but has greater flexibility and is a much more durable material. Consider cold-joining techniques such as riveting, stapling and gluing; integral tabs and slots can form ingenious constructions.

### METHOD

1. Make a paper model of the design – this will allow you to easily adjust any design flaws and determine where the scored lines will need to be.
2. Work on a self-healing cutting mat and use a sturdy metal ruler as a guide.
3. Score the plastic sheet firmly with a steel scribe, and complete the scoring process before beginning to fold the piece, because it is much easier to work on a flat sheet at this stage.
4. For tight bends or sharp angles, a small amount of plastic may need to be removed in order to allow the bend, so use a scoring tool to remove a triangular sliver from the surface of the polypropylene. This requires good judgement on your part, since removing too much material will lead to the plastic splitting when it is folded.
5. The material can be cut accurately with a sharp craft knife; be aware that it will be much easier to achieve straight lines than curves.

## RIVETING
## Acrylic

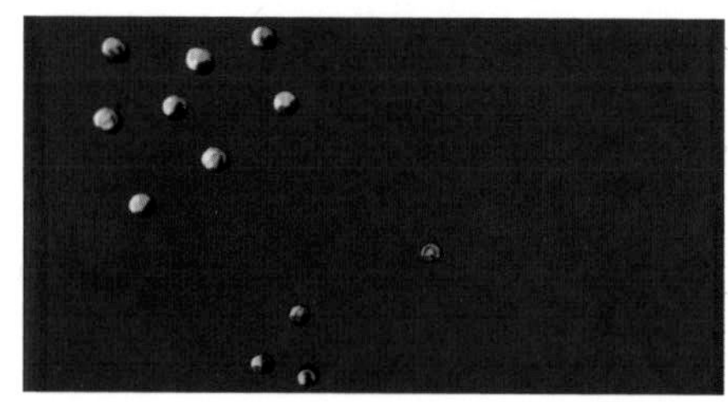

Decorative detail can be added to acrylic by riveting silver or gold wire through drilled holes. Several layers of acrylic can be joined together in this way. Decorative or tube rivets can also be used. This technique is best suited to frosted or opaque acrylic, which is less brittle and will not show the dirt or watermarks that eventually get between the layers.

### METHOD

1. Drill holes of the same diameter as the wire you will be using, and countersink both sides of each hole with a ball burr.
2. Make a rivet head on one end of the wire either by 'balling' it in a flame or while holding it in a vice, by hammering one end to spread it.
3. Push the wire through the hole and cut the end so that about 1 mm (1/32 inch) is left protruding. File the cut end so that it is flat. Working on a steel block, gently hammer the end of the wire so that it spreads to fill the countersunk area and forms another rivet head. Turn the piece over and hammer the rivet, ensuring that the countersink on each side is completely filled. Take care not to hit the plastic with the hammer as it can fracture.
4. The rivet heads can be left rounded or filed flush, then cleaned up with water and wet-and-dry paper and polished.

RIVETING
## Tube Rivets

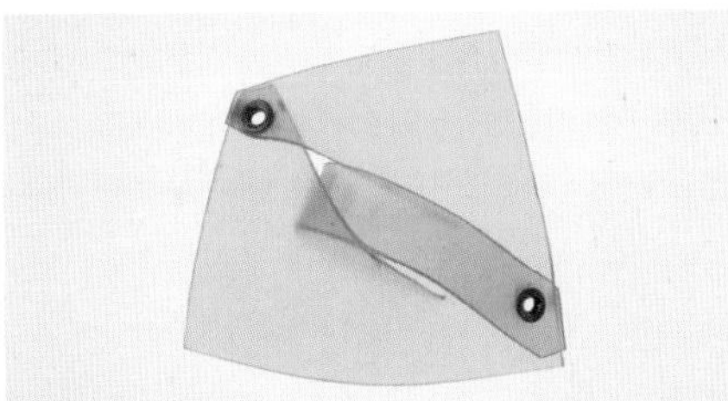

Wire rivets do not have large enough heads to cope with the flexibility of certain materials, but tube rivets provide a more durable method of cold-joining sheet plastics. Staples or metal stitching are also viable – but when using plastics to design jewellery it is a good idea to take the limitations of these materials into account.

METHOD

1 Prepare the silver tube for the tube rivets. Cut sections of tube taking into account the thickness of the material you will be riveting, and leave at least an extra 4 mm (⅛ inch) for the spread of the rivet.
2 Cut slots in the top and bottom surfaces of the tube if you like – this will help the rivet to spread more easily.
3 Anneal, pickle, clean and polish the sections of the tube.
4 Use a hole punch to make holes in the polypropylene that are the same size as the outside diameter of the tube.
5 Working on a steel block, open up one end of a tube rivet using a small doming punch and a mallet.
6 Thread the rivet through the holes in the polypropylene sheet and spread the other side of the rivet in the same way. Working alternately on both sides of the piece, continue to spread the rivet a little at a time until it lies flat against the surface of the plastic.

RIVETING
## Washers

Decorative metal washers offer versatility when cold-joining soft materials. Sandwiching rubber between layers of metal will keep it from stretching or slipping free. Many decorative techniques can be applied to metal washers, allowing a wide range of design options.

METHOD

1 Make washers according to your design – they can be circles stamped out of silver sheet, cast items or pierced shapes. The washers need to be large enough to trap enough of the plastic or rubber sheet so that it can't slip free. Wire rivets and tube rivets will both work well, provided that the diameter of the washers is large enough.
2 Drill a hole through washers of the same diameter as either the wire or the tube you will be using, and countersink the outsides of the holes.
3 Prepare the rivets by making a head on a wire rivet, or annealing pieces of tube cut to length.
4 Use a hole punch to make a slightly smaller hole in the sheet than is required for the tube rivets; wire rivets can be pushed through if the end is filed to form a point.
5 Working on a steel surface, hammer the rivet so that it is level with the washer. Turn the piece over and hammer the other side, taking care not to damage the surface of the washer. The rivet head can be left rounded or filed flush.

## LASER CUTTING

Laser-cut designs are a useful way of cutting multiple components but may only prove cost-effective for large numbers. Intricately pierced shapes can be produced easily, so consider cold-joining techniques when designing.

### METHOD

1 Supply the laser-cutting company with a computer-generated image file of your design. The design should be created in a vector-based software program such as Adobe® Illustrator® or CorelDRAW®, which will make it easier for the computer to translate. You will be charged for the time it takes to convert other file types or original artwork into the correct format.
2 When creating your jewellery concept, make the design at least twice the size you want the final result to be, and shrink the image to the correct size before sending it – this way your lines or shapes will be much crisper.

## NYLON THREAD

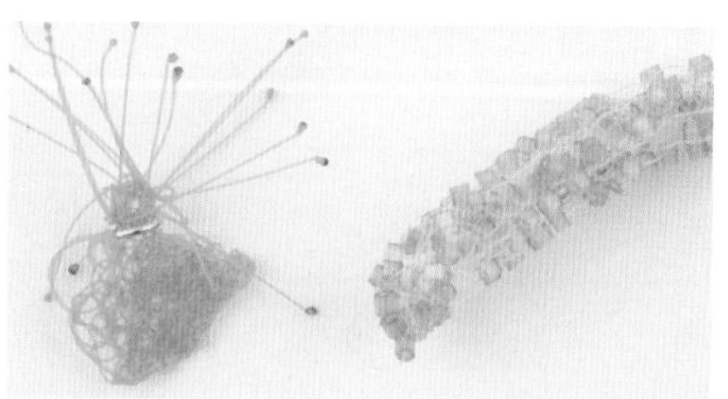

Nylon thread has a number of useful properties: it is very strong even when thin, and it can be dyed, but it is generally chemically resistant. The flexibility of nylon means that although it can be manoeuvred into tightly packed configurations, it has a memory and will try to straighten itself, and therefore will create structural three-dimensional forms.

### METHOD

1 Nylon can be knitted or crocheted in the same way as other threads, but care needs to be taken so that it doesn't unravel while it is being worked on. Wonderfully tactile net can be created in this way.
2 Secure the ends by tying a knot and then applying a flame close to the end so that it forms a ball, much in the same way as metal wire will (see page 76); this will prevent the knot from coming undone.

**KEY**        

## PLASTIC TUBING AND ROD FITTINGS

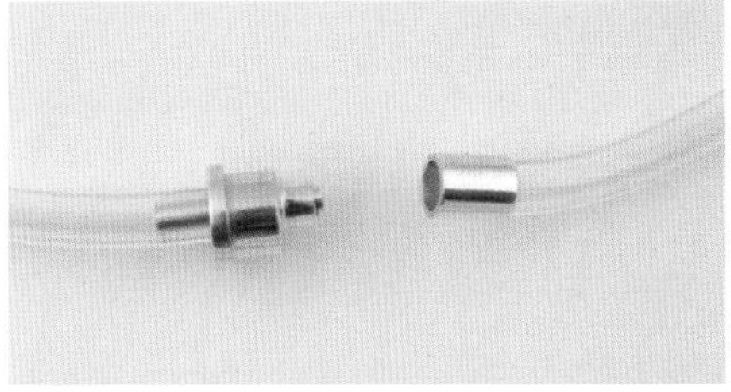

Flexible plastic tubing is a useful material, but joining or finishing the ends satisfactorily is a challenge. Capping the ends with tube, or inserting rods of the same diameter as the inside hole of the tube is one answer, and a range of glues and cements can be used to permanently attach the fixtures.

### METHOD

1 Use a piece of rod (acrylic, silver or brass, for example) of the same diameter as the inside diameter of the tubing and apply a little glue before twisting the tube over the rod. The glue you use needs to be flexible in order to account for movement of the plastic, and also transparent so that it is not obvious. Superglue is too brittle for this. There are ultraviolet reactive glues on the market, however, which will set when placed in sunlight or under an ultraviolet lamp, and these usually dry crystal-clear.

2 To cap the ends of plastic tubing you will need a metal tube that is of the same diameter as the outside diameter of the plastic tubing. Glue it into position and let it set for the required amount of time; the glue needs to be flexible but not necessarily transparent.

3 A very strong bond can be created by applying a rod to the inside of the plastic tubing with glue, and slipping a section of metal tube over the join – again, with glue.

## SANDBLASTING

Sandblasting the surface of hard plastics gives a finely frosted texture. This finish is susceptible to dirt and grease from skin, however, and should not be used for areas of a piece of jewellery that will come into contact with the body. Eventually, the surface will become shiny from use.

### METHOD

1 Mask off any areas that you do not want to be sandblasted with masking tape. Be sure that the pressure of the machine is set at the correct level, and turn on the air pump if greater pressure is required.

2 Position the piece under the nozzle of the sandblaster, and move the piece around as you fire the sand, until the whole area has been frosted evenly. A graded effect can be achieved by holding the work at an angle under the nozzle so that the sand hits the uppermost areas of the piece at a greater force than areas further away.

## POLISHING AND CLEANING UP

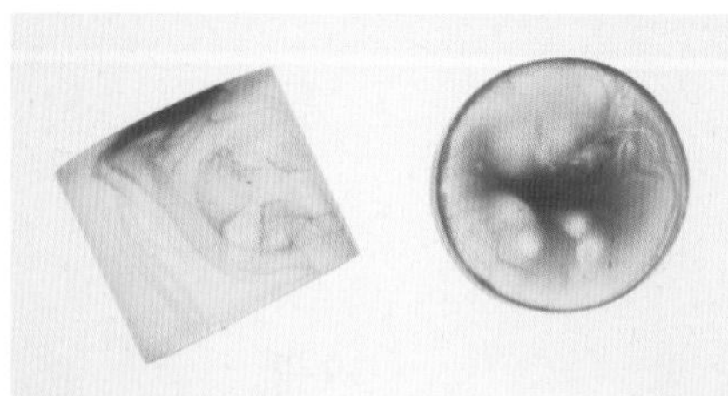

Cast resin requires careful cleaning before it can be polished or have other finishes applied. This is because the top surface will always remain tacky unless it is cleaned, and if the piece has been cast in a silicone mould, all the outside surfaces may need to be treated. Resin dissolves in acetone, so unwanted areas can be soaked away.

### METHOD

1. To remove the sticky surface residue on resin, soak the whole object in warm water and detergent for about 10 minutes or until the surface becomes milky white. This can then be scraped off.
2. Starting with 320-grade wet-and-dry paper, rub down the flat surfaces of the resin piece, using plenty of water and working on a flat surface. Ensure that any sticky surfaces have been removed before rinsing the piece and moving onto the next grade of paper, because any stray piece of coarse grit will mark the surface. The use of water during this process prevents toxic resin dust from being released into the air and also stops the wet-and-dry paper from clogging up.
3. File the piece to shape it; use an old metal file and wear a mask. It's a good idea to design castings to minimize the amount of filing required.
4. Work through the grades of paper up to 1200. The longer you spend removing the scratches from the surface, the better the surface finish will be. Any scratches remaining need to be worked out with a rougher paper before continuing with finer papers. The surface of the resin should have a fine, matt finish at this stage.
5. Resin can be polished on a polishing motor with a clean, soft mop with a grease-free, light-coloured plastic polish such as Vonax. Pendant-motor mops may not give satisfactory results, however, and if no polishing motor is available, apply a liquid plastic polish with a soft cloth and buff the piece until a good sheen is acquired.

*See step 1*

**KEY** Acrylic · Polypropylene · Nylon · Resin · Silicone · Neoprene · Polyurethane · Thermoplastic polymer

## MATT SURFACE

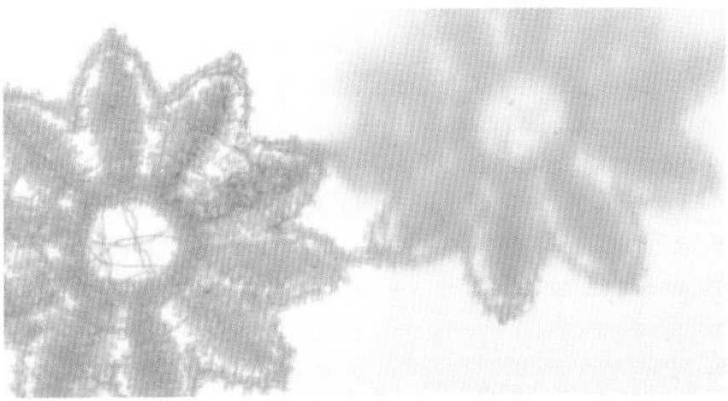

The play of light within jewellery pieces with a matt surface produces interesting results. Objects embedded in resin become slightly blurred and indistinct, and striking contrasts can be created.

### METHOD

1 Prepare the surface of the piece as you would for polishing, with wet-and-dry paper applied either in even strokes or in a circular motion. The surface can be left fine at this stage.
2 Give the surface a subtle gleam by rubbing it with water, detergent and fine wire wool or a scourer.
3 To achieve a perfectly uniform and nicely smoothed finish, tumble your piece in a barrel polisher for several hours with an abrasive barrelling medium such as grit-impregnated plastic or ceramic chips. The grade of the abrasive will determine the degree of smoothing of the form and the fineness of the finish.

## POLISHING

Plastics are relatively soft. This causes them to become scratched easily, but on the other hand, they polish quickly too. Transparent or translucent materials should be well prepared since any blemishes will be obvious once they are polished.

### METHOD

1 Remove file marks from shaping the acrylic with a fine file. Use wet-and-dry paper to round-off edges. Use plenty of water and remember to rinse the piece in between grades of paper. Work through the grades of paper up to the finest, 1200, then dry.
2 Check for any remaining scratches before polishing the piece.
3 Apply a grease-free, light-coloured plastic polish such as Vonax on a clean soft mop. While polishing the piece it is important to keep it moving continually so that there is no chance for heat to build up. Friction produced by the mop will cause the plastic to melt and smear, which will then have to be corrected with wet-and-dry paper before continuing with the polishing process. For this reason, pendant-motor mops will not give good results – the radius of the mop is so small that it causes a very fast build-up of heat, and it is difficult to achieve a uniformly polished surface.

5

# Other Media

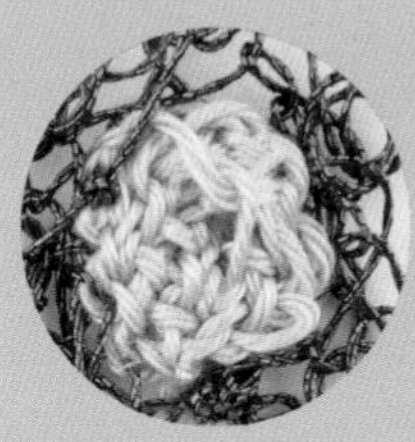
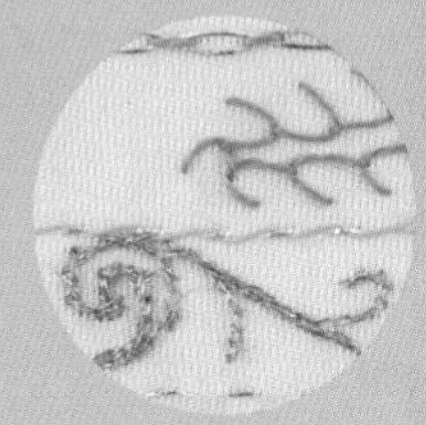

**Other Media**
pages 190–203
Cement, slate, plaster, ceramics, porcelain, glass, paper, textiles, electronic components

# Other Media

The techniques described in this section are just the tip of the iceberg. Each of the materials has particular craft practices associated with it. Do not be afraid of experimenting with or trying out new materials; they can open up a world of possibilities.

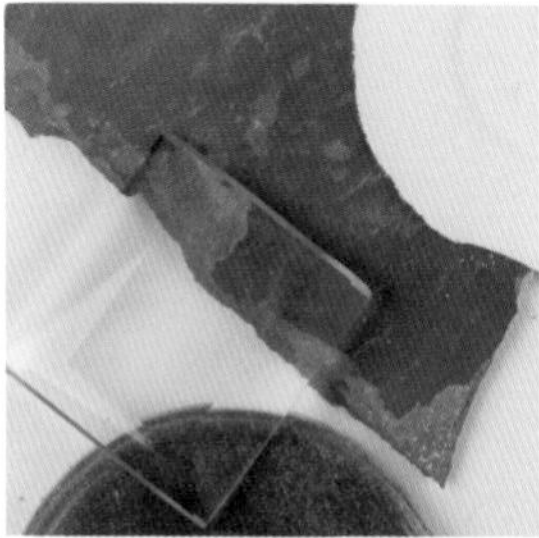

**APPLICATIONS**

With the exception of plaster, these materials are durable, water-resistant and can be used for any type of jewellery form. The main design consideration is likely to be their excessive weight – so pieces formed with these materials need to be designed on a small scale.

Many of these materials require professional knowledge and equipment, but once you learn the basics, you can overcome some of the potential difficulties. Try looking to other crafts and the manufacturing industry for suggestions. Suppliers of sculptors' materials stock many of the media described below; and found objects can provide an interesting starting point.

## CEMENT FONDUE

**Composition:** Calcium aluminate cement with aggregate (glass fibre, sand)

A type of cement, also known as 'ciment fondue', available in white or grey, that is finer in texture than standard Portland cement and will therefore cast very fine detail from a mould. Limited in its applications, but a very hard and durable material.

## CERAMICS

**Composition:** Phyllosilicate clay with minerals; kaolin

Any type of clay can be used to make components suitable for jewellery, but kaolin, a soft white clay used in the manufacture of porcelain, is the one used most due to its fineness and almost precious quality. It can be slip-cast to create hollow, thin-walled forms that are light in weight and very tactile. Porcelain is often left unglazed and then it is called 'bisque'.

## GLASS

**Composition:** Silica

The addition of boron during the manufacturing process renders Pyrex glass more durable and heat-resistant; this type of glass may be more suitable for certain jewellery projects. Glass is also often used in jewellery-making projects due to its superb optical properties, such as focusing rays of light. Actually, many techniques can be applied when working with glass.

## SLATE

**Composition:** Metamorphic rock – quartz with various embedded minerals

Stone that can be pierced or water-cut. Due to its structure, slate has a tendency to fracture, but it has an advantage: its ability to provide wonderful colour contrast when combined with precious metals.

## PLASTER

**Composition:** Gypsum

There are many types of plaster, but plaster of Paris is the one most commonly used for making open or two-part moulds. When plaster powder is mixed with water, it sets to form a solid mass. Special dental plasters will produce a much harder, denser material that very fine detail can be carved into.

## POLYMER CLAY

**Composition:** Synthetic plastic compound

A versatile modelling compound, useful for model-making and for finished pieces for occasional wear. Available in a wide range of colours and effects that can be combined. Polymer clay is baked in an oven to harden it.

△ INVENTARIUM NECKLACE
BY KATJA PRINS
*Cast and glazed porcelain elements have been combined with distressed silver forms, providing a subtle contrast of materials.*

▽ GLASS BROOCH
BY KATHRYN BONE
*Kiln-cast glass was sandblasted, ground and polished. The piece is worn with a silver pin that was lathe-turned.*

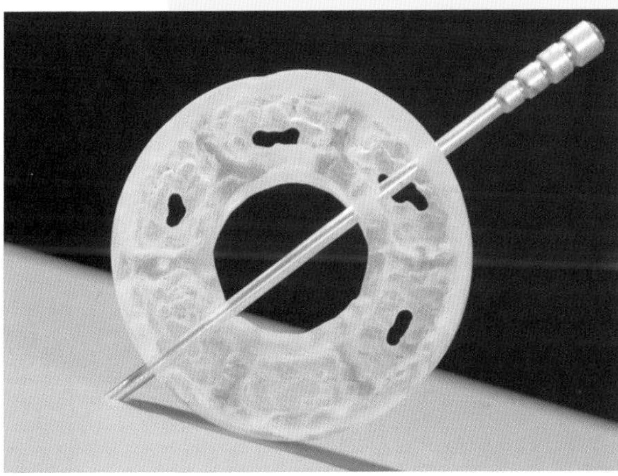

These materials are all relatively cheap and easy to use and should be experimented with to explore any possibilities the materials will allow. There is no right or wrong way to apply these materials and techniques when making jewellery.

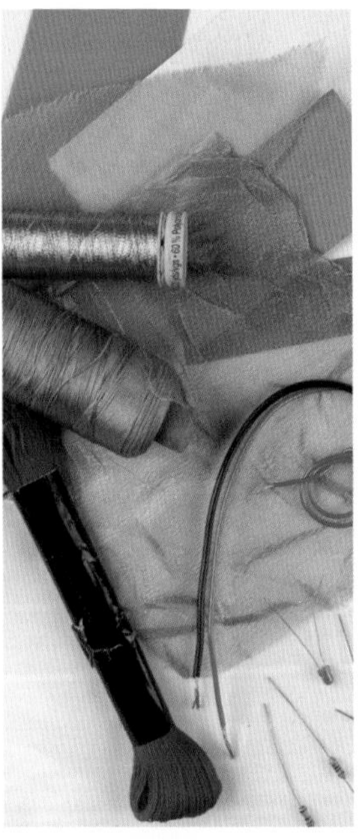

**APPLICATIONS**
Bear in mind specific considerations for each type of material when designing jewellery. Textiles, paper and electronic components are likely to suffer water damage, making them unsuitable for rings worn on the fingers.

## TEXTILES

**Composition:** Natural or synthetic fibres

Textiles can exhibit many properties, and something suitable can be found for any specific design requirement: either a single thread, or a woven, structural or printed fabric. Many techniques can be used with textiles, including some that are traditional as well as others borrowed from other disciplines.

## PAPER

**Composition:** Cellulose fibres from softwood pulp; may contain synthetic fibres

There are many types of paper with different properties that can be used to make delicate detail or construct structural forms in jewellery. Paper can be cut, folded, torn, layered or combined with almost any other material by cold-joining techniques.

## ELECTRONIC COMPONENTS

**Composition:** Various materials

Simple electronic circuits can be constructed to add sound, light or movement to pieces of jewellery. Designs will need to address incorporation of the power supply and the wearability and operability of the piece.

## MAGNETS

**Composition:** Natural magnetite or magnetized material such as steel

Commercial use of magnets in the jewellery industry is limited to fastenings and closures, usually for bracelets and necklaces. Magnetic beads are also available. Strongly magnetic components provide scope for experimentation.

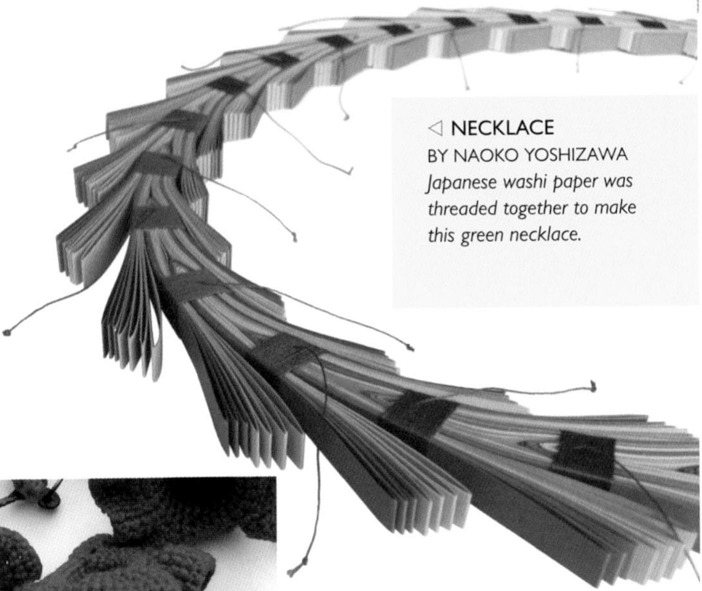

◁ **NECKLACE**
BY NAOKO YOSHIZAWA
*Japanese washi paper was threaded together to make this green necklace.*

◁ **BIG RED NECKPIECE**
BY JOANNE HAYWOOD
*These red crocheted textiles are combined with oxidized and fused silver wire, creating a contrast of colour and texture.*

▷ **ROOF DOME**
BY TAKAFUMI INUZUKA
*The pierced holes in this sculptural piece create light effects on the plastic sheet that surrounds it, with clever use of electronics and LEDs.*

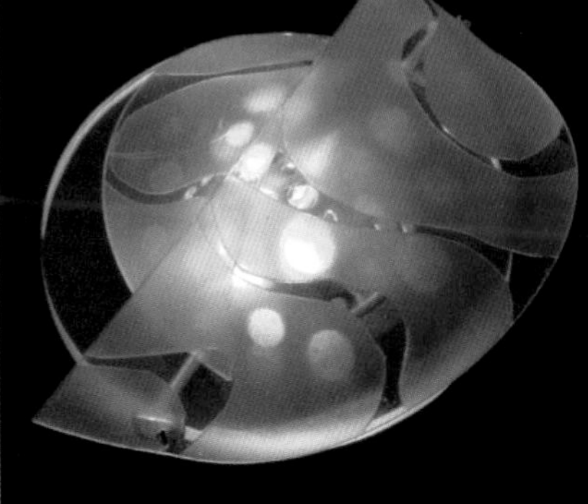

CASTING
## Cement Fondue

Cement fondue is a concrete-like substance ideal for making hard and durable forms. It can be cast solid or layered with cut fibreglass matting to make strong, hollow shapes and have objects embedded in the surface. Always wear gloves when working with this material.

METHOD

1 Use one part cement fondue to three parts soft sand or other fine aggregate, and mix well in a bowl. Add enough water to make a firm but moist consistency – when the dough is squeezed, water should appear.
2 Press the cement fondue into an open mould that has been treated with a release agent, and trim any excess from around the edges of the mould with a knife. The cement should be of an even thickness.
3 Wrap the mould in a damp cloth and leave to cure for 24 hours before removing the piece. The texture on the inside of the mould will directly affect the surface of the piece of cement fondue – a shiny mould will give a smooth surface. Plaster moulds may transfer a white bloom to the surface.

**Sample** *Cement fondue was cast into a shiny plastic mould with stone inclusions.*

PIERCING
## Slate

Although slate is a metamorphic rock, there are a number of techniques that can be applied to it. The nature of the rock means that it is brittle and prone to flaking, so it may not be suitable for some jewellery forms.

METHOD

1 Work out your design on paper and stick it to the slate with double-sided sticky tape, or use a scribe to draw directly onto the slate.
2 Use a fine saw blade (3/0 or 4/0) in the saw frame – a rougher saw blade will chip as it cuts – and make sure the tension of the blade is tight. To pierce a curve, as you move the saw frame up and down, turn the slate into the path of the blade. The faster the slate is turned, the tighter the curve will be. It is important to work slowly and keep the blade absolutely vertical so that it will not break when turning corners. The saw blade will get blunt quickly, but unfortunately, since slate is porous, it is not advisable to use any lubricant since it may be absorbed and cause a stain. Wear a mask so that you don't inhale any of the dust produced.
3 Remove saw marks with needle files – try to match the profile of the curve with the file. File the outer surfaces of curves with a flat-faced file.
4 Clean up the edges with emery paper and apply microcrystalline wax polish to seal the surface.

## MOULD-MAKING
### Plaster

Many materials can be cast into moulds, including glass, silicone, wax, resin and plaster. Avoid undercuts in the cast form or the mould will have to be broken to remove the piece.

METHOD

1 Prepare the form from which you will be casting – plasticine is an ideal material to use. Unfired clay can be used if more definition is required, and should be greased with petroleum jelly to help remove it from the mould.
2 For an open mould, place the flat-bottomed form in the base of a plastic container that has walls higher than the top of the form. Seal the edges of the form to the base to prevent leakage.
3 Place enough water in a flexible mixing bowl to fill the plastic container. Sprinkle plaster powder onto the surface of the water and allow it to settle before adding more. Keep sprinkling until the plaster begins to sit on the surface. Slowly mix the solution by hand, making sure that any lumps are dissolved.
4 Pour the mixture down one side of the plastic container and allow the mixture to cover the form you are casting, up to the top of the container wall, tapping the mould to release any trapped air bubbles. Never pour wet plaster down the sink. Allow the plaster to set before releasing it from the mould and removing the plasticine form.
5 Further details can be carved into the plaster once it is dry, but take care not to create undercuts.

**TIP:** The plaster mould should be sealed before use – apply diluted soft soap until water runs off the surface.

## HAND-FORMING
### Ceramics

Hand-forming is the basic process of modelling clay with your hands or simple tools to create forms that can be fired at high temperatures in a kiln to make robust and durable pieces. The density of ceramics means that small pieces are more suitable for jewellery forms.

METHOD

1 Prepare the clay by kneading it and rolling it out several times to ensure that there are no trapped air pockets, since these will cause the piece to shatter when it is fired in the kiln. Keep the clay damp with a mist spray as you form your pieces, referring to a design or model. To construct a cylindrical form, a spiral coil is made from a long strip of clay and the surfaces are smoothed over with wet fingers or a rubber kidney. The form can be pierced with a pointed tool to make holes, and a vast array of textures may be applied to the surface of the clay.
2 When not working on the clay, keep it tightly wrapped in plastic to retain the moisture.
3 The finished form must be left to slowly dry out before it can be fired – different clays require different firing temperatures, and ideally the kiln that is being used will have a 'ramping' programme that will allow controlled temperature changes during the firing process.

## CARVING
### Porcelain

Porcelain is a very fine-textured clay, often left unglazed after firing. Once formed, porcelain 'blanks' can be left to dry to a leathery state, and can then be easily carved with fine detail.

METHOD

1 Prepare the porcelain clay by kneading it and rolling it out several times.
2 Make the piece that will be carved, keeping the form simple – it needs to be able to support itself while it is being carved.
3 Allow the clay to dry out a bit, so that it is leathery but still flexible. It is now possible to carve the porcelain with fine detail with engraving or linoleum-cutting tools, or similar implements. Low-relief designs will work best in this medium. As you are working, do not allow the clay to dry out too much; otherwise, it will become brittle and may fracture.
4 Once the carving is complete, the finished form must be left to dry out completely before it can be fired – ideally the kiln that is being used will have a 'ramping' programme that will allow controlled temperature changes during the firing process.

## SLIP-CASTING
### Porcelain

Thin, hollow forms can be made by slip-casting a slurry of porcelain clay into a plaster mould. A shell of porcelain is formed that, once fired, can be used for larger components in jewellery because it is hollow.

METHOD

1 Mix some porcelain clay with water until it is a smooth consistency but not too thin. Have a prepared plaster mould ready for use – to make hollow forms, you will need a two-part mould that has no undercuts in the form.
2 Pour the porcelain slurry into the opening of the plaster mould, and swirl it so that the slurry coats the inside surface evenly. Pour out the excess slurry. The plaster will quickly suck the water out of the slurry, in effect drying the porcelain clay.
3 Repeat the coating process until the piece is the required thickness. Allow the piece to dry to a leathery state and carefully remove it from the mould. Trim off any flanges left by the mould and refine the surface of the form if necessary.
4 Once the piece is completely dry, it can be fired. Porcelain requires a higher firing temperature than other types of clay.

## SANDBLASTING
### Glass

Sandblasting on glass will create matt, frosted areas, and if designs have been masked off, then these opaque sections will contrast with the untouched, shiny, transparent glass. Numbers and text can be applied easily to glass in this way.

METHOD

1 Mask off any areas of the glass that you don't want to be sandblasted; masking tape, sticky-backed plastic and stickers will all work. Ensure that the tape is well stuck down; any areas that lift up during the sandblasting process will cause 'bleeding', and crisp definition will be lost.
2 Position your piece inside the sandblasting machine, holding it a few centimetres (a couple of inches) below the nozzle.
3 Check to see that the pressure is at the optimum level: compressed air is what fires the sand out of the nozzle at high speed. Close the lid and fire the sand onto the surface, slowly moving the piece so that all areas are blasted. If the piece is angled down, away from the nozzle on one side, the side nearest the nozzle will be blasted more intensely and a fading-out of the texture will occur.
4 Tap off any sand that is left on the surface and carefully remove the masking tape. Any glue residue left by the masking tape can be removed with lighter fluid applied with a cotton bud.

## DRILLING AND GRINDING
### Glass

Diamond-coated tools can be used in a number of ways on glass – to drill holes, grind areas or engrave the surface. It is important that the glass you are working on has been annealed; otherwise the stress of the process could cause it to fracture violently. Always wear goggles when working with glass.

METHOD

1 Diamond-coated drill bits are covered in a thin layer of industrial-grade diamond grit and will cut most materials. To drill glass, position yourself and your work comfortably at the bench, with the glass supported on the bench pin and with a diamond drill bit in the pendant motor. Have a small pot of water handy and dip the tip of the drill bit in it at regular intervals so that the hole is always wet. Drilling glass requires time and concentration.
2 Do not apply too much pressure, and keep the drill bit at the correct angle since any movement or slips may cause the glass to chip or the drill bit to break – and they are not cheap. For larger-diameter holes, start with a 1 mm (1⁄32 inch) diamond drill bit and work up to a 2 mm (1⁄16 inch) bit using several sizes in between so that the diameter of the hole is gradually increased. A diamond-coated ball burr can be used to bevel the edges of the drilled hole to prevent chipping.
3 Shaped diamond-coated burrs can be used to grind designs into the surface of glass, and diamond grinding pads (Diagrit) may be used for shaping pieces – always use them with water as a lubricant.

## BLOWN GLASS

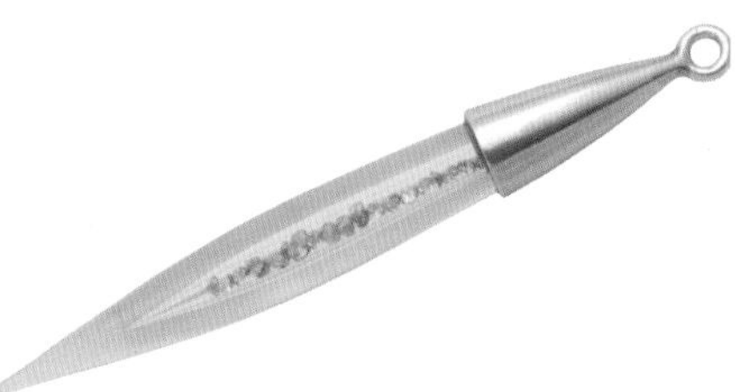

Inflated bubbles can be made from glass – where the molten glass comes into contact with air, it will harden and form a skin, but the glass inside the skin remains fluid, allowing accurate manipulation of the form.

### METHOD

1 Since glass blowing is a highly skilled technique requiring special professional equipment, it is advisable to find a company or individual to make the pieces you require. When commissioning work, always have a clear idea of exactly what it is you would like done and provide precise technical drawings. It may be necessary to compromise on your design because of technical considerations. The glass-worker will know what is possible and if this professional can understand the effect you are trying to achieve, a solution will be found more easily.
2 Glass can be blown into a mould and shaped against formers while it is rotated. The piece can be partly or entirely coloured, and it is possible to 'silver' the inside surface of a hollow form.

## LAMPWORK

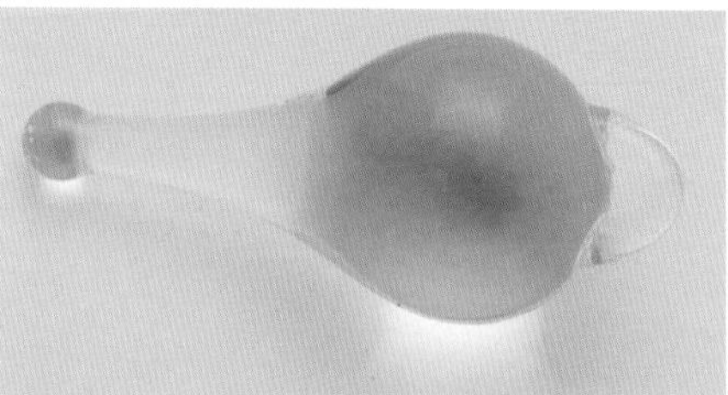

Lampwork is a technique in which an intense gas flame is used to melt or soften glass rods or tube so that they can be manipulated. The forms that can be created vary greatly, and coloured rods can also be incorporated into designs. This is a process that requires skill – there are companies that will make pieces to your specifications.

### METHOD

1 Protective eye gear must be worn, since glowing molten glass emits harmful rays.
2 Glass rods or tubes are heated in an intense flame until they are soft enough to be manipulated. The pliable glass can then be fused with other rods of different colours; squashed or rolled on a metal surface; pulled with tongs to stretch it; or have holes pierced in it. The finished item must be annealed in a kiln to relieve internal stresses before it can be used or worn safely.
3 It is advisable to have lampwork carried out by a professional.

## SPECTACLE SETTING

Although it is possible to hold glass in a bezel that has been burnished over the edges, the 'spectacle' setting used for holding lenses is a much safer method of setting since no pressure is involved and the glass is much less likely to fracture or chip during the process.

### METHOD

1 Construct a collar from sterling silver that will fit snugly around the circumference of the lens. Traditionally, the metal rim in spectacle settings is an inverted 'U' shape so that it grips the glass on both sides, but a thin wire soldered to the outside edge of each side of a narrow bezel will perform the same function.
2 Solder a piece of tube, about 4 mm (¼ inch) long, onto the edge of the bezel, ensuring that it makes good contact.
3 Once pickled and clean, use a jeweller's saw to cut through the centre of the tube across its width; file both sides of the cut. The lens can be slipped into the frame, and the ends of the bezel should meet without the lens being able to move or wobble at all. If the bezel is too big, file more metal away from the inside of the cut so that the lens is held securely. The tube can now be carefully riveted shut, or a screw thread can be cut inside it so that it can be closed with a screw.
4 This type of setting can also be used to fix other glass objects, such as a collar around the neck of a small bottle.

## MAGNETS

Magnets are most useful as joining methods. The attraction and repulsion that magnets exhibit towards one another can be exploited in ingenious ways, and this magnetic characteristic can be used to create interesting properties within a piece.

### METHOD

Concealed magnets are a very effective joining mechanism, both in practical terms and because of the fascination of the invisible forces at work. It is possible to obtain small, powerful magnets that are ideal for use in jewellery-making. These magnets can be contained and concealed inside jewellery pieces since the magnetism is strong enough to work through other materials. Experiment to determine the limitations and thicknesses of various materials that can be used. Unexpected joining mechanisms are always a pleasure, and magnets have the added advantage of being incredibly user-friendly.

## FOLDING
### **Paper**

Paper can be folded to create either delicate and fragile forms or robust and structurally strong ones. Cut-outs or paints and inks may be combined with origami techniques to make varied and interesting designs.

METHOD

1 Ensure your workspace is clean – paper will pick up dirt and grease from surfaces and fingers. Work on a self-healing cutting mat and use a sharp craft knife to cut the paper, using a metal ruler as a guide.
2 The key to neat, accurate forms is neat, accurate folds, so score the paper with a blunt point in order to help it fold more easily in a straight line. Curved folds are also possible to achieve with careful scoring, and paper will stretch a little when it is damp. Different types of paper will behave in varying ways – plastic-coated papers may not fold flat easily but will be useful for structural forms. Thin, flexible paper can have the folds in it rubbed flat in order to create finely layered pieces.
3 Cold-joining techniques must be used to attach metal fittings and findings. When riveting paper, take care not to compress it too much, and work on a clean steel block.

## LASER CUTTING
### **Paper**

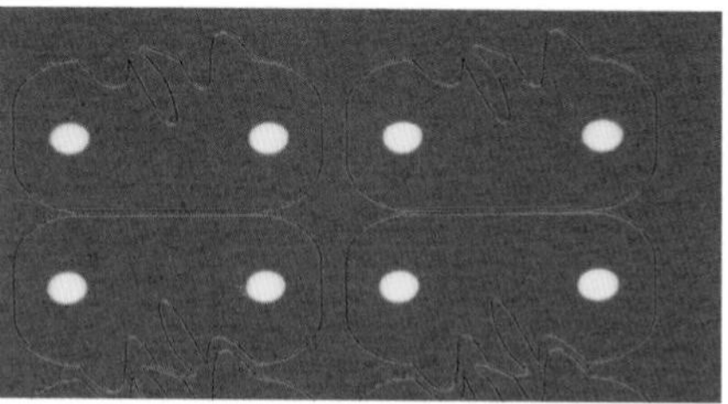

Laser cutting can be used to produce multiple identical shapes, which may be layered or grouped in large quantities. The slight burn marks produced during the process will show more on light-coloured paper but could be incorporated as a design feature.

METHOD

1 You will need to provide a digital file of the image that you would like to be laser-cut. The design must be produced in a computer software package that uses vector lines, such as Abode® Illustrator®. Most companies will accept original artwork, but will charge a fee for converting it into a digital format.
2 The laser cuts along the centre of the vector line, with the width of cut usually being about 0.26 mm (0.01 inch), which allows very delicate tracery or an intricate scheme of slots and tabs to be followed.
3 The intensity of the laser can be accurately controlled – a more intense beam may be required to cut through some materials, and slight scorching around the edges of the cuts can occur.

EMBOSSING
## Paper

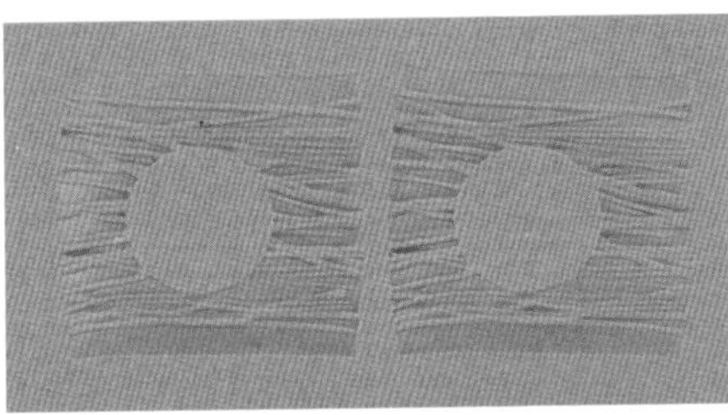

Paper can be put through a rolling mill along with a pierced template or a rolling mill texture in metal. The result is a low-relief texture that can also accept paints, inks and dyes applied to it. Thick paper such as watercolour paper will give the best results.

### METHOD

1. Sandwich the piece of paper you will be embossing with the template in between two sheets of clean metal. This is to protect the paper from any dirt on the rollers of the mill.
2. Adjust the distance between the rollers so that the sandwich of metal and paper can be rolled through the mill without too much pressure. If the template is pushed into the paper with too much force, the paper becomes too thin and can easily split.
3. Some types of paper will compress more than others during the process, and the same template may produce satisfactory results with one paper but not another. It is possible to achieve very detailed low-relief patterns on paper – try using metal rolling mill textures when embossing the paper.

KNITTING/CROCHET
## Textiles

Knitted or crocheted forms can be incorporated into jewellery pieces in a number of ways, and may form the entire piece. Be clear about the statement you are making, and use attention to detail and careful choice of thread to express your ideas.

### METHOD

1. These techniques can be used to construct structural or linear forms either from a pattern or by working freely and seeing where the form leads you.
2. Different types of thread or cord can be used and will greatly influence the outcome of the finished article, as will the size of the needles or hook used to form the structure. Large needles and fine thread will produce a loose, flexible piece, whereas thick cord worked on fine needles will make a densely woven structure with some rigidity.
3. Textile elements are often combined with a metal framework or findings – consider how the two materials will join together successfully.

FABRIC

## Construction

Segments of fabric can be stitched or glued together to make three-dimensional forms. Stiff fabrics that will keep their shape well are best used for geometric designs; stretchy fabrics supported with padding will produce more organic forms.

### METHOD

1 For structured forms, work out templates for the sections you need and make up a rough model first. Cut around the templates in the fabric that will be used for the final piece, leaving a border of 12 mm (½ inch) all the way around.
2 Pin the pieces back to back and tack them in place with a running stitch. A sewing machine is useful for its speed of stitching, but it may be easier to work on small-scale pieces with hand-stitching. Leave one end or edge of the form unstitched so that the fabric can be turned right side out, fill the form with a padding material if desired and neatly stitch the open edge closed.
3 Organic forms can be more freely constructed, and soft padding will mean that stitches can be run through the piece in order to pull areas in and distort them.
4 When choosing fabric, consider the properties of a particular material – fabric jewellery should not be liable to pick up dirt and oils readily, or if it does, should be easily washable.

## EMBROIDERY

Beautiful decorative effects and textures can be created on the surface of fabric with embroidery thread. The embroidery may be applied before or after construction of a piece and may take the form of graphic, abstract or figurative designs.

### METHOD

1 The fabric that the embroidery is worked on will have a significant influence on the overall effect. Loosely woven fabrics may be more easily worked but will not be as luxurious as a fine satin.
2 The choice of threads and colours is also important. Embroidery silks are available in every shade, but they are not hard-wearing. Synthetic threads may be a better choice and are also more colourfast.
3 The design can be marked out on the fabric with tailor's chalk, a soft pencil or iron-on transfers. Secure the fabric in an embroidery frame that will hold it taut while it is being worked.
4 A wide range of different stitches and variations can be used, including chain stitch, backstitch, knotting, weaving and appliqué. Always keep the ends of the thread on the reverse of the piece so that when the embroidery is complete, an iron-on facing can be bonded to the fabric to prevent knots or thread ends from unravelling,

ELECTRONIC COMPONENTS
## LEDs

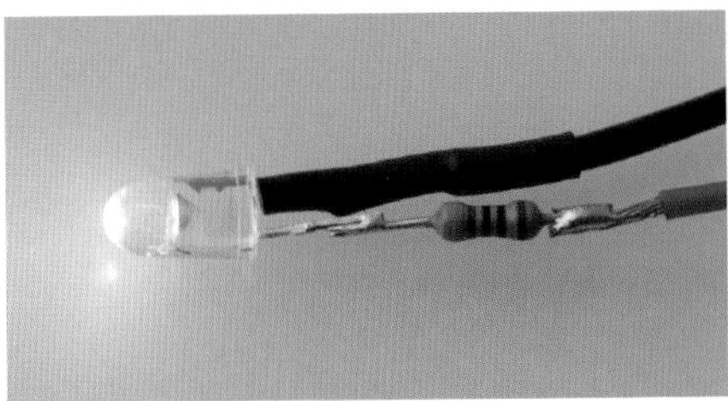

Light Emitting Diodes, or LEDs, are available in a range of colours, as well as clear, ultraviolet and infrared. In jewellery, LEDs are often used in conjunction with other materials such as plastics to make full use of the optical effects that can be produced.

METHOD

A basic knowledge of electronic circuits is a necessity for this technique, since the components must be joined in the correct positions for them to function. A piece of jewellery containing electrical components must be meticulously designed to incorporate the elements; have non-conductive surfaces so the circuit does not short; and be easily operated by the wearer. Containing the battery or power supply is the biggest problem but has become less of an issue as technology progresses, and newer, small circuits do not require a great deal of power. The equipment needed is inexpensive and once the basics have been mastered, electronic circuits with differing functions can be used to great effect.

ELECTRONIC COMPONENTS
## Fibre Optics

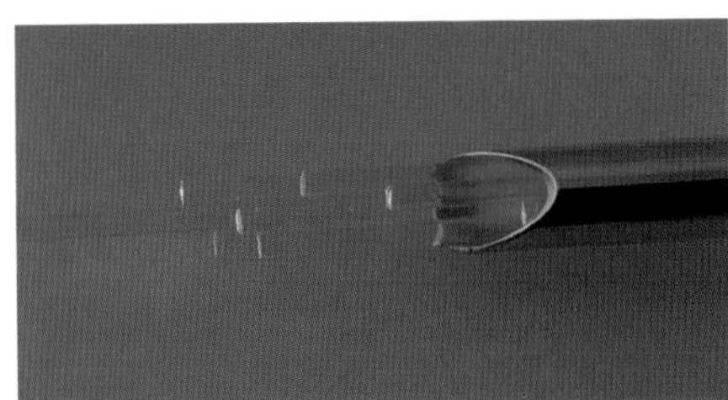

Fibre optics are linear strands that will transport light from one place to another. The light-source is usually an LED, which will provide an intense beam when focused through the fibre-optic material.

METHOD

1 As with LEDs, this technique involves electrical components, so many of the same problems arise – the piece of jewellery must be designed so that the function of the components is not compromised.
2 Fibre-optic material is easily available, but much more expensive than transparent acrylic rod that will also bounce light along its length and project a beam. The rod must make good contact with the LED for the light to be transmitted successfully.
3 The combination of coloured plastics and coloured LEDs can give interesting results, with the light accentuating parts of the body when the jewellery is worn.

# 6

# Stones and Settings

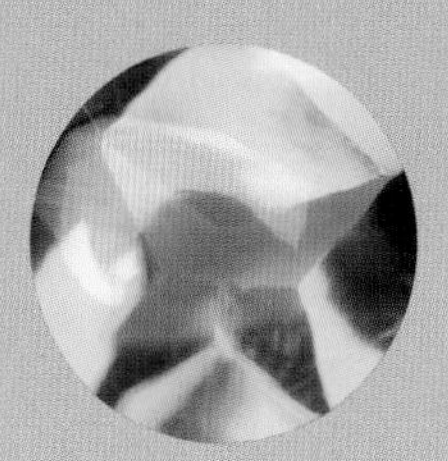

**Stones**

pages 206–229

White/colourless, black, brown, red, orange, yellow, green, blue, violet, pink, mixed/optical effects

**Settings**

pages 230–241

Stone shapes, straight-sided gemstone cuts, stone settings

## DIAMOND

*Brilliant-cut diamond*

### SPECIFICATIONS

**Hardness:** 10 Mohs

**Specific Gravity:** 3.14–3.55

**Refractive Index:** 2.417–2.419

**Crystal Form:** Diamond crystals belong to the cubic or isometric system; chemical composition is crystallized carbon.

**Properties:** Strong adamantine lustre.

**Pricing:** All diamonds marketed by De Beers are classified into standards of quality, which directly affect the price. Many diamonds are laser-marked with an inscription invisible to the naked eye. Factors that will affect the price are clarity, colour, weight, fluorescence, cut and shape.

Buy from a reputable dealer.

Alternatives are white sapphires, which have less fire but are durable and reasonably priced, or cubic zirconia which are cheaper but can scratch.

**suitable for ultrasonic cleaning**

## PEARL

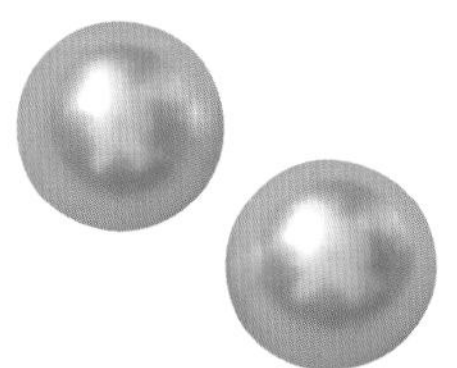

*Cultured pearls*

### SPECIFICATIONS

**Group:** Organic

**Hardness:** 3–4 Mohs

**Specific Gravity:** 2.68–2.79

**Refractive Index:** 1.53–1.68

**Crystal Form:** Orthorhombic

**Properties:** Pearl colour is a mixture of body colour and lustre (overtone).

**Pricing:** The main factors are whether the pearls are natural or cultivated; saltwater or freshwater. Cultivated pearls are widely available in many shapes, colours and forms and are usually sold as strings of 40 cm (16 inches). Individual pearls are also available, as full round, half-drilled or beads. A pair will cost more than two individual pearls since they have been matched.

**heat and chemically sensitive/ not suitable for ultrasonic cleaning**

## ROCK CRYSTAL

*Dandelion-cut rock crystal*

### SPECIFICATIONS

**Group:** Quartz

**Hardness:** 7 Mohs

**Specific Gravity:** 2.65

**Refractive Index:** 1.544–1.553

**Crystal Form:** Crystalline quartz appears as single crystals in a trigonal system.

**Pricing:** Inexpensive, although larger or special cuts will be more expensive as the stone is quite brittle and difficult to work with. Care must be taken when setting the stone to avoid damage.

**heat and chemically sensitive/ not suitable for ultrasonic cleaning**

## DIAMOND

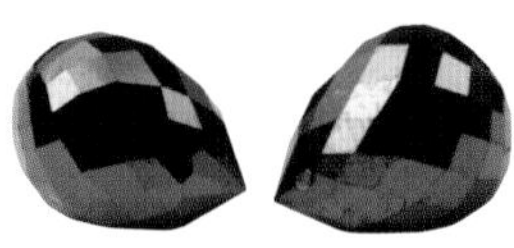

*Black diamond briolettes*

### SPECIFICATIONS

**Hardness:** 10 Mohs

**Specific Gravity:** 3.14–3.55

**Refractive Index:** 2.417–2.419

**Crystal Form:** Diamond crystals belong to the cubic or isometric system and their chemical composition is crystallized carbon. Black diamonds derive their colour from black mineral inclusions. The material is often fibrous and is difficult to cut and polish; the girdle and facet edges often become chipped.

**Pricing:** Prices reflect the quality of the stone, and it is possible to find stones at reasonable prices. A great deal of black diamond material is treated; it is irradiated or heated under very high temperatures. Synthetic black diamonds look virtually identical to natural ones and are much cheaper.

**not suitable for ultrasonic cleaning**

## PEARL

*South Sea baroque pearl*

### SPECIFICATIONS

**Group:** Organic

**Hardness:** 3–4 Mohs

**Specific Gravity:** 2.68–2.79

**Refractive Index:** 1.53–1.68

**Crystal Form:** Orthorhombic

**Properties:** Tahitian pearls from the black-lip mussel, *Pinctada margaritifera*, are the only natural black pearls that exist; all other black pearls are dyed. The 'black' can vary from silver to dark grey and may have pink and green overtones.

**Pricing:** The price of a row of Tahitian pearls is high, reflecting the difficulty of finding and matching enough pearls of the same shape, size and colour. Black South Sea baroque pearls measure between 9–20 mm (3⁄8–3⁄16 inch).

**heat and chemically sensitive/ not suitable for ultrasonic cleaning**

## HEMATITE

*Hematite crystal*

### SPECIFICATIONS

**Hardness:** 5.5–6 Mohs

**Specific Gravity:** 5.12–5.28

**Refractive Index:** 2.94–3.22

**Crystal Form:** Trigonal

**Properties:** Hematite has a conchoidal fracture and no cleavage, but there is a natural parting on two planes. The material needs to be treated carefully during polishing since it can chip.

**Pricing:** The low cost of hematite makes it suitable for beads, cabochons and carvings.

**heat and chemically sensitive/ not suitable for ultrasonic cleaning**

## DIAMOND

*Brilliant-cut cognac diamond*

### SPECIFICATIONS

**Hardness:** 10 Mohs

**Specific Gravity:** 3.14–3.55

**Refractive Index:** 2.417–2.419

**Crystal Form:** Diamond crystals belong to the cubic or isometric system and their chemical composition is crystallized carbon.

**Properties:** Strong adamantine lustre.

**Pricing:** Brown- and cognac-coloured diamonds are good value and the colours are beautiful, ranging from light golden copper to fiery orange to deep cognac to dark brown.

**suitable for ultrasonic cleaning**

## HESSONITE

*Grade-faceted hessonite*

### SPECIFICATIONS

**Group:** Grossular garnet

**Hardness:** 6.5–7.5 Mohs

**Specific Gravity:** 3.49–4.16

**Refractive Index:** 1.69–1.89

**Crystal Form:** Cubic

**Properties:** As a result of its brown-orange to brown-yellow colour, hessonite garnet is called cinnamon stone in Africa. The stone has distinctive, swirling, molasses-like inclusions, most of which are small crystals of apatite.

**Pricing:** The high specific gravity of hessonite will make its cost slightly higher than for other gemstones of the same size and carat.

**not suitable for ultrasonic cleaning**

## ZIRCON

*Brilliant-cut zircon*

### SPECIFICATIONS

**Hardness:** 6.5-7.5 Mohs

**Specific Gravity:** 3.93–4.73

**Refractive Index:** 1.81–2.024

**Crystal Form:** Tetragonal

**Properties:** Adamantine lustre, strong double refraction (dichroism). Zircon contains traces of uranium and thorium, and as a result can differ in hardness, specific gravity, refractive index and colour. Colour distribution is often uneven.

**Pricing:** High zircon is yellow-brown in colour and a harder, more desirable stone than low zircon, which has radioactively decayed to a greenish-yellow or greenish-brown shade. As it can chip easily, zircon is relatively affordable.

**heat and chemically sensitive/ not suitable for ultrasonic cleaning**

## RHODOLITE GARNET

*Faceted rhodolite garnet*

### SPECIFICATIONS

**Group:** Garnet

**Hardness:** 6.5–7.5 Mohs

**Specific Gravity:** 3.49–4.16

**Refractive Index:** 1.69–1.89

**Crystal Form:** Cubic

**Properties:** Rhodolite has a beautiful, violet-red colour with few inclusions. Its composition is considered to be superior to pyrope since the colour is brighter.

**Pricing:** The high specific gravity of rhodolite will make its cost higher than other gemstones of the same size and carat. Rhodolite is mid-priced within the garnet group.

**not suitable for ultrasonic cleaning**

## PYROPE GARNET

*Pyrope cabochon*

### SPECIFICATIONS

**Group:** Garnet

**Hardness:** 6.5–7.5 Mohs

**Specific Gravity:** 3.49–4.16

**Refractive Index:** 1.69–1.89

**Crystal Form:** Cubic

**Properties:** Pyrope has a blood red colour with few inclusions. The best stones have a fiery red colour that does not darken too much once set in jewellery.

**Pricing:** The high specific gravity of pyrope will make its cost slightly higher than other gemstones of the same size and carat. Despite this, garnets are relatively inexpensive.

**not suitable for ultrasonic cleaning**

## RUBY

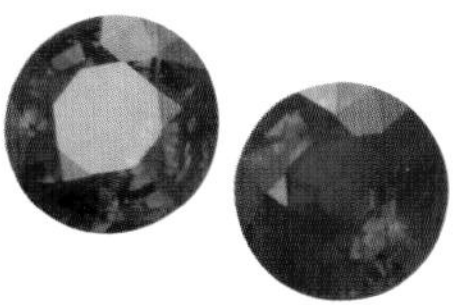

*Brilliant-cut rubies*

### SPECIFICATIONS

**Group:** Corundum

**Hardness:** 9 Mohs

**Specific Gravity:** 3.97–4.05

**Refractive Index:** 1.762–1.778

**Crystal Form:** Hexagonal prisms, tables and rhombohedrons.

**Properties:** Strong pleochroism.

**Pricing:** The most desirable (and therefore most expensive) type of ruby is the Burmese ruby – pure red with a hint of blue. Thai rubies have a darker purplish-red colour but are 'cleaner' stones overall, having less rutile needle inclusions and more lustre than Burmese rubies. Rubies are priced according to colour, clarity, size, cut and proportions. Larger gems are more expensive, but small stones with good colour and clarity have a reasonable value.

**suitable for ultrasonic cleaning**

## RUBELLITE

*17.36ct rubellite*

### SPECIFICATIONS

**Group:** Tourmaline

**Hardness:** 7–7.5 Mohs

**Specific Gravity:** 3.01–3.06

**Refractive Index:** 1.614–1.666

**Crystal Form:** Trigonal

**Properties:** Stones should be an intense hot-pink to red with a violet to blue tone, with no muddying yellow or brown tones. Lower-grade rubellite is often heat-treated to intensify the colour. The effects of treatment can fade over time, so check which processes, if any, have been applied.

**Pricing:** A few fine inclusions make the stone more desirable than one in which the inclusions are clearly visible. This is the most desirable and expensive tourmaline.

**heat sensitive/not suitable for ultrasonic cleaning**

## SPINEL

*Flame spinel*

### SPECIFICATIONS

**Hardness:** 8 Mohs

**Specific Gravity:** 3.54–3.63

**Refractive Index:** 1.712–1.762

**Crystal Form:** Cubic crystal system, usually occurring in octahedral form.

**Properties:** Vitreous lustre.

**Pricing:** The most popular and sought-after colour of spinel is bright red-orange, like that of a poppy or a flame. Stones of this colour are called flame spinels, and their price tag is far higher than spinels in other colours. It is rare to find spinels of more than four carats and the majority of faceted stones are quite small, weighing between 0.5 and 2 carats.

**suitable for ultrasonic cleaning**

## CORAL

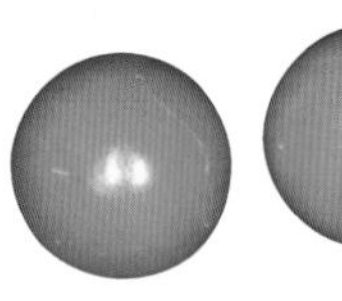

*Sardegna coral*

### SPECIFICATIONS

**Group:** Organic

**Hardness:** 3–3.5 Mohs

**Specific Gravity:** 2.68

**Refractive Index:** 1.49–1.66

**Crystal Form:** Trigonal and microcrystalline. Has a banded structure similar to a tree trunk.

**Pricing:** The pricing of coral depends on its quality, colour, shape and size. It is sold by gram weight. Coral twigs are much cheaper than round beads, and beads over 6 mm (¼ inch) in diameter jump up in price because more rough coral is needed to make them. Large pieces of coral are rare and expensive. Synthetic coral or alternatives such as porcelain, stained bone or glass may be used as a substitute.

**heat and chemically sensitive/not suitable for ultrasonic cleaning**

## CARNELIAN

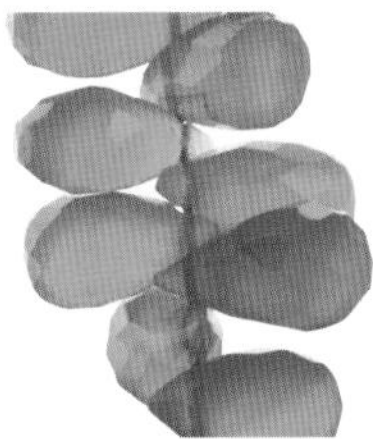

*Carnelian briolettes*

### SPECIFICATIONS

**Group:** Chalcedony

**Hardness:** 6.5–7 Mohs

**Specific Gravity:** 2.58–2.64

**Refractive Index:** 1.53–1.54

**Crystal Form:** Trigonal – mainly fibrous aggregates with a porous nature.

**Properties:** The colours in carnelian range from a pure, intense red-orange to softer brownish oranges and reds. High-quality material is semi-transparent with an intense colour that seems to glow. The colours can be enhanced by heating and dyeing. Natural carnelian should have a cloudy distribution of colour, without any banding or colour zoning.

**Pricing:** Except for the best red-orange material, it is relatively inexpensive.

**heat and chemically sensitive/ not suitable for ultrasonic cleaning**

## DRAVITE

*Mirror-cut dravite*

### SPECIFICATIONS

**Group:** Tourmaline

**Hardness:** 7–7.5 Mohs

**Specific Gravity:** 3.01–3.06

**Refractive Index:** 1.614–1.666

**Crystal Form:** Trigonal

**Properties:** Dravite is normally yellow-brown to orange-brown in colour; its colouring agent is magnesium and it often appears alongside yellow tourmaline in gem gravels. It has strong dichroism, showing two distinct colours from different angles. The colour of dravite is sometimes lightened using heat treatment.

**Pricing:** This is an inexpensive colour of tourmaline, and is good value for money.

**heat sensitive/not suitable for ultrasonic cleaning**

## SUNSTONE

*Faceted sunstone*

### SPECIFICATIONS

**Group:** Feldspar

**Hardness:** 6–6.5 Mohs

**Specific Gravity:** 2.56–2.62

**Refractive Index:** 1.52–1.53

**Crystal Form:** Triclinic and monoclinic.

**Properties:** Opaque cabochon material is usually a shimmering brownish-orange to reddish-orange. Facet-grade sunstone is transparent to slightly translucent and ranges from a soft pinky orange to a fiery bright red. It has become more widely available in recent years.

**Pricing:** The redder a sunstone is, the more it will cost.

**heat and chemically sensitive/ not suitable for ultrasonic cleaning**

## AMBER

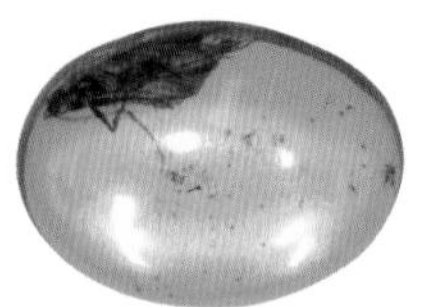

*Yellow amber cabochon*

### SPECIFICATIONS

**Group:** Organic

**Hardness:** 2–2.25 Mohs

**Specific Gravity:** 1.05–1.09

**Refractive Index:** 1.54–1.55

**Crystal Form:** Amorphous. Small, irregularly shaped masses with a cracked and weathered surface.

**Properties:** Colours of amber vary from milky white to yellow to red to black. Much amber is reconstituted, sometimes with synthetic resins. Real amber will produce smoke that smells a bit like incense when tested with a hot needle.

**Pricing:** Amber is a low-priced stone and the different colours have only minor variations in cost, with bright yellow transparent being the most desirable and expensive.

**heat and chemically sensitive/not suitable for ultrasonic cleaning**

## CITRINE

*Square-faceted citrine*

### SPECIFICATIONS

**Group:** Quartz

**Hardness:** 7 Mohs

**Specific Gravity:** 2.65

**Refractive Index:** 1.544–1.553

**Crystal Form:** Crystalline quartz appears as single crystals in a trigonal system.

**Properties:** Citrine ranges in colour from pastel lemon yellow to deep reddish brown and amber. The most common natural colour is golden and tends to be pale. Supply is plentiful, and large-size stones are available.

**Pricing:** The darker the colour, the more expensive the natural material becomes, though it is still much less expensive than topaz.

**heat sensitive/not suitable for ultrasonic cleaning**

## DIAMOND

*1.57ct fancy diamond*

### SPECIFICATIONS

**Hardness:** 10 Mohs

**Specific Gravity:** 3.14–3.55

**Refractive Index:** 2.417–2.419

**Crystal Form:** Diamond crystals belong to the cubic or isometric system and their chemical composition is crystallized carbon.

**Properties:** Strong adamantine lustre.

**Pricing:** The more intense the yellow, the more expensive the stone – canary yellow is the most valuable. Lighter shades of these diamonds can look like capes (diamonds of a low-grade colour).

**suitable for ultrasonic cleaning**

## HELIODOR

*Faceted heliodor*

### SPECIFICATIONS

**Group:** Beryl

**Hardness:** 7.5–8 Mohs

**Specific Gravity:** 2.69–2.80

**Refractive Index:** 1.57–1.59

**Crystal Form:** Beryl has a hexagonal, prismatic structure and occurs in granites and pegmatites as well as in alluvial deposits of gravel. It has a vitreous lustre.

**Properties:** The colour of 'golden beryl' ranges from pale lemon to yellow-green to a rich, warm gold. Heliodor may contain fine, tube-like inclusions that can create a cat's-eye effect when cut in cabochon form.

**Pricing:** Like all beryls, the critical factor in pricing is intensity of colour.

heat and chemically sensitive/ not suitable for ultrasonic cleaning

## SAPPHIRE

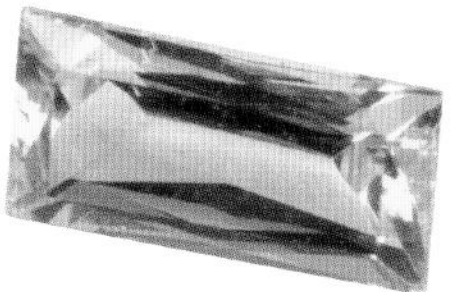

*Baguette-cut sapphire*

### SPECIFICATIONS

**Group:** Corundum

**Hardness:** 8–9 Mohs

**Specific Gravity:** 3.95–4.03

**Refractive Index:** 1.762–1.778

**Crystal Form:** Trigonal

**Properties:** Yellow sapphires are quite common and range from pale yellow to intense amber. Pure golden yellows are rare, so many sapphires are heated to a golden colour.

**Pricing:** Prices for yellow sapphires are reasonable.

suitable for ultrasonic cleaning

## TOPAZ

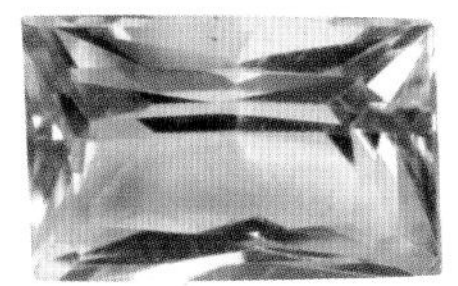

*Champagne topaz*

### SPECIFICATIONS

**Hardness:** 8 Mohs

**Specific Gravity:** 3.49–3.57

**Refractive Index:** 1.609–1.643

**Crystal Form:** Orthorhombic

**Properties:** Yellow is the most common natural colour of topaz, which is often treated or irradiated to improve the colour. Topaz can be found in large sizes.

**Pricing:** Generally good value for money.

heat and chemically sensitive/ not suitable for ultrasonic cleaning

## AVENTURINE

*Aventurine quartz cabochon*

### SPECIFICATIONS

**Group:** Quartz

**Hardness:** 7 Mohs

**Specific Gravity:** 2.65

**Refractive Index:** 1.544–1.553

**Crystal Form:** Crystalline quartz appears as single crystals in a trigonal system.

**Properties:** Semi-translucent.

Aventurine has a lovely medium to dark green colour and can contain tiny sparkling flecks of green fuchsite mica. Makes attractive cabochons and beads.

**Pricing:** An affordable stone.

**heat and chemically sensitive/ not suitable for ultrasonic cleaning**

## BERYL

*Bent-bar cut beryls*

### SPECIFICATIONS

**Group:** Beryl

**Hardness:** 7.5–8 Mohs

**Specific Gravity:** 2.69–2.80

**Refractive Index:** 1.57–1.59

**Crystal Form:** Has a hexagonal, prismatic structure and occurs in granites and pegmatites as well as in alluvial deposits of gravel. It has a vitreous lustre.

The majority of green beryl is transformed into blue aquamarine at high temperature. Emeralds are a strong deep green, bluish-green or yellow-green. Green beryl is pale green or pale yellow-green. It often contains inclusions similar to the fibres, rods or cloudiness in emeralds.

**Pricing:** Depends on intensity of colour.

**heat and chemically sensitive/ not suitable for ultrasonic cleaning**

## CHRYSOPRASE

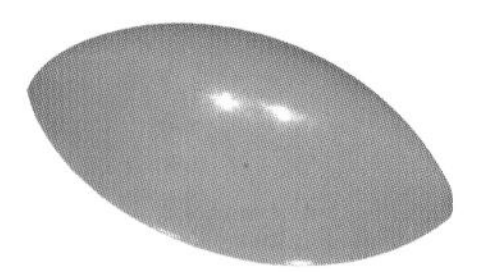

*Chrysoprase cabochon*

### SPECIFICATIONS

**Group:** Chalcedony

**Hardness:** 6.5–7 Mohs

**Specific Gravity:** 2.58–2.64

**Refractive Index:** 1.53–1.54

**Crystal Form:** Trigonal

**Properties:** The best chrysoprase has an intense apple-green colour and is translucent. Chrysoprase often varies in colour, depending on its nickel content, and it can be pale green, emerald green or dark green. The stone's translucency also varies. Colour tends to be evenly spread. Black or brown speckled deposits can occur and give a jade-like appearance.

**Pricing:** The popularity of the intensely coloured chrysoprase has made it more expensive, but lower-grade colours are moderately priced.

**heat and chemically sensitive/ not suitable for ultrasonic cleaning**

## EMERALD

*Colombian emerald*

### SPECIFICATIONS

**Group:** Beryl

**Hardness:** 7.5–8 Mohs

**Specific Gravity:** 2.69–2.80

**Refractive Index:** 1.57–1.59

**Crystal Form:** Beryl has a hexagonal, prismatic structure and occurs in granites and pegmatites as well as in alluvial deposits of gravel. It has a vitreous lustre.

**Properties:** Distinct dichroism.

Heat treatment to improve colour is standard practice. Certain cuts are more prone to cracking than others; take care when setting and never expose the stone to heat.

**Pricing:** Clarity, colour intensity, flaws and size are important factors. Lower-grade material is used for cabochons and beads.

**heat and chemically sensitive/ not suitable for ultrasonic cleaning**

## INDICOLITE

*Scissor-cut indicolite*

### SPECIFICATIONS

**Group:** Tourmaline

**Hardness:** 7–7.5 Mohs

**Specific Gravity:** 3.01–3.06

**Refractive Index:** 1.614–1.666

**Crystal Form:** Trigonal

**Properties:** Many-faceted indicolites have step cuts or scissor cuts to display the best colour and bring light into a potentially dark stone.

**Pricing:** This is the rarer indicolite, the highly desirable blue-green coloured variety.

**heat sensitive/not suitable for ultrasonic cleaning**

## NEPHRITE JADE

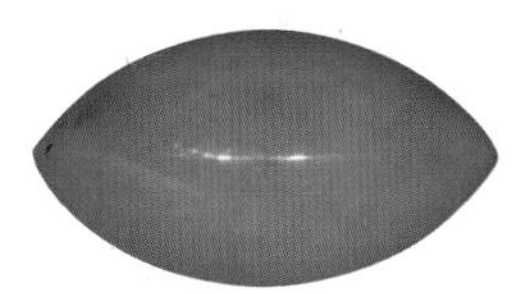

*Russian nephrite jade*

### SPECIFICATIONS

**Hardness:** 6.5 Mohs

**Specific Gravity:** 2.96

**Refractive Index:** 1.61–1.63

**Crystal Form:** Monoclinic. It has a greasy to pearly lustre. The crystal structure is tougher than steel.

**Properties:** The colours are less delicate and pure than those of jadeite, and range from dark green to cream. The colours can be banded, blotchy or homogenous. The typical shade of green in nephrite is spinach or sage.

**Pricing:** The jade-carving industry is huge and the main cutting centres are in China and Taiwan. The fact that so many dyed and poor-quality nephrite jade goods are on sale results in its devaluation as a gemstone.

**heat and chemically sensitive/ not suitable for ultrasonic cleaning**

## JADEITE JADE

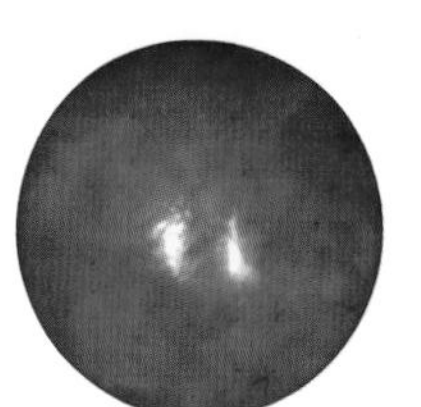

*Green jade*

### SPECIFICATIONS

**Hardness:** 7 Mohs

**Specific Gravity:** 3.33

**Refractive Index:** 1.66–1.68

**Crystal Form:** Monoclinic. Jadeite has a greasy to pearly lustre.

**Properties:** Jadeite is a precious gem. In its pure form it is white but can also occur in a wide range of colours, which tend to be pastel and mottled. The exception to this is imperial jade, which is a vibrant, rich, emerald or apple-green colour.

**Pricing:** Imperial jade can be translucent to near transparent and is highly prized and extremely valuable.

**heat and chemically sensitive/ not suitable for ultrasonic cleaning**

## MALACHITE

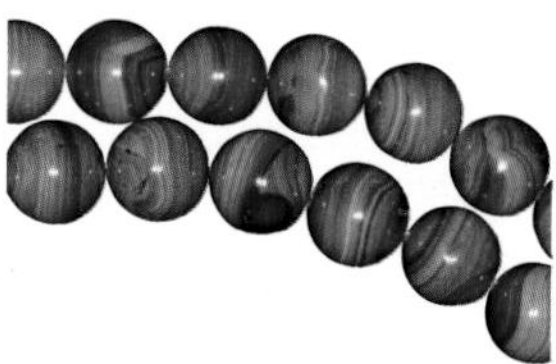

*Malachite beads*

### SPECIFICATIONS

**Hardness:** 4 Mohs

**Specific Gravity:** 3.8

**Refractive Index:** 1.65–1.90

**Crystal Form:** Monoclinic. Malachite is described as a secondary mineral because it is created by a chemical reaction between minerals that have already formed.

**Properties:** Malachite is soft and easy to carve and shape. It is readily available in bead and cabochon form. The lustre ranges from vitreous to dull.

**Pricing:** Malachite is a mineral in abundant supply, but much material on the market is synthetic, dyed or treated. Resin-bonded or plastic-impregnated malachite consists of fragments glued together with resin.

**heat and chemically sensitive/ not suitable for ultrasonic cleaning**

## PERIDOT

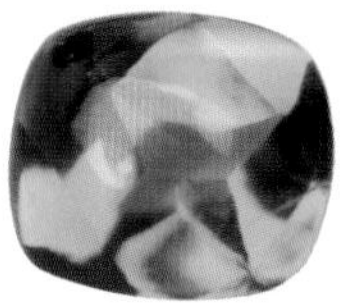

*Buff-top cut peridot*

### SPECIFICATIONS

**Hardness:** 6.5–7 Mohs

**Specific Gravity:** 3.27–3.37

**Refractive Index:** 1.64–1.69

**Crystal Form:** Orthorhombic. Peridot appears as flat prismatic crystals with distinct striations along the length.

**Pricing:** Faceted peridot is readily available in pale colours, which are moderately priced. The higher cost of large, intensely coloured stones reflects the rarity of good-quality material. Lower-grade material is used for cabochons and beads.

**heat and chemically sensitive/ not suitable for ultrasonic cleaning**

## PREHNITE

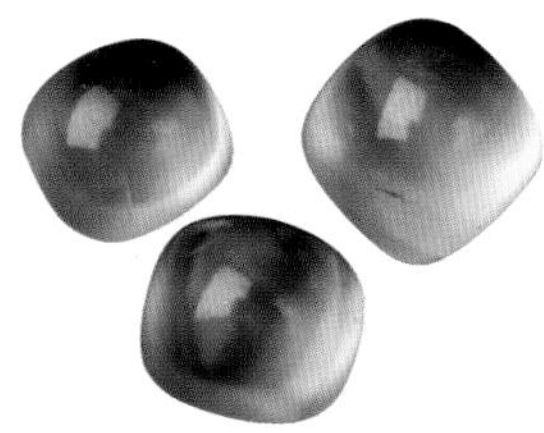

*Prehnite cabochons*

### SPECIFICATIONS

**Hardness:** 6–6.5 Mohs

**Specific Gravity:** 2.82–2.94

**Refractive Index:** 1.611–1.669

**Crystal Form:** Orthorhombic. Individual crystals are rare.

**Properties:** Chatoyancy (cat's-eye effect) in cabochon.

**Pricing:** Prehnite beads and cabochons are inexpensive and readily available.

**heat and chemically sensitive/ not suitable for ultrasonic cleaning**

## TSAVORITE

*Faceted tsavorite garnets*

### SPECIFICATIONS

**Group:** Grossular garnet

**Hardness:** 6.5–7.5 Mohs

**Specific Gravity:** 3.49–4.16

**Refractive Index:** 1.69–1.89

**Crystal Form:** Garnet is a group of structurally and chemically related mineral species that crystallize in the cubic system. This system has the highest symmetry; crystals can take the form of a cube, octahedral or pentagonal dodecahedron. Garnet has a vitreous, glass-like lustre.

**Properties:** High lustre

**Pricing:** This is the transparent lime-green to emerald-green variety of grossular garnet. There is low public awareness of tsavorite, so the stones can be extremely valuable yet provide a viable alternative to emerald, since they have better clarity, are more durable and less expensive.

**not suitable for ultrasonic cleaning**

## VERDELITE

*Forest-green verdelite*

### SPECIFICATIONS

**Group:** Tourmaline

**Hardness:** 7–7.5 Mohs

**Specific Gravity:** 3.01–3.06

**Refractive Index:** 1.614–1.666

**Crystal Form:** Trigonal

**Pricing:** The most common shades of verdelite are bottle and yellowish green, but emerald green, bright leaf green and chrome green are the most sought-after colours – and the hardest to find; consequently, their value is high. Although it is possible to find the various shades of green in small sizes, or to find stones that have inclusions or that are too dark or too pale, it is quite a challenge to find a clean, green tourmaline of more than five carats.

**heat sensitive/not suitable for ultrasonic cleaning**

## ALEXANDRITE

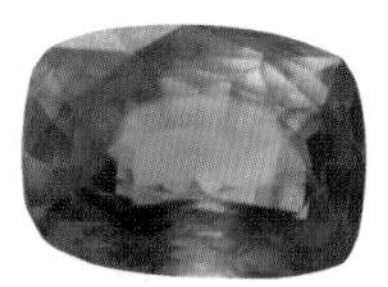

*Faceted alexandrite*

### SPECIFICATIONS

**Group:** Chrysoberyl

**Hardness:** 8.5 Mohs

**Specific Gravity:** 3.7–3.78

**Refractive Index:** 1.746–1.763

**Crystal Form:** Orthorhombic system. A hard, durable stone, normally faceted. Some cat's-eye alexandrites also exist in cabochon form. These are small, but with colour-change properties.

**Properties:** A transparent gem with colour-change properties; it appears blue-green in daylight and red or red-brown in artificial incandescent light. The best colour changes occur in thick stones.

**Pricing:** Usually comes in small sizes, and gemstones are, on average, between 1 carat and 1½ carats of weight. Stones over 2 carats are scarce and extremely expensive.

**suitable for ultrasonic cleaning**

## AQUAMARINE

*Nigerian aquamarine*

### SPECIFICATIONS

**Group:** Beryl

**Hardness:** 7.5–8 Mohs

**Specific Gravity:** 2.69–2.80

**Refractive Index:** 1.57–1.59

**Crystal Form:** Beryl has a hexagonal, prismatic structure and occurs in granites and pegmatites as well as in alluvial deposits of gravel. It has a vitreous lustre.

**Properties:** Aquamarine is dichroic, so the intensity of the colour changes depending on the angle it is viewed from. Aquamarines have a much better clarity than emeralds. It is easier to find clean stones at a good size, and fewer inclusions and cracks mean the material is less brittle.

**Pricing:** The more intense the colour, the higher the value.

**heat sensitive/not suitable for ultrasonic cleaning**

## BLUE CHALCEDONY

*Blue-lace agate*

### SPECIFICATIONS

**Group:** Chalcedony

**Hardness:** 6.5–7 Mohs

**Specific Gravity:** 2.58–2.64

**Refractive Index:** 1.53–1.54

**Crystal Form:** Trigonal

**Properties:** This can be a really beautiful stone, offering floral tones ranging from delicate lilac to periwinkle blue to smoky lavender.

**Pricing:** The best material is transparent; lower-grade chalcedony can have some clouds. The enormous increase in the popularity of blue chalcedony over the last few years has pushed its prices up, and top-quality intense blue material can be expensive.

**heat and chemically sensitive/not suitable for ultrasonic cleaning**

## DIAMOND

*Treated blue diamond*

### SPECIFICATIONS

**Hardness:** 10 Mohs

**Specific Gravity:** 3.14–3.55

**Refractive Index:** 2.417–2.419

**Crystal Form:** Diamond crystals belong to the cubic or isometric system and their chemical composition is crystallized carbon.

**Properties:** Blue diamonds are rarely bright blue; the stones typically have a greyish blue tone caused by boron. A treated blue diamond is closer to greenish blue.

**Pricing:** Natural blue diamonds are more expensive than pink, yellow or cognac. Treated diamonds are more affordable, cut from lower-grade material and often only available in smaller sizes. Heating and irradiating have uncertain results, and it can be hard to achieve certain or consistent colours. The colour can be muddy.

**heat sensitive/suitable for ultrasonic cleaning**

## INDICOLITE

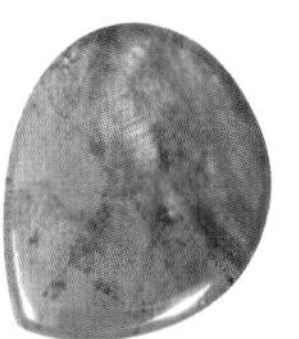

*Blue indicolite*

### SPECIFICATIONS

**Group:** Tourmaline

**Hardness:** 7–7.5 Mohs

**Specific Gravity:** 3.01–3.06

**Refractive Index:** 1.614–1.666

**Crystal Form:** Trigonal

**Properties:** Indicolite shows dark blue from one angle and light blue from another. The stone can often appear very dark so needs to be faceted carefully to allow the lighter tone to dominate.

**Pricing:** Blue indicolite is one of the most desirable and expensive tourmalines, though the dark, inky blues are unpopular and are often heat-treated to lighten them.

**heat sensitive/not suitable for ultrasonic cleaning**

## KYANITE

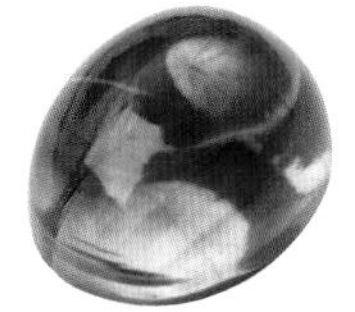

*Kyanite cabochon*

### SPECIFICATIONS

**Hardness:** 4.5–5 or 7 Mohs

**Specific Gravity:** 3.55–3.69

**Refractive Index:** 1.712–1.734

**Crystal Form:** Triclinic

**Properties:** Gem-quality material is transparent to translucent, and the lustre ranges from vitreous to pearly. A great deal of bead and cabochon material contains inclusions of quartz, pyrite crystals, hematite flakes and fibres of ilmenite and rutile. Kyanite has a moderate double refraction and is trichroic, showing colourless, violet-blue and cobalt blue.

**Pricing:** The availability of kyanite is good and there is a wide choice of quality and prices in bead form. The better quality is not cheap, but the colour and clarity compensate for the price.

**heat and chemically sensitive/not suitable for ultrasonic cleaning**

## LAPIS LAZULI

*Lapis lazuli pendeloque*

### SPECIFICATIONS

**Hardness:** 5–6 Mohs (depending on composition)

**Specific Gravity:** 2.38–3.00 (higher if high pyrite content)

**Refractive Index:** 1.50–1.55 (depending on composition)

**Crystal Form:** Isometric. Lapis lazuli has three main mineral components: lazurite, hauyne and sodalite. Calcite and pyrite are found in varying degrees.

**Properties:** Natural lapis lazuli is opaque and often contains small gold or silver pyrite veins or layers. Finest quality lapis is an even, deep blue with a purplish tint and is free of pyrite inclusions.

**Pricing:** Since there is so much dyed and treated lapis on the market, buy from a reputable dealer. Natural, good-quality lapis is valuable whereas dyed material is not.

**heat and chemically sensitive/ not suitable for ultrasonic cleaning**

## SAPPHIRE

*Cushion-cut sapphire*

### SPECIFICATIONS

**Group:** Corundum

**Hardness:** 9 Mohs

**Specific Gravity:** 3.95–4.03

**Refractive Index:** 1.762–1.778

**Crystal Form:** Barrel-shaped, double-pointed hexagonal pyramids, and tabloid shapes.

**Pricing:** The purity and intensity of the blue is critical. Ideally, it should possess a violet overtone with no sign of grey or green. The lightness or darkness of a stone, colour zoning and clarity all need to be considered; irregular colour zoning detracts from a stone's value and beauty. Larger gems are more expensive, but small stones with good colour and clarity can still have a reasonable value.

**suitable for ultrasonic cleaning**

## SPINEL

*Burmese spinel*

### SPECIFICATIONS

**Hardness:** 8 Mohs

**Specific Gravity:** 3.54–3.63

**Refractive Index:** 1.712–1.762

**Crystal Form:** Cubic crystal system, usually occurring in octahedral form.

**Properties:** Vitreous lustre.

**Pricing:** Spinel can be used as an alternative to blue sapphire because it is durable, brilliant and affordable – the price is similar to that of aquamarine and tourmaline. Spinels also occur in a cobalt-blue colour.

**suitable for ultrasonic cleaning**

## TOPAZ

*Irradiated blue topaz*

### SPECIFICATIONS

**Hardness:** 8 Mohs

**Specific Gravity:** 3.49–3.57

**Refractive Index:** 1.609–1.643

**Crystal Form:** Orthorhombic

**Properties:** Topaz has high brilliance and vitreous lustre. Irradiated material comes in a light sky-blue, a vibrant Swiss-blue and a dark grey-blue called London-blue.

**Pricing:** Topaz is often heat-treated or irradiated to enhance the colour. Demand for topaz remains high despite concerns about the treatment process, but the abundance of material keeps the price relatively low.

**heat and chemically sensitive/ not suitable for ultrasonic cleaning**

## TURQUOISE

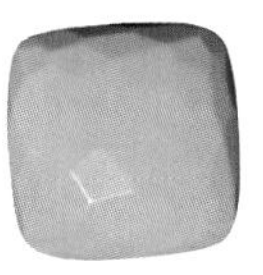

*Sleeping Beauty turquoise*

### SPECIFICATIONS

**Hardness:** 5–6 Mohs

**Specific Gravity:** 2.80

**Refractive Index:** 1.61–1.65

**Crystal Form:** Triclinic

**Properties:** Turquoise is opaque to semi-translucent and has a waxy to dull lustre. Unfortunately, it has a high porosity, which can lead to the material fading and cracking over time.

**Pricing:** Much turquoise on the market is treated by dyeing, coating or reconstituting with resin, and can even have a fake matrix. This material should be inexpensive. The quality of natural turquoise is based on colour, intensity and the presence of any matrix rock. A piece of Sleeping Beauty turquoise that is free of any matrix and is an intense dark blue is deemed ideal.

**heat and chemically sensitive/ not suitable for ultrasonic cleaning**

## ZIRCON

*Treated blue zircon*

### SPECIFICATIONS

**Hardness:** 6.5-7.5 Mohs

**Specific Gravity:** 3.93–4.73

**Refractive Index:** 1.81–2.024

**Crystal Form:** Tetragonal

**Properties:** Adamantine lustre, strong double refraction (dichroism). Zircon contains traces of uranium and thorium, and as a result can differ in hardness, specific gravity, refractive index and colour. Colour distribution is often uneven. Treated blue zircon has a distinct turquoise colour that is not easily confused with other stones. Its brilliance, fire and intensity set it apart from stones such as topaz or aquamarine.

**Pricing:** Relatively affordable due to its susceptibility to wear and tear, especially following heat treatment.

**heat and chemically sensitive/ not suitable for ultrasonic cleaning**

## AMETHYST

*Faceted amethyst*

### SPECIFICATIONS

**Group:** Quartz

**Hardness:** 7 Mohs

**Specific Gravity:** 2.65

**Refractive Index:** 1.544–1.553

**Crystal Form:** Crystalline quartz appears as single crystals in a trigonal system.

**Properties:** Amethyst is slightly dichroic, meaning that its colour has either a bluish or a reddish tone. Amethyst can be found in all shades of purple, from light lavender to intense Siberian amethyst that displays highlights of magenta when faceted.

**Pricing:** Intensely coloured stones are more valuable than paler ones, which are very reasonably priced.

**heat sensitive/not suitable for ultrasonic cleaning**

## CHALCEDONY

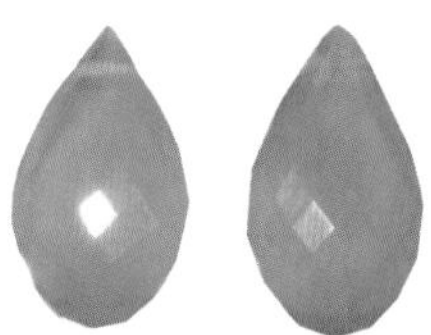

*Lilac-coloured chalcedony*

### SPECIFICATIONS

**Group:** Chalcedony

**Hardness:** 6.5–7 Mohs

**Specific Gravity:** 2.58–2.64

**Refractive Index:** 1.53–1.54

**Crystal Form:** Trigonal

**Pricing:** This can be a really beautiful stone, offering floral tones ranging from delicate lilac to periwinkle blue to smoky lavender. The best material is transparent; lower-grade chalcedony can have some clouds. Natural-colour stones are more expensive than dyed ones.

**heat and chemically sensitive/ not suitable for ultrasonic cleaning**

## IOLITE

*Faceted iolite*

### SPECIFICATIONS

**Hardness:** 7–7.5 Mohs

**Specific Gravity:** 2.53–2.78

**Refractive Index:** 1.522–1.578

**Crystal Form:** Orthorhombic

**Properties:** Trichroic

**Pricing:** Most of the available iolite is a medium violet-blue. AA-grade iolite with the exceptional blue-violet colour is close to the price of good-quality faceted tourmaline. Lower-grade iolite is often included and usually cut as cabochons, and it is rare to find large pieces that are free of inclusions.

**heat and chemically sensitive/ not suitable for ultrasonic cleaning**

## SCAPOLITE

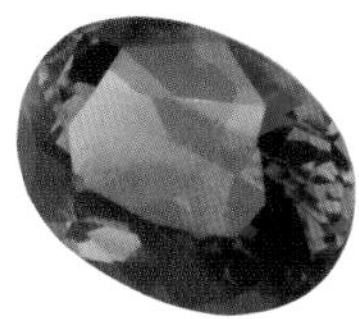

*8.14ct oval scapolite*

### SPECIFICATIONS

**Hardness:** 6–6.5 Mohs

**Specific Gravity:** 2.5–2.74

**Refractive Index:** 1.540–1.600

**Crystal Form:** Tetragonal system. Scapolite is not suitable for ring stones as the cleavage and brittle fracture mean that faceted stones have to be treated with care during setting and polishing and will quickly be damaged with wear.

**Properties:** Good violet scapolite can range from a soft lilac to a velvety blackberry – lower-grade material tends to be dark or grey in tone.

**Pricing:** The availability of scapolite is increasing and prices should reflect that by dropping. However, it is not a particularly expensive stone.

**heat and chemically sensitive/ not suitable for ultrasonic cleaning**

## TANZANITE

*Baguette-cut tanzanite*

### SPECIFICATIONS

**Group:** Zoisite

**Hardness:** 6.5–7 Mohs

**Specific Gravity:** 3.30–3.35

**Refractive Index:** 1.69–1.70

**Crystal Form:** The material has perfect cleavage, making it soft and brittle, and so it is not suitable for everyday wear.

**Properties:** The stone is heat-treated to produce a more attractive and intense blue. Faceted tanzanites exhibit pleochroism, in which different colours and intensities can be seen when the material is viewed from different angles.

**Pricing:** The high price of intense colours has meant that more pale lilac and lavender is being used – to great effect. The gentler colours are not only cheaper, but are more versatile to work with.

**heat and chemically sensitive/ not suitable for ultrasonic cleaning**

## LAVENDER JADE

*Lavender jade cabochons*

### SPECIFICATIONS

**Group:** Jadeite Jade

**Hardness:** 7 Mohs

**Specific Gravity:** 3.33

**Refractive Index:** 1.66–1.68

**Crystal Form:** Monoclinic. Jadeite has a greasy to pearly lustre.

**Properties:** Jadeite is a precious gem. In its pure form it is white, but can also occur in a wide range of colours, which tend to be pastel and mottled.

**Pricing:** The purity and strength of colour affect the price – darker shades of lavender are more valuable than paler varieties.

**heat and chemically sensitive/ not suitable for ultrasonic cleaning**

## DIAMOND

*Fancy pink cushion diamond*

### SPECIFICATIONS

**Hardness:** 10 Mohs

**Specific Gravity:** 3.14–3.55

**Refractive Index:** 2.417–2.419

**Crystal Form:** Diamond crystals belong to the cubic or isometric system and their chemical composition is crystallized carbon.

**Properties:** Strong adamantine lustre. A vivid pink diamond can produce stunning orange highlights, but the colour is more usually pastel.

**Pricing:** Pink diamonds have become very popular and therefore very expensive. Treated pink diamonds are more affordable, but the colour is often a little 'dirty'.

**heat sensitive/suitable for ultrasonic cleaning**

## KUNZITE

*14.7ct faceted kunzite*

### SPECIFICATIONS

**Group:** Spodumene

**Hardness:** 6.5–7 Mohs

**Specific Gravity:** 3.15–3.21

**Refractive Index:** 1.66–1.68

**Crystal Form:** Monoclinic – prismatic tabular. Kunzite has an uneven brittle fracture and a strong vitreous lustre.

**Properties:** Kunzite is generally pale. To achieve more attractive pink colours it is common for stones with brownish tones to be heated to 150°C (300°F).

**Pricing:** Kunzite is good value as a gemstone; its moderate cost allows jewellery-makers and designers to use large stones for dramatic effect. Any naturally intensely coloured stones are rare though, and carry a premium.

**heat and chemically sensitive/ not suitable for ultrasonic cleaning**

## ROSE QUARTZ

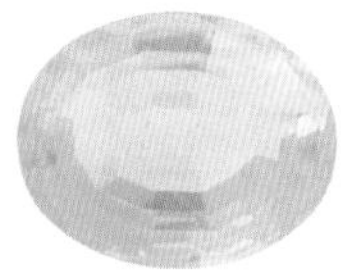

*Faceted rose quartz*

### SPECIFICATIONS

**Group:** Quartz

**Hardness:** 7 Mohs

**Specific Gravity:** 2.65

**Refractive Index:** 1.544–1.553

**Crystal Form:** Crystalline quartz appears as single crystals in a trigonal system.

**Properties:** Rose quartz ranges from pale pink to deep peach. Most is included or cloudy, with a translucent appearance. Despite its brittleness, a great deal of rose quartz is used in carvings and beads.

**Pricing:** Clear 'gemmy' material is limited and can be more expensive. The lower-grade material is brittle and can be full of cracks and flaws, so be careful when buying cheaper materials since cracks may open up.

**heat and chemically sensitive/ not suitable for ultrasonic cleaning**

## SAPPHIRE

*Faceted pink sapphire*

### SPECIFICATIONS

**Group:** Corundum

**Hardness:** 8–9 Mohs

**Specific Gravity:** 3.95–4.03

**Refractive Index:** 1.762–1.778

**Crystal Form:** Trigonal

**Properties:** Pink sapphire has become very popular and appears regularly in jewellery designs. The colour can range from soft baby pink to hot bluish-pink. Ideally, it should be a uniform, intense pink with no lavender or brown tones.

**Pricing:** Natural hot-pink sapphires have risen in cost significantly and are selling at prices similar to medium-grade blue sapphire.

**heat sensitive/suitable for ultrasonic cleaning**

## SPINEL

*Russian rose-pink spinels*

### SPECIFICATIONS

**Hardness:** 8 Mohs

**Specific Gravity:** 3.54–3.63

**Refractive Index:** 1.712–1.762

**Crystal Form:** Cubic crystal system, usually occurring in octahedral form.

**Properties:** Vitreous lustre. Spinel is a good material for small, faceted stones, especially if they are being gypsy set. Its hardness prevents the stone from crumbling or splintering when pressure is applied onto the girdle. Spinel is also excellent for engagement rings or any piece of jewellery that is going to be worn every day.

**Pricing:** Similar to that of aquamarine or tourmaline. Larger sizes are more expensive because of their scarcity.

**suitable for ultrasonic cleaning**

## TOPAZ

*3.5ct precious pink topaz*

### SPECIFICATIONS

**Hardness:** 8 Mohs

**Specific Gravity:** 3.49–3.57

**Refractive Index:** 1.609–1.643

**Crystal Form:** Orthorhombic

**Pricing:** Natural pink stones are rare, so yellow material is heated to pink. As a result, natural pink stones carry a higher value.

**heat and chemically sensitive/not suitable for ultrasonic cleaning**

## BANDED AGATE

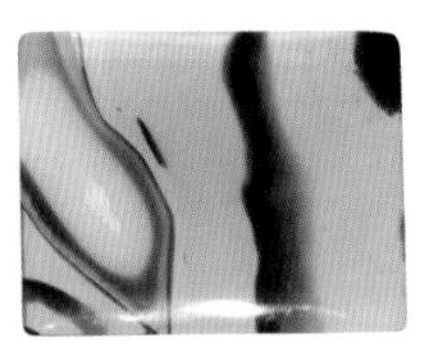

*Agate slice*

### SPECIFICATIONS

**Group:** Agate

**Hardness:** 6.5–7 Mohs

**Specific Gravity:** 2.58–2.64

**Refractive Index:** 1.53–1.54

**Crystal Form:** Trigonal – mainly fibrous, porous aggregates. Waxy, dull lustre.

**Properties:** Banded agates have distinct colour banding in rounded layers of different thicknesses, and often contain white quartz crystals. The band colours depend on the impurities present and, being porous, the material is frequently stained and dyed.

**Pricing:** Natural-colour agates are more expensive, while low-grade, cheaper material is normally dyed.

**heat and chemically sensitive/ not suitable for ultrasonic cleaning**

## DENDRITIC AGATE

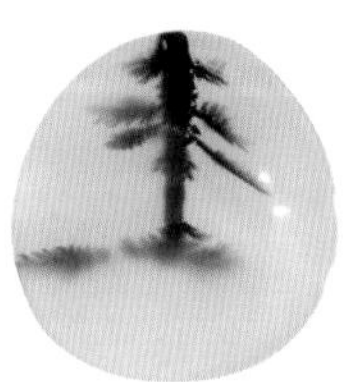

*Agate cabochon*

### SPECIFICATIONS

**Group:** Agate

**Hardness:** 6.5–7 Mohs

**Specific Gravity:** 2.58–2.64

**Refractive Index:** 1.53–1.54

**Crystal Form:** Trigonal – mainly fibrous, porous aggregates. Waxy, dull lustre.

**Properties:** The translucent, pure white agate contains 'scenes' of black or dark brown dendritic (tree-like) inclusions, caused by iron oxides and hydroxide. The black dendrites might look organic, but in fact they have a similar structure to the ice crystals that build up in patterns on glass. Dendritic agate is usually cut as slices and polished to be made into pendants and brooches.

**Pricing:** The more attractive and detailed the scene, the more the stone costs.

**heat and chemically sensitive/ not suitable for ultrasonic cleaning**

## RUTILATED QUARTZ

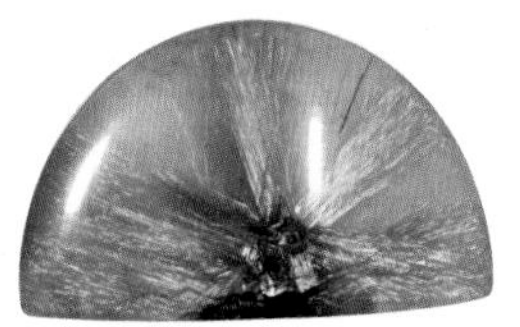

*Half-moon cut quartz*

### SPECIFICATIONS

**Group:** Quartz

**Hardness:** 7 Mohs

**Specific Gravity:** 2.65

**Refractive Index:** 1.544–1.553

**Crystal Form:** Crystalline quartz appears as single crystals in a trigonal system.

**Properties:** This quartz contains yellowish-brown or gold-coloured needles that sometimes sweep, hair-like, through the stone, which gave rise to the old name of Venus-hair stone. The inclusions in tourmalinated and rutilated quartz look best when the quartz is completely clear without any 'foggy' veils.

**Pricing:** Valued according to its inclusions – the more beautiful the pattern, the pricier the gem.

**heat and chemically sensitive/ not suitable for ultrasonic cleaning**

## TOURMALINE

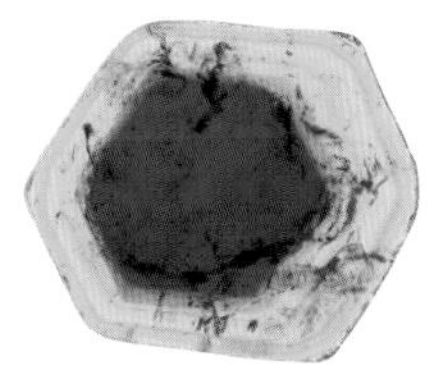

*Tourmaline crystal*

### SPECIFICATIONS

**Group:** Tourmaline

**Hardness:** 7–7.5 Mohs

**Specific Gravity:** 3.01–3.06

**Refractive Index:** 1.614–1.666

**Crystal Form:** Trigonal

**Properties:** Many tourmalines consist of two, three or more colours. The most well-known combination is watermelon tourmaline, in which the crystal has a pink centre and a green rim. The variation of colour combinations is vast and some crystals have a definite colour contrast while others have just a tonal difference. Multicoloured tourmalines are cut to show off the colour combination; cutters usually use a step-cut octagon or baguette cut.

**Pricing:** The better the colour contrast and cleaner the stone, the more expensive it is.

**heat sensitive/not suitable for ultrasonic cleaning**

## RUBY-IN-ZOISITE

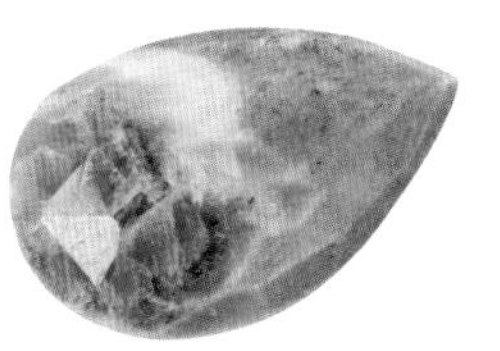

*Faceted drop*

### SPECIFICATIONS

**Group:** Zoisite

**Hardness:** 6.5–7 Mohs

**Specific Gravity:** 3.3–3.35

**Refractive Index:** 1.69–1.70

**Properties:** Discovered in Tanzania in 1954, this opaque, green zoisite rock contains black hornblende inclusions and large, low-grade, opaque rubies. It has an attractive colour contrast that works well in carvings, beads and cabochons.

**Pricing:** Despite containing rubies, it is of moderate value.

**heat and chemically sensitive/not suitable for ultrasonic cleaning**

## MOONSTONE

*African blue moonstone*

### SPECIFICATIONS

**Group:** Feldspar

**Hardness:** 6–6.5 Mohs

**Specific Gravity:** 2.56–2.62

**Refractive Index:** 1.52–1.53

**Crystal Form:** Triclinic and monoclinic. The lustre is vitreous to silky.

**Properties:** Rainbow moonstone has a patchy, milky appearance. When the stone catches the light, the reflection off the layers and inclusions produces a rainbow effect.

**Pricing:** Transparent and crystal-clear with a floating blue schiller on the surface is the most valuable type. The more intense the schiller, the more desirable the stone. Rainbow moonstone is much cheaper.

**heat and chemically sensitive/not suitable for ultrasonic cleaning**

## OPAL

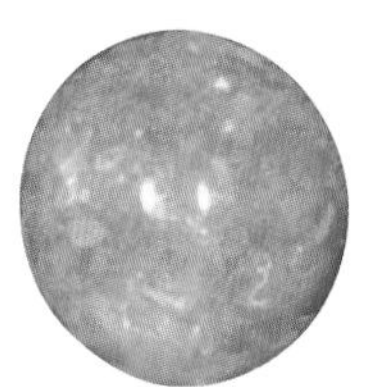

*Precious white opal*

### SPECIFICATIONS

**Group:** Opal

**Hardness:** 5.5–6.5 Mohs

**Specific Gravity:** 1.98–2.50

**Refractive Index:** 1.37–1.52

**Crystal Form:** Amorphous, composed of hydrated silica gel with a water content of five to thirty per cent.

**Properties:** White opal can have a strong colour-play. Many look pale and insipid, requiring closed-backed bezel settings to maximize iridescence. Doublets and triplets are synthetic composite opals. In a doublet, the top is precious opal; the base common potch opal. A triplet has a base of common opal, a middle of precious opal and a top of rock crystal.

**Pricing:** The more even the colour, the higher the value.

**heat and chemically sensitive/ not suitable for ultrasonic cleaning**

## FIRE OPAL

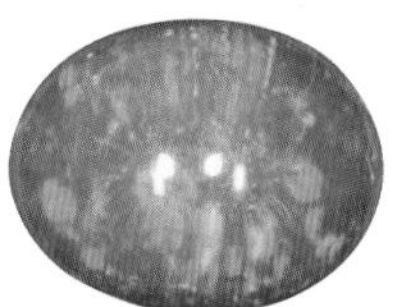

*Fire opal cabochon*

### SPECIFICATIONS

**Group:** Opal

**Hardness:** 5.5–6.5 Mohs

**Specific Gravity:** 1.98–2.50

**Refractive Index:** 1.37–1.52

**Crystal Form:** Amorphous, composed of hydrated silica gel with a water content of five to thirty per cent.

**Properties:** Fire opal ranges from yellow to red, with orange to red the most unusual and red the most desirable. Iridescent material is rare. Quality stones are transparent with a vitreous lustre; not milky or opaque. Fire opals are often faceted.

**Pricing:** Large, transparent stones with good colour have increased in value, but fire opal does not attain the selling prices of precious opal.

**heat and chemically sensitive/ not suitable for ultrasonic cleaning**

## STAR RUBY

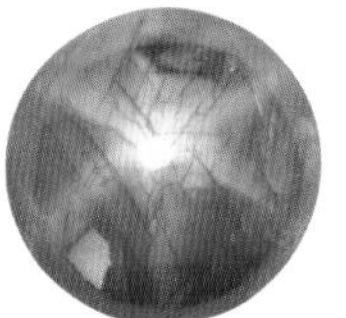

*Star ruby cabochon*

### SPECIFICATIONS

**Group:** Corundum

**Hardness:** 9 Mohs

**Specific Gravity:** 3.97–4.05

**Refractive Index:** 1.762–1.778

**Crystal Form:** Hexagonal prisms, tables and rhombohedrons.

**Properties:** When the rutile needles in a ruby are aligned, asterism occurs in the form of a six-ray star. Rubies may also have a cat's-eye effect, but this is rare. Synthetic star rubies have been sold since 1947 and are popular; synthetic star cabochons are usually cut shallow, unlike the natural star rubies.

**Pricing:** The higher-market star ruby will be translucent red rather than the opaque brownish purple usually available. The rays should be sharp, silvery-white lines that extend to the base.

**suitable for ultrasonic cleaning**

## CHRYSOBERYL CAT'S-EYE

*Cat's-eye cabochon*

### SPECIFICATIONS

**Group:** Chrysoberyl

**Hardness:** 8.5 Mohs

**Specific Gravity:** 3.70–3.78

**Refractive Index:** 1.746–1.763

**Crystal Form:** Orthorhombic

**Properties:** Cut as a cabochon, with a pronounced silver-white cat's-eye effect, which moves from side to side when rotated. The colours range from honey-yellow and brown to yellowish-green and bright green. The ideal colour is a light golden-brown with a darker shadow that produces the cat's-eye effect. The stone should be translucent and have a velvet to silk-like lustre.

**Pricing:** Dependent on the size, colour and quality of the optical effect. Large stones are expensive and rare; smaller stones are much cheaper.

**heat sensitive/not suitable for ultrasonic cleaning**

## QUARTZ CAT'S-EYE

*Cat's-eye cabochon*

### SPECIFICATIONS

**Group:** Quartz

**Hardness:** 7 Mohs

**Specific Gravity:** 2.65

**Refractive Index:** 1.544–1.553

**Crystal Form:** Single crystals in a trigonal system.

**Properties:** Quartz cat's-eyes are unusual. They can be found in green to yellowish-green, grey-green, yellow-brown and deep grey and have a sharp white cat's-eye streak down the centre. This streak is the result of parallel wavy fibre-like inclusions of asbestos. The stone has to be cut so that the fibres are parallel to the cabochon base. It has a soft, silky lustre.

**Pricing:** Good value compared to chrysoberyl cat's-eyes.

**heat and chemically sensitive/not suitable for ultrasonic cleaning**

## TIGER'S-EYE

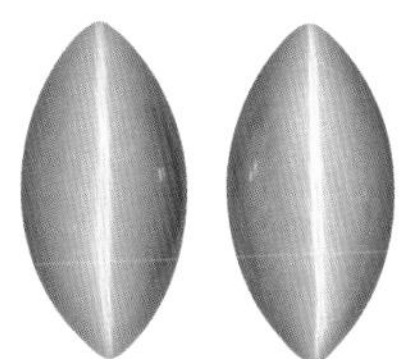

*Tiger's-eye cabochon*

### SPECIFICATIONS

**Group:** Quartz

**Hardness:** 7 Mohs

**Specific Gravity:** 2.65

**Refractive Index:** 1.544–1.553

**Crystal Form:** Single crystals in a trigonal system.

**Properties:** Tiger's-eye comes in brownish yellow, golden-yellow, reddish-brown and greenish to brown. Hawk's-eye is similar, but with a darker bluish to black colour. These stones have a striking optical effect from the replacement of closely packed blue asbestos fibres by quartz; the fibrous quartz structure makes the surface shimmer. The material is cut flat, into slabs or plates, to show off the optical effect.

**Pricing:** Inexpensive.

**heat and chemically sensitive/not suitable for ultrasonic cleaning**

# Stone shapes

## PARTS OF A FACETED GEMSTONE

These are the terms for different parts of a round, brilliant-cut gemstone. Their varying proportions will affect the brilliance, beauty and colour of the stone.

**Girdle** The outer edge of a stone, where the crown meets the pavilion.

**Crown** The top portion of a stone, above the girdle.

**Pavilion** The lower part of a stone, from the girdle to the culet.

**Table** The flat surface on top of a stone; the largest facet or face.

**Culet** The lowest part of the stone, which appears as a point or a ridge.

Upper girdle
Kite
Star
Table

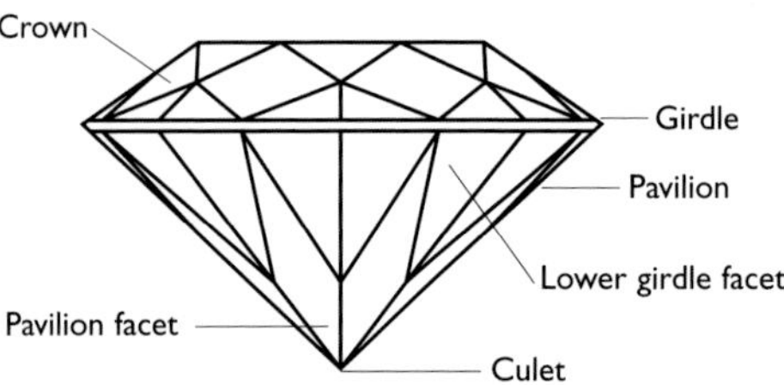


## BRILLIANT CUT

The brilliant cut has been developed as an ideal cut of mathematically calculated proportions. This cut maximizes a stone's natural light dispersion, bending light rays towards the centre of a stone and then reflecting them out again to produce 'fire' and brilliance.

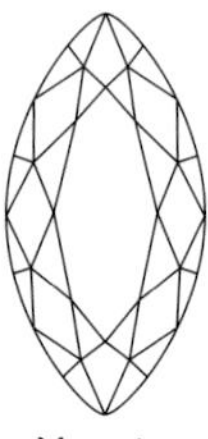
Marquise

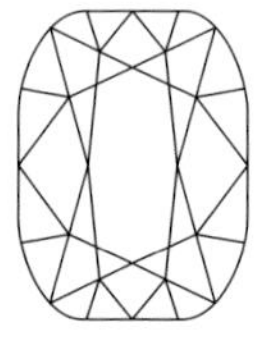
Antique cushion

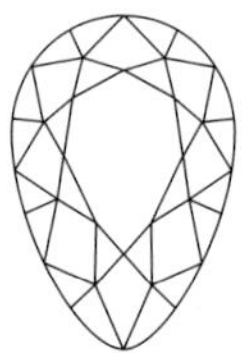
Pear shape

## BRIOLETTE CUT

This is effectively a double rose cut, with an elongated cone-shape upper crown and rounded pavilion covered with triangular or rectangular facets.

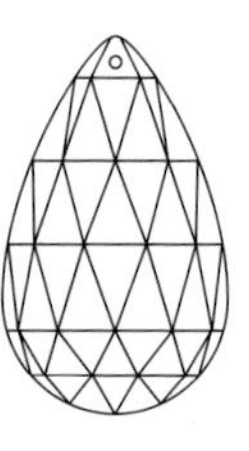
Briolette

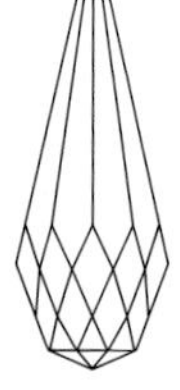
Drop

# Straight-sided gemstone cuts

## STEP CUT

The step cut does not produce the brilliance of a brilliant-cut stone, but it does show off colour very effectively. Variations on the step cut include baguettes, which are elongated rectangles; the emerald cut, which is a rectangular step cut with corners cut diagonally to make an octagonal shape; the scissor or cross cut in which the steps are divided into triangular facets; and the French cut, which is used on small stones.

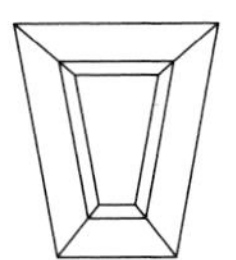
Step-cut trapeze baguette

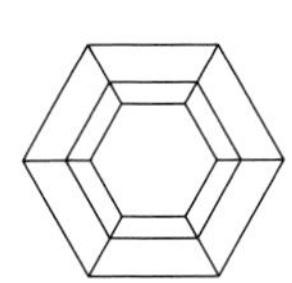
Step-cut hexagon

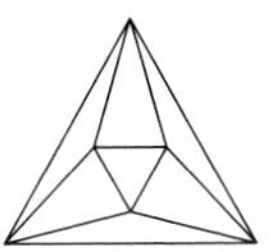
French-cut equilateral triangle

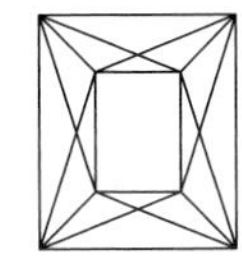
Cross-cut rectangle

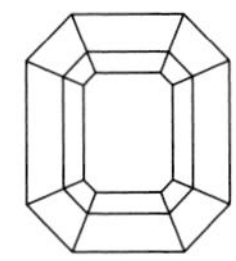
Emerald cut with two crown steps

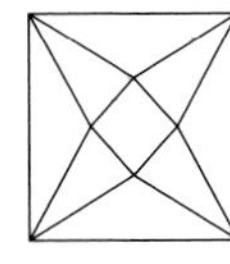
Square French cut with square table

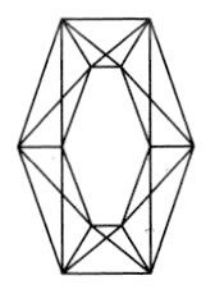
Cross-cut long hexagon

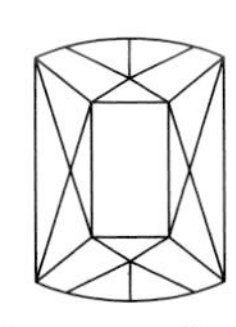
Cross-cut pillow (barrel)

## FANCY CUTS

Fancy cuts were originally devised to retain maximum weight in irregularly shaped crystals, but nowadays are design-driven. They create different optical effects such as mirror and prism cuts and may also be variations of existing cuts.

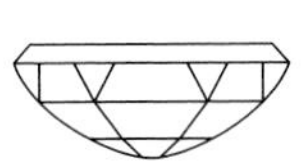
Flat top with step-cut pavilion (side view)

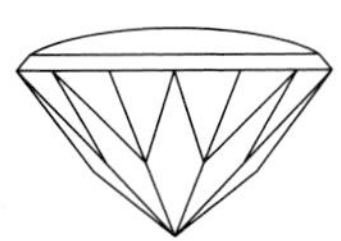
Buff top with brilliant-cut pavilion (side view)

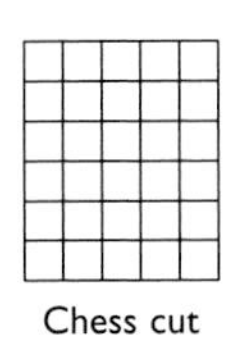
Chess cut (plan view)

Bent top rectangle triangle cut (plan view)

## CABOCHON CUTS

Cabochon cuts can vary in both outer girdle shape and the convex curve of the surface. The surface profile can range from a flat slab to a high-domed bullet. The base can be flat, or rounded as a double cabochon to increase colour density in light-coloured stones.

Low dome

High dome

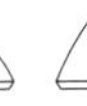
Cone

Bullet

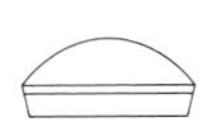
Double bevelled

Hollow/carbuncle

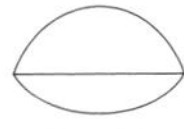
Double

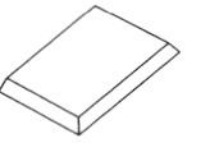
Flat cut/slab

Buff top

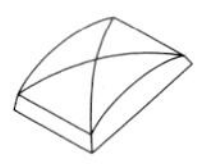
Buff top (cross-vaulted)

# Settings

## BEZEL SETTING

This type of setting is most commonly used to set cabochons, but can be used for faceted stones if a ledge, or bearer, is made inside the bezel on which the stone can sit. It provides a protective band of metal around the circumference of the stone that holds it in place. Fine silver should be used to make a bezel for soft or fragile stones.

A strip of 0.5-mm (1/64-inch) thick silver sheet is used to construct a bezel, and the join is soldered. The bezel should be loose enough so that the stone can be dropped into it from above, but tight enough that the stone does not wobble. The bezel is then soldered onto a base sheet and pierced out around the outside edge to make a 'cup'. The base may be pierced out, leaving a ledge for the stone to sit on. Once filed to shape and cleaned up, the bezel cup can be soldered onto the piece of jewellery.

The metal is set around the stone using a flat-ended 'pusher'. Work 'north, south, east, west' around the bezel with the pusher, then 'northeast, southeast, southwest, northeast', and so on. This will force the metal to compress evenly, leaving no gaps. A burnisher is used to smooth the metal around the stone. Support the piece in a ring clamp or sink it into setter's wax while working.

*A simple bezel-set cabochon is the focal point of this silver ring.*

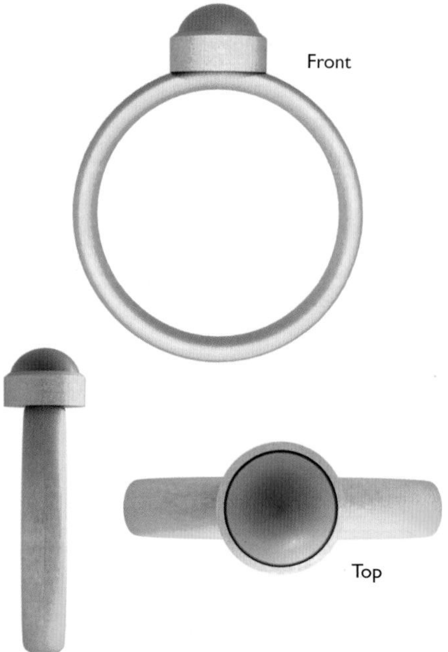

Bullet cabochons have been set into the ends of these tubular drop earrings.

## TUBE SETTING

Although the effect of tube setting is similar to bezel setting, the fabrication of the piece is different. The open back of this setting means that more light can reach the stone.

A tube is soldered onto a ring shank and the end is filed flush. Metal is removed from the inside of the tube with a round burr that is exactly the same diameter as the stone, so that the stone can sit in the recess far enough down so that the girdle is just below the surface. The tube must have a wall that is thick enough to allow the inner portion to be removed, leaving a wall at least 0.5 mm ($\frac{1}{64}$ inch) thick to set the stone. The rim of the tube can be thinned on the outside with a file, if necessary, so that it will be more easily rubbed over the stone with a pusher. The setting must be well cleaned and polished inside before setting the stone. Support the piece in a ring clamp or sink it into setter's wax while working on it. This is a good way to set cabochons and faceted stones.

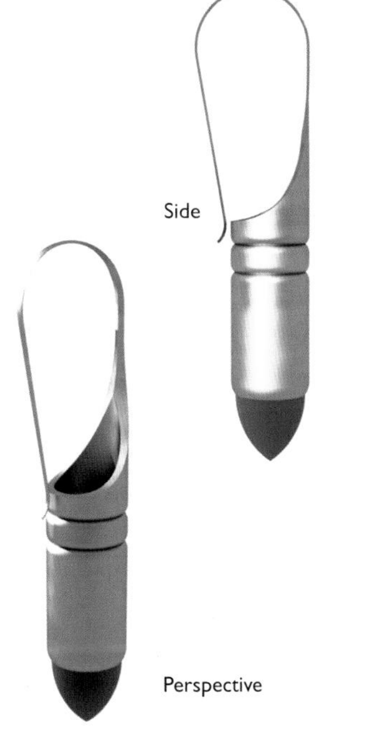


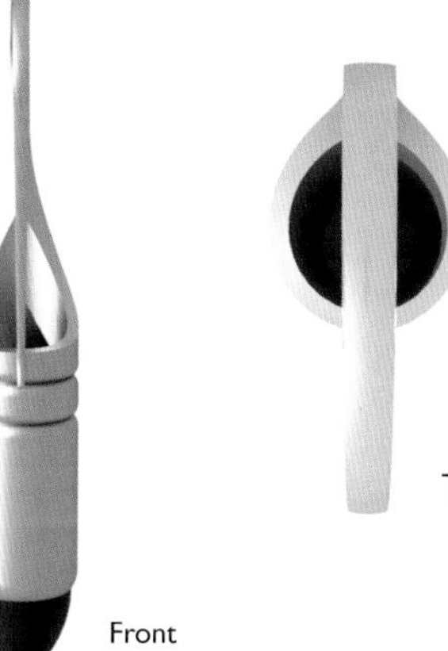

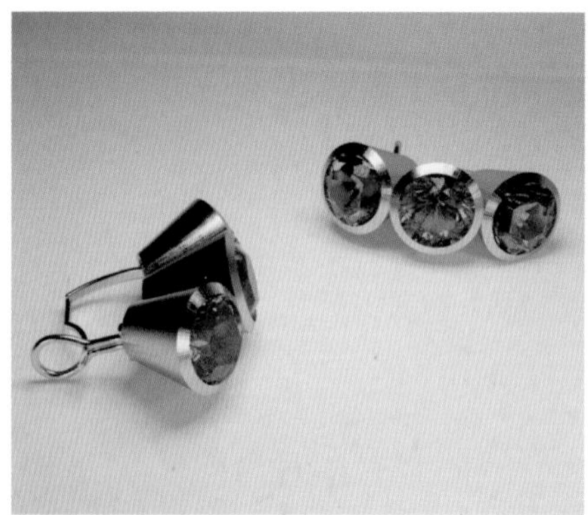

*Three collet settings have been combined to form the structure of these gold earrings.*

## COLLET SETTING

A variation on the tube setting, a collet setting can be carefully filed to divide it into claws, or left intact and used as an elegant rub-over setting that echoes the shape of the stone with its tapered sides.

A piece of cut tube or a form made from a curved strip of sheet is placed in a collet block. The size and shape of the stone will determine the type of collet block used, whether the collet is angled at 17 or 28 degrees and is round, oval, navette or square. The collet must be deep enough so that culet does not protrude from the base – the stone will sit lower in the collet than is first apparent.

Once the collet has been shaped in the collet block, it is filed to shape and cleaned up. The setting is then soldered into a ring shank and the inside of the setting is burred out so that the stone will sit below the top of the collet. The top edge of the collet is thinned with a file so that it can be more easily pushed over the stone with a flat-ended pusher.

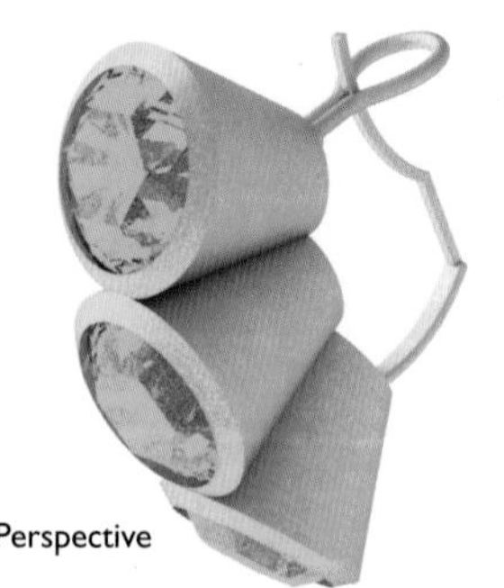


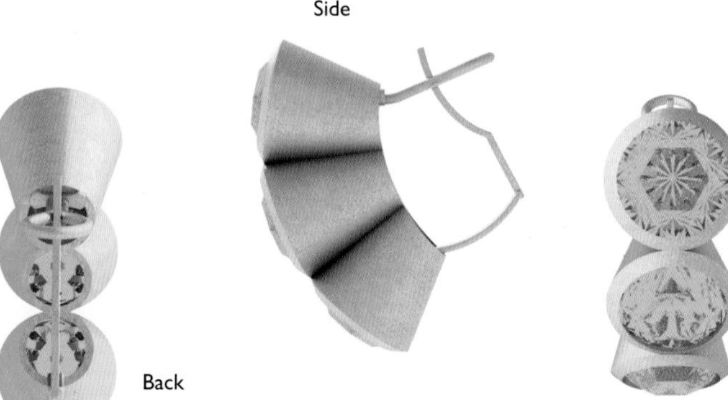

## CLAW SETTING

The claw setting is commonly used with transparent, faceted stones as it elevates and displays the stone while keeping the surrounding metal to a minimum. The prongs are attached to a bezel to maintain shape and stability, and at least four claws should hold the stone. Decorative detail can be added, such as splitting the prongs to create forked claws or setting small diamonds into the top of the claws.

This type of setting is best constructed from gold or platinum. Each prong should have a groove engraved or cut with a burr a short way down from the tip, and in which the stone can sit. The tip of the claw should be thinned and polished before the stone is inserted between the prongs.

Setting is performed by pushing the ends of the claws over the edge of the stone above the girdle with a prong pusher. The metal is burnished down so that it sits flush with the surface of the stone.

*Traditional claw settings can be used to effectively display faceted stones.*

## FLUSH SETTING

Flush setting, also known as 'gypsy setting', is popular because of its clean, minimal look. Faceted stones are sunk into the surface of the metal and held in place by a thin rim of metal pushed over the stone's edge. It is easier to work on a slightly domed surface than a flat one, and also easier to clean up the metal after setting the stone.

Holes are drilled that are smaller than the diameter of the stone and a round burr the same size as the stone is used to cut away metal deep enough for the girdle of the stone to be below the metal's surface – the table should be about the same height as the surface of metal. A burnisher is used to push metal down onto the stone, working 'north, south, east, west' to pin it in position so that it doesn't move during setting. The point of the burnisher is used around the inside edge to make a neat circle. Emery paper is used to clean up any marks left on the metal from setting, taking care not to scratch the stone.

*Highlights have been created in this domed pendant by using flush-set white and brown diamonds.*

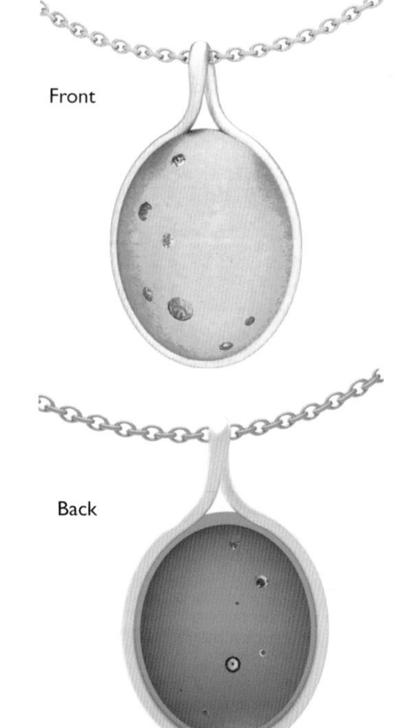


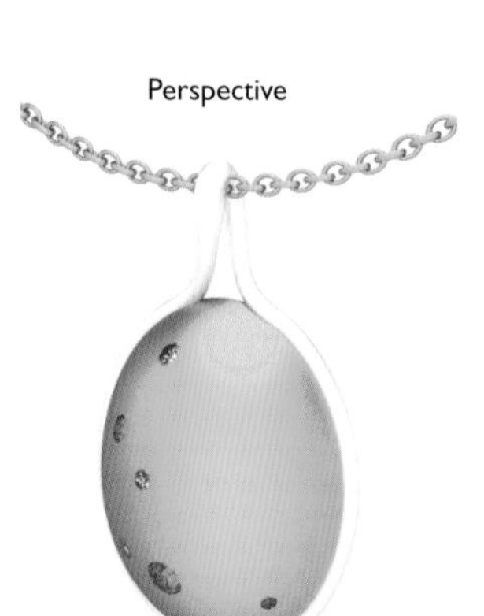


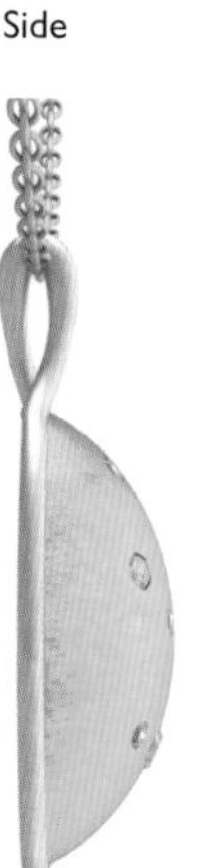

## CHANNEL SETTING

A channel setting is used for securing rows of square or baguette step-cut stones. Ledges are cut in the edges of the channel and metal is folded over to grip the girdle of the stones on two sides. This allows for gems to be butted up, giving a continuous effect. The setting demands accuracy, as the stones have to match in colour and be a calibrated size.

The setting must be fabricated to match the precise specifications of the stones that are being used. The channel, or ledge, is engraved inside so that the stones fit snugly in and all sit at the same height. With the stones in the channel, and no gaps or metal in between them, the metal wall is pushed over the stones to set them in position.

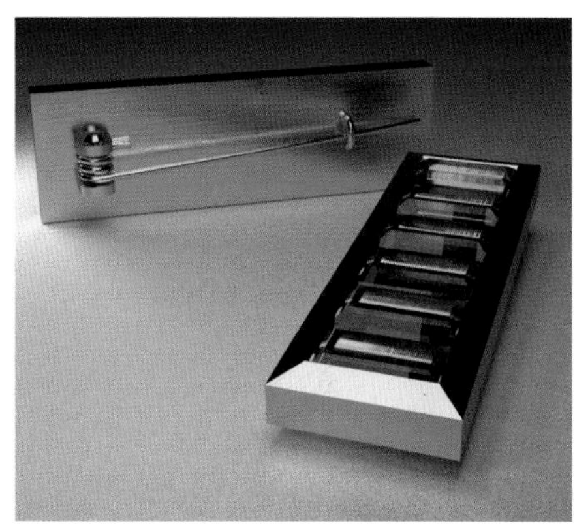

*A simple box brooch is channel set with baguette-cut emeralds.*

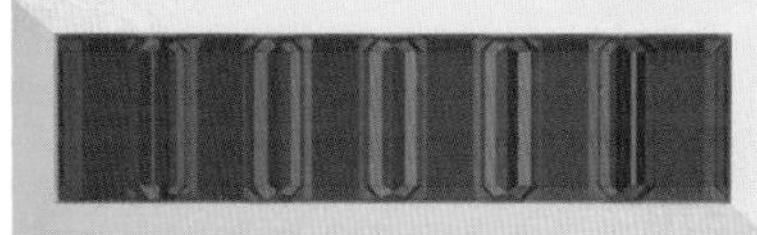

Front

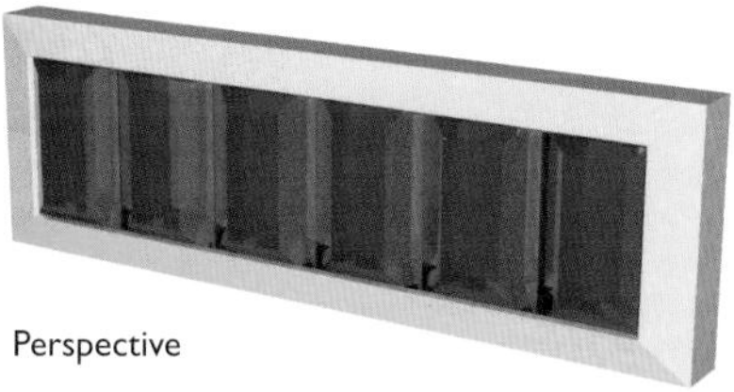

Perspective

Back

Side

*Stones have been used to add detail to this pendant, which was constructed from sheet metal.*

## GRAIN SETTING

A grain or bead setting can be used for cabochons, faceted stones and full or half pearls. The metal is recessed to take the stone, which is held in place by a number of tiny beads. These are made by chiselling up metal slivers with a graver and shaping them into rounded beads with a graining tool, which has a small domed cavity in its end. The grains sit just over the edge of the stone, fixing it in place. Faceted stones will need to sit in a burred-out recess so that the girdle is flush with the surface of the metal. The metal around the stone is often carved with a flat graver to reflect light back in towards the stone and to tidy up the marks left from raising the grains. Support the work in a ring clamp or sink it in setter's wax while working on it.

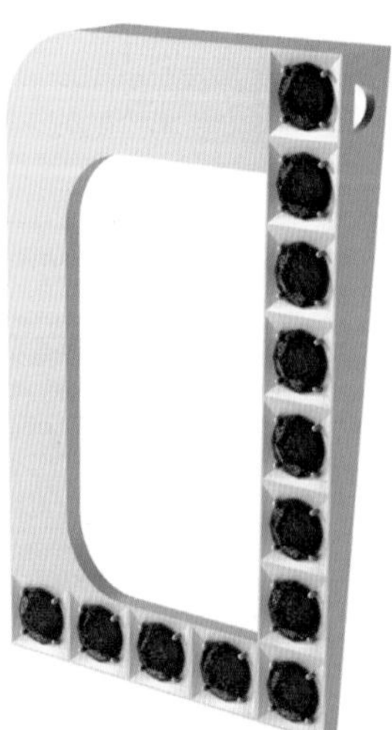

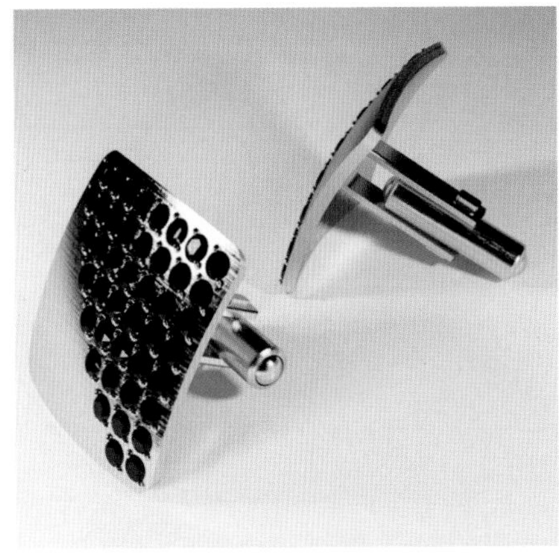

*A carpet of rubies embellishes these gold cufflinks.*

## PAVÉ SETTING

This type of setting also uses bead or grain setting. Small stones are arranged very close together, with a tiny amount of metal visible between them and secured by beads that are carefully raised from the base material. The surface of the metal appears 'paved' with stones. A similar effect can be created with prongs rather than grains.

Holes are drilled into the metal close together, but allowing for the diameter of the stones. A ball burr is used to open up the holes so that the stone's girdle is flush with the surface. The grains are raised with a graver and then pushed over and neatened with the correct-size beading tool, and the metal surrounding the stones is engraved to tidy any cut marks. Grains can be raised to fill any gaps that may remain.

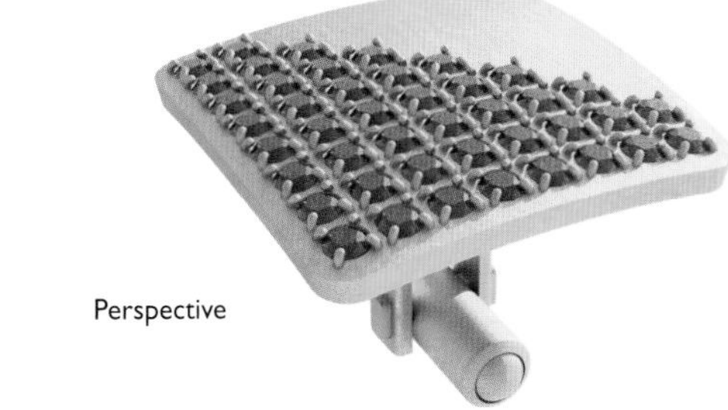

Perspective

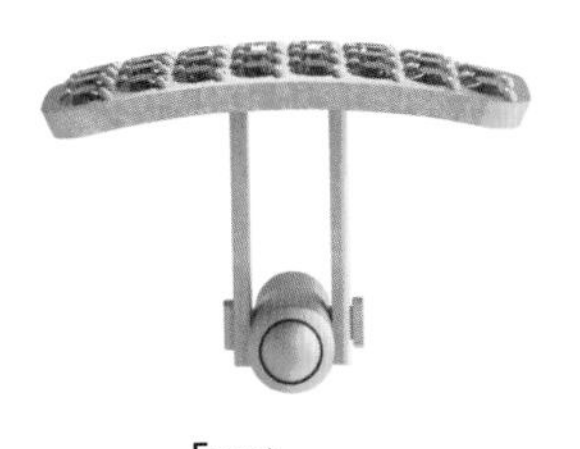

Front

Side

Top

*In a clean and minimal tension setting, almost all of the stone is visible.*

## TENSION SETTING

This type of setting relies on the tension of the shank to keep a stone in place with just two points of contact securing it. The shank should be made from white gold, platinum or stainless steel since silver and other metals do not have the tensile strength necessary to keep the stone in place for long, and it will eventually get loose and fall out. The shank also needs to be made of metal thick enough to contain the height of the stone so that the culet does not press uncomfortably into the finger when the ring is worn. A groove that has been burred or engraved onto both metal faces will help the stone to be held more securely in the ring.

Once the shank has been made and sufficiently work-hardened, it can be opened up enough to allow the stone to be slipped into position with a mandrel or a ring stretcher. When released, the shank will tightly hold the stone.

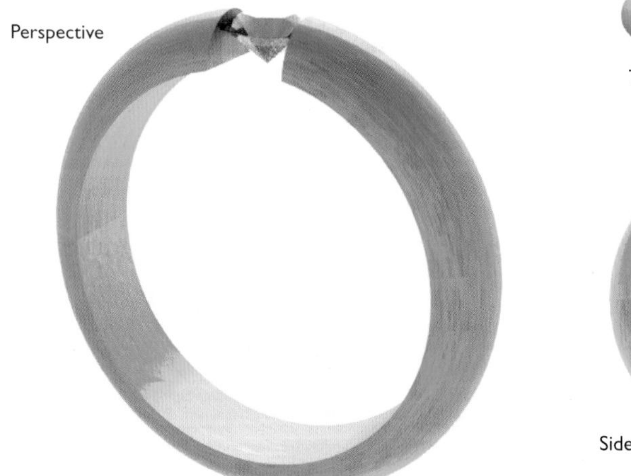

## ILLUSION SETTING

Illusion setting is an advanced stone-setting technique that uses carved facets in the metal surrounding the stone to reflect light in a way that confuses the eye and makes the stone appear larger than it really is. A small stone is set into a hole in a larger metal disk, using raised grains to hold it in position. The metal is then carved with gravers to produce polished facets that mimic the reflections in the stone, creating the illusion.

For the best effects, use a colourless transparent stone in a white-coloured metal such as white gold or platinum, and have the piece plated with white rhodium.

*Highly polished surfaces are necessary for the illusion in this type of setting to work successfully.*

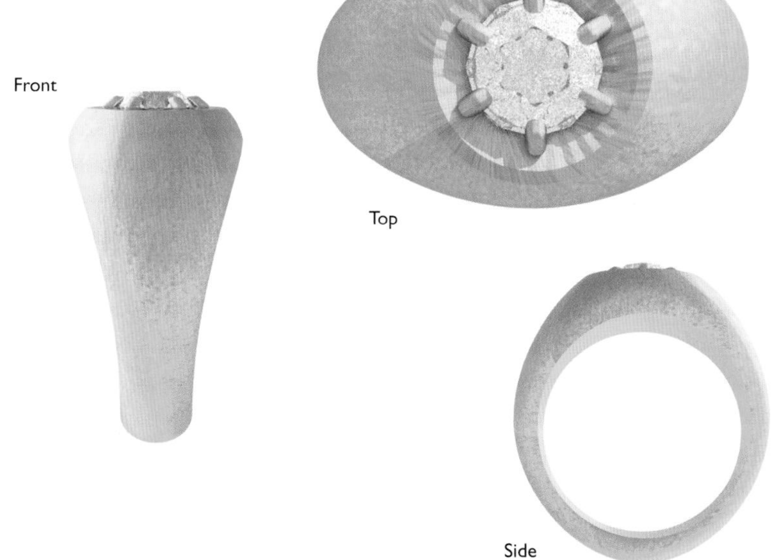

# Recipes

The following chemical solutions are referred to throughout the book and are listed here under the material and technique to which they correspond. Make sure you use the correct solution for your jewellery project.

## NITRIC ACID

**Caution:** Always add acid to water when mixing etching solutions and work in a well-ventilated area. Use the solution in a glass dish with a low centre of gravity so that it cannot easily be knocked over.

TIP: Acid solutions can be used many times before the saturation of dissolved metal will inhibit the action of the acid, and they should be stored in a clearly marked and sealed bottle. Solutions mixed up for specific metals should be kept separate – do not etch copper in a solution mixed up for steel.

If a new etching solution works too slowly to begin with, try adding a small amount of an old solution to give it a kickstart.

BASE METALS: **COPPER, BRASS and GILDING METAL**
p23 **Etching with nitric acid**

**Recipe:** One part nitric acid (70% reagent grade) to one part water

BASE METALS: **STEEL**
p48 **Etching**

**Recipe:** One part nitric acid to six parts distilled water

PRECIOUS METALS: **SILVER**
p94 **Etching: Stop-out varnish resist**
p96 **Etching: Aquatint**
p96 **Etching: Sticky-backed plastic**

**Recipe:** One part nitric acid (70% reagent grade) to three parts water

NATURAL MATERIALS: **BONE, IVORY and SHELL**
p145 **Etching**

**Recipe:** One part nitric acid to five parts water

## COPPER NITRATE

BASE METALS: **COPPER, BRASS and GILDING METAL**
p34 **Copper nitrate**

**Recipe:** 200 g (7 oz) of copper-nitrate crystals in 1 litre (1 quart) of warm water

**Method:** Stir until the crystals are completely dissolved. Store the solution in a sealed glass jar and pour out a suitable amount into a high-sided glass jar when required.

## FERRIC NITRATE

BASE METALS: **COPPER, BRASS and GILDING METAL**
p34 **Ferric nitrate**
PRECIOUS METALS: **SILVER**
p95 **Etching: PNP**

**Recipe:** One part ferric-nitrate crystals to three parts water

**Method for ferric nitrate:** See copper nitrate, above.

**Method for etching PNP:** Add the crystals to the warm water at 40°C (104°F) and mix until dissolved. A cold solution will work much more slowly than a warm one. The solution can be reused by heating in an outer container of hot water – never heat it directly.

## AQUA REGIA

PRECIOUS METALS: **GOLD**
N.B. This recipe does not feature in the book but is the correct solution to use when etching gold.

**Recipe:** One part nitric acid to three parts hydrochloric acid

This mix is specifically suited for etching gold – it is known as 'aqua regia' because it's the only solution that will work on gold. Because gold is so expensive, etching is not usually used to remove metal, since it is not easily recovered from the solution.

TIP: Adapt your design so that engraving or rolling mill textures could be used instead, and you will not 'waste' as much gold.

## LIVER OF SULPHUR

PRECIOUS METALS: **SILVER**
p121 **Oxidation:** Liver of sulphur

**Recipe:** Dissolve a tiny (pea-size) amount of potassium sulphide in 100 ml (3 fl oz) warm water, or 25 ml (1 fl oz) of liver of sulphur solution per litre (quart) of water at 60–70°C (145–160°F)

**Method:** Immerse the piece for 20 seconds and rinse well in water. Repeat if necessary.

## FERRIC CHLORIDE

BASE METALS: **COPPER, BRASS and GILDING METAL**
p28 **Etching with ferric chloride**

**Recipe:** 250 g (9 oz) ferric chloride crystals to 0.5 litre (1 pint) warm water at 40°C (104°F)

**Method:** Mix crystals with 333 ml (0.6 pint) of hot tap water until dissolved; add more water to top up to 500 ml (1 pint). A cold solution will work much more slowly than a warm one. The solution can be reused by heating it in an outer container of hot water – but never heat it directly.

## TOURMALINE-BLACK ANTIQUING FLUID

BASE METALS: **COPPER, BRASS and GILDING METAL**
p32 **Tourmaline-black antiquing fluid**

**Recipe:** One part tourmaline-black to ten parts water

TIP: The diluted solution can be stored in an airtight plastic bottle and reused as required.

## TOURMALINE-BROWN ANTIQUING FLUID

BASE METALS: **COPPER, BRASS and GILDING METAL**
p32 **Tourmaline-brown antiquing fluid**

**Recipe:** One part tourmaline-brown to ten parts water

TIP: The diluted solution can be stored in an airtight plastic bottle and reused as required.

## BLACK PATINA

BASE METALS: **STEEL**
p54 **Black patina:** Hematite

**Recipe:** One part hematite to ten parts water

**Method:** Immerse the piece in the solution for two minutes.

TIP: The diluted solution can be stored in an airtight plastic bottle and reused as required.

# Suppliers

## UNITED KINGDOM

### TOOLS

**BUCK & RYAN**

Victoria House
Southampton Row
London WC1B 4AR
Tel: 020 7430 9898
www.buckandryan.co.uk

**H.S. WALSH**

234 Beckenham Road
Beckenham
Kent BR3 4TS
Tel: 020 8778 7061
—OR—
44 Hatton Garden
London EC1N 8ER
Tel: 020 7242 3711
www.hswalsh.com

### ENAMELLING SUPPLIES

**VITRUM SIGNUM**

Gresham Works
Mornington Road
North Chingford
London E4 7DR
Tel: 020 8524 9546
www.vitrumsignum.com

### PRECIOUS METALS

**J. BLUNDELL & SONS**

16 Hatton Wall
London EC1N 8JH
Tel: 020 7404 0744
www.jblundell.co.uk

**COOKSON PRECIOUS METALS LTD**

49 Hatton Garden
London EC1N 8YS
Tel: 0845 100 1122
www.cooksongold.com

**RASHBEL UK LTD**

24–28 Hatton Wall
London EC1N 8JH
Tel: 020 7831 5646
www.rashbel.com

**JOHNSON MATTHEY METALS LTD**

40–42 Hatton Garden
London EC1N 8EE
Tel: 020 7269 8400
www.matthey.com

### BASE METALS

**FAYS METALS**

Unit 3, 37 Colville Road
London W3 8BL
Tel: 020 8993 8883

**SCIENTIFIC WIRE COMPANY**

18 Raven Road
London E18 8HW
www.scientificwire.com

### GEMSTONES

**CAPITAL GEMS**

30B Great Sutton Street
London EC1V 0DU
Tel: 020 7253 3575
www.capitalgems.com

**R. HOLT & CO**

98 Hatton Garden
London EC1N 8NX
Tel: 020 7405 5284
www.holtsgems.com

**LEVY GEMS**

Minerva House
26–27 Hatton Garden
London EC1N 8BR
Tel: 020 7242 4547
www.levygems.com

**A. E. WARD & SONS**

8 Albemarle Way
London EC1V 4JB
Tel: 020 608 2703
www.aewgems.co.uk

### CASTING

**WEST ONE CASTINGS**

(gold, silver)
24 Hatton Garden
London EC1N 8BQ
Tel: 020 7831 0542

**WESTON BEAMOR**

(platinum, fine casting)
3–8 Vyse Street
Birmingham B18 6LT
Tel: 0121 236 3688
www.westonbeamor.co.uk

### ELECTROFORMING

**RICHARD FOX**

8–28 Milton Avenue
Croydon
Surrey CR0 2BP
Tel: 020 8683 3331
www.foxsilver.net

### OTHER MATERIALS

**4D MODELSHOP**

The Arches
120 Leman Street
London E1 8EU
Tel: 020 7264 1288
www.modelshop.co.uk

### MAPLIN ELECTRONICS LTD

218 Tottenham Court Road
London W1T 7PX
Tel: 020 7323 4411
Over 140 stores nationwide.
www.maplin.co.uk

### PENTONVILLE RUBBER

104–6 Pentonville Road
London N1 9JB
Tel: 020 7837 7553
www.pentonvillerubber.co.uk

### HAMAR ACRYLIC FABRICATIONS LTD

238 Bethnal Green Road
London E2 0AA
Tel: 020 7739 2907
www.hamaracrylic.co.uk

### ALEC TIRANTI

27 Warren Street
London W1T 5NB
Tel: 020 7380 0808
www.tiranti.co.uk

### BARNETT LAWSON (TRIMMINGS) LTD

16–17 Little Portland Street
London W1W 8NE
Tel: 020 7636 8591
www.bltrimmings.com

### STUART R. STEVENSON

68 Clerkenwell Road
London EC1M 5QA
Tel: 020 7253 1693
www.stuartstevenson.co.uk

### FALKINER FINE PAPERS

76 Southampton Row
London WC1B 4AR
Tel: 020 7831 1151
www.falkiners.com

### GPS AGENCIES LTD

Unit 3–3a Hambrook Business Centre
Cheesmans Lane
Hambrook
West Sussex PO18 8XP
Tel: 0123 457 4444
www.ivoryalternative.com

## AUSTRALIA

### PRECIOUS METALS

### A. & E. METAL MERCHANTS

104 Bathurst Street, 5th Floor
Sydney
NSW 2000
Tel: +00 61 2 9264 5211
Fax: +00 61 2 9264 7370
www.aemetal.com.au

### JOHNSON MATTHEY (AUSTRALIA) LTD

339 Settlement Road
Thomastown
VC 3074
Tel: +00 61 3 9465 2111
www.matthey.com

## USA

### TOOLS

### ALLCRAFT TOOL AND SUPPLY

666 Pacific Street
Brooklyn
NY 11207
Tel: +00 1 718 789 2800
www.allcraftonline.com

### ANCHOR TOOL AND SUPPLY COMPANY

PO Box 265
Chatham
NJ 07928
Tel: +00 1 201 887 8888

### ARMSTRONG TOOL & SUPPLY COMPANY

31747 West Eight Mile Road
Livonia
MI 48152
Tel: +00 1 800 446 9694
Fax: +00 1 248 474 2505
www.armstrongtool.com

### FREI & BOREL

PO Box 796
126 Second Street
Oakland
CA 94604
Tel: +00 1 510 832 0355
Fax: +00 1 800 900 3734
www.ofrei.com

### INDIAN JEWELER'S SUPPLY CO

601 E Coal Ave
Box 1774
Gallup
NM 87305–1774
Tel: +00 1 505 722 4451
Fax: +00 1 505 722 4172
www.ijsinc.com

### METALLIFEROUS

34 West 46th Street
New York
NY 10036
Tel: +00 1 212 944 0909
Fax: +00 1 212 944 0644
www.metalliferous.com

### MYRON TOBACK

25 West 47th Street
New York
NY 10036
Tel: +00 1 212 398 8300
Fax: +00 1 212 869 0808
www.myrontoback.com

### PAUL GESSWEIN & CO

255 Hancock Avenue
PO Box 3998
Bridgeport
CT 06605–0936
Tel: +00 1 203 366 5400
Fax: +00 1 203 366 3953
www.gesswein.com

### RIO GRANDE

7500 Bluewater Road NW
Albuquerque
New Mexico 87121–1962
Tel: +00 1 800 545 6566
Fax: +00 1 800 965 2329
www.riogrande.com

### SWEST INC

11090 N. Stemmons Freeway
PO Box 59389
Dallas
TX 75229–1389
Tel: +00 1 214 247 7744
Fax: +00 1 214 247 3507
www.swestinc.com

## PRECIOUS METALS

### DAVID H. FELL & CO

6009 Bandini Blvd
City of Commerce
CA 90040
Tel/Fax: +00 1 323 722 6567
www.dhfco.com

### T.B. HAGSTOZ AND SON

709 Sansom Street
Philadelphia
PA 19106
Tel: +00 1 215 922 1627
Fax: +00 1 215 922 7126
www.silversmithing.com/hagstoz

### HANDY AND HARMAN

1770 Kings Highway
Fairfield
CT 06430
Tel: +00 1 203 259 8321
Fax: +00 1 203 259 8264
www.handyharmanproducts.com

### HAUSER AND MILLER COMPANY

10950 Lin-Valle Drive
St. Louis
MO 63123
Tel: +00 1 800 462 7447
Fax: +00 1 800 535 3829
www.hauserandmiller.com

### C.R. HILL COMPANY

2734 West 11 Mile Road
Berkeley
MI 48072
Tel: +00 1 248 543 1555
Fax: +00 1 248 543 9104

### HOOVER AND STRONG

10700 Trade Road
Richmond
VA 23236
Tel: +00 1 800 759 9997
Fax: +00 1 800 616 9997
www.hooverandstrong.com

### BELDEN WIRE AND CABLE COMPANY

PO Box 1327
350 NW N Street
Richmond
IN 47374
Tel: +00 1 765 962 7561
www.belden.com

## BASE METALS

### NASCO

4825 Stoddard Road
PO Box 3837
Modesto
CA 95352–3837
Tel: +00 1 800 558 9595
Fax: +00 1 209 545 1669
www.enasco.com

### REVERE COPPER PRODUCTS

PO Box 300
Rome
NY 13442
Tel: +00 1 315 338 2554
Fax: +00 1 315 338 2070
www.reverecopper.com

# CANADA

## TOOLS

### BUSY BEE MACHINE TOOLS

2251 Gladwin Crescent
Ottawa, ON
K1B 4K9
Tel: +00 1 613 526 4696
10 stores.
www.busybeetools.com

### LACY AND CO

55 Queen Street East
Toronto, ON
M5C 1R6
Tel: +00 1 416 365 1375
Fax: +00 1 416 365 9909
www.lacytools.ca

## PRECIOUS METALS

### IMPERIAL SMELTING & REFINING CO

451 Denison
Markham, ON
L3R 1B7
Tel: +00 1 905 475 9566
Fax: +00 1 905 475 7479
www.imperialproducts.com

### JOHNSON MATTHEY LTD

130 Gliddon Road
Brampton, ON
L6W 3M8
Tel: +00 1 905 453 6120
Fax: +00 1 905 454 6869
www.matthey.com

# Resources

## USEFUL MEASUREMENTS AND INFORMATION

### Table of Ring Sizes

| UK | US | Ring blank length* (mm) | Ring blank length* (inches) | Inside diameter (mm) | Inside diameter (inches) | UK | US | Ring blank length* (mm) | Ring blank length* (inches) | Inside diameter (mm) | Inside diameter (inches) |
|---|---|---|---|---|---|---|---|---|---|---|---|
| A | ½ | 40.8 | 1.61 | 12 | 0.47 | N | 6¾ | 57.8 | 2.25 | 17 | 0.67 |
| B | 1 | 42.0 | 1.65 | 12.4 | 0.49 | O | 7 | 58.4 | 2.30 | 17.2 | 0.68 |
| C | 1½ | 43.2 | 1.70 | 12.8 | 0.50 | P | 7½ | 59.5 | 2.35 | 17.6 | 0.69 |
| D | 2 | 44.5 | 1.75 | 13.2 | 0.52 | Q | 8 | 60.9 | 2.40 | 18 | 0.71 |
| E | 2½ | 45.8 | 1.80 | 13.6 | 0.54 | R | 8½ | 62.3 | 2.45 | 18.4 | 0.72 |
| F | 3 | 47.2 | 1.85 | 14 | 0.55 | S | 9 | 63.4 | 2.50 | 18.8 | 0.74 |
| G | 3¼ | 48.3 | 1.90 | 14.2 | 0.56 | T | 9½ | 64.8 | 2.55 | 19.2 | 0.76 |
| H | 3¾ | 49.5 | 1.95 | 14.6 | 0.57 | U | 10 | 65.9 | 2.60 | 19.6 | 0.77 |
| I | 4¼ | 50.8 | 2.00 | 15 | 0.59 | V | 10½ | 67.4 | 2.65 | 20 | 0.79 |
| J | 4¾ | 52.7 | 2.05 | 15.4 | 0.61 | W | 11 | 68.6 | 2.70 | 20.4 | 0.80 |
| K | 5¼ | 53.4 | 2.10 | 15.8 | 0.62 | X | 11½ | 69.9 | 2.75 | 20.8 | 0.82 |
| L | 5¾ | 54.6 | 2.15 | 16.2 | 0.64 | Y | 12 | 71.2 | 2.80 | 21.2 | 0.83 |
| M | 6¼ | 56.0 | 2.20 | 16.6 | 0.65 | Z | 12½ | 72.4 | 2.85 | 21.6 | 0.85 |

* *Always add the thickness of the metal you are using to the length of blank required for a particular size, to ensure accurate results.*

◁ MEASURING
*There is a wealth of devices available for measuring fingers and rings – from expensive boxed sets to disposable card or plastic gauges.*

**BOOKS**

*New Directions in Jewellery*
Astfalck, J. and Derrez, P.
Black Dog Publishing, 2005

*Ornament and Object: Canadian Jewellery and Metal Art*
Barros, A.
Boston Mills Press, 1998

*Engraving on Precious Metals*
Brittain, A. and Morton, P.
NAG Press, 1958

*New Directions in Jewellery II*
Clarke, Beccy
Black Dog Publishing, 2006

*Jeweller's Directory of Gemstones*
Crowe, Judith
Firefly, 2006

*Electroforming*
Curtis, Leslie
A&C Black, 2004

*Hydraulic Die Forming for Jewelers & Metalsmiths*
Kingsley, Susan
20-Ton Press, 1993

*Enamels, Enameling, Enamelists*
Matthews, G. L.
Krause Publications, 1984

*Complete Metalsmith*
McCreight, Tim
Brynmorgen Press, 2004

*Metals Technic: A Collection of Techniques for Metalsmiths*
McCreight, Tim (Ed.)
Brynmorgen Press, 1997

*The Art of Jewelry Design: From Idea to Reality*
Olver, Elizabeth
North Light Books, 2002

*Wire Jewellery*
Stofer, Hans
A&C Black, 2005

*Jewelry Concepts and Technology*
Untracht, Oppi
Doubleday, 1982

**WEBSITES**

www.klimt02.net
Klimt02: international community for jewellery and design.

www.metalcyberspace.com
Metalcyberspace: information and resources.

www.ganoksin.com
Ganoksin: archive of technical articles, and much more.

**ORGANIZATIONS**

Society of North American Goldsmiths
www.snagmetalsmith.org

Hand Engravers Association of Great Britain
www.handengravers.co.uk

Association For Contemporary Jewellery
www.acj.org.uk

Crafts Council
www.craftscouncil.org.uk/photostore

Craft Central
www.craftcentral.org.uk

The Goldsmiths' Company
www.thegoldsmiths.co.uk

Benchpeg newsletter
www.benchpeg.com

Jewellers Association of Australia
www.jaa.com.au

**FURTHER READING**

Art Jewelry magazine
www.artjewelrymag.com

Bead&Button magazine
www.beadandbutton.com

Beadwork magazine
www.interweave.com

Benchpeg newsletter
www.benchpeg.com

Lapidary Journal Jewelry Artist
www.jewelryartistmagazine.com
www.lapidaryjournal.com

Metalsmith
www.snagmetalsmith.org

National Jeweler
www.nationaljewelernetwork.com

Scale of approximate hardness based on resistance to abrasion

| Mohs' Scale of Hardness | |
|---|---|
| **1** Talc | **6** Feldspar |
| **2** Gypsum | **7** Quartz |
| **3** Calcite | **8** Topaz |
| **4** Fluorite | **9** Corundum |
| **5** Apatite | **10** Diamond |

Standard sizes for common jewellery forms

| Standard sizes of: | mm | inches | mm | inches | mm | inches |
|---|---|---|---|---|---|---|
| Diameter of earring posts and wires | 0.8–0.9 | 0.031–0.035 | | | | |
| Necklace lengths | 400 | 16 | 450 | 18 | 500 | 20 |
| Bracelet lengths | 175 | 7 | 190 | 7.5 | 200 | 8.5 |
| Bangle diameters | 60 | 2.4 | 65 | 2.6 | 70 | 2.8 |

# Glossary

**Abrasives**
The natural or man-made sand-like particles used to smooth or clean away marks on a surface, as can be found adhered to abrasive papers such as emery or wet-and-dry.

**Acetone**
A flammable liquid used to remove setter's wax/cement, permanent-marker-pen ink and resin.

**Adhesive**
A sticky substance, such as glue, used for fixing things together.

**Alloy**
A mixture of metals.

**Ball-peen hammer**
A hammer with one flat end and one ball end used for shaping and texturing metal.

**Base metal**
A non-precious metal such as aluminium, brass, copper, gilding metal, nickel, pewter, steel and titanium.

**Bevelled**
On a slant or inclination.

**Bezel**
The rim of metal that is used to secure a stone in a rub-over setting.

**Bezel pusher**
Also Pusher
A tool used in stone setting to push metal over the stone.

**Billet**
A thick stack of fused metal sheet, used in mokume gane.

**Binding wire**
Iron or steel wire used to secure components together during soldering.

**Blocking**
In repoussé, the work done on the back of the metal.

**Borax**
A type of flux.

**Bronze**
A pale yellow metal used for casting, which is generally an alloy of copper and tin.

**Buffing wheel**
See Mop

**Bullion**
Gold and silver.

**Burnish**
To polish by rubbing, usually with a polished steel tool.

**Burr**
Metal tools for grinding, for use with a pendant drill or a flexible shaft motor.

**Centre drill**
A specialized drill with a 60-degree-angled section and a narrow tip.

**Centre punch**
A pointed punch used to make an indent in metal prior to drilling.

**Chenier**
Tubing.

**Chips**
See Pallions

**Chuck**
The jaws of a drill or a lathe that hold a tool or piece of work.

**Countersink**
The enlargement of the entry to a hole.

**Creasing hammer**
A steel hammer with a double wedge-shaped head, having two long narrow faces that sit at a 90-degree angle to the handle.

**Crosslock tweezers**
See Sprung tweezers

**Cross-peen hammer**
A steel hammer with one thin face that sits at a 90-degree angle to the handle, and one flat face.

**Curing**
The process of liquid components turning solid – resin, for example.

**Dapping block**
See Doming block

**Die**
Tools used for shaping by stamping, or a cutting tool used for cutting screw threads.

**Dividers**
Two pointers hinged like a pair of compasses, with an adjusting screw. Dividers are used for scribing arcs and for scribing a line parallel to an edge.

**Doming block**
Also Dapping block
A steel form with hemispherical depressions used to form domes.

**Doming punches**
Also Dapping punches
Steel punches with rounded heads used with a doming block to make domes.

**Draw plate**
A steel tool comprised of a series of tapered holes of diminishing sizes through which wire is pulled to transform its shape.

**Ductile**
A term used to describe a material that is yielding or pliable.

**Emery stick**
A small wooden stick with emery paper stuck onto it. May be flat or curved.

**Exothermic**
A chemical reaction that gives off heat as a by-product.

**Faceted**
A term used to describe gemstones that have been cut so that their form is covered in small, polished, flat surfaces.

**Ferrous**
Containing iron.

**Fibre-grip tweezers**
See Sprung tweezers

**Fibre grips**
Protective covering used to protect material from being damaged by the steel jaws of a vice.

**Findings**
Commercially made jewellery fittings.

**Finish**
The cleaning up of a piece by sanding and polishing.

**Firescale**
See Firestain

**Firestain**
Also Firescale
A layer of subcutaneous discoloration on sterling/standard silver that is the result of annealing or soldering.

**Fittings**
Functional components such as catches, clips and joints, as used in jewellery.

**Flux**
A chemical used as an antioxidant as part of the soldering process.

**Former**
Also Triblet
A form, generally made of steel, used to support metal while it is being formed.

**Fretwork**
A sheet that has been pierced with a number of holes or shapes to make an ornamental pattern.

**Fume cupboard**
A glass-fronted cupboard that has an extraction or air-filtration system inside, in which chemical processes such as etching are done.

**Gauge**
A standard of measurement, such as the thickness of sheet or the diameter of wire.

**Glass brush**
An abrasive brush made from glass-fibre filaments. It is useful for achieving a smooth, satin surface on metals and for cleaning purposes, especially in preparation for enamelling.

**Gold size**
An adhesive used to apply gold leaf. It has a slow drying time, and must be left to go tacky before the leaf is applied. Available in oil-based or acrylic forms.

**Grain**
A rounded bead of metal that has been formed to hold a stone in place.

**Gravers**
Steel tools used to cut away metal in engraving and setting.

**Hammer**
A tool for beating or striking metal.

**Imperial**
Non-metric standard of measure or weight.

**Join/joint**
The meeting of two or more pieces, often in terms of soldering.

**Jump ring**
Plain ring forms used in jewellery, not including finger rings.

**Laminate**
Layers of material that are sandwiched together.

**Lathe**
A tool used for cutting rotary objects.

**Linisher**
Machine with a rotating sanding belt.

**Malleable**
A material that can be readily formed or rolled.

**Mallet**
A non-metal-faced hammer, often made from wood, plastic or hide.

**Mandrel**
Also Triblet
A tapered steel rod, usually with a circular cross-section, used for shaping or stretching rings or bracelets.

**Metric**
Relating to measurement based on the decimal system.

**Moh's scale**
A scale of approximate hardness based on resistance to abrasion.

**Mop**
Also Buffing wheel, Polishing bob
A fabric wheel used for polishing, usually with a polishing compound applied to it.

**Moulds**
A hollow form into which molten wax, resin or metal can be poured for casting.

**Needle file**
Small file, usually used without a wooden handle and available in a wide variety of cross-sections and grits.

**Non-ferrous**
Metals not containing iron.

**Ormolu**
An oil-based varnish traditionally used over gilding.

**Outwork**
Processes or special professional services that are performed by someone else, for example laser cutting and engraving.

**Pallions**
Also Chips
Pieces of solder, taken from the French word for 'flake'.

**Patina**
A surface finish that develops on metal or other material as a result of exposure to chemicals or handling.

**Pickle**
A chemical solution used to remove the oxides that are a result of heating.

**Pin**
A piece of wire with a sharpened end used to fasten an object.

**Pitch bowl**
A heavy, round-bottomed metal bowl filled with pitch, for holding metal during chasing or repoussé.

**Planishing**
Polishing or flattening by hammering with a mirror-finished hammer face.

**Polishing bob**
See Mop

**Precious**
A term used to describe diamonds, sapphires, rubies and emeralds when referring to stones or gold, silver and platinum when referring to metals.

**Prong**
A tine or spur, made in a claw-stone setting, for example.

**Prong pusher**
A small metal tool used in stone setting. It is rectangular in cross-section with a channel cut into the end.

**Pumice**
A powdered form of volcanic rock used with water to abrade and clean the surface of metals.

**Punches**
Hardened steel tools used in forming or texturing metal.

**Pusher**
A small metal tool used in stone setting. It is usually rectangular in cross-section with a wooden handle.

**Pyrex™**
A type of glassware resistant to heat.

**Quench**
Dropping hot metal straight into water, or a mixture of oil and water, for rapid cooling and hardening.

**Raising hammer**
A steel hammer with two long cylindrical faces set at a 90-degree angle to the length of the handle.

**Reverse-action tweezers**
See Sprung tweezers

**Ring clamp**
A hinged clamp with leather-lined jaws that is tightened either with a wingnut or a wedge.

**Rivet**
Wire or tube used to join two or more pieces when its headless end is hammered.

**Rod**
A straight, solid wire.

**Rub-over setting**
A type of stone setting that uses a bezel.

**Sandbag**
A leather cushion filled with sand, used to support tools or pieces of work.

**Setter's cement**
See Setter's wax

**Setter's wax**
Also Setter's cement
A hard substance that can be softened by warming, used to support jewellery pieces for stone setting.

**Shank**
Straight or plain section of a ring or twist drill bit.

**Sheet**
A piece of metal that is normally of uniform thickness.

**Sinusoidal stake**
A 'snake-like' stake, specifically used for anticlastic raising.

**Solder**
A fusible alloy for joining metals.

**Sprung tweezers**
Also Crosslock tweezers, Reverse-action tweezers, Fibre-grip tweezers
Tweezers that close when you release them, used as a soldering aid.

**Stakes**
Polished metal formers used by the jewellery-maker to support the work being planished or forged.

**Stick feeding**
A method of soldering that uses a long, thin piece of solder held in a pair of insulated tweezers. The solder is touched onto the end of the seam when the metal reaches the correct temperature and the solder flows to fill it.

**Sweat soldering**
A method of soldering large pieces of metal and long, continuous seams together face to face. The pallions of solder are fused to one or two of the surfaces before the pieces are placed together and reheated to join them.

**Tang**
The end of a file, graver or tool; often fitted into a wooden handle.

**Tap**
A tool used for cutting a screw-thread in a hole.

**Temper**
To alter the hardness of steel.

**Template**
A shaped, thin plate used as a guide to define a form.

**Triblet**
See Former and Mandrel

**Undercut**
Areas of a three-dimensional form that have been recessed and may inhibit easy removal from a mould.

**Vernier gauge**
A sliding scale used for accurate fractional measurement.

**Work-hardening**
The hardening of a material by manipulation.

# Index


## A

abalone leaf 35
abrasive barrelling mediums 117
acetone 186
acrylic 166, 182
  rod 174
agate
  banded 226
  dendritic 226
alexandrite 218
aluminium 36, 37, 39–42
  leaf 35
aluminium and refractory metals 36–43
amber 212
amethyst 222
ammonia 33
annealing
  aluminium and refractory metals 37
  copper, brass and gilding metal 12
  gold 61
  silver 58
  steel 44
anodizing 40
  resists 41
anticlastic raising 91
antiquing fluid
  tourmaline-black 32, 243
  tourmaline-brown 32, 243
aqua regia 243
aquamarine 218
aquatint 23
aventurine 214

## B

balled wire 76
bamboo 128
banded agate 226
barrel polishing 28
barrelling 117
base metals
  aluminium and refractory metals 36–43
  copper, brass and gilding metal 12–35
  steel 44–55
beech 134
bending 134, 146
beryl 214
bezel setting 148, 232
binding 162
bleaching 163
blown glass 198
blue chalcedony 218
boiling leather 155
bone 140
bone, ivory, shell, horn and jet 140–149
borax 18, 31, 120
branding 157
brass 12–15, 17, 18, 25, 32
  brushes 117
brilliant cut 230
briolette cut 230
burr walnut 132
burring and grinding 38

## C

cabochon cuts 231
CAD/CAM 108
carnelian 211
carving 131, 143, 196
carving and grinding 50
casting
  cement fondue 194
  plastics and rubber
    dyes 179
    embedded objects 179
    marbled colours 180
    metal leaf 181
    metallic powders 180
    resin 178
    silicone 177
  other materials 181
  silver and gold
    finishing 105
    with moulds 106
    multiples 106
    soft wax 105
cat's-eye
  chrysoberyl 229
  quartz 229
cement fondue 190, 194
ceramics 190, 195
chain 77
chain-mail 78
  variations 78
chalcedony 222
  blue 218
channel setting 237
chasing and repoussé 89
chemicals 9, 32, 107, 124
cherry wood 129
chrysoberyl cat's-eye 229
chrysoprase 214
citrine 212
claw setting 235
cleaning up (plastics and rubber) 186
coconut 128
collet setting 161, 234
combining materials
  collets 161
  setting 160
  tube setting 160
Convention on International Trade in Endangered Species of Wild Fauna and Flora (CITES) restrictions 150
copper 12, 13, 15, 17, 18, 22, 23, 26, 31, 32, 34, 45, 242
  leaf 35
  nitrate 34, 242
copper, brass and gilding metal 12–35
copper plate 120
coral 210
cotton wool 33
crochet 80, 201
cutting (leather) 152

## D

decorative rivets 110, 182
dendritic agate 226
diamonds 206, 207, 208, 212, 219, 224
disc-cutter: hole punch 62
doming 85
dravite 211
draw plates 84
driftwood 128
drilling 14, 62, 130, 170, 197
dyeing (leather) 153
dyes
  aluminium and refractory metals 41
  bone, ivory, shell, horn and jet 148
  fabric 138
  feathers, hair and quills 163
  plastics and rubber 179
  wood 138
    wax resist with dyes 138

## E

ebony 129
electroforming 23, 107
electronic components 192
  fibre optics 203
  LEDs 203
elm 134
embedded objects 179
embossing 156, 201
embroidery 202
emerald 215
emery paper 29, 52, 116
enamelling
  copper, brass and gilding metal 26
    foil 27
  silver and gold 100
    basse-taille 97, 102
    champlevé 101
    cloisonné 102
    gold foil 103
    plique-à-jour 59, 101
engine turning 97
engineered wood 128
engraving 15, 98, 99, 136
epoxy resin 166
etching
  aquatint 96
  bone, ivory, shell, horn and jet 145
  with ferric chloride 28
  with nitric acid 23

pens 28
PNP 95
steel 48
stop-out varnish 95
stop-out varnish resist 94
eyelets 156

F
fabric: construction 202
faceting 147
fancy cuts 231
feathers 158
feathers, hair and quills 158–163
ferric chloride 243
etching with 28
ferric nitrate 34, 242
fibre optics 203
filigree 79
fire opal 228
flick wheel 30, 118
flush setting 236
fold-forming 90
folding 43
paper 200
and scoring 182
forging
spreading 93
tapering 92
twisting 93
upsetting 94
forming leather 154
French knitting 80
frosted surfaces 30
fusing 18, 70, 71

G
garnet
pyrope 209
rhodolite 209
gas torches 9, 53
'gilding leaf' 35
gilding metal 12, 14, 17, 18, 32
glass 190, 191
blown 198
drilling and grinding 197
sandblasting 197
glossary 250–252
glue construction 135
gold
9-carat yellow 60
14-carat yellow 60
18-carat yellow 59, 60, 61
22-carat yellow 61
rose 13
white 60, 125
gold dust 71
gold foil 27, 71
gold leaf 123, 151
leather 157
transfer and lacquer 123
gold plating 60, 61
gold powders 157
grain setting 238
granulation: silver 76
grinding glass 197
grinding wheels 50

H
hair 158
*see also* feathers, hair and quills
hammer textures
ball-peen 67
cross-peen 66
planishing 67
raising 16, 66
textured 16
handforming: ceramics 195
hardening (steel tools) 49
hardwoods 128, 131, 136
head pins 76
health and safety 8–9
heat colouring 137
heat patina 30, 40, 52, 53, 119
heat texturing 174
raised 175
heat-treated leaf 35
heliodor 213
hematite 54, 207
hessonite 208
hickory 134
horn 141
*see also* bone, ivory, shell, horn and jet
hydraulic press 88, 154

I
illusion setting 241
image transfer 42
indicolite 215, 219
inlay
bone, ivory, shell, horn and jet 144
gold on silver 73
gold pieces 74
inlaying wire 74
milled 19
plastics and rubber 171
silver solder 20
wood 132
iolite 222
ivory 132, 140, 242
synthetic 140, 141
vegetable 140
*see also* bone, ivory, shell, horn and jet

J
jade
jadeite 216
lavender 223
nephrite 215
jet 141
*see also* bone, ivory, shell, horn and jet
jeweller's wax 103, 106
jump rings 77, 78

K
'keum-boo' 71
kilns 9, 53
knitting 79, 201
kunzite 224
kyanite 219

L
laminating 133, 172
lampwork 198
lapis lazuli 220
laser cutting 133, 142, 184, 200
latex 168
lathe 84
lavender jade 223
leather 150–157
chemically tanned 150
full grain 150
suede 150
top grain 150
vegetable-tanned 150
vellum 150
LEDs 193, 203
lining gravers 25

M
machines 8
magnets 192, 199
malachite 216
marbled colours 180
marquetry 133
marriage of metals
copper, brass and gilding metal 19
silver and gold: gold combinations 75
matt finish
copper, brass and gilding metal 29
plastics and rubber 187
silver and gold 115
pumice powder 115
steel 51
measurements 247, 249
medium-density fibreboard (MDF) 128
metal leaf 35, 181
metallic powders 124, 180
Mohs' Scale of Hardness 249
mokume gane
concentric circles 22
silver and gold 75
wood-grain effect 21
mould making
impression 175
plaster 195
polymorph 177
silicone 176
moonstone 227
mother-of-pearl 132, 141
*see also* bone, ivory, shell, horn and jet

N
nacreous shell see mother-of-pearl
nail varnish 28
natural materials
bone, ivory, shell, horn and jet 140–149
feathers, hair and quills 158–163
leather 150-157
wood 128–139
neoprene 168
nephrite jade 215
nickel 12

niobium 37, 39
nitric acid
etching with 23
recipe 242
nylon 167, 184

## O

oil 139, 149
opal 61, 228
fire 228
other media 190–203
overlay 161
oxidation 32
liver of sulphur 121
pariser-oxide 122
platinol 122

## P

paints, oil-based 138
palladium leaf 35
paper 192
embossing 201
folding 200
laser cutting 200
patchwork leaf 35
patina
ammonia 33
black 243
hematite 54
'bucket' 33
heat see heat patina
iridescent 121
pickle 35
red heat 31
patination fluids 33
pavé setting 239
pearls 169, 206, 207
pendant motor textures
with burrs 112
deep impressions 114
with diamond burrs 113
silicone points 113
pens
'etching' 28
permanent marker 28
peridot 151, 216
photoetching 97
pickle patina 35
piercing
bone, ivory, shell, horn and jet 142
copper, brass and gilding metal 14
plastics and rubber 170
silver and gold
curves 63
straight lines 63
steel 46
wood 130
other materials: slate 194
piqué work (wire inlay) 144
plaiting 83, 162
plaster 191
plastic tubing and rod fittings 185
plastics
acrylic 166
epoxy resin 166
nylon 167
polyester resins 166
polypropylene 167
polyurethane 166
sticky-backed 23, 96
plastics and rubber 166–187
plating 124
rhodium 125
rubbed back 125
platinum 125
platinum leaf 35
plywood 128
PNP paper 23
polishing
aluminium and refractory metals 39
bone, ivory, shell, horn and jet 149
copper, brass and gilding metal 28
leather 154
plastics and rubber 186, 187
silver and gold 114
semi-polished finish 117
steel 51
wood 139
polyester resins 166
polymer clay 191
polymorph 177
polypropylene 167, 182
polyurethane 166
porcelain 191, 196
precious metal clay (PMC) 107
precious metals: silver and gold 58–125
prehnite 217
press forming
copper, brass and gilding metal 22
silver and gold
die matrix 85
die matrix and insert 86
die matrix and resist 86
objects 88
punch 87
'press 'n' peel' (PNP) paper 95
printing 42
pumice powder 29, 51, 115
punches see stamps and punches
pyrography
leather 157
wood 137
pyrope garnet 209

## Q

quartz
rose 224
rutilated 226
quills 158
see *also* feathers, hair and quills

## R

raised rolling mill textures 15
recipes 242–243
red heat patina 31
refractory metals see aluminium and refractory metals
repoussé see chasing and repoussé
resin 178, 186
resources 247–249
reticulation 17, 69, 70
rhodium 125
rhodolite garnet 209
ring sizes 247
riveting
bone, ivory, shell, horn and jet 147
copper, brass and gilding metal 24
plastics and rubber
acrylic 182
tube rivets 183
washers 183
silver and gold 109
wood 134
rivets
decorative 110, 182
leather 156
tube 110, 182, 183
rock crystal 206
rolling mill textures 15, 64, 65
rose quartz 224
rubber 168
latex 168
neoprene 168
silicone 168
vulcanized 168
see *also* plastics and rubber
rubellite 210
ruby 129, 209
star 228
ruby-in-zoisite 227
rust 54
with mask-off 55
rutilated quartz 226

## S

sandblasting 39, 118, 119, 135, 185, 197
sanding leather 155
sapphire 61, 129, 151, 213, 220, 225
satin circular finish 116
satin finish
copper, brass and gilding metal 29
silver and gold 116
steel 52
satinwood 132
sawdust 33
scapolite 223
scouring pads 29, 52
scraped texture 38
screw threads 111
settings 230–241
sewing (leather) 153
shading tools 25
shagreen (stingray hide) 155
sharpening 47
shell 141
see *also* bone, ivory, shell, horn and jet
silicone rubber 168
casting 177
mould-making 176

silver
Britannia 58
fine 58
sterling 58, 70
tarnish-resistant alloys 58
silver and gold 58–125
silver dust 18
silver foil 27
silver solder 20
slate 191, 194
slip-casting: porcelain 196
softwoods 128, 131, 134, 136
soldering
aluminium and refractory metals 37
copper, brass and gilding metal 12, 18
gold 61
gold and silver 72
silver 58
steel 44, 48
spectacle-setting 199
spinel 159, 210, 220, 225
spot welding 49
stains 148
stamping (leather) 152
stamps and punches
bone, ivory, shell, horn and jet 145
copper, brass and gilding metal 17
silver and gold 68
letters and numbers 69
texturing 68
wood 136
stapling 43
star ruby 228
steel 44–55
burnisher 51, 115
mild 44, 49, 54
stainless 44, 45, 54
tinplated 45
tool (silver or carbon) 44, 54
wool 52
stencils 71
step cut 231
stitches 25
stone settings 232–241
stone shapes 230
stones 206–229
straight-sided gemstone cuts 231
studs 156
suede 150
sunstone 211
suppliers 244–246

**T**

tantalum 36, 39
tanzanite 223
tempering (steel tools) 49
tension setting 240
textiles 192, 201
thermoforming 173
acrylic rod 174
thermoplastics 166
tiger's-eye 229
titanium 36, 37, 38, 39, 40, 43
tobacco, rolling 33
topaz 213, 221, 225
torches 52
gas 9, 53
oxyacetylene 53
tortoiseshell 140, 141
*see also* bone, ivory, shell, horn and jet
tourmaline 227
tsavorite 217
tube rivets 110, 182, 183
tube setting 233
turning 131, 146, 171
turquoise 221
twisted wire 81
flattened 82
simple 82
twisted wire tube 81

**V**

varnish 139, 149
stop-out 23
vellum 150
veneers 132
verdelite 217
verdigris 33, 34
vulcanized rubber 168

**W**

walnut 134
washers 183
washi paper 193
watchmaker's lathe 146
watercolour paper 15, 201
wax 139, 149
wax carving 103
rings 104
wax resist with dyes 138
weaving 83
welding 112
wet packing 26
wire wool 29
wood 128–139

**Z**

zircon 208, 221

# Credits

**Additional samples by:**
Paul Wells, Frieda Munro, Chris Howes, Olga Kosica, Tracy Furlong, Megumi Sakamoto, Tatjana Gretschmann, Mary Van de Water

**The author would also like to thank:**
Giles Last, Chris Howes, Paul Wells, Martin Hopton, and the staff at Central Saint Martins College of Art and Design, London, for their help and support during this project; 4D Modelshop Limited for kindly supplying the laser-cut samples; and Leon Williams for the stone setting illustrations.

**Finished pieces by:**
t = top; m = middle; b = bottom; l = left; r = right

Anastasia Young **p2, p88, p98, p129t, p140, p159b, p173** www.anastasiayoung.co.uk; Paul Wells **p13t, p90, p92**; Drew Perridge **p13m**; Melissa Hansom **p13b, p59bl**; Chris Howes **p21, p45b**; Arthur Hash **p37t**; Jenni Caldwell **p37m**; Melanie Eddy **p37b**; Suzi Tibbetts **p45t, p55** www.iclimbtrees.co.uk; Takafumi Inuzuka **p45m, p141bl, p167t, p193b**; Erik Tindäng **p45b**; Sonja Seidl **p59tr** www.sonjaseidl.com; Kelly McCallum **p59tl** www.kellymccallum.com; Regina Aradesian **p59m** www.aradesijewellery.com; Barbara Christie **p61t**; Hayley Friel **p61m** haylee@oheffie.co.uk; Nutre Arayavanish **p61b** www.nutrejeweller.com; Mette T. Jensen **p129m** www.mettetjensen.com; Martin Hopton **p129b, p141br**; William Vinicombe **p151t&m**; Tomasz Donocik **p151b** www.tomaszdonocik.com; Tracy Furlong **p159t**; Jana Reinhardt **p167m**; Tina Lilenthal **p167b**; Min-Ji-Cho **p169t&m** www.minjicho.com; Frieda Munro **p169b**; Katja Prins **p191t** www.katjaprins.com; Kathryn Bone **p191b**; Naoko Yoshizawa **p193t**; Joanne Haywood **p193m** www.joannehaywood.co.uk

**We would also like to thank the following photographers:**
Stephen Bone **p191b**; Eddo Hartman **p191t**; Erik Tidäng **p45b**; Rama **p169m**; Joel Degen **p59m, 129m**; Frank Thurston **167b**; Suthiphong J. **p61b**